Terry M. Mulcahy

Dominican College

San Rafael

California

by John Robinson Beal

PEARSON OF CANADA
THE SECRET SPEECH
JOHN FOSTER DULLES

MARSHALL IN CHINA

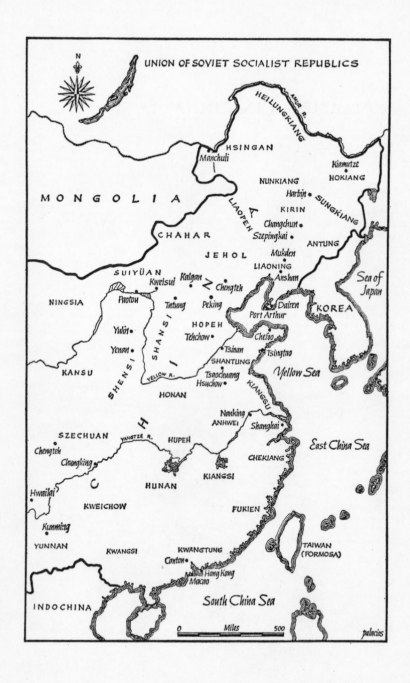

MARSHALL IN CHINA

by John Robinson Beal

DOUBLEDAY CANADA LIMITED
Toronto
Doubleday & Company, Inc., Garden City, New York
1970

LIBRARY OF CONGRESS CATALOG CARD NUMBER 69–12220
COPYRIGHT © 1970 BY JOHN R. BEAL
INTRODUCTION COPYRIGHT © 1970 BY DOUBLEDAY &
COMPANY, INC.

To Betty, John, Bill, and Carolyn,
who shared with me some of the experiences
of learning to know China and its people
during a critical year.

CONTENTS

*or nine tenths solved." Assassination of two Chinese lib-
erals in Kunming arouses U.S. indignation. In face of
government determination to oust Communists from positions threatening Nanking and Shanghai, Marshall
abandons further efforts to restore constantly ruptured
truce.*

INTRODUCTION

Perhaps Jack Beal could have performed an even greater public service had he published this volume earlier in our involvement in Vietnam. It is a record which everyone interested in East Asia could read with profit. Fortunately it is not too late to draw inferences which are invaluable to consideration of current Asian problems.

In 1947 I happened to be in Moscow with General Marshall, then Secretary of State, in a conference on German and Austrian affairs. We had been in contact during World War II regarding North Africa and Europe. I have never met a more honest and straightforward individual or one who had greater abhorrence of duplicity. In Moscow he was fresh from his Chinese experience and whenever he had a free moment his thoughts reverted to that abortive mission. Its failure weighed heavily on him, but I am not sure whether he even then understood the chasm which separated his ideas and purposes from those reservations and fears inherent in Chiang Kai-shek, who for many years had lived with the Communists and later broke with them.

The author suggests that Chiang Kai-shek had twenty years of experience in dealing with the Communists, but Secretary of State Byrnes and the American public were just beginning that experience. This made for different assessments of tactics, with Chiang utterly convinced that the Communists were untrustworthy, and Washington still willing to believe that Russian intransigence was only temporary.

The author's fascinating account relates to the agonizing prelude to the Communist takeover of the world's most populous nation, and developments affecting the United States which flowed from that event. As an example, it is safe to assert that the United States would not be involved in Vietnam today nor would it have had to fight in Korea without that development.

The author skillfully portrays the delicate web of the three-cornered relationship in which the United States sought to maneuver in its futile effort to reconcile the Nationalist forces, civil and military, with the recalcitrant Mao element operating with the encouragement and support of the Soviet Union.

The text reveals certainly that American policy was governed by friendly and constructive thoughts. The American government and people wished the Chinese well, and there was inclination in Washington to regard the Chinese Communists as just another local political party with traditional ambitions. It seems not unfair to say that we totally underestimated those ambitions which concerned dominance of China, the destruction of the existing political and social structure, and opposition to the democratic regime we envisaged and toward which the Nationalists made faltering steps. To General Marshall and to an impatient President and policy makers in Washington, the Chinese problem seemed restricted to reconciliation between warring factions; they worked for an end to civil war, and for reconstruction after the frightful devastation of the Japanese occupation with the ensuing horrendous suffering. We had not comprehended the broader implications of Mao's favorite slogan—the only avenue to power is through the barrel of a gun. We clung stubbornly to the belief that the Communists would give up their private armies even after they were equipped with the mass of Japanese weapons captured by the Russians in the process of stripping industrial Manchuria.

We were innocents abroad concerned with promoting the unity of China in the interest of world stability. The fact that the Communists were dead set against our brand of

Chinese unity never seemed to occur to us at the time. Mr. Beal's account reflects Washington's inability then to provide to General Marshall and to Ambassador Leighton Stuart the fundamental direction which the precarious situation demanded. Of course, Washington did not provide that guidance. The predicament was similar to that during World War II when American foreign service officers on duty in China, some serving as advisers to Chinese forces which included Communists, were not provided with sound and essential guidance. American policy still bore the imprint of President Roosevelt's grand design of cooperation with the Soviet Union. That central idea alone would have prevented all-out support of the Chinese Nationalists and obliged a straddle for non-partisan approach to chimerical reconciliation of the two Chinese factions.

Mr. Beal's story is revealing in its analysis, which shows that the Kuomintang failed not because of inadequate American aid but rather because of fatigue and decay, lack of will to fight, and loss of popular support. By the same token the Communists through ruthless discipline and fanatical zeal presented themselves to the Chinese people as their "Liberators." His account demonstrates that the Chinese Communists in their determination to triumph relied on the disintegration of the Chinese Nationalists, the terrible poverty gripping the masses then living in the nightmare of a runaway inflation, and the devastation wrought by the Japanese occupation. The intense, widespread misery alone was sufficient to cause the people to lose confidence in the Nationalist Government.

All of this correctly assumed that American public opinion would not in any event have supported direct military intervention on behalf of the Chinese Nationalists against the Communists. It is also possible that such intervention would not have been accepted by many Chinese. After years of Japanese occupation widespread xenophobia was prevalent.

The sad fact is that the civil war in China was beyond the control of the United States.

In 1946 General Marshall obeyed his instructions and loyally attempted to restore peace in China. During months a long series of proposals and counterproposals were made which had little or no effect upon the course of military activity and produced no political settlement. Probably no one except General Marshall could have accomplished what he did—the cease-fire agreement, Executive Headquarters, the Demobilization and Reorganization Agreement. But all of this came to naught. He displayed limitless patience and willingness to promote an agreement between the Chinese Nationalists and the Chinese Communists. Perhaps he failed to recognize that the Chinese Communists were fanatically committed to the domination of all China for reasons of ideology, hatred, and the ambitions of their leadership, enjoying as they did the approval of Moscow. It is easy enough in retrospect to believe that they intended to destroy totally the bourgeois Chinese political and social structure.

It is impossible to read Mr. Beal's absorbing account of his activity as a consultant of the Nationalists and a very useful intermediary between them and the Marshall Mission without analogy to Vietnam. In both situations there emerges the factor of substantial Russian support. In the case of China, Russian ability to support the Chinese Communists of course was limited by immediate postwar supply problems. After all, this was the period when the Soviet Union stripped industrial and other equipment from a large part of China. In recent years the Soviet Union from its vast arsenal has been able easily to provide North Vietnam with modern equipment without which it would have been obliged long ago to quit. There are also visible in the present account the familiar charges of corruption in the Kuomintang rather than concern with the ruthless terrorism and brutality practiced by Communist elements. It is easy to note a similarity of emphasis in some current reports of corruption and black markets in Saigon, and criticism of the inadequacies of an imperfect but developing democratic regime together with an American tendency to ignore the Hanoi terroristic dictatorship, the real road block to peace. The similarity is marked.

In reluctantly laying down Mr. Beal's narrative I regret that he was not able to continue the story until the departure of Chiang Kai-shek for Taiwan.

Robert D. Murphy

FOREWORD

In 1946, when the United States was just beginning to relax from the strain of the Second World War, blissfully ignorant as a nation that it had acquired enormous world-wide responsibilities with its new power, General George C. Marshall was sent to China by President Truman. The basic thought underlying his assignment was that the "civil war" which had broken out as soon as the Japanese surrendered must not be permitted to distract the United States from its primary task of helping Europe to rehabilitate itself. The method chosen to stop the fighting was to promote a coalition government, so that Mao Tse-tung's Communist minority would join Chiang Kai-shek's Kuomintang in ruling the country and set its course on the paths of democracy. Americans who have suggested using this formula to settle the war in Vietnam would do well to restudy the American experience on the mainland.

Quite abruptly I found myself in the midst of the 1946 operation as an independent adviser under contract to the Chinese government. As a Washington newsman I was current on the major events, but sudden immersion in them day to day was a completely different matter. In a very short space of time I had to meet people bearing what to me were very strange names, and identify their roles. I learned, for example, that Chang Chun was an individual, governor of Szechuan Province, and one of the Kuomintang representatives in the early negotiations presided over by General Marshall; and Changchun a city, the capital of Manchuria, possession of which was a major objective of both sides in the fighting. It took me much longer to distinguish between Wu Tieh-cheng, Secretary-General of the National Government, and Wu Ting-chang, Secretary-General of the Kuomintang (Nationalist) Party; one a Brezhnev, the other a Kosygin in terms of the division of power in Russia after Khrushchev.

There is a hoary cliché about the difficulty Americans have in telling Chinese apart. George Yeh, an urbane and cultured man who later became Foreign Minister, once made ironic allusion to it when he was asked by correspondents how Chinese police could have mistaken the identity of an American they had arrested. "I don't know," he said, smiling a bit as he added: "Maybe all Americans look alike to Chinese."

All this is by way of advising the reader to take a relaxed approach to the Chinese names he encounters. Old China Hands will recognize most of them, and researchers may find footnotes to history in their activities. But this book was not written primarily for Old China Hands. It is a story told chronologically and, being chronological, introduces characters from time to time who have only walk-on parts in the larger drama. The principals and the supporting cast will make themselves apparent as the narrative goes on.

The two most prominent Americans were, of course, General Marshall and Ambassador John Leighton Stuart. The Chinese were Generalissimo Chiang; Madame Chiang; Dr. T. V. Soong, the Prime Minister that year; Chou En-lai, head of the Communist delegation in Nanking; Chen Li-fu, one of two brothers heading what was known as the "CC clique," a powerful faction within the Kuomintang. Among other Chinese the names of Dr. Peng Hsueh-pei, the Minister of Information, and Dr. Lee Wei-kuo, his vice-minister, are disproportionately evident in this account because they were two officials with whom I dealt more frequently than others of equal or higher rank.

Americans still mystified by what went on in that critical year about which there has been much bitter dispute among the experts are invited back of the scenes to see events from the unique vantage point I occupied. It should help them form their own opinion as to the wisdom of American policy; perhaps they will find parallels that apply to Vietnam today.

J.R.B.

CHAPTER ONE

*General George C. Marshall is drafted by President Truman
at end of 1945 to undertake mission to China. Truman statement directs him to work for an end to hostilities between
Chiang Kai-shek's Kuomintang government and Mao Tse-
tung's Communists; to speed Japanese repatriation; and to urge
political conference that would return China to "effective
Chinese control." After initial success in Chungking, Marshall
returns to consult Washington on needs of united China seeking to recover from World War.*

There are times when one's life can take an unexpected and
completely new course virtually overnight. General George
C. Marshall, after a lifelong career as a professional soldier,
turned over his command as Chief of Staff to General Dwight
D. Eisenhower one morning, and was drafted that same afternoon to start a new career in diplomacy. President Truman,
in his memoirs, recalls the circumstances under which he
picked the distinguished war leader to undertake his mission
to China. Mr. Truman had learned of the unexpected resignation of Ambassador Patrick J. Hurley; he went to the telephone in the Red Room of the White House and put in a
call to General Marshall at his home in Leesburg, Virginia.
Without any preliminary he said: "General, I want you to go
to China for me." Marshall said, "Yes, Mr. President," and
hung up. Two days later the general explained to the President why he had been so abrupt, but Mrs. Marshall gives a
more poignant account in her book, *Together,* describing her
life as an army wife. She told of the sense of relief with which

they drove from Washington on that late November day of
1945, and how they had stood for a few minutes on the portico
of their stately home, enjoying the peace of their sunlit, tree-
shaded surroundings. Then they entered the house and she
started upstairs for a brief rest before dinner. Halfway up she
heard the telephone ring. When she came down an hour later
the radio was carrying a news broadcast announcing the appointment. Marshall said, "That call was from the President.
I couldn't bear to tell you until you had had your rest."

Peaceful retirement for Marshall was not to be, even
though he had earned it many times over as the nation's top
soldier during its greatest war. Nor was there to be real peace
for the world, even though the surrender of Japan the previous August had brought the conflict officially to an end.
Fighting broke out immediately on the Asian continent between Chiang Kai-shek's Nationalist Government and the
Chinese Communists led by Mao Tse-tung. Only three
months had elapsed since V-J Day and already it was
apparent that China was going to be a continuing source of
trouble in the world's search for peace.

Marshall's departure from Washington took place on December 15. Mr. Truman set forth his mission in a statement
issued the same day, the essence of which was expressed in a
passage which said the United States Government believed it
essential

"1. That a cessation of hostilities be arranged between the
armies of the National Government and the Chinese Communists and other dissident Chinese armed forces for the
purpose of completing the return of all China to effective
Chinese control, including the immediate evacuation of the
Japanese forces.

"2. That a national conference of representatives of major
political elements be arranged to develop an early solution
to the present internal strife—a solution which will bring
about the unification of China."

The Chinese government was making plans to move its

capital to Nanking in May, but at the time it was still operating from the wartime capital of Chungking in the interior province of Szechuan, and it was to Chungking that Marshall went. In remarkably short order he had won approval of three agreements which seemed to accomplish the basic purpose of his mission. On March 11, 1946, he returned to the United States for consultation.

"He was of the opinion," explained the State Department's 1949 White Paper, *United States Relations with China*, "that he should make a brief visit [to Washington] to obtain financial and economic facilities to aid China and return to China in time to assist in adjusting differences which were certain to arise over the major problems connected with the agreements reached. It was his opinion that steps had to be taken to assist China and its people in the increasingly serious economic situation and to facilitate the efforts being made toward peace and unity in China and toward the establishment of a unified defense force."

In the initial period of approximately three months, though there had been spectacular progress on the major problems, several incidents took place which distressed Marshall. The government had suppressed some Communist newspapers. There had been a raid on a Communist delegation headquarters where signal equipment was used to communicate with Mao Tse-tung in Yenan; the raiders were unknown, but government agents were suspected. Theodore H. White and Annalee Jacoby were about to publish a book, *Thunder Out of China*, a stinging indictment of corruption and inefficiency in the Chiang Kai-shek regime, and Marshall had been told that it was banned in China. He felt these and similar incidents would arouse unfavorable reaction in the United States, where book-banning and censorship were usually disapproved.

Marshall reasoned that throughout its period of postwar reconstruction China needed the support of the U.S.—of its people as well as its government—and that such incidents

obviously would get in the way of good relations. He and his
staff could protest to Chinese officials and point out the
harm they were causing, but Marshall felt cautionary advice
would be more effective if the government heard it from
someone independent of his mission. The Chinese, he concluded, needed an adviser familiar with both U. S. Government thinking and American public opinion. Accordingly he
suggested that they hire an American adviser for this purpose. The Chinese government promptly agreed but since it
was his idea they asked him to find a suitable candidate. He
assigned the job to a member of his staff, and thus it was
I was approached.

It was, to me, a most surprising proposition. I knew no
more about China than the average American, and certainly
claimed no expertise in the area. It was explained that the job
did not call for a Far East expert but someone familiar with
American politics and public opinion. For the previous
twelve years I had been a Washington correspondent, covering the U. S. Congress and other capital news sources, and
had joined the Washington staff of *Time* just two years before. When I learned that the magazine was willing to grant
a leave of absence I accepted. In due time I got a call from
the Chinese Embassy saying that the Prime Minister, Dr.
T. V. Soong, had instructed that I be offered a contract to
serve as an adviser to the National Government.

Marshall's emissary had gone into the incidents that had
prompted the general to suggest the job, and discussed the
reasoning behind it. "Your mission," he said, "will be to keep
the Chinese out of trouble with the United States."

It was an exciting assignment. I felt that the U.S. and
Russia were more directly confronting each other in China
in working out their postwar relationships than they were in
Europe, where a number of other politically advanced states
were involved. At the same time I had misgivings based on
the vagueness of the mission as expressed in the capsule in-
struction given me. How did one keep a government "out of

trouble with the United States"? Indeed, how *could* one? In theory, it seemed to me, it behooved an adviser to give his employer a completely independent judgment on questions put to him, and his effectiveness would depend on how cogently he could argue his case; his effectiveness would be nil if he tempered his advice to what he thought the employer wanted to hear. But it was hard to picture how this theory would translate in action. If I had any political opinion at the start it was influenced by the impression, widespread in the U.S. at the time, that the Chinese Communists were not really Communists, or puppets of the Russians, and were in fact the type of honest, frugal, incorruptible administrators who really ought to be running the country. It was scarcely reassuring when a State Department official, who was giving me what seemed to be a factual and serious briefing on Chinese affairs, blurted out at the end: "Of course T. V. Soong is the greatest crook in the world." I could get no specifics from him: "Everybody knows it." Stunned as I was by such statements, I could only conclude that some private, angry frustration had led him into what at worst could only be wild exaggeration; but that one remark was in the back of my mind all the time I was in China.

I had little time for reading or briefings. Marshall, who was in Washington for consultation at the time, was about to go back and he thought I should get to China as fast as possible. I made one decision. In view of the uncertainties I faced I would keep a diary. This I did throughout my stay; each night I wrote myself a full report of what I had witnessed that day and of conversations in which I had taken part. My two years of indoctrination in the *Time* system of reporting led me to do it in great detail, describing the looks of the individuals I dealt with, the surroundings, and my own impression of what they said. Some entries ran to thousands of words; some days a few lines sufficed. It is from this personal journal and related papers I collected that I draw the following account of events which so fatefully affected subsequent U.S. policy.

In San Francisco, on the eve of my departure for China by the Naval Air Transport Service, I looked up a family friend who had been a teacher in China at one time. Had I, he inquired, read Nathaniel Peffer's *Prerequisites to Peace in the Far East?* I had not even heard of it, nor of Peffer, a professor at Columbia University. My friend said, "If you can read only one book about the Far East, it should be Peffer's *Prerequisites to Peace,* and if you can read only one chapter of it, you should read Chapter Six." There was no chance of getting a copy before my departure, and my friend said he would have one of his students type out Chapter Six and mail it to me. He also told me I could not get better guidance in China than from J. Leighton Stuart, president of Yenching University at Peking, where he had taught. Peffer's book, published by the Institute of Pacific Relations in 1940, made eminent sense in Chapter Six, "The Internal Needs of China," when I finally got it, and so it would today if only history had some way of accommodating the real needs of the world's people. I saw Peffer several times during my stay in China, and Stuart became the U.S. ambassador soon after my arrival.

Also while in San Francisco I noted in the papers that Henry Wallace was in town to address a dinner of labor politicians. In Washington I had covered his activities as Vice-President, as well as the 1944 Democratic convention at which President Roosevelt had dropped him from the national ticket in favor of Harry S Truman. Remembering that in early 1944 he had undertaken a mission to China for Mr. Roosevelt, I dropped in on a press conference he was holding at the Palace Hotel, and stayed behind afterward to talk to him. Wallace had joined forces with political activists in the organized labor movement who eventually backed his Progressive candidacy for President in 1948, and some of his press conference had been devoted to "party discipline" among the Democrats.

I told him that some of the limited reading I had done

indicated that after his trip to China he had informed the President that the Chinese Communists were likely to take over the country. Was this true?

"I know nothing about the Communists," said Wallace. "I did not visit them. I did see Madame Sun Yat-sen and Dr. Sun Fo. They are sympathetic to the Communists."

In that case, I asked, did he have any knowledge to indicate that Mao's people were tied up with Russia?

Wallace did not answer directly. He said he had talked to an American, a correspondent for one of the big New York banks, who was caught in Peking at the time of Pearl Harbor. "The only way he could escape," Wallace recounted, "was through the territory of the Chinese Communists. It took him about nine months. He thinks they are agrarian reformists, interested in lowering interest rates and things like that."

He seemed unwilling to commit himself on a personal basis. He looked at me with what I thought was a pitying expression and said: "You are going into a very complicated situation. Talk about party discipline! You'll have Gestapo and thought police. You'll have to keep your mouth tight shut and your ears very much open."

I left him feeling rather disquieted.

CHAPTER TWO

U.S. public is not in a mood to accept nation's suddenly acquired global responsibilities. Popular "get the boys home" pressure is matched by demobilization riots and near mutinies at bases abroad. Allied capitals striving for cooperation toward building peace are alarmed by Russia's postwar demands, but both Washington and American public remain uncertain as to "agrarian" nature of Chinese Communists and their armed revolt against reputedly corrupt government.

Flying the Pacific in April 1946 was mainly the task of military transport aircraft, as was also the case over the Atlantic. The sleek, comfortable, swift commercial jet, with its pre-dinner cocktails, juicy steaks, and attentive stewardesses, was still years in the future; when I first flew the Atlantic in 1952 by commercial airline in a Constellation I marveled at the progress in speed and comfort accomplished in six years. For that matter, looking back nearly a quarter of a century in the light of the race to land on the moon, it is amazing to recall that it was only in January 1946 that the U. S. Army Signal Corps first bounced a radar signal off the moon, from Belmar, New Jersey. It was hailed as an important discovery in communications, demonstrating that high frequency impulses could penetrate the ionosphere.

For my flight to Shanghai the Chinese Embassy had arranged a B priority with the Naval Air Transport Service. It meant travel aboard the relatively slow C-54 wartime transports, fitted with what were known as MacArthur seats, being slipcovered, forward-looking chairs instead of the wartime inward-facing cold aluminum bucket seats. It was not uncomfortable but involved overnight stops in Hawaii, Kwajalein, and Guam, as well as some intermediate island-hopping for meals—breakfast, for example, in Okinawa after a midnight take-off from Kwajalein, before the final leg to the Chinese mainland. It took five days and I had plenty of time to ponder my assignment.

As one of the two superpowers which had emerged from the Second World War the United States was, I felt, confronted by Soviet Russia and by Communism on mainland China in a much more direct way than on the other side of the world. In Europe the confrontation involved other politically developed nations with long histories of democratic tradition. In China a largely illiterate peasant mass scarcely a generation removed from life under despotic imperial rule was undergoing all the stresses inherent in leaping virtually overnight from the oxcart to the airplane. There was not the same buffer to soften confrontation in the Far East.

The American public, as distinct from the government, was however only dimly aware of the global responsibilities which the nation had inherited from the war. Barely a decade before, in the depression of the 1930s, the country had been seeking "new frontiers" to overcome what looked like economic stagnation; the average citizen in 1946 did not yet realize they had been found, unwittingly, in places like Berlin and Korea. Domestically the public was preoccupied with quick demobilization and return home of the armed forces. From the Philippines to Europe troops were demonstrating against slowness in their repatriation; in Frankfurt one such protest was quelled by threat of bayonet. President Truman felt obliged to issue a formal White House statement. "The critical need for troops overseas has begun to slow down the army's rate of demobilization," he said. "The future of our country now is as much at stake as it was in the days of the war." There was a nationwide steel strike and a less crippling

—economically—but more personally inconvenient telephone walkout.

The United Nations General Assembly was holding its first meeting in London. Secretary of State James F. Byrnes was seeking to devise means of transferring the Western monopoly in atomic energy to international control, and considering suggestions for the assignment of national forces for use under direction by the Security Council to subdue aggression if it broke out again. Originally the concept, developed during the war, was that an international force could be employed punitively at the UN's behest, and committees studied the idea but it finally emerged, first in an emergency alliance forged to deal with Korea, and ten years later in the watered-down version of an emergency force sent to Suez to separate the combatants. The new international organization's first major problem was that of Iran, where the Soviet Union was refusing to pull out her troops and Andrei Gromyko was claiming UN discussion of it was "illegal." At the same time Russia was being very sticky about pulling out of Manchuria, but this did not get the same attention.

The democratic world had expected cooperation from the Soviet Union in the making of a lasting peace and was becoming uneasily puzzled by Russian actions which thwarted its hopes. The secrets of Yalta were just emerging; a Russian claim to the Kurile Islands and southern Sakhalin as war booty from Japan caused Byrnes to search the State Department records and discover it was true that Roosevelt and Churchill had agreed to it. Another Yalta secret—the award to Stalin of Russia's czarist rights in China's Manchurian railways and a naval base at Port Arthur—was kept secret at the time even from Chiang Kai-shek. When informed of it, at U.S. instigation he sent T. V. Soong, who was then Foreign Minister, to negotiate a treaty. Soong was presented with additional demands which he was unwilling to accept, but with Byrnes backing China on sticking to the Yalta terms, a treaty later was signed by Soong's successor, Dr. Wang Shih-chieh.

There was a slowly gathering resentment over Communism's grasping imperialism, particularly in Europe, but in the public mind it was still subliminal. Truman and other Western statesmen were learning that Communists talked a strange new language, in which the introduction of "democratic elements" in the postwar governments of Central Europe—a consummation devoutly sought by the U.S.—meant the infusion of totalitarian Communist control. But unwillingness to believe the worst of the Russians was such that not until his speech on St. Patrick's Day of 1948, outlining the "Truman Doctrine," did the President make so bold as to state in so many words what the country already knew—that it was Russia which was causing all the trouble. It was still two years before Communism's cynical takeover of power in Czechoslovakia, which prompted the creation of NATO as a mechanism for collective defense.

Even so, Stalin's Communism, mysterious as it appeared to the diplomats attempting to cope with it, was crystal clear in comparison with the murky nature of its oriental cousin. U.S. officials seeking guidance from Stalin about Mao Tse-tung and his followers were told that they were "oleomargarine" Communists—leading Ambassador Patrick J. Hurley to the conclusion that they were a sort of political kin to the minority Republicans in his then solidly Democratic home state of Oklahoma. Certainly the impression prevailed in the United States that "Communist" was the wrong label for the Chinese variety: they were agrarian reformers and quite possibly the democratic hope of China as an alternative to what was regarded as the corrupt and inefficient regime of Chiang Kai-shek. Although I was infected by this impression as I flew the Pacific, I was unwilling to accept it without seeing for myself.

The final leg of the flight was through mist and drizzle that kept visibility to a minimum. As the airplane descended to circle for its landing at Shanghai's Kiangwan Airport I could dimly make out on the ground through the haze seemingly endless acres of transport planes, an enormous junk heap of war. Literally thousands of C-47s, C-46s, and C-54s were strewn helter-skelter, apparently waiting to be discarded for good or cannibalized for civilian use. I thought of the words of Charles Dickens which had characterized another era: "It was the best of times, it was the worst of times . . ." and they seemed most apropos on that rainy Sunday morning of April 28, 1946. The advent of peace gave promise for the future, but the world had been left in such devastation that the job of reconstruction was greater than anything it had ever faced before.

CHAPTER THREE

Arrival in Shanghai gives vivid introduction to inflation and widespread gossip about corruption. Prime Minister Soong shows interest in trend of American politics and U.S. reaction to Russian policy. In Nanking, Marshall describes how mistrust on both sides has eroded military truce and political agreements he supervised in Chungking. Correspondents released from Communist capture in Changchun report Mao's armies have taken most of Manchuria with Russian help and intend to stay. First meeting with Generalissimo Chiang.

Shanghai was a coming down to earth mentally as well as physically. Emerging from the aircraft, I had the impression of having learned the truth of that old cliché about being in "the middle of nowhere." It was 9:18 A.M., local time, and it was drizzling. There was no terminal building in sight, though I thought I could make out the shape of a control tower at some distance through the mist. When the flight started in San Francisco the passenger list had consisted about half of military personnel and half of hard-hat construction workers en route to projects at various parts of the Pacific, but as we changed planes at stops along the way the hard hats peeled off to other destinations. Of the original company of travelers, only one fellow civilian, Ernest Musselwhite of Standard Vacuum, remained. Suddenly it came over me that I was a stranger in a strange land at the far end of $936 worth of airplane ride, and it was not a comfortable feeling. As we stood wondering what to do next Musselwhite said, "For two cents I would climb right back on that plane and go home." I told him two of us felt exactly the same way.

In a moment three stake trucks rumbled up through the mist, come to pick up the army, navy, and marine arrivals. There was nothing to do but pile our baggage on the navy truck and climb aboard. We were told it would take us to a reception center at "the Glenline building," whatever that was. Nothing so far had provided any impression of being in China, but as we proceeded, the sights and sounds of the Far East came gradually through the mist: first the sight of coolies with their conical straw hats, then Chinese soldiers guarding an ammunition dump as we left the airfield—giving the vague impression that fighting was going on somewhere near. Then came occasional glimpses of the distinctive curved-tile roof of a Chinese building and finally a rickshaw pulled by a coolie. When we reached the built-up sections there were flags and pennants everywhere and a bustle of activity.

At the Glenline building Musselwhite got in touch with the local Standard Oil representative, who claimed not to have received any cable about his arrival. The Washington Embassy had informed me it had cabled the date of my departure and I could expect to be met and provided with hotel accommodation. But on reflection I realized that the Foreign Ministry could not have known the date of my arrival, uncertain as it was when I started out, owing to transfers of planes in the Pacific. Rather than try to run down a local ministry representative on Sunday I telephoned my friend Bill Gray, bureau chief for *Time* and *Life* in Shanghai —I was puzzled not to find a listing for *Time* in the phone book until someone pointed out it was a directory left over from the Japanese occupation, none having been printed since—and was invited to accept *Time*'s hospitality for the time being. Bill told me to hire a pedicab, the tricycle version of the ricksaw, and tell the driver, "Broadway Mansions." Every coolie in Shanghai knew where it was, he said. And thus, with my flight bag and briefcase at my feet and my portable typewriter on my lap, I was pedaled to my first stopping place in China.

Before I checked in next day with the Foreign Ministry's local office I ventured out to learn about Chinese inflation. The official exchange rate at the time was 2020 yuan CNC (Chinese National Currency, commonly referred to as so many dollars CNC by the Americans) but the exchange shops were offering more. For $15 U.S. I got 36,000 CNC at a rate of 2400. For 16,000 CNC I sent off a cable to Washington informing my family of my arrival and for 210 CNC per half ounce I dispatched some air mail letters. In equivalent U.S. currency these prices were not out of line, but when I had to pay 2000 CNC, or about $1.00 for a fifteen-cent tin of U.S. smoking tobacco—one which obviously had come from an army PX—I realized I would have to adjust to a different scale of values. When I returned to the *Time* ménage that evening I learned that as the day progressed the CNC rate had gone up: George Silk, a *Life* photographer, had got a rate of 2440, and later Bill Gray got 2500; the Shanghai *Evening Post & Mercury* said it reached 2600 during the day. Gray said there was 10 trillion currency outstanding, and paper currency was being printed at the rate of 100 billion a month.

My visit to the ministry office resulted in an appointment for me next day at 9:30 A.M. with Prime Minister Soong. I recorded it as follows:

SHANGHAI, April 30—I went to the offices of the Executive Yuan on the second floor of the Bank of China building and was taken to a sort of directors' room, wood-paneled, with a large table and green tapestry chairs. Hot tea was brought for me in a glass. A man who introduced himself as Jim Brennan came in to meet me. He turned out to be an associate of Tommy Corcoran, the Washington lawyer who represents Soong in the United States. Soon I was beckoned in to Soong's office, similar in décor to the directors' room, though with black leather chairs.

Soong greeted me cordially. He was bigger than I expected—

tall and proportionately broad. His black hair was combed back pompadour style with a sort of flattened effect, and he wore shell-rimmed glasses. His blue pin-stripe suit was rather rumpled and so was his white shirt, giving him an air of being hard at work. He had three telephones on his desk and four little push buttons in a black stand.

Brennan sat in while we talked, but left about halfway through. Dr. Soong was interested in the political situation in the United States. I reviewed it at some length: Truman's popularity had dropped; the independents in the Roosevelt coalition he had inherited were uncertain where to turn; Southern Democrats were leagued with Republicans in Congress to hamstring Truman's program; the Democratic split encouraged Republican conservatives to think in terms of someone like John Bricker for the presidential nomination in 1948. Dr. Soong was interested in Harold Stassen's chances. I said I thought they were poor. Under his questioning I added that I saw little chance that Truman would be unseated by the Democrats and little chance that a third party would develop, though if one did the best bet would be Henry Wallace, who had considerable popular support although he was politically inept.

Dr. Soong inquired about U.S. feeling toward Russia, and about Byrnes and how he was doing as Secretary of State. I told him my judgment was that distrust of Russia was growing; that Byrnes seemed to be growing in the job and doing better, and apparently friction between him and Truman had been smoothed over. Dr. Soong asked if I knew David Lu, and said he was thinking of getting him out here. [Lu was head of the Washington bureau of the Central News Agency of China, and a good friend of mine; he had covered Soong's trip to Moscow when he negotiated the Sino-Soviet Treaty.] I said it was a wonderful idea. He seemed pleased and said Dave and I would work as a team. I will be stationed in Nanking, he went on, since the government was in the process of moving from Chungking and would make the transfer official on May 5. He himself will be flying to Nanking Thursday or Friday and he invited me to go with him. He said President Chiang Kai-shek (to whom he referred as "the Gissimo"; the *Time* people call him "the Gimo") wanted to meet me and would ask me many questions about U.S. reaction. "Give it to him straight," he said. "We all—the Gissimo, you, and I—have the same aims, but sometimes the Gissimo doesn't calculate the political reactions."

We talked half an hour or more. It was a very friendly reception, and made me feel better about the outlook here.

Shanghai, I was soon to learn, was interested in subjects different from, and rather incidental to, what absorbed Nanking. The foreign residents, especially those who remembered the days when the city was divided into foreign concessions and run by their respective governments, were interested in politics only as it bore on their business interests. Foreign businessmen spent their time discussing the shortcomings of the Chinese government and passed along whatever gossip they picked up—gossip the accuracy of which they could not possibly be in a position to know. I was given a fascinating glimpse of it that night at dinner with the *Time* people, where I was introduced to three other guests who were attempting to establish an air freight business between Australia and Shanghai. The head of the business was a former U. S. Air Force pilot. My journal recorded the evening thus:

SHANGHAI, May 1—His story at dinner last night is somewhat fabulous as a shoestring enterprise proposition; with his friends he saved enough from his pay to acquire a surplus DC-3 and buy some secondhand clothing in the U.S. which he flew to China. But Chinese will not buy three-button suits or sweaters with octagon designs on them (they look like turtles, a symbol of cuckoldry in China) and they lost $25,000 on the deal. They flew some other cargo to Australia, making enough to pay for the gasoline, then flew back with woolen goods, and made $60,000— enough to buy another surplus plane.

He was beefing to me about (1) inflation, which brought business to a standstill, and (2) the squeeze, which cost him as much as customs duty on his last load—some $3300 U.S. He was full of stories about Soong family venality: "everyone in China below the Generalissimo is out to make a killing"; the Soongs were the wealthiest family in the world, with a billion dollars cached away in the U.S., etc. He repeated a story I've heard before to the effect that a plane dispatched from Chungking for Washington with "important secret documents" had to ditch in the river when it caught on fire; when salvaged, what it proved to have was U.S. currency which the Soong family was sending to the U.S.

I listened as he spouted on: every time T. V. Soong comes to Shanghai the CNC market rises or falls. The rumor is that it will go to 10,000 this time. "Mark my words," he said, "within six weeks it will rise and then fall below the official rate while they make their killing."

He wanted to know my opinion on Russia. His was that we could whip Russia now but not in ten or fifteen years, and at that time we will have to fight them. He thinks U.S. foreign policy was all wrong because we have renounced such extraterritoriality as the International Settlement in Shanghai, which, when it existed, was a well-run municipality. Now, under the Chinese, it is graft-ridden, as per above.

The same entry noted that the Shanghai papers of the last two days had carried stories charging that seventeen rice merchants had used a $1 billion CNC government loan to corner the rice market and, by withholding rice during this time of need, had profiteered to the extent of nearly $1 billion CNC. Bill Gray, reading about it, commented: "You know, I believe that."

SHANGHAI–NANKING, May 2—Jim Brennan called to say that Dr. Soong was planning to leave for Nanking at 2 P.M. A car was sent to pick me up at twelve-fifteen and take me to Dr. Soong's home —a most pleasant, spacious house with a large lawn and garden,

where I met Madame Soong and a Chinese gentleman named
Mr. Lee. Madame Soong is young, beautifully groomed, and very
attractive. It was a Western-style lunch—sliced goose as the main
course. Mr. Lee, Jim told me later, is a Shanghai playboy (his
gray hair made the term seem inappropriate) who likes to gamble
and whose hobby is planning gardens. He planned Dr. Soong's
Shanghai garden (T.V. plans to spend weekends in Shanghai)
and was being taken to Nanking to make over the garden at No. 1
House, official residence of the Prime Minister.

We left in several cars for the airfield. The Chinese National
Air Corporation had a special plane, a DC-3, ready (Dr. Soong's
travels always tie up the airline's schedules) and the party loaded
aboard. The twenty-one seats were almost all filled.

T.V. has an imperious sort of walk. It was stifling hot in the
plane at first and after take-off T.V. stood up to take off his coat
and vest. On a waist holster, strapped over his left hip, was a re-
volver. It startled me, but served to remind me that China is unsettled politically and a dangerous land. He stood for a moment
looking back through the plane with the air of a man accustomed
to ruling others.

The flight was smooth but a dense haze prevented much view
of the ground. I only noticed what an immense amount of irri-
gation there was—canals and ponds everywhere. We flew across
the Yangtze several times, finally crossed the low mountain near
Nanking, and landed at the small airport within the city wall.
From there we drove to No. 1 House. Madame Soong said
they have a house of their own on the highest hill in Nanking,
from which the city lights can be seen at night. There was tea
immediately, and some good, creamy ice cream.

Dr. Soong then took me over to the offices of the Executive
Yuan in a spacious, Chinese-style building, and sent for the Minister of Information. But Dr. K. C. Wu had not yet arrived from
Chungking, and it was a subordinate official who answered the
summons. He did not speak English and was accompanied by a
thin young man named Charles C. H. Wan, who told me he had
attended the Columbia School of Journalism and once worked

for the New York *Herald Tribune*. Wan translated for him; the
official was probably facing the dread T. V. Soong for the first
time in his life and appeared to be frightened out of his wits.
T.V. ordered him to find me a place to live, so I went off with
him and Wan to the Central Hotel, where a room was produced.

What a room! It had a private bath, complete with tub and a
toilet that flushed, but no light, no hot water, not even toilet
paper. The bedroom had sickly green walls of stucco; there was
a four-poster brass bed (without bedding), a couple of chairs, a
table, a dresser. It adjoined a balcony overlooking a central courtyard. One weak bulb, hanging from the ceiling on a pulley con-
trivance which permitted it to be hauled down close to the table,
was the only illumination. I felt the official was so unnerved by
having been summoned before Soong that I would not prolong
his agony, reasoning that, if the correspondents could live there,
I could get along for the time being, and sent a room boy to get
bedding. I dined, thank God, with the Soongs, for the hotel was
not serving meals. The Minister of War, General Chen Cheng,
and his wife were guests but neither of them spoke English and
T.V.'s attempts to converse with me occasionally were rather desultory. He asked, for example, what was responsible for the great
success of *Time*. I had never thought about it particularly, but I
quickly totted up eight reasons in my mind. T.V. listened to the
first but by the time I was ready to launch on the second he was
talking Chinese again to the Minister of War.

Both housing and food were initial problems for a newcomer. In Washington I had been warned that houses would
be scarce, and it was part of my contract that the government
would find me a suitable place to live with my family as soon
as they could arrange a sailing. As for my own temporary accommodations, I did not think about them particularly in
advance. While I subconsciously expected adequate food and
housing in a great Western port city like Shanghai, I would
not have been surprised had I encountered postwar hardships
of one kind or another. I frankly did not expect the luxury of

being a guest in a sixteenth-floor penthouse suite in Shanghai's Broadway Mansions, one of the Far East's finest hotels, waited on hand and foot by servants, relieved of coping with the problem of ordering meals in Chinese restaurants. Perhaps because I had enjoyed several days of this the squalor of Nanking's Central Hotel was more of a letdown than I expected. I was not surprised to learn later that during the war it had been the chief brothel for Japanese officers. After one night in the place, and after Charlie Wan's help next morning in finding myself a not too appetizing but standard American breakfast of scrambled eggs, toast, and coffee in a restaurant called the New Moon Café, I telephoned General Marshall's residence to request a chance to see him and also to inquire if I could get into the Metropolitan Hotel, which was occupied by officers of the U. S. Military Assistance Group in China (MAGIC).

Word came back that Marshall was tied up for the day with a visit from Herbert Hoover and a call on the Generalissimo but would see me next day. Meantime, I was told, I could move any time to the Metropolitan, which I did before lunch. It was such a psychological prop to be among fellow Americans and eating American meals at the outset that I rather outstayed my welcome, but I shamelessly brazened it out. Gradually, however, I grew very fond of Chinese food, which can be the equal of any cuisine in the world. Colonel David Barrett, an Old Army China Hand, confided one secret of its enjoyment: "Taste it, and if you like it, eat it; just don't ask what's in it."

Since my appointment with Marshall next day was not until 5 P.M. I spent the morning preparing a memorandum for Dr. Soong based on beefs I had heard from the correspondents so far in Shanghai and Nanking. Phil Potter, of the Baltimore *Sun*, and Bill Gray had both asked me to help them get interviews with Dr. Soong, but this was part of a policy of greater access to Chinese officials by foreign newsmen I wanted to discuss with him personally, and I dealt mainly with the complaints I had heard from Fritz Opper of ABC and George Moorad of CBS. In Shanghai they had told me there was such a lack of radio broadcast facilities in China—U.S. television, incidentally, was still a couple of years in the future—that they were both pulling out to cover the forthcoming atom bomb tests at Bikini atoll and would not come back. "Their beef," I had noted, "was total lack of interest by Chinese officials, administrative and technical incompetence, nepotism, and lack of coordination in the Chinese communications setup. They cited a news story saying that China had bought six tons of signal material, including radio equipment, and said T.V. was the only man in China capable of bringing order out of the chaos in communications." I passed along to Soong their argument that satisfactory equipment existed but it would take direct orders from him to the Minister of Communications to get it utilized for effective results, and I offered to work with the minister on the problem. Then, having dispatched the memo to the Executive Yuan, I rode off to meet Marshall in the car which the Ministry of Information had provided for me —a right-hand-drive vehicle of such ancient vintage that I was unable to determine the make, but complete with chauffeur and footman. "It must be fifteen years old, at least," I recorded in my journal, "and it rattles like hell." Cars of any age were at a premium in Nanking. My record of the session with Marshall reads:

NANKING, May 4—General Marshall is occupying the home of the former German ambassador. It is Chinese style outside, and modern, comfortable, and spacious inside—probably the best in Nanking. The general invited me out on the terrace and we dragged a couple of wicker chairs near the edge, overlooking the lawn and garden.

Marshall seemed distant at first but he warmed up. We talked about an hour and a half, and covered so many things it is hard to remember them. Also, I was able to follow him only vaguely, because I have been all but blacked out on detailed news for some time, first because of the five days on the Pacific flight, and since then because of poor coverage by the papers available.

While he recited all the difficulties, all the stalemates in the political negotiations between the Kuomintang and the Communists as they exist, his general air was distinctly not hopeless, as is that of the correspondents to whom I have talked. He said there has been bad blood on both sides—broken faith, total mistrust. Chiang Kai-shek recently (I hadn't seen it) made a statement saying the Communists were not to be trusted—just as Marshall had a U.S. loan all fixed for signing within twenty-four hours. It knocked the loan out the window, temporarily, I gather; discussing the loan was one reason for his trip to Washington.

I asked how I could help. Marshall said by watching for just such statements and heading them off. He said he had told the Gimo that I was well recommended and the only thing he did not know about me was whether I would be aggressive enough in arguing my case in just such circumstances.

"I probably have not properly represented the interests of the United States," he said. "I feel that I am representing the Chinese people," meaning that in the clash between the Kuomintang and the Communists the Chinese people are being lost sight of.

For my ears only, Marshall said that Chiang's current terms for settlement are exactly what Chou En-lai offered him four weeks ago. They were, he said, the four points given in the newspapers last week, attributed to Marshall, but which actually were given out by the Gimo. Chou, he said, knows they were put out by the Gimo. This meant nothing to me, since I had not seen the points, and was not sufficiently cued in to understand; perhaps I should have asked him to elaborate, but I thought I could fill myself in.

Marshall regards the "CC clique" as his enemies in this deal, and has so told the Gimo, with considerable emphasis. They (the CC) sabotaged the peace negotiations by stirring up anti-Communist demonstrations; by breaking into and sabotaging the Communist radio in Canton. It is now, he said, in the quarters of an American officer. Chou wasn't even permitted a radio until Marshall supplied him one to communicate with Yenan. The Chinese offered to let him use theirs for his messages—a ridiculous proposal. Also, he said, they had failed to provide for Chou's move from Chungking to Nanking, until finally Marshall provided his own plane and borrowed one for himself.

Finally, said Marshall, Chou came to him with evidence that the Nationalists were about to sabotage the railroad (the name of the place was strange to me and I failed to catch it) and make it look like a Communist plot, further to inflame the situation. Chou was appealing to Marshall to get in there with an inspection team, and Marshall had told him Brigadier General Henry A. Byroade would be in there tomorrow—Sunday. Chou would send someone, perhaps himself, but the Gimo was stalling and Marshall had told him that unless the Nationalists sent a member too he would go himself, as a means of causing the Nationalists to lose face.

If the reader is confused at this point by references to the CC clique as enemies of Marshall, or wondering why the Chinese government should transport Chou En-lai to Nanking, or what an inspection team was, he is only a shade more confused than I was myself at the outset as I plunged into a complicated situation. I wrote in my journal only what I understood and had to fill in the rest as I went along.

What I did understand was the agreements reached with Marshall's assistance in Chungking during his original three months in China. They were basic to what was happening, although no one was more aware than Marshall that on their adoption a great deal of work would be required to implement them and straighten out differences of interpretation.

The first agreement was signed on January 10 between the Kuomintang government and a Chinese Communist delegation headed by Chou En-lai. In this compact both sides, whose armies were fighting at various points in China, had agreed to cease fire at midnight January 13. It also created an

Executive Headquarters in Peking (EHQ), consisting of three commissioners, one representing each side and one representing the United States. EHQ was to have an operations staff similarly composed of three members, comprising field teams available to oversee observance of the truce and to carry out directives of headquarters. Although fighting had meanwhile broken out in Manchuria, Chou's request to Marshall was for a team to investigate a specific incident to forestall what he claimed was a Kuomintang plot to create trouble and blame the Communists.

The second agreement was embodied in resolutions adopted January 31 by a Political Consultative Conference (PCC). The political elements in this conference were the Kuomintang (KMT), the Chinese Communist Party (CCP), the Democratic League, the Youth Party, and some independent political personages.

In American terms, it was hard to think of these groups as political parties. The Kuomintang had been founded by Sun Yat-sen, leader of the revolution which overthrew the Manchu dynasty in 1911 and created the Chinese Republic. Sun's belief was that three stages would be required to consummate the revolution: first, the fighting to overthrow the dynasty; second, a period of "political tutelage" during which the Kuomintang would educate the masses in self-government; and, third, the advent of democratic government. It was as political tutors that the KMT was running the country. The Communists differed from a minority opposition party in that they ran their own government in the region they occupied and had their own army. Both these parties had large popular following, but the Democratic League, a group of left-wing individuals, had no real popular support and had status only because of the prominence and activity of its "leaders." The League faithfully followed the Communist line and was useful as a front organization with intellectuals. The Youth Party, which did have a rank and file, was under the thumb of the Kuomintang. In effect, therefore, it was the

Kuomintang vs. the Communists in the PCC, a body created—with American prodding—to bring about the third stage of Sun's revolution by coalescing the KMT and the Communists and creating a new multiparty government for China.

The PCC adopted resolutions on the organization of such a government and set forth civilian philosophy on military problems. The most pregnant of them dealt with the basic power conflict created by the existence of a Communist army independent of the government: "The army belongs to the State . . . [it] shall be established in response to the necessities of national defense." A resolution on peaceful national reconstruction held that "political disputes must be settled by political means"—an indirect commitment by both sides not to continue their fighting—and listed the rights of the people to include "the freedoms of person, thought, religion, belief, speech, the press, assembly, association, residence, removal, and correspondence."

All of these resolutions were adopted as guidance in amending a draft constitution initially put forward in 1936 but never acted on because the Japanese war interrupted. The constitution itself, which was intended to end the period of political tutelage, was to be written by a National Assembly called for May 5 in Nanking, but postponed because the Communists refused to name delegates to it.

The third and most remarkable of the Chungking agreements was one on military reorganization, signed on February 25. It provided for reduction of both the government and the Communist forces, down to a ratio of five to one. After twelve months the government would undertake to cut down its army to ninety divisions and the Communists to eighteen; in another six months there would be a further reduction to fifty government and ten Communist divisions. The reduced forces were to be integrated and deployed over five general areas of China. The object was to separate the army from politics. Marshall said of this pact when it was signed: "This agreement, I think, represents the great hope of China. I can only trust that its pages will not be soiled by a small group of irreconcilables who for a selfish purpose would defeat the Chinese people in their overwhelming desire for peace and prosperity."

Marshall was doing more than utter a pious hope in making this statement. Official statements, drab and uninformative as they may seem to the lay public, usually contain nuances of meaning for the people to whom they are primarily directed. Nowhere is a nuance more quickly recognized than in China, where the literature is built on nuances of thought. Marshall's reference to a "small group of irreconcilables" was a shaft aimed at the Kuomintang's "CC clique," so called because it was headed by two brothers named Chen, Li-fu and Kuo-fu. The CC clique was the largest single political element within the Kuomintang, a disciplined bloc that opposed the whole concept of coalition with the Communists. Despite the fact that their party leader, Chiang Kai-shek, had welcomed Marshall's mediation in the effort, they never ceased to believe that the only solution for China was complete eradication of the Communists and they were capable of disruptive action in secret. They were suspect every time an anti-Communist incident took place, such as the raid on the Communist radio station in Canton which Marshall had mentioned, though it was never possible to prove who was responsible for these incidents. Blame was invariably put on the CC clique but inevitably the government had to take the responsibility. As in Russia, where the Communist Party runs the government but is technically separate in its organization, the Kuomintang Party gave directives to the government. Chiang was head of both organizations, but in the government he had a number of officials representing the less potent "Political Science clique," rivals to the CC, and composed of Western-educated intellectuals.

As for the government's responsibility for moving Chou En-lai to Nanking, during the period of negotiation he was head of an official delegation in Kuomintang territory and thus entitled to treatment as a guest.

But at the time I was more interested in what Marshall had to say about the Russians and the Communists in Manchuria, since it seemed this was where Soviet and American interests confronted each other. The account of that first interview with Marshall goes on:

May 4 (continued)—Marshall finds no overt act by the Russian government in aid of the Communists, but aid is being given them by the local Soviet commanders. The anti-Communist agitation of the CC clique produced reaction among the political commanders with the Chinese Reds and they began exerting control in Manchuria. In violation of the January 10 agreement they took over territory, receiving rations from the Russians as well as the opportunity to seize Japanese munitions, thus gaining strength.

Other items: Herbert Hoover, who came through here yesterday, discovered that T. V. Soong had sold UNRRA goods (rice?) in Shanghai to hold down the CNC rate. Hoover was plenty sore about it and it won't be permitted again. Speaking of UNRRA, Marshall said the political postponement of the atom bomb test at Bikini atoll had affected China relief; it interfered with freight shipments that would otherwise be here, and will reduce the amount of food available to prevent famine.

One deal had been worked out which pleased Marshall very much. The Chinese wanted to acquire $15 million in dock facilities from the U. S. Navy and pay for it by offsetting against what the U.S. owes China, but the navy was against this form of payment. At a conference with Admiral Cooke, Commander of the Seventh Fleet, Marshall thought of this: why not let them pay in services? That was how it was worked out, with the price cut down to $5 million. The benefits are that the U.S. will have access to docking facilities in Shanghai and Tsingtao, where otherwise the nearest fleet repair station would be Guam: it does not require a treaty; the Foreign Liquidation Commission gets rid of surplus for which there was only one purchaser.

A houseboy brought us old-fashioneds as we neared the end of our talk. Marshall said he would send me the U.S. editorial summary he gets of everything pertaining to his mission, prepared for him every day in Washington.

The capsule account of what had been happening in Manchuria which I put down after the talk needed elaboration. A lot had happened while I was blacked out on news during the trip, and the accounts in the three Shanghai English-language papers did not give a connected picture of developments. As I filled it in later against the background of the cease-fire agreement, the Yalta agreements, and the terms of the Japanese surrender, the situation was as follows:

Despite the concessions made at China's expense by the Big Three at Yalta, there had been one benefit: Stalin had pledged himself to treat Chiang's government, not the Communists, as the legal representative of all China. The terms of the Japanese capitulation had provided that Chiang's commanders would receive the surrender of Japanese troops everywhere on Chinese soil. Yet in Manchuria, which the Russians had occupied after their six days of fighting at the very end of the war, they were timing their withdrawals so that the Communists could take over before the Nationalists had time to move in sufficient troops.

In early January General Tu Li-ming, Nationalist New Sixth Army commander for Manchuria, flew to Mukden with a forward echelon of officers to make contact with the Russians for the takeover. A few units of airborne troops were sent ahead by air to the Manchurian capital of Changchun. In Shanghai the New Sixth comprising 26,000 men, prepared to leave for Manchuria by ship.

Negotiations for takeover began in Changchun, and the Russians demanded more than they had been promised in the

Sino-Soviet Treaty. That document had given them joint partnership with China for thirty years in the Chinese Eastern Railway and the South Manchurian Railway, a joint naval base at Port Arthur, and the promise that Dairen would be a free commercial port. At Changchun they demanded, additionally, joint control over certain Japanese-developed heavy industry, commercial air rights and the construction of airfields throughout the former Japanese-occupied provinces; also a telephone line from Dairen to Manchuli on the Siberian border. Meanwhile fighting broke out in provinces to the west and south of Manchuria as the Communists moved to block the movement of government troops. On January 20 Chungking announced that fighting was going on in seven places, each of them involving points along a railroad, and the Communists broadcast from Yenan (but did not circulate in the *New China Daily News* which they were permitted to publish in Chungking) a charge that they had intercepted an order from Chiang Kai-shek to his generals prior to January 10 saying that a truce was about to be signed and advising them to beat the deadline by seizing strategic points in Jehol Province.

The Russians stalled on notifying the government of their withdrawal schedule—they were stripping Manchuria of its Japanese-built heavy industrial plant, as China and the U.S. subsequently discovered—and when they suddenly pulled out of Mukden on March 10 the Communists fought with Nationalist troops, though they did not take the city.

In late March and early April government forces entered various cities along the railway to Changchun as well as the capital itself, where they reported the Communists had surrounded the city and were dug in awaiting the Russian withdrawal. On April 4 a government spokesman said the Russian evacuation would take place within a few days and that Soviet authorities had given the Communists a schedule of their withdrawals which had not been provided to the government. The Nationalists sent additional troops toward Changchun from Mukden and reported that they had clashed with 25,000 Communists armed with Japanese weapons; farther south, between Peking and Mukden, the Communists were reported mounting an all-out offensive to prevent the government from reinforcing its troops and exercising its takeover rights in Manchuria. On April 14 the Russians completed evacuation of Changchun, where the Nationalist garrison consisted of a Peace Preservation Corps of only 7000 built around 4000 regular troops, and three days later the city fell to the Communists. A New York *Times* dispatch from Chungking announcing the capture said, "Obviously the Communist strategy in the Northeast [the name by which the Chinese knew Manchuria] is developing in accordance with a long-pursued plan, in the working out of which the Communists have closely coordinated their activities with the moves of the Russians."

Hearing Marshall's account of current activities made me feel I had made a beginning in catching up with what I needed to know, but I still had to meet the Generalissimo and that was not to come for several days. The next day, May 5, was devoted to the official investiture of Nanking as the capital. In company with a number of Chinese from the Ministry of Information I attended an outdoor meeting at which I got my first look at Chiang, as well as Madame Chiang. The Gimo, wearing a plain military uniform and cap, seemed to me not very oriental in facial cast; Madame Chiang eyed me in the midst of the Chinese crowd with what I thought was some curiosity. Later the Chiangs held a reception for the diplomatic corps and the Chinese thought it might be appropriate for me to attend, but I decided it would be better to await my set appointment.

Meantime I got word from Jim Brennan that Dr. Soong had accepted my recommendations about communications and an order had been drafted for the ministry. Brennan said T.V. had exploded over the recollection of how hard he had tried, unsuccessfully, during the war, to get signal equipment for China at a time when Britain and France were getting it, but signed the order nevertheless. It included arrangements for the foreign correspondents to have blanket filing privileges over the Chinese Government Radio Administration facilities; I had noted that their permits were currently unnecessarily restricted to filing from certain specific points and were of no value when they traveled. Brennan's news was followed by an appointment with Dr. Soong, at which I got a chance to talk about the need for readier access to Chinese officials by the foreign press. One reason the Communists get a good press in the U.S., I explained, was the ready availability of Chou En-lai or some other member of the Communist delegation whenever they needed information. I asked him to see Phil Potter of the Baltimore *Sun*, who was in town to do a story on the inflation situation, and he set an appointment for the next day. Soong was annoyed by a story in Shanghai's *China Press* under a UP dateline from Washington which he thought took a patronizing tone as to conditions on which the U.S. would insist if it made a loan to China. He asked me to draft a statement he could issue in reply, which I did afterward, but with a note saying that on second thought I believed it would be better for him to ignore it.

About this time it was decided I should have a Chinese name. The system is to pick one of the "hundred names" which sounds closest to the foreign name, so that it can be printed in Chinese ideographs. The "hundred names" are the group of surnames by which virtually all Chinese are known. The nearest approximation to Beal which a scholar of the ministry could work out was one that sounded to me like making it into two syllables, "Be Er," which was written thus:

The "Be" was a fairly common Chinese surname, and meant nothing; the "Er" meant "ear," but in some fashion I did not follow, it was connected with the philosopher Lao-tse, and therefore intended to be flattering. Both these sounds, however, were capable of being expressed in other characters.

The Chinese written language never failed to fascinate me. The word for "adviser" was made up of two characters meaning "wish think."

NANKING, May 9—Phil Potter had his interview with T.V. on inflation, and told Jim Brennan afterward that he was very impressed, though I have not had a chance to talk to Phil yet. I had phoned Jim that it would be a good idea to ask T.V. to take off his pistol and put it in a drawer until afterward, but Jim said he would be wearing his coat. Later, when I went to the Executive Yuan, Jim said T.V. was subject to constant ribbing by the Gimo because he refused to attend the regular Monday morning meetings at Sun Yat-sen's tomb where officials bowed three times to Sun's picture. "While the rest of them are doing that he is working," said Jim.

T.V. asked me to ride with him to the Gimo's where he was to attend a luncheon for General Eisenhower, here on a brief visit. He apparently has accepted my advice to forget the patronizing *China Press* article. One characteristic of him that shows to date is his pride in Chinese sovereignty and dignity. He is quick to resent any slur reflecting on China as a self-capable nation.

He said he had been considering my idea that he should hold periodic press conferences—Jim Brennan worked on him last night—and would hold one at regular intervals. Then he told me some government administrative changes are coming up. There is to be a new Minister of Information, Peng Hsueh-pei. The present minister, K. C. Wu, is going to be mayor of Shanghai. (I recalled that Phil Potter told me K.C. had said privately that T.V. had been importuning him to take this job, but he didn't want to because he felt the government was not stable enough.) Yu Ta-wei is to be Minister of Communications (replacing Yui Fei-peng), and Wang Yun-wu will become Minister of Economics (replacing Wong Wen-hao). Before T.V. dropped me at the Gimo's gate to ride back in the chauffeured jeep which has replaced my old rattletrap we agreed to put out the news at a tea-press conference Wednesday, May 15, at which T.V. would elaborate on the statement: the new appointments are designed to improve administration and emphasize civilian control of the government. Yu Ta-wei, for example, is a general of ordnance, but only in the same sense that General Motors' Bill Knudsen was a wartime lieutenant general in the U. S. Army. As I left T.V., I passed Marshall and Eisenhower as they arrived in the former's five-star staff car.

K. C. Wu, the smooth and jolly Information Minister who was well known to the correspondents from the days at Chungking, held his first press conference in Nanking and I attended. Potter told me he was nicknamed "wordless Wu" by the press corps because he never told them anything, and this fitted with Dr. Wu's mention to me in a conversation about smoking that he took up cigarettes as minister because the pause to light up gave him time to think up a cautious answer to a troublesome question. But I thought he handled himself well. Among the correspondents were two just returned from Changchun, who were among five captured by the Communists when they took the city and who have just been released. They were Henry Lieberman of the New York *Times* and Charlotte Ebener of International News Service. After the conference they stayed, with Phil Potter, to tell their story to K.C. and me. The recital took two hours; what it added up to is that the Communists have taken over most of Manchuria, with Russian help, and intend to stay. Lieberman feels they cannot be dislodged. He has written his story in a series for the *Times*, listing the facts of Russian aid as he saw them. He disagreed, however, with Miss Ebener's statement that they were "puppets of Russia." I didn't quite follow the distinction he drew, but I think it was in effect that they were Chinese first. But generally the story is very depressing. He saw no hope for cooperation with Russia by the U.S. on the basis of the Chinese Communist attitude. I telephoned Colonel Hart Caughey suggesting that Marshall might like to hear their story.

K.C. had me to dinner tonight, my first Chinese meal. Thanks to my prior coaching by Dr. and Mrs. Tan of the Washington

Embassy, I handled my ivory chopsticks without trouble. In addition to Bob Smyth, acting U.S. chargé d'affaires, and his wife the guests were Chinese newspaper editors and publishers and ministry officials. Madame Wu, slender and short and a gracious hostess, speaks charming English. There were God knows how many dishes, "time" fish, so called because they appear only at certain times of the year, bamboo shoots, and others I've forgotten, served with warm yellow Chinese wine in small cups. There was a good deal of "*kanpei*," or bottoms up, though Smyth insisted he was a "*sui bien*" man, sipping at it, since waiters refilled the cups the instant they were empty. K.C. said his porcelains, silver, and linens had survived the war buried in packing cases at Hankow. He half apologized for the show by saying that a thrift campaign would start tomorrow, but in honor of the Smyths, who are being transferred, and myself, it had to be done right. It was a delightful evening.

NANKING, May 10—I took Henry Lieberman and Charlotte Ebener around to see General Marshall this morning. They spent from nine-thirty to eleven o'clock recounting their experiences. He listened without comment, except that he interrupted once to get a map of Manchuria so as to follow their account, and again to get a stenographer to take down what Lieberman had heard from the Communist garrison commander at Changchun. I thought they spread it out a bit thin, but he didn't indicate boredom. Later I dropped in to see K.C. at the Ministry of Information, who at that moment got a phone call from T.V. saying the Generalissimo wants to see me at 4:30 P.M. tomorrow.

Around five o'clock I dropped around to the Nanking Hotel to see what was doing among the correspondents. Miss Ebener and Gordon Walker, of the *Christian Science Monitor*, were looking for transportation to the airport to meet Byroade, due in from the truce team inspection near Hankow that Marshall had told me about, so I provided it. General Chou En-lai arrived in the first plane. He greeted the correspondents genially but turned them over to a spokesman who said something about finding "light skirmishes" in the area in question. Chou's face struck me as having more of a Gallic cast to it than Chinese. Byroade, in the second plane, refused to talk, but did give Miss Ebener a copy of the agreement signed at Hankow. Who the Nationalist representative was, and which plane he was on, I did not find out; apparently he had nothing to say. Gordon Walker deduced that there was little if any fighting and that Byroade's silence was due to a desire not to make the Communists lose face, since they had charged attack by the government troops and the government had categorically denied it. Dined with five of the correspondents at a place called DD's Café, where I had good vegetable soup and a surprisingly good tenderloin with french fries, peas, fruit soufflé, and coffee for something less than $6000 CNC. Got a lift back to the hotel (my chauffeur, Yang, having disappeared) with Captain Young of Byroade's staff.

Nanking sits on the flood plain of the mighty Yangtze River, a city mostly flat, surrounded by an ancient wall built of the characteristic large bricks still bearing the "chop" or identification mark of the Ming dynasty. At that time the wall was in disrepair, with large ruined sections where Japanese shells had blasted through, but there were long stretches wide enough for a car, where one could walk on top and look out over the canals and ponds between the city and the river. There were a few hummocks of rising ground here and there, and one prominent landmark, Purple Mountain, outside the wall. The Chinese custom was to bury great men in mounds, with funeral alleys leading to them guarded by statues of animals on either side. The greater the man, the bigger the mound. To the Republic of China, Sun Yat-sen was its greatest man, and his mausoleum was situated well up the slope of Purple Mountain, the biggest mound in the whole area and a majestic backdrop to the city.

On the morning of Saturday, May 11, the mountain was wreathed in fog and it was surprisingly cool. By noon it was drizzling slightly. Rain grew steadily heavier as the day wore on. I lunched with Walter Logan of the United Press, who wanted to discuss UP's desire to get favorable rates for a daily morsecast time on the government radio. After lunch he suggested we go by the palace of the Japanese puppet emperor, Wang Ching-wei, which he thought would make a good press hostel. We looked over one wing where the layout permitted seven suites of two rooms and bath, and a common dining room.

The press hostel had been an invention of wartime Chungking—well known at the time—created to compensate for the woefully inadequate housing available in the war capital and to provide a place for the foreign correspondents to live and maintain a common mess. Since it was to China's advantage to assist the foreign press in getting its story out to the world from the beleaguered city in the interior, the hostel was a heavily subsidized operation. The correspondents did pay nominal fees for room and board, but they were very nominal.

It surprised me that any of them should consider the government obligated to continue the press hostel practice once the war was over, but it was true that adequate housing was in short supply in both Shanghai and Nanking, and I held my tongue. I could not help reflecting, however, that for the foreign press in China to expect to be accommodated in the most elegant resident in Nanking was as if the foreign correspondents in Washington—the British, the French, the Tass men, and others—requested the U. S. Government to put them up in Blair House. This was almost the case in Shanghai, where six top floors of Broadway Mansions had been turned over to the representatives of foreign news media and they operated a club in the seventeenth-floor penthouse.

I was told by an official how the Wang Ching-wei palace happened to be vacant: the committee sent from Chungking to survey Nanking for homes and office space picked it as the appropriate residence for the Generalissimo. But he refused to accept such elegance and said he would live in a relatively small two-story brick house in the compound of National Defense Headquarters. Since the head man had turned down the palace, naturally no lesser official could lay claim to it. The project for making it into a press hostel never got beyond the correspondents themselves; it was turned over to the U. S. Army for use as an officers' club, and later purchased by the U.S. to become the embassy.

NANKING, May 11—It was raining fairly hard by 4 P.M. when K.C. and I set out in his Plymouth sedan for the Chinese Army Headquarters—once a cadet training center—where the Gimo lives. We went to the quarters of the Gimo's aide to await the scheduled time of four-thirty. The Gimo, we were told, was in a meeting. Finally we were summoned to the residence, waiting briefly in an anteroom full of Chinese chairs. Soon President and Madame Chiang appeared in an adjoining room and Madame Chiang said, "The chairs are more comfortable in here," so we joined them.

Generalissimo Chiang was wearing khaki uniform without insignia or decorations of any kind; Madame Chiang had on a black Chinese-style dress with a flower design in dark red, and a black bolero. The room seemed to be the Gimo's office. At one end was a desk which looked as if someone worked at it. The walls were beige and the carpet blue. We sat around a low table, Madame Chiang and I at opposite ends of a davenport, the Gimo at ease in an overstuffed chair, and K.C. sitting on the edge of his, waiting to interpret.

The President opened with the usual courtesies: he was glad to have me here and was sure I could help the Republic in the matter of publicity. He wanted to know how long I had been here and such, still warming up. Had I talked over publicity with T. V. Soong? I said I had, and with General Marshall, a thoughtless remark I regretted instantly since it tended to depreciate the independence of my status. But maybe I was just too tense.

Then he floored me with what seemed a blockbuster: what did I think of the situation? Here I had been in China not quite two weeks and the man wanted to know what I thought of the situation. I didn't feel I really knew what the situation was, let alone what I thought of it. I temporized: did the Generalissimo mean the political situation? He said: political, economic, general.

Well, I said, I was scarcely in a position to speak about any of them, but—I was reaching desperately for some way of answering —it happened that two American correspondents who had been captured by the Communists at Changchun had just been released and had arrived in Nanking with their stories, which I had heard. They seemed to think that the Communists had occupied Manchuria intending to stay, and they believed it meant a military stalemate. I added that in discussing events with the American correspondents generally I had found belief that the political situation was hopeless, but I had talked to General Marshall and thought him not so pessimistic, though the way he put it was that a solution would be found because it must be found.

K.C. took so long translating my reply that I had a moment's hysterical recollection of those comedy scenes in the movies where a court interpreter listens to five minutes of jabber by a foreign-speaking witness and then informs the judge: "He say no." But I realized he was ad-libbing detail about the correspondents, for I heard him mention their names and I had not done so.

Next the Gimo wanted to know what I thought of the future of international relations, an equally disconcerting question. My answer, I guess, was equally strained: I thought Russia and the U.S. were drifting on a course toward war, chiefly because they distrusted each other so completely. I thought there was a disposition in the U.S. to look objectively at Russia's current actions and examine them on their merits, but no feeling that Russia was using similar good faith in trying to see problems from the American point of view. This, I went on, was tending to undermine the acceptance of Russia built up in the United States when they were wartime allies. I added that there was a disposition in America to believe the Chinese Communists were more Chinese than Communists, but that Lieberman's account of their current attitudes indicated differently.

I studied the Gimo during K.C.'s translation, and he seemed to be listening intently, reflecting between questions. He is a relatively short man, very alert, trim of figure, and his head so close-cropped that it may have been shaved or at least clippered. I reflected on all the recent Chinese history that has swirled around him but it was hard to feel particularly awed when you have to deal through an interpreter. In a way, though, he did awe me.

Madame Chiang asked K.C. to tell the servants to serve tea. They brought in small Chinese cakes and bran muffins with it, and she urged me to take one of each. She asked a few questions about my family which she translated for her husband, but otherwise left it to K.C.

The Gimo said he wanted a house found for me. He wanted me to review Chinese internal publicity as well as publicity abroad, to make weekly reports, and hold meetings of criticism. Madame Chiang commented that the Chinese understand only the Russian brand of publicity—the use of slogans, etc.—and do not understand the subtler type. She thought the best kind was to tell the truth and put it in the best light. The Gimo said I could call on him whenever I wanted, and could telephone Madame to arrange it, and with every cordiality from both of them we were dismissed.

I felt it was a rather strained introduction to the Gimo, especially since I am not quite sure what he intends by his instructions, but apparently it went well enough to satisfy K. C., for on the way back he warmed up as he has not done before and told me an anecdote about his own experience as secretary to the Gimo, years ago—for three days. He showed up the first morning at six o'clock only to discover the Gimo had already seen two visitors. Since he had just been married he found the long hours a dismal prospect, and managed to get himself transferred elsewhere. I hope K.C.'s successor is as friendly and as knowledgeable about Western affairs.

CHAPTER FOUR

Baltimore Sun *dispatch stating Marshall mission has "failed" draws rebuke from Truman. Effort to curb conflicting military claims by confining releases to Marshall's Executive Headquarters teams comes to nothing. Meeting Chou En-lai. Government captures Changchun, closes Communist newspaper in Peking.*

It was a Sunday, just two weeks since I had set foot in China, though it seemed more like two months. I decided on a lazy day, sleeping and reading, but around five o'clock out of sheer boredom I went to the Nanking Hotel in search of someone to have dinner with. My journal recorded the result:

NANKING, May 12—It turned out that Chou En-lai had held a press conference in which he accused "certain Kuomintang elements" (meaning the CC clique, doubtless) of promoting civil war with the Communists in the hope of dragging the U.S. in on the Kuomintang side, of sabotaging Marshall's military agreement, and of seeking to water down the PCC resolutions. Gordon Walker and Phil Potter, in telling me about it, both said they believed it very likely some such plot was true. The correspondents went out to file their stories, but six of them showed up at the Metropolitan for the army movie. Around 10 P.M. I signed off to go to bed, but when I found the Shanghai Sunday morning papers, just delivered to my room, I came down again. Potter was as interested as I was. Saturday evening's Shanghai *Post & Mercury* had a report that Wellington Koo, Ambassador to the U.K., would get the Ministry of Foreign Affairs in a cabinet

shuffle; the story also forecast creation of a National Defense
Ministry with Chiang Kai-shek assuming the post of Minister for
Defense, with the incumbent Chief of Staff, General Ho Ying-
chin, and General Chen Cheng, Minister of War, mentioned as
"both ranking nominees" for Chief of the General Staff. The
same story said that Dr. Wong Wen-hao would continue as vice-
president of the Executive Yuan, and predicted there would be
changes in the education and industry portfolios. Potter noted a
confusing contradiction in a paragraph which said that General
Chen Cheng would be appointed head of the Generalissimo's
Northeast Headquarters. He commented: "If Ho Ying-chin is out
as Chief of Staff, it means that the Gimo is going to fight, and
there will be civil war."

The *China Press* had an Agence France Presse dispatch from
Nanking quoting *Ta Kang Pao* (the *Strength Daily*) as forecasting
K. C. Wu's appointment as mayor of Shanghai; the story also
said the Ministers of Communications and Economics had resigned. "The government is yielding to CC pressure," said Potter
as he read it. "Wong is one of the most liberal men in the government. The CC clique is getting ready to fight." Potter asked if I
could arrange an interview for himself and four others with General Ho and also with Chen Li-fu, one of the two brothers heading the clique. I said I would try.

NANKING, May 13—K.C. was not at the ministry in the morning; I was told he had gone out to Purple Mountain with the rest
of the officials for the weekly Monday morning report at the tomb
of Sun Yat-sen. He came in about 3 P.M., but simultaneously got
a summons from T.V. so I went along to talk to him in the car.
I suggested that Chou En-lai's statement called for reaction, and
the best way of doing it was to arrange press conferences by General Ho and Chen Li-fu, since the correspondents had asked
specifically to talk to these men. K.C. agreed. "What should they
say?" he asked. I told him, "That depends on what the facts are."
He probably sensed my suspicion, for he protested there was no

"plot" such as Chou had charged, and was still protesting when we arrived at the Executive Yuan.

We saw Soong together, then K.C. was with him privately, then I saw him alone. He had called K.C. originally to discuss his forthcoming press conference, and asked us what the correspondents wanted to talk about. I said one topic was the company law [a new law containing restrictions on foreign businesses]. T.V. shuddered. He remarked that he didn't know all about it and would have to find out. I said another topic was inflation. "Perhaps I had better not have a press conference," he said, adding that the new appointments could be revealed in a statement. In view of the leakage, I did not feel, at the moment, like arguing the point. He asked to see the handout by noon tomorrow and invited K.C. and me to have lunch with him afterward.

When he had me in for a private session he said Marshall had told him about receiving the Changchun correspondents, and he wanted to know what their story was. I gave him a résumé. He was interested in Lieberman's account of Russian cooperation with the Communists, and asked if he had said anything about how the Nationalist troops fought, remarking that they were outnumbered and were not regular troops.

As a means of getting his comment on the appointments coming up I described Potter's reaction to the weekend stories. T.V. belittled the idea that the changes were intended to strengthen the CC clique. The men filling the Communications and Economics posts, he said, are non-party members; K.C. is "theoretically" a Political Science man, and as a civilian is replacing a general as mayor of Shanghai. He passed up an opportunity to comment on Ho Ying-chin; but, on the way back to the MOI [Ministry of Information], K.C. said his best information was that Chen Cheng will be the new Chief of Staff and that Ho will leave the country to work for six months with the UN's military commission.

T.V. seemed unimpressed by my warning that the news leaks over the weekend undermined the news value of his announcement. "There has been a lot of gossip," he said. "Now this is official." He did say there was nothing to the story about Wellington Koo, and he confirmed the National Defense Ministry setup, which K.C. said would be somewhat similar to the U.S. plan for integrating the army, navy, and air force. Chiang Kai-shek, he added, positively will not take that portfolio.

By the time K.C. and I got back to the ministry it was almost five o'clock. Potter, rather annoyed over the wait, had already arranged a five-thirty press conference with Chen Li-fu. K.C. quickly arranged one with General Ho at six-thirty.

Phil Potter and Tillman Durdin, of the New York *Times*, dropped in at the hotel around 10 P.M. Phil was pleased as punch over the strong statements made by the two officials. He said General Ho, in response to his question, announced his resignation as Chief of Staff. "This is good," said Phil. "These fellows are saying what they think. It gets the government's case to the American people. These people haven't been talking before. I believe the American people can decide things for themselves if they have the facts." He and Durdin pressed me hard for information on the rumored government changes, but I felt it unwise to set myself up as a leak and put them off.

NANKING, May 14—At noon K.C. and I went to the Executive Yuan to show T.V. the handout on the new appointments, which covered the ones we had originally been told about. T.V. said a supplementary statement could be prepared on military changes, as something that probably could be announced but would have to await the result of a cabinet meeting tomorrow. He said that on Chiang's proposal it had been decided to abolish the National Military Council and substitute a Ministry of National Defense consolidating the land, sea, and air forces. General Chen Cheng—I now have him placed as the red-cheeked little man with stomach ulcers who was at T.V.'s at dinner my first night in Nanking—will become Chief of Staff and General Pai Chung-hsi gets the new Defense Ministry.

We then went to lunch with T.V. at his residence, with some

other guests. T.V. is obviously tired. Someone attempted to bring up a question of business, to which he replied, "Oh, let me digest my food."

Aroung six o'clock I went to the Nanking Hotel and knocked on Phil Potter's door. He apparently had been sleeping, for his eyes were bloodshot and he appeared tired. He asked me what I thought all the government changes meant. I said I didn't feel sure enough to say anything positively, but my impression was they were moves toward coalition with the Communists. Why? Because they tended to conciliate radical KMT and Communist elements and gave no encouragement to the CC clique.

"I dope it out just the opposite," he said. He produced carbons of the story he had filed. It began: "General Marshall's mission to China has failed." It continued that the Third World War had already started, just as the Second started in China in 1931, and would flow from the civil war that was certain to come now in China. The country faces partition, etc.

What basis, I asked, did he have for reaching such sweeping conclusions? He explained it roughly thus: the Gimo called off —postponed, anyway—the National Assembly because to hold it with Communist boycott would be a farce. Now he was reshuffling his cabinet and not including any Communists; he was getting his government ready for war.

Limited as my knowledge of the situation is, I can't agree with him. He has been brooding on this too long, and he is tired. Certainly it would be useless to hold a National Assembly without the Communists, and as for putting them into the government now, it would be an act of political folly to do it short of the outcome of the negotiations. The Communists would disown anyone appointed by the government under such circumstances. I took Potter to the hotel for dinner, after which we got into a talk with an officer who seemed gravely worried by Phil's account of what he had filed. After Phil left, the officer urged me to call Colonel Caughey so that Marshall could get the story killed. I refused—it was 11 P.M. anyway—since I disapproved of any such attempts to censor him. But I must see Marshall again as soon as possible.

One thing I had noticed about Potter's reaction to the rumors of cabinet changes: at first he saw the possibility of hopeful results, particularly if General Ho was removed as Chief of Staff. Ho, like Chen Li-fu, was known as irreconcilably anti-Communist—both were called "reactionary" and "fascist" in the terms picked up from the Communists. He did resign, but Potter chose in the end to believe the worst of the government's intentions. This, I think, was because the only people from whom the correspondents could get detailed political anaylsis were the Communists, who either from innate suspicion or from private designs of their own always believed the worst of the government.

NANKING, May 15—First thing this morning I called Marshall's office for a date and was told he was just leaving the house to fly to Shanghai, where Mrs. Marshall is taking some sort of medical treatment. So I asked for a date as soon as he got back.

In midmorning K.C. told me the original handout involving the civilian ministries plus the mayor of Shanghai stood up as the result of the Executive Yuan meeting, and also the supplementary release on military changes, but he had to wait for a phone call to release the second.

Before dinner Lieutenant M. S. Auerbach showed up at the hotel with two Communists, whom he introduced to me. [Auerbach was head of a small Special Services Unit mission in Nanking whose job was to maintain liaison with the Communists, SSU being the successor to the wartime OSS.] One was a thin young man named Chang Wen-chin who is spokesman for and secretary to Chou En-lai, and the other a man named Liao who was released some four months back from a KMT prison, first political prisoner let go under the PCC agreement. They asked me if I was optimistic about my mission. I said not entirely, but it got me to thinking that I had better separate out and put down my various aims, as they appear to me, for obviously if I confine myself to what I am asked to do by the Chinese I will be wasting my time.

NANKING, May 16—I went by the Executive Yuan on the way to work to talk to Jim Brennan about a good time to have a lengthy, relaxed discussion with T.V. about my job. I suggested a good opportunity might be flying down to Shanghai with him tomorrow, since Madame Soong was not going along.

As I figure it, unless I want to get bogged down in the petty affairs of the Information Ministry, I must decide for myself what I should do. I reason that I should do three jobs in increasing order of importance: (1) give such technical advice on the improvement of MOI as requested, since this was what popped into their heads first when they sought to figure out what to do with me; (2) advise on how best to channel Central Government news to the foreign press on the basis of getting out facts that they now neglect to publicize; (3) advise on high-level policies which would have unfavorable effect abroad—arguing them out of such policies, remembering General Marshall's remarks about being aggressive.

Had a long talk after lunch with Lieutenant Auerbach, who is going to be an extremely valuable contact because of his SSU work keeping in touch with the Chinese political situation. He told me the Communist reaction to the government changes: (1) with non-partisans in the posts wanted by the Communists, when the time comes to include Communists the KMT can withdraw and tell the Communists to fight it out with the non-partisans; (2) the KMT is seeking to create the impression abroad that it is liberalizing itself, when actually the non-partisans are pro-KMT. Chou's delegation is amused and still wary. Chen Cheng as Chief of Staff and Pai Chung-hsi as War Minister are only a shade less objectionable to the Communists than Ho Ying-chin.

NANKING, May 17—Dr. Peng Hsueh-pei took office as Minister of Information today, after which H. P. Tseng, head of the MOI's international department, took me to meet him. Peng asked if he could call on me in my hotel. I was favorably impressed—I don't know why I was expecting not to be. The heartening thing to me was the unexpected air of confidence he displayed in talking to me. Someone—either T.V. or K.C.—has told him I am okay, indicating confidence on the part of that person. Also heartening was Peng's volunteered statement that, unlike the Communists, who kept making charges and spreading rumors, he believed in a policy of telling the truth. It remains to be seen whether he means it, but it's a good basis on which to start.

Peng said that KMT policy was to retrench and therefore he was going to cut the MOI personnel from three hundred to sixty, but he was not planning to cut the international department. He plans to attack the communications problem by making some sort of a deal with one or more of the banks (which have their own radio networks) so as to provide a network covering the principal cities. This will be very necessary to the correspondents if the USIS, which they are using now, fails to get a further appropriation from Congress and is forced to close down June 30. Peng plans to continue K.C.'s practice of holding press conferences Wednesday afternoons.

Peng seems to have an orderly mind. He had thought out five or six topics and he discussed them in order. Unlike K.C., who is friendly as a puppy and bounces around in talk so much it is hard to deal with him connectedly and consecutively, Peng stays put long enough to cover ground in conversation. I invited him to dinner tonight, and we made a date to go walking at three o'clock Sunday.

Jim Brennan phoned to say that Truman's food mission representative had got in last night and had kept them busy until midnight at the Executive Yuan drafting memoranda, etc., with the net result that I would have no chance to talk to T.V. either on the plane or in Shanghai this weekend. But I could go along for the ride and a Shanghai weekend if I wanted. I decided against it, in view of the fact that Peng was taking over and it would have been discourteous to disappear.

Auerbach told me he suspects Peng is a CC man, but he based this only on the fact that KMT members who are relatively unknown generally turn out to be CC; also on some gossip he heard

from the Communists about Peng. I think he is overly suspicious.
To me, Peng appears to be a T. V. Soong man.

Events were beginning to pile up, from my viewpoint.
Phil Potter's story in the Baltimore *Sun* aroused widespread
editorial interest in U.S. papers and President Truman denied
at a press conference that Marshall's mission had failed.

Stories were printed in the U.S. that General Albert C.
Wedemeyer was about to be appointed U.S. ambassador to
China. Marshall, though he had the rank of ambassador, was
not the man accredited to the government of China. That
post had been vacant since Pat Hurley's impetuous resignation which prompted Truman to phone Marshall on the afternoon of the day he retired as Chief of Staff. The general was
acting as the President's personal representative on a particular mission.

Jim Brennan told me that Marshall held a personal veto
over the $500 million U.S. loan he had gone back to Wash-
ington to arrange after the agreements successfully arrived at
during his initial months in the wartime capital of Chungking.

All these items raised questions in my mind and I felt it was
time to request another session with Marshall. The general
had a habit of dominating a conversation and I did not get
all my questions asked, but he answered most of them without
prompting from me.

NANKING, May 18—Marshall gave me a date for two-thirty but
at eleven o'clock Captain Soong of his staff called to ask if I could
make it noon instead and stay for lunch afterward. The general
began on the topic of political negotiations. The status is that
there still is "a possibility" of success. His putting it that way was
rather startling and depressing. He revealed that actually he has
withdrawn from the negotiations since he left Chungking and is
refusing to mediate in a situation where neither side will concede
anything. Now, he said, Chou is beseeching him to get back in

and he is still refusing, but by outlining all the reasons why he can't, so that Chou gets the idea what he has to give in on.

A great deal has been made in the KMT press of the fact that Marshall is demanding that the Communists give Changchun, the captured Manchurian city, back to the Nationalists. The fact is that Marshall never proposed this; he merely transmitted this demand on behalf of the Generalissimo. Chou is well aware of the true state of affairs. Nevertheless this has caused a propaganda campaign by the Communists against Marshall which they are now trying to counteract, and possibly has made the CC clique look on him more favorably.

The KMT has made numerous stupid mistakes, some of them apparently by design of CC elements. The Communists, for one thing, have a spy system that is just about a hundred per cent perfect. Everything the Gimo tells his officers they learn and report to Marshall. They learn many things that stir them up; they had a complete (uncut) version of the Gimo's interview with Peg Vaughn [Miles W. Vaughn, an official of UP] before it was published, and it contained many harsh statements about the Communists.

Here, for example, is the inside on two stories in the news recently: at Pao Tou Nationalists attacked and wiped out 300 Communists, charging they were planning to open a dyke and flood some land; actually the break they were planning was somewhere else. Naturally the Communists massed strength and wiped out the Nationalist forces in revenge. At another place a CNRRA man [CNRRA was the Chinese counterpart of UNRRA], under cover of taking relief supplies to a Nationalist group, tried to take money —army pay—and food to KMT soldiers. The Communists discovered the plot and that was why they seized the stuff [20 million CNC, 1000 bags of flour, and 20 boxes of milk] and killed the KMT member of an Executive Headquarters field team. This sort of stuff is probably engineered by the CC and is more subtly effective than what the Communists are doing, since it stirs the Communists to retaliation that gets publicized.

It gets worse and worse. Marshall said both sides seem to lose sight of how awfully close they are to an abyss, and the KMT has no alternative to offer. Even people like T.V., he said, don't seem to realize that obstruction in political affairs doesn't mean the end of all government, or abdication. Sure, the Communists would obstruct once they got into the government, but the government would go on in the inefficient way of democracy as in the U.S. and Britain with the people able to express their will. What he was trying to convey to me, therefore (and he threw in that he was not trying to play both ends against the middle through me), was that it's up to me to convince some of these people that acceptance of the Communists in a constitutional government doesn't mean the end of everything.

Marshall made no mention of the status of General Wedemeyer.

We had lunch in the sun on the terrace. Colonel Caughey, his assistant, Colonel Hutchin, and Tillman Durdin joined us. Durdin, it turns out, has been hired by Marshall to write his reports to the State Department, and has taken a two months' leave from the New York *Times*. Marshall asked his opinion on a demonstration—parade, etc.—by the Seventh Fleet in its forthcoming visits to Shanghai and Tsingtao: would the Communists seize on it as propaganda to prove we were trying to display our military might against them? Durdin thought it wise to avoid such display, and so did I. Caughey and Hutchins both said they thought it would make no difference. After some discussion, Durdin and I both agreed with them. Marshall said, having heard all opinions, he would act, but he didn't say how. He bewailed the navy's insistence on awarding a DSM to General Tai Li, the wartime commander who was killed in an airplane crash several months ago, saying it would have a bad political effect.

Dr. Peng came to dinner with me at the hotel. He has set up a weekly appointment for both of us with the Gimo, at 4:30 P.M. on Saturdays whenever the Gimo is in town. Peng is going to be all right from the standpoint of operations and the question is, can I convert his thinking with respect to the long-range, over-all wisdom of what Marshall plans for China?

NANKING, May 20—Dr. Peng had a tea for the Chinese and foreign press at three at the International Club. He made a brief speech in English and Chinese, citing recent municipal elections in Shanghai, Chungking, and elsewhere as evidence of democracy. Dick Lauterbach of *Time* and *Life* commented that they were stacked and machine-run.

I came back to the hotel to meet a Chinese tutor Dr. Searle Bates, a local missionary, found for me, a tall, clean-looking, earnest young Nanking University student named Li Chung-mih.

After Li left I got a rather frantic phone call from Dr. Peng. He said Marshall had issued a statement and he had not yet seen the text but he wanted me to find out the intentions behind it. I phoned Marshall's and Captain Soong read it to me. It amounted to an appeal to both sides to desist from warlike statements while he was trying to prevent warfare in North China from spreading everywhere. Peng said he had told the government agency, Central News, not to print it. I read the statement to him and he agreed there was nothing harmful in it. I suggested it was essential that Central News carry it, else the foreign correspondents would note the fact and put it in their stories. I asked him to come to the hotel at seven-thirty for a talk, and he said he would.

Around eight-thirty his assistant Henry Tseng arrived, said that Dr. Peng had been delayed, had not eaten, and would I come along with him. I did, and nibbled at a bowl of rice while Peng ate. He said that after learning of the statement he called on General Marshall. He seemed very impressed by Marshall's candor and cordiality. It was a beautiful buildup for my argument. I led up to Marshall's argument that the KMT had to be conciliatory toward the Communists and that taking them into the government would mean obstructions and difficulty but would help bring stability. I thought I did it diplomatically, since I was talking to the KMT and not chewing the fat with another American, and he took it very well, agreeing with most of it, but he gagged on letting the Communists into the government. They would, he claimed, eventually take over. This was hard to answer, in view of privately expressed opinions of some officials to me that the Communists in power would be good for China. I merely pointed out to Peng that coalition would have the advantage of avoiding civil war, regaining sovereignty over the industrial complex of Manchuria, which it did not have now; and that the KMT, numerically stronger, should not fear opposition under democratic procedures. He agreed that bringing Manchuria back under central government control was worth another try to negotiate with the Communists. He said, however, that one fear was that the Communists might use Marshall's negotiations to gain time, strengthen themselves, and at the end present a *fait accompli* when all Marshall could do was denounce them. Some thought, he said, that now the KMT had a fifty-fifty chance of beating them, which would dwindle with the passage of time.

So I don't know for sure whether he is a CC man or one of the die-hards who want to fight to a showdown with the Communists; I'm inclined to think not. One thing I did was to make damn clear that if any of this crowd had the idea they could get the U.S. into war on their side they had better think again; also that they might as well disabuse themselves of the idea we would use the atomic bomb to help them out—a fantastic suggestion recently made in one of the local newspapers, which I showed him. He said the editor was an anti-Russian crackpot. He agreed that I should see all handouts of the international department before they are put out.

So the first step is in the works. I emphasized how important it was to base every decision on the greatest amount of information possible—knowledge of what is happening in the KMT, what Marshall is thinking, what the Communists are thinking, if I can find out—and he agreed. It all took until eleven o'clock, interrupted by some calls he made to the Gimo with respect to Marshall's statement. He notified Central News, by the way, to print the statement and told two government newspapers, *Central Daily News* and *Peace Daily*, to print editorials promising to comply.

NANKING, May 21—The Chinese press can scarcely be said to have toned down much. *Central Daily News* was somewhat quieter, but *Peace Daily* was rather rabid. At Dr. Bates's suggestion I am paying Li Chung-mih 25,000 CNC a month for my Chinese lessons, and transportation by my jeep, subject to upward revision if food prices go up. First news I've had from Washington came today, a note from Frances Henderson in the *Time* bureau forwarding Larry Sears's transcript of Chapter Six of Peffer's *Prerequisites to Peace*. She said Betty had not received my arrival cable until May 7.

NANKING, May 22—Bill Costello, Far Eastern manager of CBS, wanted to talk to me about Chinese radio facilities and I dropped by the Nanking Hotel. His story was pretty much that of Opper and Moorad, though he had investigated further and had learned from T. C. Loo, head of the broadcasting activities in Shanghai, that a second station capable of reaching the States is in process of being put together and lacks only a few materials. Also, a 150,-000-watt Westinghouse station, with some new principle which folds the upper half of the band into the lower and adds power, is on order in the U.S. Costello's point is that China needs a network covering the principal cities here, plus an international outlet in Shanghai that will compete with the best in the Orient—50 KW. U.S. pickups are based on strength of signal and China cannot just get by with weak strength. I told him to wait and see Peng after today's press conference.

Till Durdin came for lunch. On inflation, he said the CNC rate compared with prewar should be 6000 or 7000 to $1, and the government is keeping it down in the market with the help of UNRRA imports, which require no drain of gold out of the country. He hears that 5000 CNC notes already have been printed.

Peng did fairly well at his first press conference, although on the first question he walked into a trap laid by Dick Lauterbach and Phil Potter. The question was: Have any minority parties protested the appointment of General Pai Chung-hsi? Forgetting that Pai's new appointment had not yet been officially admitted, his answer was, "No. General Pai is one of the ablest generals in China." Since Peng insists on written questions in advance, I suggested he let me see his prepared answers before the conference.

Afterward he saw Costello, who does a good sales job. As a hint about getting him moving on finding me a house I told Peng the Metropolitan was asking how soon I could get out. Pen is a golfer, and I told him I had met an officer who offered army help to repair the old golf course here, neglected since before the war, if American officers could play. That really interested him.

NANKING, May 23—Dr. Peng said that Chou En-lai called on him yesterday to suggest that military news be released only by EHQ. Peng agreed in principle, but suggested that a majority of two of the three-man committee decide when the news is given out, lest no news come out at all. He is going to see him again to-morrow. I suggested that I should go along, but Peng demurred. It seemed to me, however, that if any policy is to be decided it is the kind of thing I must be in on, and I insisted. It turned out that what he was worrying about was the necessity of translating the whole conversation. I said that would not be necessary, but that I would be on hand to consult. On that basis he agreed readily enough and said he would stop by at 9 A.M. to pick me up.

Had a talk today with Lee Wei-kuo, California- and Columbia (Ph.D.)-educated Vice-Minister of Information. He seems a friendly and very intelligent fellow. He once served as the Gimo's first secretary, and during the war had a general's commission in the army for nine months. He also attended the San Francisco conference setting up the United Nations. He said with some pride, "I was raised by the Gimo," meaning raised politically, and thus a neutral in the clique-beset KMT but on friendly terms both with Chen Li-fu of the CC and General Chang Chun, head of Political Science and governor of Szechuan Province, of which Lee is a native. As one unfamiliar with the labels and customs of politics here but familiar with politics in terms of human motivations, I thought his description of the KMT made eminent sense.

He pictured the Gimo as ruler of a coalition in the same sense that F.D.R. was as leader of a conservative Southern wing and Northern liberals and radicals.

Lee emphasized that in both the Chinese government and the KMT party organization there was a mixture of Sun Yat-sen's original democratic concepts acquired from Anglo-Saxon experience, and the influence of Russian ideas through his Soviet advisers, Galen and Borodin. He described it as a mongrel product which is causing China trouble today. To illustrate, he said he had been told by party elders how China adopted such a mixture. Sun was approaching an election to the KMT Central Executive Committee and Borodin came to him with a list of names of people to be elected. Sun demurred at such undemocratic procedure but Borodin insisted that was the way it had to be done—those selected must be elected. Sun finally agreed and thus the Russian "leadership" system was grafted on an organization built originally on democratic principles. Now, he said, the CEC makes proposals to the Gimo but the Gimo has the right of veto. Lee noted parenthetically that Chen Li-fu favors the Russian system. We are going to continue our talks.

NANKING, May 24—Dr. Peng did call for me at nine o'clock, but he renewed his objections to taking me with him to see Chou En-lai. We finally compromised on a separate, exclusive interview for me. He asked me to wait for him at the MOI, and meantime line up an appointment with Marshall. Riding downtown, he told me some big news: Changchun had been captured by government troops, and the Gimo had gone to Mukden. Changchun was entered yesterday morning, although the news was not received here until last night.

Although Marshall was very busy, Colonel Caughey fixed me up for 5 P.M. Peng got back to say that I was to see Chou at 4 P.M. and that he would see me again at two-thirty, after consulting his military sources, before I went. Sometime later Chou's secretary, Chang Wen-chin, the thin young man I had met, called to say Chou regretted he had to make another appointment for four and what other time was convenient for me? I said 8 P.M.

I called Jim Brennan to say I would be tied up and unable to see Dr. Soong, since he was leaving for Shanghai at noon, and that I would give him a complete fill-in after his return. Then, having wanted to eat a Chinese meal for some time, I took a group from the MOI to the Six Flowers Spring restaurant in the Confucius Temple district. I couldn't identify the dishes they ordered for the party at my request, but what fascinated me was the way they all cracked watermelon seeds with their teeth (spitting the hulls on the floor). I tried it but couldn't seem to master the technique. The meal came to 37,000 CNC with tip.

In my second conference with Peng he asked me to register certain objections with Chou. He said he would like to go along with me to see Marshall, and I called Caughey from his phone. The colonel said it would be okay if I didn't let Peng drag it out, since the general was tired.

We met Marshall at five, out on his terrace. I related the chronology of the negotiations with Chou for a propaganda truce (Marshall had a typewritten memo of what I had told Caughey on the phone earlier) and of the dispute over Chou's proposed ban on military news except that which was put out by the EHQ, or a field team, by unanimous consent. On this point Marshall objected that: (1) it would turn EHQ into a news-gathering agency; (2) such official news was too late to satisfy the press; (3) there were any number of places where there were no field teams and therefore no way of putting out official news. As to Chou's insistence on unanimous consent, he commented that Chou obviously wanted to avoid a precedent that would impair his similar insistence on unanimous consent with respect to field team operations in Manchuria.

I was forced to admit that I was not familiar enough with the operations of EHQ, and I agreed with Marshall that on that basis any such program would mean a news blackout and was out of the question. I suggested, however, that it might have a good effect, particularly in China, if he were to make a statement that both

sides had agreed to abate their propaganda war. He said that
perhaps he owed it to them both, and asked me to draft some
suggestion of what he might say.

Then, directing himself to Peng, he began to harangue the fellow on how fearful he was that the taking of Changchun would
ruin a truce agreement he had agreed on last night. He obviously
wanted Peng to carry this thought back to the KMT people. He
threw in the surprising statement that last night Chou had agreed
to a Communist evacuation of Changchun on condition that the
Nationalists stay out and the city be occupied by an advance section of EHQ, and later given over to Nationalist control. Government occupation, he feared, might upset the whole thing.
Chou had agreed, he said, but Chiang did not know it yet; and
then Marshall read Peng a stern lecture on not divulging that bit
of information to anyone in the KMT, not even the Gimo, with
a parenthetical warning to me also. Throughout, Marshall dwelt
on the faults, the blunders, of the KMT and how they had
brought reaction from the Communists and in what awkward position they put him. Since it was the third such recital I had heard,
I began to see the pattern. He apparently gives each side the idea
that its aberrations have ruined a painfully built up agreement,
and thus tries to keep each in line.

He said, incidentally, that he had been privately advised from
Washington today that an attack on him personally is about to be
launched in Washington, charging that he had "sold out to the
Communists."

At eight o'clock on the dot I arrived at Chou En-lai's residence,
Villa of Plum Blossom Garden. It was a drab place. I was led to
a room without a carpet, with dusty wooden floors, but with comfortable living-room furniture covered with blue slipcovers. First
to enter was Chang Wen-chin, the thin young man with thick
eyeglasses who acts as his English secretary. Soon came Chou, a
short, trim, alert-looking youngish man I would judge to be only
a few years, if any, older than I. Peng tells me Chou was a student
in Paris when he was.

With Chou was Lu Ting-i, a frail, mop-headed little man who

is the CCP's Minister of Information. Chou took a chair adjoining
mine, folded his arms, and sat back with the air of a man on guard
for anything that might come up. He wore a black suit. His eyes
are brown and he seems a man of force.

Knowing they had expressed curiosity to General Marshall as to
what I was doing in China, I began by telling them frankly. I
then launched into a discussion of the propaganda truce terms
Chou had proposed, outlining Peng's suggestions. Chou commented candidly and made his points clear; obviously he has a
very orderly mind. We ended in disagreement on his proposed
handling of military news, but I explained that I was not com-
mitting anybody and that Peng would get in touch with him.
Then I repeated my opening gambit: I did not know China but
I did know the U.S. If at any time he felt the need of consulting
me I wanted him to do so. I was employed by the government of
China but I felt that unless I went beyond the routine of duties
of adviser I wasn't fulfilling anything worth while. He, Lu, and
Chang listened with what I thought was interest to this recital.
There was an air of cordiality in my departure and he accom-
panied me to the gate.

One thing struck me. In nothing specific he said but in his attitude when he discussed the Manchurian fighting it was obvious
to me that in his mind there was not the resentful reaction to the
taking of Changchun that Marshall seemed to fear. It made me
feel that the situation is now hopeful, from the Communist side,
with respect to a successful truce. In fact at one point Chou indicated belief that the fighting would be over this month. He
took my English without translation, but relied on Chinese himself, with occasional English. Chang, translating this point, said
the general expected the fighting to end in a month. "No," Chou
interrupted, "in *this* month," and he jabbed a forefinger into the
arm of his chair to emphasize that he meant the seven days left
in May.

Auerbach came to my room at the hotel later, eager to hear
what Chou was thinking. In the course of discussion my casual
reference to Changchun informed Auerbach for the first time of

its capture. He was greatly excited. This led him into a long dissertation on what it could mean, in the light of the previous day's briefing he had had at the embassy. And the Gimo's trip to Mukden. He finally concluded it could mean good or bad; good if the Communists felt they had demonstrated they could whip the government and had withdrawn because they now want to resume political and truce negotiations; bad if the Gimo and his generals, encouraged by Changchun, would decide to push on and clean up the Communists. He is convinced the Communists see political advantage to be gained in coalition with the KMT, also that they are inclined—and would be more so in power—to be more pro-American than pro-Russian.

NANKING, May 25—Had another long talk with Peng's Vice-Minister, Lee Wei-kuo. Chiang, he says, is legally entitled to Harbin, Tsitsihar, and the rest of Manchuria, and may have the military power to go on and take it, but he must decide whether it is politically wise, and that is why he has gone to Mukden. Lee sees the KMT on trial if there is coalition. It must win the support of the mass of the people in political competition with the Communists or it isn't entitled to power. This sounds to me like sound doctrine. I asked him to read and comment on, later, the chapter from Peffer's book which I had received, and a piece in a recent *New Yorker* by John Hersey saying China has collapsed and all of Chiang's horses and all of Chiang's men cannot put it together again. Lee is my man at least until David Lu arrives. He says he would like to get out of politics and go into teaching.

This morning's *China Press* carried an accurate account of the propaganda truce agreement and the government's backdown on negotiations, quoting Lu Ting-i.

On Dr. Soong's return from Shanghai I had an unsatisfactory session with him about the press conference he was supposed to have. He listened to my arguments but said he didn't want to talk about inflation and it would be premature to discuss relief. Anyway, he said, he would be too busy with the Gimo out of town; maybe next week.

I had another long talk with Lee Wei-kuo, who endorsed Peffer's *Prerequisites* chapter and agreed with a good deal of Hersey's *New Yorker* piece but held that the major blame in the present conflict lies with the Communists. He cited, confidentially, many incidents in support of his argument.

Peng had his second press conference, at which he said the government's attitude was that the Communists must carry out the three Chungking agreements, after which political questions could be easily disposed of. I was not aware that although the government had submitted a list of its proposed initial military reductions, under the cutback agreement, the Communists had never complied with this requirement. I was of course aware that the Communists were blocking the holding of the National Assembly by the simple process of refusing to name delegates to it.

NANKING, May 30—Tonight the *China Press* reports via UP from Peking that the official Communist Hsin Hua News Agency and the party's official daily newspaper, *Chieh Fang Pao* [the *Emancipation Daily*], were closed down by the municipal government "on instructions from Nanking." A pretty discouraging beginning for me. Tried to call Peng to inquire about it, but got no response. Last night the cabinet was with Dr. Soong until midnight; he may be there again tonight.

Earlier I had a long talk with Peng. I judge he is pretty much in the CC frame of mind. Seems to think it will take only a few more days of pursuit to annihilate the Communists. He says they were practically wiped out before the war, and thrived only because the populace hated the Japs. The people hate the Russians even more, he said, because Russian troops quartered in Manchuria were "primitive" and went in for looting and raping. He said there is considerable feeling in the cabinet that Marshall's efforts are only helping the Communists.

Lu Ting-i, the mop-headed Communist information man, was

at the hotel for dinner with Lieutenant Auerbach and asked if he could see me tomorrow. At the time I did not know about the newspaper suppression; I imagine that's it. I told him I'd call him after I knew what time I was to see General Marshall. Later Captain Eng called from Marshall's residence to fix twelve o'clock and to say I was invited to stay for lunch.

NANKING, May 31—By the time I showed up at noon, General Marshall had received a protest from Chou En-lai about Peng's handling of the propaganda truce. Chou complained because Peng had refused to agree to his proposal on unanimous release of military news, complained because at his press conference Peng said the government was acting unilaterally to tone down its propaganda, and claimed that while the Communist press had moderated its tone, the KMT had not. It was a distorted protest. I gave Marshall a transcript of what Peng had said, and said that to my observation the KMT had moderated its tone considerably. Till Durdin, who also was present, agreed. Marshall asked, what about the proposal that EHQ put out as many reports as it could? I said that as far as I knew Peng seemed to have been cooled off by his own people and didn't go back to treat further with Chou after my report to him, though he had indicated he would.

Marshall showed interest, of course, in the Peking newspaper suppression. I told him of having tried to reach Peng last night and of having left word with Peng that I wanted to see him today. I think this is something I shall have to carry to the Gimo and thrash out. In the moment I had with Peng before I had to leave for Marshall's he took a most casual view of the suppression. He said "our explanation is" that the government could not permit the paper and agency to operate while the Communists were actively fighting. I had no time to argue about the professions of free press in the PCC resolutions to which the government had adhered.

Marshall showed a favorable response to my informal inquiry on Peng's behalf whether China could buy the USIS radio network operating in China in the event that Congress did not appropriate funds for its continuance. He thought China would have priority. I also told him that Lieutenant Auerbach had found a house for his unit and in view of my temporary status at the Metropolitan had invited me to move in until the MOI found one for me and my family; I wanted to know what he thought of the propriety of living with the SSU under the circumstances. He seemed to think it would make no difference. At lunch Marshall avoided business, as he usually does, and reminisced about Virginia hunt days.

At two-thirty Chou En-lai's secretary, Chang Wen-chin, came to see me; I had been expecting Lu Ting-i. Chang wanted to discuss the newspaper suppression and the propaganda truce. I said I was working on the former, and took occasion to point out my task was not made easier by the fact that the Communists permit no opposition press in their territory, or by the fact that they are fighting the government. He repeated the usual Communist line that they welcomed an opposition press but I suggested we be realistic on that point. On the propaganda truce I said I would ask Peng to get in touch with him again, but if Chou really wanted a showdown on his proposal he could raise it officially in the Committee of Three.

The MOI had one of its men take me to see various possible houses, and that day I was shown one out near the north wall, a large yellow stucco building containing four apartments, each with eight rooms and bath. It was occupied at present, I was told, by "representatives of Tibet" who had come to attend the National Assembly. Indeed it was—there were seventy of them in the four apartments, bursting the place at its seams. Where, I inquired, were the Tibetans going to go? Oh, said my guide nonchalantly, they would be squeezed into three of the apartments to make the fourth available. As politely as possible I told him I was not that crazy about having seventy Tibetans for neighbors.

That evening Dr. Peng threw a dinner at a Szechuanese restaurant for the foreign press and some of the Chinese editors. Cuttlefish and sharks' fins were among the dishes. I was pleased to find myself seated next to a quiet, roly-poly little man with thick-lensed glasses who looked like a Chinese version of *The New Yorker*'s Alexander Woollcott. He was Hu Lin, editor-in-chief of *Ta Kung Pao*, the country's most respected newspaper, which prided itself on its journalistic objectivity and carried beneath its Chinese logotype the French word summing up its guiding principle: *L'Impartial*. He gave me a delightful lesson in Chinese modesty. Through an interpreter I told him that someday I wanted to learn all about his paper. He replied that I was interested out of all proportion. No, I insisted, everyone in China had told me his paper was the best. He said I shouldn't consider it that important.

Ta Kung Pao was not to be confused with Nanking's *Ta Kang Pao*, (though confusion was the idea behind establishment of the latter).

CHAPTER FIVE

Fighting intensifies in Manchuria. Meeting Chen Li-fu, head of "CC clique," and other prominent political figures. Marshall achieves new truce of limited duration early in June. Generalissimo's views on freedom of press for Communists during armed rebellion.

All this time fighting was going on along the railroad that runs northeast into Manchuria via Mukden, Changchun, Kirin, Harbin, and Tsitsihar. The confusing claims invariably put out by two sides in any warfare, and the strangeness of place names, made it difficult to picture what was happening, especially since I was deeply wrapped up in trying to master details of the political situation. I did become aware that fierce fighting had been in progress for about a month at the rail center of Szepingkai. When word came of its capture I asked an American military attaché how long it would take, assuming the Nationalists maintained their momentum, for government troops to reach Changchun. He guessed that "on the basis of logistics" it would require a month or more.

When Changchun fell within a few days it was unexpected and puzzling. I had been impressed first by Marshall's feeling that it blew a hard-won agreement toward truce which he almost had in hand—wrecked it because now, he feared, the Communists would refuse further political bargaining, would complain again of "bad faith" on the government's part. But immediately after that Chou En-lai led me to believe Changchun was relatively unimportant. I took his attitude to be a hopeful omen: the Communists were not going to be as intractable as Marshall thought.

Next day, however, Lee Wei-kuo told me about a confidential military briefing for top editors which he had attended. As shown in the journal entry below, this indicated that the really significant victory had been the one at Szepingkai, not Changchun, and its effect on the political negotiations was to enhance government confidence that the Communists could be pursued and disposed of. Instead of stiffening Communist resistance, defeat had led them to look for relief to the negotiating table. For the government, victory seemed to bring into sight complete rout of the Communists and encouraged those who believed in pressing on while they had the upper hand.

NANKING, June 1—An operations officer named Liu told of the Battle of Szepingkai. The Nationalist strategy was to absorb as many Communist units as possible while government troops attacked another Communist unit near Fushun, which apparently was wiped out with little or no attention in the press. The Communist troops in Manchuria number around 300,000, of which 100,000 are good troops, Russian (or Japanese) equipped. Another 100,000 are unemployed factory workers indentured by the Communists. The good troops are the New Fourth and part of the Eighth Route armies. The Nationalists attempted a flanking movement to encircle the Communists, who discovered it and retreated. Communist casualties at Szepingkai were 40,000 plus the desertion by thousands of the untrained factory workers. Now government troops are pursuing some of the remnants toward Harbin, but the main body of Communists is withdrawing eastward toward Korea and Vladivostok.

As the Communist decision came to withdraw from Szepingkai after a month's tough fighting in the face of the Nationalist threat of encirclement, a Communist colonel named Wong who was chief of operations for General Lin Piao carried out a plan to desert that he had been formulating. He loaded all the documents of Communist plans he could get together onto four mules and, armed with four revolvers and a leaflet promising safe conduct (dropped by Nationalist planes), he escaped to Nationalist lines with several enlisted men.

From him and from a captured officer the Nationalists learned that during the planning conferences for the Battle of Szepingkai there was considerable complaint by Communist officers on two points: (1) Russia was not providing enough help; (2) Russia had harmed the Chinese Communist cause by looting Manchuria of machinery. These men also said the Communist leaders had never told the army that it was to be partly demobilized and integrated with the Nationalist Army under the military agreement of February 25.

Next (continued Lee) the editors were told about certain intercepts of messages between Lin Piao and Mao Tse-tung which were part of the haul. They began with what was believed to be the second in an exchange, a message from Mao to Lin. Referring to what apparently had been an original recommendation from Lin that peace negotiations begin immediately, Mao's message said they must be held up for a month to give the Communists time to breathe and recoup strength. Russia, it added, is not able to help much because it does not feel capable of challenging the U.S. at present. The next message, from Lin to Mao, purportedly gave an account of Russian Marshal Malinovsky's reasons for pulling out and leaving the Communists to shift for themselves: (1) Russia had supplied arms and training and the Chinese Communists still are not very good; (2) they were supposed to take Tsingtao, and could have taken it, but didn't. For these reasons Malinovsky advised Moscow against providing further help.

Then Chen Cheng spoke to the editors, presenting the alternatives facing the government in the current situation. They are: (1) peace; (2) war; (3) further delay. Chen said the government preferred peace, to avoid further bloodshed. But if it had to be war, as a second alternative, let it be all-out war and be done with it. Delay was to be avoided as the worst alternative for the government, and by delay he indicated he meant letting the situation float and handling incidents as they arose. Chen stressed, said Lee, that the government wanted peace and was in a position to be conciliatory but firm with the Communists. Lee noted that this same line was voiced by Sun Fo, a good liberal, in a Shanghai newspaper interview, according to an AP dispatch which Lee sent for and read to me, translating from the Chinese text.

I suggested to Lee that General Marshall should be told all this if he hasn't already, and later I called Till Durdin to suggest it would be better to hear it from Lee than to filter it through me, though I would be glad to convey it if he wanted. How much of it to believe it's difficult to judge. It's improbable that all of it is true, or that none is true. Most suspicious, from their context, are the "intercepts" between Lin and Mao. If they are faked, what is the precise motive? Remembering Chou's charge of a Communist plot to drag the U.S. into war against Russia, one can suspect it would be calculated in that direction, possibly to encourage U.S. belief that Russia would be an easy target right now. Yet that would seem a superficial guess; the same people eager to mop up on the Communists now would be those Peng describes as anxious to get the U.S. out of the picture on the ground that it is only helping the Communists by urging truce and thus delaying their annihilation.

But other things were going on beside the fighting, and my journal entry for that day also recorded a talk with Peng about the newspaper suppression:

June 1 (continued)—I knew Peng would be anxious to hear about Marshall's reaction to his tentative inquiry about buying the USIS radio network, so I saved that as a teaser and discussed first my housing situation. I said I really didn't feel like sharing a four-unit building with seventy Tibetans. He took it philosophically and said they would look further.

Then I went into the press suppression, without making much of a dent on him. The sticking point was his argument that no nation at war permits an enemy press to operate in its territory.

I said the government might have thought of that sooner, but he brushed that off by saying the Communists had been warned from the first and had gone ahead anyway, so that the time finally had come (decided on before he took over, he said; he seems inclined under pressure to pass the buck) to make them cease and desist. The argument that seemed to impress him most was that EHQ officially recognized the New China News Agency. He said he would have to look into that. Finally I said I would insist on taking it up with the Generalissimo and asked him to make a date. He said we'd see the Gimo next Saturday anyway, but he might be able to arrange it prior to that.

I took up Chou's protest via Chang about his failure to communicate further on the proposed propaganda truce. He said he had nothing to say to Chou and didn't want to see him; as for Marshall's suggestion that EHQ be instructed to publish as many incident reports as possible, that was beyond his authority as minister.

Finally I told him I thought Marshall reacted favorably on the sale of the USIS network, but that I had heard from a USIS man that the Senate had put $16 million into the appropriation bill to continue U.S. operation and it looked as if the item might stick in conference with the House. To my private amusement, Peng thought that if the U. S. Government were tipped it had a customer for the network, Congress would kill the appropriation.

After I got back I saw the morning's Shanghai papers. The *North China Daily News* had a UP story quoting "a high government official" as saying it was government policy not to permit Communists to publish while they were fighting the government.

NANKING, June 2—Had lunch with Lieutenant Auerbach and his assistant in the SSU's newly acquired local headquarters at 4 Kuling Lu. They have a house and servants but no furniture, though some is being made for them. In midafternoon Auerbach left for the airport to meet a colleague from Shanghai who was bringing money to pay for the furniture. He missed connections, for a short while later a young man rushed excitedly into the house, asked for Auerbach, and then rushed out again, saying: "I've got $8 million CNC in the truck and I'd better get it." He came back lugging a huge laundry bag full of paper currency.

NANKING, June 3—Talked separately with Jim Brennan and Till Durdin about my feeling that unless I can get some reversal on the policy of suppressing Communist publications I should quit and go home. Brennan agreed that from my standpoint it was important to present my case; Till felt I need not go to that extreme and that a letter to Peng would serve to keep my record straight.

NANKING, June 4—Naturally, freedom of the press figured in the questions submitted for Peng's press conference tomorrow. We renewed our argument in the preparing of his answers. He said he had a telegram from Peking saying that in addition to the two Communist outfits seventy-five non-Communist publications were suppressed for the same reason—lack of proper registration. Furthermore, he said, the Communists refused to submit to residence identification, a regulation that is in effect in many cities, including Nanking.

I went to his house at 9 P.M. for further conference. As I arrived he said the Gimo had just summoned him. He asked me to wait; I asked to go along. He demurred and finally we agreed that I would ride out with him and stay in the car; if the opportunity presented—if the Gimo did not seem too occupied with other questions—he would ask if I could be called in. As we approached the military headquarters in the dark, Peng's chauffeur switched on the interior light of the car and soldiers converged on it at the entrance. There was considerable discussion in Chinese, during which I caught references to "wish think." Finally the guards were satisfied and flagged us in. We drove to the house where the sentries stopped us short of the driveway. I paced outside, waiting. It was a brilliant Nanking night, with a quarter moon and bright stars.

Peng was back again in about twenty minutes, very apologetic.

The Gimo, he said, was "adamant" on the press item, and spent all his time outlining what he wanted Peng to say about the possibility of a political settlement. He wanted it stated that since the Communists had failed to live up to their original agreements, this time he wanted a concrete program agreed to, with a timetable for repairing of railroads, etc.; also, he wanted Marshall, and the American EHQ team members below him, to be given arbitration authority with respect to EHQ decisions.

NANKING, June 5—After thinking over the situation overnight I renewed my request of Peng that he arrange an interview with the Gimo for me to present my views. He refused, saying the Gimo considered it of no importance, and said I could go ahead and make my own appointment. Through Jim Brennan I asked if T.V. would do it for me. Jim phoned back that Soong also refused; he "had no heart" for any such task. Till Durdin, whom I consulted by phone, thought I might phone Madame Chiang, but Lee Wei-kuo advised against it on the ground that it would cause ill feeling. Also, he said, Madame Chiang was likely to be more adamant than her husband. So I drafted a memo, going the limit in accepting the government's argument, probably further than I should have, but still making my own pitch for freedom of the press. I delivered the memo and went to the ministry in time for Peng's conference.

To my surprise, the correspondents let Peng get by with his answer on the press suppression with practically no questions. Hank Lieberman told me later he considered the answer "damning" and was content to let it speak for itself.

There was a party at the American Embassy to bid farewell to the Smyths and welcome their successors, Mr. and Mrs. W. Walton Butterworth, Jr. I left early to bathe and eat, since I had an 8:30 P.M. appointment with Chen Li-fu which had been set up by Lee Wei-kuo. The army movie for tonight was a mystery, *Spiral Staircase*, which I had wanted to see, but as I left for Chen's I thought that meeting the formidable Chen Li-fu was quite as much of an attraction.

Chen's house, buried in one of the native sections, was a gray brick affair sharing a compound with another which I later learned was that of his brother, Chen Kuo-fu. It was furnished in what for Nanking is comfortable style, but it was not luxurious. Most garish item of décor was the white globe lighting the living room, decorated longitudinally and latitudinally by two glass Saturn-like rings.

Chen turned out to be nothing like anyone's picture of a man who runs his own secret police. He is small in stature, with white streaks in his black hair, and a ruddiness to his complexion that reminded me of Senator Harry Byrd's. He seemed a man of considerable personal charm. He spoke of having been in politics fifty years, which would suggest he was about seventy, but his skin was as smooth as a woman's, and one man at the ministry told me he is actually around fifty-four. Having heard from Auerbach and Phil Potter accounts of Chen's lifelong fight against the Communists, I had hoped to lead him into a discussion of the political situation, but he insisted on telling me about his long struggle. At ten-ten I looked discreetly at my watch and decided to quit asking questions in the hope that he would quit telling secrets of Communist organization and tactics that I had already heard from the Dies Committee in Washington; but still I wasn't able to get away politely until around eleven-thirty.

He understood my English and started replying in Chinese through Henry Tseng of the ministry (he had his own man, Wu, on hand as a check) but as he warmed to his obviously consuming interest in exposing Communism he answered in English and lapsed only occasionally into Chinese. One of these lapses was to give some definitions in connection with the Communist charge that he is a "conservative." The definitions, as translated by Wu: "Those who discover Communist intrigues before they happen are conservatives. Those who discover Communist intrigues after they happen are progressives. Those who never discover Communist intrigues are members of the Democratic League." He laughed immensely over it.

I tried to get his slant on U.S. policy in China. It was hard to figure out, for some of the things he said contradicted other things. I guess he may have been saying, in the net, that Hurley's policy—support for the Kuomintang—was the right one. He saw the American attitude as having three phases: (1) indifference while China fought Japan alone; (2) overweening sympathy after Pearl Harbor, when China was the brave ally fighting Japan; (3) overweening disgust when the men who came over to help in the fighting began writing home telling about all the squeeze, graft, and inefficiency.

Chen thought China had no reason to fear Russia, but reason to fear the Chinese Communists, in this respect: Russia is realistic; when she sees the Chinese Reds are weak—i.e., when she fears she may be backing the wrong horse—she will be friendly to China. If the Chinese Communists grow strong, she will use them to heckle China. There probably is a good deal to his theory. Yet at the same time he seemed to be saying that if the Communists come into the government they can be absorbed and become more Chinese than Communist.

He had some surprising things to say about history. He claimed, for example, to have been the negotiator with Russia and the Chinese Communists at the time of the Gimo's kidnaping in 1936. He said he had forced the Russian negotiator to cable Moscow he would be killed if the Gimo were harmed. He said he had discovered a Communist plot to seize power from the Gimo at Canton—discovered it just an hour before it was to go into effect—and moved first. He also claimed to have converted 23,500 persons from Communism, including one whose wife and children were buried alive in retaliation by the Communists in Shanghai.

Auerbach said later this is the set three-hour speech Chen is prepared to deliver to anyone. Perhaps, having got this out of his system with me, he can proceed further next time.

NANKING, June 6—I told Lee Wei-kuo I had sent the Gimo a memo on the press suppression issue. He patted me on the back and said I would have to learn about China and not take things so hard.

I phoned the MOI to find out what was going on and was astonished to learn that Peng was holding a press conference at eleven o'clock. I immediately phoned Peng: what was it to be about? He evaded, saying he would have to "check up at the last minute." So I alerted the correspondents and, thoroughly annoyed at his attitude, went to the ministry in time for it.

It turned out to be the Gimo's announcement of a fifteen-day truce in Manchuria. But the correspondents had got wind of it yesterday and filed stories which were in the morning Shanghai papers which I had not yet seen. Afterward I saw Peng and asked him when he learned of it. He may have been lying: he said from the Gimo this morning—but added that "a Communist" had told him about it at the American Embassy cocktail party. I presume either Chou or Lu Ting-i, both of whom I saw there. I doubt that the Gimo had decided when he summoned Peng night before last.

Peng was furious because T.V. apparently jumped him for transferring me to him in the effort to get to the Gimo. I assured him I had acted on my own basis and he seemed mollified, conceding it was just a "zigzag," his favorite word for mistake.

I feel that for the time being my tactics should be: (1) with Soong, not to go near him; (2) with Peng, sit back for a while and let him spend his money letting me perfect the grammatical construction of his English statements. I'm tired anyway and can stand an easing of pace. Maybe I'm taking Lee Wei-kuo's advice. I knocked off for the afternoon and moved from the Metropolitan to Auerbach's SSU ménage at 4 Kuling Lu, where I was given a room which had an army cot, mosquito-netted, and no other furniture whatever.

NANKING, June 7—Things were disorganized this morning as a result of Auerbach's plans to leave at 8 A.M. for Yenan with Chou En-lai in Marshall's airplane. At the airfield Colonel Caughey refused to let him go, or Potter, who was trying to sneak away from the rest of the correspondents. Caughey said Marshall did not want any Americans along while Chou went to headquarters to consult.

Peng asked me to draft an informal memo to Marshall offering to buy the USIS network, a job that took only a few minutes. Then he asked if I would talk to the correspondents about a house the ministry could provide them for a press hostel, it being tacitly understood that they could share in its expenses now that the war was over. It had four bedrooms and one Japanese-style bathroom; the owner required a 10 million CNC deposit (key money), it would take 5 million CNC to repair, and the rent would be 1 million CNC a month. I rounded up a group of correspondents for lunch and was not surprised when they invited me, not too diplomatically, to come around again when I had something they could afford.

The first "formal" truce since my arrival—supposedly restoring the formal truce announced in the January 10 agreement in Chungking—was the main topic of conversation in Nanking. Everyone with whom I talked discussed the possibilities of extension and what would happen next. Lee Weikuo thought the chances of peace were not too bad. He judged that the Gimo would be willing to extend the fifteen days, but that he did have a right to expect *some* progress on a concrete program, *some* specific agreements by the Communists, before agreeing to an extension. Jim Brennan took a dim view; all they were now negotiating, he said, was an extension. "All agree," I noted in recording these and other conversations, "that the government cannot carry on full-scale civil war—which is pretty obviously the alternative to peace, although the tactic of delay and delay may be accomplished—without foreign aid. This puts it up to the U.S. Shall we make up our minds to help the government, or shall we pull out of China? The latter would leave a void Russia would be sure to fill in time."

There soon were charges that the truce had been violated.

The Nationalists claimed that the Communists had attacked at Lafa and Tehchow, and had blown up a bridge on the Grand Canal. Though I suspected the Nationalists had been doing some attacking themselves here and there, I concluded that on the whole the Communists were ignoring the truce where it suited them and where they saw a chance for advantage.

The SSU unit, which now had the house furnished, was having guests for lunch and dinner who talked of war, peace, and politics. Eric Chou and Kao Chi, both reporters for *Ta Kung Pao* (*L'Impartial*), came with their wives to lunch; both thought that political settlement was hopeless. One evening the guests were three leaders of the Democratic League: Lo Lung-chi, a disagreeable fellow who acted as the League's spokesman, Carson Chang, a gentle, gray-haired man who reminded me of American Federation of Labor's President Bill Green, and Huang Yen-pei, Chinese without a trace of the West. Auerbach had warned me that a clash of opinions might come up, and I held my tongue when Lo Lung-chi sounded off immediately on how American aid was keeping the civil war going. Lo repelled me from the start; in fact he was the only man in China to whom I took an active and lasting dislike. He had been educated at the University of Wisconsin, and impressed me as one in whom intellectualism and liberalism had soured. Carson Chang seemed a reasonable, intelligent liberal and very much in contrast to Lo. Huang was to me the most delightfully Chinese of the three, expressing his opinions with gestures that made me think of him as a character in a Chinese opera. Using Lo as an interpreter, he told me he wanted to explain the situation.

The Kuomintang was so corrupt, said he, that it was driving the people to the Communists. The corruption was terrible, worse than before the war. Why? He said the answer was complicated, but he proceeded to explain: the KMT kept party members in office regardless of competence. The

KMT suspected people who were honest, and worked hard, and wore poor clothes, of being Communist. He said he knew four poor but honest magistrates who were killed by the KMT under suspicion of being Communists. And oh! the vice-mayor of Shanghai was *so* corrupt! In the takeover from the Japanese he had found a safe deposit box full of jewels he kept for himself. He was even more corrupt than T. V. Soong, so Soong removed him and he was now working to overthrow Soong. The KMT incited workers to strike in order to gain leadership over them. Huang's story, with gestures, was a most charming performance.

Talks with Lee Wei-kuo and with the SSU guests gave me insights into Kuomintang politics in this period. T. V. Soong, I learned, was without any political support in China itself. His sole influence rested with the Generalissimo, and was based on his reputation for connections with American financiers. I was told he disliked having men around him who were politically influential, and hoped to squeeze out O. K. Yui, Minister of Finance, and Wang Shih-chieh, Foreign Minister, because both were members of the Political Science clique, which was the more influential clique in the government (as opposed to the CC clique, more influential in the KMT party). There was frequent speculation that Soong would be ousted, and his most likely successor would be a Political Science man, General Chang Chun, governor of Szechuan. I could understand the Chinese assessments of Soong from the viewpoint of Chinese politics, but a good friend of mine in Washington who knew him well had told me, "Soong is a very able man, and you can't keep an able man down"; and I felt I had an additional perspective on him.

Another Saturday rolled around and Peng and I had another appointment to keep with the Gimo. I had been wondering whether my memo on press suppression would affect it, but a note from Peng informed me we were expected at the usual time of 4:30 P.M.

NANKING, June 8—This time we saw him at the big red brick building with Chinese-style roof and eaves decorated like totem poles that is the administrative headquarters for the Officers' Moral Endeavor Association (OMEA), roughly equivalent to a military YMCA. Peng introduced me to a huge man with a pleasing English accent, General Huang, who heads the outfit.

The Gimo was in a room in the southeast corner, where his walnut desk, glass-topped, was bare of gadgets except for a marble or onyx desk set. The furniture consisted of red leather chairs and davenport; opposite the Gimo was a gilt-framed painting of Sun Yat-sen; there was a bookcase, some pots with cactuslike plants, and a brown rug on a checkered linoleum floor. Peng was all set to interpret, but before he could start the Gimo's English secretary, Shen Chang-huan, came in to take over that job. Another secretary, not introduced or known to me, came in with a notebook in which, during the conversation, he occasionally jotted notes. Before we had gone far, T. T. Hsiao, the head of the Central News Agency—he reminds me vaguely of U. S. Supreme Court Justice Robert H. Jackson—arrived also.

The Gimo was no less cordial than usual, and apparently to give me an opening he asked how my work was going—had I encountered any difficulties? I said the only one was the suppression of the Communist papers, about which I had sent him a memo, which I hoped he had received.

Shen translated: the President had read my memo and he agreed with my views. My recommendations would be put in effect.

This floored me completely. I wondered if it was a case of saving my face or something. In flustered fashion I thanked him and said I was happy over his action. Then came the rest: right now, however, a fifteen-day truce was in effect and it was thought best to await the outcome of that. I nodded, knowing that if the truce ended in another deadlock and another outbreak of fighting there was no hope of convincing him anyway; if a settlement was arranged, the Communists would be reinstated. I could not quarrel with that.

Then the Gimo continued: one thing I didn't understand about the Chinese Communist press. He believed in a free press and felt they had a right to propagandize the Marxist line and express editorial opposition to the government; but the Chinese Communists based their publications on distortions of the truth and spreading of rumors that create unrest among the population.

Feeling not quite equal to convincing him that one man's fact is another man's propaganda, I tried this gambit: I had, indeed, noted some distortions of truth in Communist propaganda; but after all, didn't that sort of thing defeat its own purpose in the long run? People believed it for a while but they soon learned its falsity and then lost confidence in the source of the propaganda. I went on to reiterate the arguments I had made in the memo, adding one I hadn't made: that the very fact that this matter was not considered important by the government but was considered important by me was an indication I was sensitive to something on which I could give the government some advice; I could contribute an understanding of foreign reaction.

To my first point the Gimo replied: it was very true that false propaganda defeats itself in the long run, but there was also this about China: many of its people were illiterate, many others very poorly educated, so that they were not capable of judging the falsity of the Communist propaganda.

This ended his very polite lecture on things I did not know about the press in China. He changed the subject. What was my opinion of his truce announcement? I said I thought it an act of statesmanship. Legally the government was entitled to take over Manchuria under the Sino-Soviet pact and surrender terms, and militarily it appeared to be capable of doing it, but it was wisdom to forbear while giving General Marshall time to work for peaceful settlement. I added, perhaps incautiously, that initial foreign reaction seemed to be good. He was quick to pick this up. Would I elaborate? I said I had seen only a very brief review this afternoon, and could not remember that it quoted any specific newspaper comment (I checked later in the stuff

Marshall had sent me and found none) but it was generally favorable. I promised to elaborate when I got more information.

He went on: had I read the text of the editorial in the Yenan *Emancipation Daily*? I had read what the Communists had put out—I was not sure it was the full text—and said I was frankly at a loss to explain why, at the start of a truce period, the Communists should become so vituperative toward the Americans. But it coincided with a setup of attacks by Moscow on the United States in the last few weeks, and Moscow's motives were hard to penetrate. The Gimo agreed, and asked that I analyze the Yenan text as translated by the MOI.

Abruptly he asked how I was standing the heat. It was ninety today and very muggy. I told him I was used to such weather in Washington, but today was the equal of Washington's worst. He said that any time I could not stand Nanking's heat to let him know and I could go to Kuling, and he would send word and see that I was taken care of. He repeated this invitation at the close of the interview, after some Chinese discussion with Peng, adding that I was to feel free to give him advice at any time. This made me feel that while I had made no impression on the newspaper suppression he did not take it amiss; he does not insist on hearing only his own opinions.

In the car driving back Peng said the Gimo apparently is going to Kuling, which meant that he could go too. It is the coolest place in China, he said, though not as high as Kunming; some two thousand meters. Then, after a stop at the MOI, he took me along to a British Embassy reception—and en route he observed: "You don't understand about Chinese politeness. The Generalissimo said he agreed with you, but he was just being polite. He has told me the Communists cannot be permitted to publish, but that the Communist paper at Chungking will not be suppressed." I said nothing. If Peng is right—and he probably is—it means the attitude will still be, even granted peace, that the government will take its own sweet time before permitting the Communists to publish again.

A week later Peng and I had another session with him, after a period during which the papers were full of stories about what was going on in the negotiations, but so fragmentary I could get no clear picture of it. An appointment with Marshall was canceled because of his involvement in the talks, and I felt cut off from information I needed.

NANKING, June 15—The Gimo received us in the same room of his residence where I first met him. But since then the rug has been removed, the easy chairs covered with tan slipcovers, and some maps and scrolls have been hung on the walls so that it looks more like a Chinese office-conference room. He wore a mandarin costume this time: wool, for the day was cool and rainy. He was cordial as usual, but more nervous than I have seen him, as if under the strain of the current negotiations. He has a habit, when his legs are crossed, of wiggling his free foot or drumming his fingers on the chair arms during translations, and sometimes ran his hand over his fuzz-bald pate. There was more of an air of business to be done as we began. Abruptly he asked what I thought of the situation and what advice I had to offer. I said I was very discouraged on the basis of what I knew—I have been trying to hammer home my need for more information on the inside of negotiations—and though it looked as if the Communists were being intransigent and ruining the last hope for peace, I felt my information was too meager to give advice at this stage.

He was quick to pick that up. Had I not seen General Marshall? I said I had not attempted to see him since the fifteen-day truce began, feeling he was too busy with the negotiations, and that my last appointment was canceled because he got involved in them. I felt like adding, but did not, that I needed my information from the government side as well as from Marshall. The Gimo seemed to sense that, however, and proceeded to give what seemed like a bit of news—what I suppose he would consider was all I needed to know. He said that in his opinion the Communist proposals were fake, and they were not to be trusted. They wanted to discuss restoration of communications but not military reorganization.

Still thinking in terms of getting information from every source I could, I said I would like to talk to the Communists and see what they had in mind. For Peng's benefit I asked if the Gimo approved of that. Again there was a quick question first: had I met any of the Communists? I told him of having talked to Chou En-lai, Lu Ting-i, and Chang Wen-chin in connection with the propaganda truce. The Gimo replied: my plan had his approval.

He pressed me a second time for advice on what to do in connection with the negotiations. In desperation I dragged out a proposal Peng had talked about during our ride down to the residence: have a military spokesman issue daily news to keep the Communists from getting the jump on the government with their claims of having been attacked. This was apropos of a remark he had made complaining that the Communists were leaking incorrect versions of the negotiations to the press.

Then he went into a Chinese discussion with Peng, and a servant brought in tea, and creamy ice cream in a lacquered cup, and the Gimo urged me to eat while he talked to Peng. Toward the end of the discussion he motioned in my direction and Shen Chang-huan, the interpreter, broke in to say that Peng had brought up a political problem and the Gimo had asked him to consult me about it afterward.

Riding back to the ministry, Peng said his question was whether, in case there was no settlement during the truce, it would not be best to call the National Assembly and proceed on the basis of coalition with all the minority parties except the Communists. My off-the-cuff reaction was that it would put pressure on the Communists to join in or be left out in the cold, but I said if the call were made it should be done with the door left open to the Communists.

Auerbach had invited three Communists to dinner. One of them was Wang Ping-nan. Wang, educated in Germany, is a sinister-looking character. The talk was inconsequential.

NANKING, June 16—Talked to Till Durdin to get a line on the negotiations. He said there had been an agreement to send a field team into Manchuria to deal with the military reorganization. (Peng had told me this last night; it was a step toward attempting to restore the Chungking military agreement.) Durdin said the Gimo was wrong in saying the Communists had not discussed military reorganization, because Chou and Byroade had talked about that just last night. He thought the Communist fighting in Shantung was merely a reflex from Manchuria. There they had been exposed as not being as strong as they had claimed, and they were attacking the government where it was weak in an attempt to regain the bargaining power of a military threat elsewhere.

I got a call from Peng, who said the Gimo wanted him to put out another statement and would I come down to the ministry at four-thirty? In the meantime I saw the Shanghai papers and noticed that someone had leaked what purported to be a five-point Communist proposal and a five-point government proposal. Naturally this had blanketed Peng's statement of the previous day, which was relegated to one paragraph in an AP story. I mentioned this to Peng and said I had to know as much as the correspondents did, and should not have to keep bothering Marshall when I should be getting such information from the government. His only explanation and excuse was that there was a girl reporter on *Hsin Min Pao* whose sister was the wife of Lin Piao, the Communist general, and on the basis of this family connection she got a daily report from Chou. The girl herself was not a Communist "yet," Peng volunteered.

NANKING, June 18—I saw General Marshall at ten, mentioning that the Gimo had asked my opinion of the peace negotiations and that I did not know enough about them to speak properly. Marshall said the thing I could tell him was that the foreign correspondents here feel that the Nationalist commanders do not regard the current fifteen-day truce as of any importance. Further, that they think they can easily dispose of the Communists. This attitude, which is indicated in their talk, tends to make the Communists believe that the government wants war rather than peace.

Refuting what the Gimo told me, he said it was not true that Chou was refusing to discuss military reorganization. He said he had received the Gimo's conditions only the night before, and that he considered them to be too stiff. The Communists, he said, would never agree to them. The Gimo wants the Communists to remove their troops from southern Chahar and Jehol, and also from North Kiangsu. But as he was telling me, an aide brought in a map and he noted that the presence of Communist troops there posed a threat to Peking and Nanking respectively. He ordered a study to be made of the effect of the removals Chiang had suggested—a removal by September 1.

Marshall showed me an SSU report from Tsingtao indicating that Nationalist defeats in Shantung, and the reported attempts of Communists to land at Tsingtao by junks, were a clever Nationalist plot to make themselves seem the victims of aggression. This suspicion was based, however, on the fact that the Nationalists, who usually refuse to concede the loss of a town for a day or more, were in this case announcing losses within an hour or so, almost as if the stories were prepared in advance. Yet this may be just Communist propaganda, or nothing more than a KMT attempt to capitalize on their defeats for propaganda purposes.

Marshall also showed me a memo reporting that Eugene Vinogradov, third secretary of the Russian Embassy, in a dinner conversation with a member of the U. S. Embassy, said that Russia regards U.S. moves in China as offensive and her attitude unfriendly. Someone in Nanking has told me that Vinogradov is the only member of the embassy, including the ambassador, who is permitted to circulate socially in Nanking by himself, all others going in pairs. This would indicate he is the real boss of the Russians here, which would give his remarks more significance than otherwise.

Next I went with Peng to see Soong. T.V. wanted to advance his press conference to 4 P.M. Wednesday, so we decided to wash out Peng's usual Wednesday stint. I tried out Henry Lieberman's most embarrassing questions on T.V., together with a few of my own, and he wasn't fazed in the slightest. If I had been on my toes I might have deduced something from his reaction to one whether Tommy Corcoran handled T.V.'s investments in the U.S. It was something to the effect that it wouldn't be a crime if he did have investments but that if he gave a dollar (?) to Corcoran he would be a crook. His interest in my opinion on the negotiations and his frank give-and-take on embarrassing questions had their effect on Peng. We discussed what tone he should take with respect to the *Time* article [a recent story by Bill Gray critical of China's administration and referring to its "incestuous economy"] and I advised a good-humored one. "Well," said T.V., "if I can buy the press this way, I'm going all out."

I told T.V. that public relations was more than press relations. I had heard much criticism because he refused to go before the Legislative Yuan. "The president of the Executive Yuan has never gone before any other Yuan," he said, as if that were sufficient explanation. He said, however, that he had been invited to appear at an informal meeting of the PCC, but could send a deputy. I urged him to go himself. He indicated he might, but was not final about it.

While we were there, Hsu Kan, Minister of Food, came in and talked in Chinese. On the way back to the MOI Peng told me Hsu had asked T.V. to intercede with the Gimo to have the press lay off the rice dealers arrested in connection with charges they cornered the Shanghai market with the help of a government loan. He said T.V. had agreed. Peng added that he did not believe the Gimo would issue strict orders, but might ask the press to play it down and have the dealers released under bond. I asked if the Gimo would interfere with the courts in the case. Peng said no. He went on to say that Hsu was by far the most unpopular man in the government, and would be removed except that no one would be likely to accept the job, since it was the target of great criticism.

I told Peng I thought the government was taking the wrong

tack by continually claiming that the Communists were insincere, did not really want peace, and were out to ruin the country in the hope of seizing advantage from that. He said that, confidentially, the Gimo was fearful that the negotiations would fail and that the government would be blamed. This was the most depressing scrap of information I have received so far, since for success everyone concerned must enter with the same attitude as Marshall— that the talks must succeed because the alternative is war. It contradicts my feeling last Saturday that the Gimo was thinking in the perspective of a man who has struggled for some eighteen years or so to unify China. I told Peng I felt the government's line tended to stiffen the Communists and make negotiations harder, and I felt I should mention this to the Gimo, and he agreed.

NANKING, June 19—This has been an interesting day. Peng and I went to the Executive Yuan just before four o'clock. T.V. seemed just a trifle apprehensive. "You aren't nervous?" I asked him. "Oh no," he said, "I've handled the press before." To my mind his conference was a complete success. He was utterly candid, down to the point of admitting, when at the end Lieberman expressed the thanks of the press for access to him, that he did it because he was under attack. The correspondents were surprisingly reserved and under restraint in their questioning, holding the queries to inflation and economics. T.V. got a chance to say everything he wanted to, and did it with just the right amount of acting: calm, candid replies, repetition for emphasis. The phrase "incestuous economy" in Bill Gray's *Time* article seemed to stick in his craw and he described the piece as "the outpourings of a lascivious mind." What seemed the best point to me was his iteration of the great need in China for peace—*real* peace. I remembered he told me Monday that the economy here cannot stand another six months of the present uncertainty. The papers in his hand trembled a bit when it was over. I told him I thought it was a good show, and left Peng to superintend the Chinese conference following immediately.

As I was driving back to the MOI I had an object lesson in what is eating China now: a battalion of artillery troops, carrying full gear, was heading down Chung Shan Road north toward Sun Yat-sen Circle, apparently off for the wars. Their mules were loaded down and their howitzers were trundling along behind them. It was a vivid illustration of T.V.'s reminder, a few minutes before, that military expenditures are taking nearly 80 per cent of China's budget.

My jeep disappeared during my call at the ministry, and as I waited for the chauffeur to return I watched the people on the street. A little fellow who could have been anywhere from eight to fourteen years old was going along with a basket full of toys made of bamboo and paper, tooting his identifying tune on a little bamboo flute. Children stopped him once and crowded around, but I did not see any buy. He took his brave and pitiful wares and proceeded. He seemed neither downcast nor glad— just a kid who seemed to accept that he had to make his own living and was doing it with a certain self-confidence.

After dinner I worked until eleven preparing a memorandum for the Gimo on the peace negotiations. I felt I could think more concisely on paper, and if I awaited Saturday's appointment the truce period would have expired.

NANKING, June 20—Marshall showed me a transcript of talks he has had with Leighton Stuart, in which Stuart was reporting on his own conferences with the Gimo and Chou. [Stuart was the retiring president of Yenching University who had spent his life in China and was widely respected by all factions; toward the end of the war the Japanese asked him to persuade Chiang to intercede with the Americans on peace terms.] Chou was objecting to the Gimo's proposed disposition of troops in Manchuria, though he indicated he was willing to negotiate that later; he was objecting to the proposed deployments in North China, which he called unreasonable; and he opposed the arbitration power proposed for Marshall. He wanted joint operation of railways without any Nationalist railway police. Whether this meant a mixed KMT-Communist operation, or separate operation of sections, I could not tell from Stuart's account. I returned home and redrafted my memo to the Gimo in what I felt was a respectful but more positive form, and dispatched it to him.

NANKING, June 21—Li Chung-mih, my Chinese tutor, arrived saying that his fellow students were in despair over the morning papers, which made it look like war with the Communists when they wanted peace. We spent quite a bit of time discussing the situation. Afterward I dropped in to see Dr. Soong, having received a request from Richard Johnston of *Time* for an interview with him and having Lieberman's request for a separate interview on hand. T.V. fixed 5 P.M. for Hank and five-thirty for Johnston, subject to cancellation if he were summoned by the Gimo.

The correspondents were all invited to a buffet Chinese lunch with General Wu Tieh-cheng and Chen Li-fu, at the general's house. Wu is secretary-general of the KMT. The ministry's Moe Votaw says Wu is independent in politics, respected by practically everyone. Chen Li-fu shows enough interest in me these days to make me suspect he may have learned something of the ideas I am feeding the Gimo. He drew me aside to tell me the Communists are bluffing, and besides they can be licked in three months. He was sure there would be peace, that they would give in. I told him I thought he was wrong, at least on a three months' campaign. He pointed out that the last time the KMT fought the Communists they did not have an air force, and went into history to recall that actually the KMT had never really fought the Communists more than three months. I asked him if he thought the economy could stand the strain, and fed him a bit of what T.V. has been telling me—you never can count on the outcome of a war.

During lunch a phone call came saying that Peng was holding a special press conference at 2 P.M. I knew T.V. had gone to a war council at the Gimo's lunch, and suspected that Peng had a truce extension to announce. That was what it was—extension for eight days, to June 30. He also announced that the government had receded from asking arbitration power for Marshall and wanted a majority, instead of unanimous, deciding vote in the Committee of Three, in EHQ, and in the field teams. Obviously it is a concession to the Communist claim that arbitration would infringe sovereignty, but also I am sure Marshall refused to accept arbitration power lest he embroil the U. S. Government too closely. I remarked facetiously to Lieberman it was unfair to the U.S.—the two Chinese would outvote the American.

Peng says this eight-day extension is final, though for politeness' sake that was fudged over. I think my memo may have driven home one more nail in the argument for extension that Marshall and Stuart have been putting up.

NANKING, June 22—At ten o'clock I dropped in at Marshall's to see if there was anything I needed to know before seeing the Gimo today. Marshall was looking over some material preparatory to the first Nanking meeting of the Committee of Three which originally had been set up at Chungking. He said he had insisted on holding a formal meeting because he felt both sides were talked out in individual conversations, and could by formal meeting check off the things they already had agreed on informally, to get them out of the way. Yet, he said, the KMT member, General Hsu Yung-chang, had been ordered not to attend and Marshall had to argue the Gimo out of it.

Chou En-lai had always refused to discuss differences point by point while the Communists had the upper hand in Manchuria, Marshall said, while the Nationalists refused to make a comprehensive agreement. Now it was the other way around; the Gimo insists on a three-way settlement while Chou, under continuing Marshall pressure, has finally agreed to settle point by point. But Hsu talks and talks and refuses to commit the government to anything. Marshall said that when I saw the Gimo I should tell him: "Don't encourage him," meaning Hsu. He asked if I had sent the memo I showed him and I said I had redrafted it after talking to him.

The Gimo seemed much more relaxed today than he was last

week. The session was, to me, a pretty desultory affair. We disagreed whether the Communists preferred peace to war. I asked whether he thought negotiations would be speeded if the Communists accepted the proposal to decide things by majority vote in the Committee of Three. He thought it would be a great help. I asked if he would like me to try to persuade the Communists on this point. Peng smiled as he translated, and the Gimo, in good-humored indulgence, replied that he thought the Communists would not accept it except in a limited way that would not mean anything, but I could go ahead. I added that it seemed to me the National Government had nothing to fear from this proposal, while the Communists, as a minority group, could rely on protection from Marshall. This drew agreement from the Gimo, who said he was not complaining but it was a fact that the Communists got about 60 per cent of the breaks.

On the way home Peng brought up a confidential point. He said that secretly a small group which included Sun Fo was considering two alternative moves in the present situation. One was an announcement that the government would abide by the PCC resolutions. This, I take it, is a yielding to Chou's pressure for deciding political questions at the same time as military. Chou has been charging that the KMT intended to go back on the political settlement, and while he has no specific proof of this he knows the CC clique is trying to sabotage it. But if such an announcement fails in its effect, the secret group favors calling the National Assembly for October 10 and going ahead with a coalition government without waiting for the Communists.

CHAPTER SIX

Riot at Nanking railroad station ascribed to activities of CC clique. Government negotiator gives inside account of talks. Chou En-lai professes hope for success. Marshall warns Chiang against taking advice of "militarists." Truce extended at end of June but Chou indicates alarm to Marshall over vagueness of terms.

While Marshall in his constant round of meetings was seeking desperately to persuade Chiang he must resist his war-minded followers who wanted to clean up on the Communists while they had the advantage, a riot broke out at the Nanking railroad station on the night of June 23.

A delegation from Shanghai, arriving to petition the Generalissimo for peace, was met by a group of anti-Communist refugees. Furious argument between them soon developed into fist fights. Among those injured was Kao Chi, a reporter for *Ta Kung Pao*, and a girl who worked for *Hsin Min Pao—* a girl who, according to Peng, was sister-in-law of Communist General Lin Piao.

It was the kind of incident guaranteed to arouse unfavorable U.S. reaction. The peace delegates claimed to have no connection with the Communists, saying their sole interest was in stopping civil war. At the time there was even more disposition to take such protestations at face value than there is today. The finger of blame pointed immediately toward the government because police were slow to move in and stop the melee. If it was a clever Communist provocation, its effect was to picture the KMT once again as a harsh, repressive government.

I watched to see what effect it would have on the peace negotiations. In terms of positions between the two sides, I could discern none; its only effect was to give Marshall another incident about which to complain to Chiang. If the government was behind the refugees, I wanted to know such things. This was precisely the type of incident I had to head off, if I could.

I realized I was having to dig out information for myself as to what was going on. Marshall was extremely helpful whenever I took the initiative to ask him, but he was not obligated in any way to keep me advised. I picked up information incidentally in talks with the Generalissimo, and by contact with Peng, who was reasonably candid in answering my questions, and sometimes volunteered significant points. But I felt the Chinese had no appreciation of the extent to which an adviser "needs to know" to be of much help.

NANKING, June 24—Last night's riot occurred when ten delegates of an anti-civil war organization, apparently a Communist front, arrived to petition Chiang Kai-shek (and, it is now said, also Marshall and the Communists) for an end to the fighting. The "refugees from northern Kiangsu" where middle-class home- and landowners have been driven out by the Communists may have been genuine refugees, though some of them wore silk gowns and others Western clothes.

The Shanghai delegates appear to be genuine liberals rather than actual Communists, although they seem to be lending themselves to the standard Communist tactic of propaganda protests.

The Communists charge that the beatings were caused by KMT "gestapo." It looks to me as if the government itself is involved, though only through the negligence of the police, gendarmes (garrison troops), and railway guards, who normally swarm around the station and who presumably could have prevented the argument from turning into physical encounter. But I doubt that the government is responsible for the men who got away with administering the beating. Rather, I would judge it is the work of Chen Li-fu's "renovationists."

Chen disclaims connection with the "renovationists" but his daughter told someone—I think the ministry's Moe Votaw—that Daddy was very busy these days with the renovationists. I can't help recalling Chen's definition of a "conservative" and thinking that this protest would be his idea of a "Communist intrigue" which it behooved the renovationists to discover beforehand, and squelch. This policy seems utterly stupid to me because the end result is to give the Communists a propaganda issue. I think the government is liberal enough (or at least fearful enough of adverse reaction) not to want to engage in such violent tactics, but that at heart, now that it has occurred, most sections of it approve.

Correspondents asked for comment from the ministry and Peng put out a statement tending to hold aloof, deploring the incident and cautioning against such demonstrations at a time when "the government and our American friends" are striving so hard for peace.

NANKING, June 25—The station riot is creating a big stink, as well it might. In midafternoon I got a call from the Executive Yuan. Dr. Soong wanted me to come over. I found him very worried about it. I said I was tempted to try seeing Chen Li-fu again to tell him he was hurting China by such tactics. T.V. seemed to accept my assumption that the CC people were behind it.

What he chiefly had on his mind, however, was a lunch Thursday, off the record, for five or six selected correspondents. "Our group which is trying to hold China together has nothing to hide," he said, "and I think we ought to talk to the correspondents often." I listed those I thought should be invited and he told me to fix it up for 1 P.M. at No. 1 House.

I picked up Hessel Tiltman of the London *Daily Herald* and took him out to see Dr. Sun Fo. I talked privately to Dr. Sun beforehand, explaining that Henry Wallace had mentioned him as one he had met on his trip to China. I had wanted to ask him about the secret plan to go ahead with coalition government without the Communists but felt it unwise to do so directly, so I inquired if he thought there was any possibility of coalition in case the Communists refused to join. He did not rise to the bait. He said he saw none.

From one of the correspondents I ran into at the Officers' Club I learned that the "Kiangsu refugees" were planning a counter-demonstration at Communist headquarters at 9 A.M. tomorrow. I came home and tried to phone Soong but could not get him. I reached Peng, who said he had heard of it and had checked police and the gendarmes. He said no permit had been issued, and if one came in no more than twelve demonstrators would be permitted to take part.

NANKING, June 26—At his press conference Peng got a well-deserved grilling from the correspondents on the station riot in the face of his bland statement, though it seemed to me they let him off easily at that. He announced that Wei Tao-ming had been appointed vice-president of the Legislative Yuan.

NANKING, June 27—T.V. put on a good show at his luncheon for the correspondents at No. 1 House. Ronald Stead of the *Christian Science Monitor*, whom I had invited by wire from Shanghai, failed to get the telegram in time and he was the only one to miss it. T.V. was a candid, affable host. The menu was soup, steak,—a splendid steak—potato cakes and peas, and lemon meringue pie. Talk was free and informal and I think everyone was impressed. T.V. told about his experiences at poker: he won $215 U.S. the first time he played, on a boat en route to Hong Kong, and quoted a Chinese proverb to the effect that "the gods of chance protect a novitiate." He prefers stud to draw. He discussed the appointment of a Britisher named Pritchard as customs inspector in Shanghai and said he intended to hew to the line of doing what he thought best regardless of criticism. His argument was that Pritchard was the best possible man he could find for the post, one who had spent thirty years in customs work in Hong Kong. Customs, of course, is the worst scandal of the government—one of the worst, anyway, with pilferage, squeeze, and inefficiency rampant. He said rent control was under consideration for Nanking, at four hundred times prewar prices. Rents are up several thousand times now. He had some minor bits about diplomatic appointments.

The correspondents are still complaining about housing. Walter Logan of UP complained that the price is too high for the house which the MOI has finally found, which will house six or eight. I promised to drop everything else tomorrow to see what I could do, chiefly because I felt everyone was in a good mood at present, including T.V.

NANKING, June 29—Peng has agreed to provide the house the correspondents want for a hostel on the following terms: room for six correspondents at $500 U.S. or $75 a month each—i.e., $500 if only one stays. Repairs by owner with three months' rent in advance; furniture from alien property stocks; all subject to: (1) completion of agreement with owner; (2) eviction of present occupants. This is satisfactory to the correspondents, who will form a committee to run the house and hire a manager to oversee the mess. Logan is happy, temporarily, anyway.

I saw Marshall briefly just before he left for the Gimo's. He waxed indignant over the station riot, suggesting that I tell the Gimo no one in America will believe the government is not implicated because of the long abstention from interference by the police.

After he left, Till Durdin gave me a fill on the negotiations. The situation is still fluid, with Marshall making the rounds: Gimo, Chou. But, said Till, there was now the basis for settlement if the Gimo will take it. The Communists have agreed to withdraw from southern Chahar except for Kalgan; from southern Jehol south of Chengteh.

This removes the threat from Peking because mountain ranges intervene and the Nationalists, by garrisoning the passes, can hold them off. Further, an agreement providing authority for the Americans to make certain important decisions on the field teams tends to give assurance that the military and other agreements will be carried out; at least it provides a basis for branding the Communists as violators before the world if they violate their provisions. He thought I might point out to the Gimo the incentives for trying a workable plan: (1) peace from fighting, giving China a chance for economic recovery; (2) firm American support; (3) approval of the U.S. loan.

On the station incident, I picked up an interesting scrap of information from Colonel Hutchin: Marshall's office was notified of the disturbance by the Communists—by Chou's secretary, Chang Wen-chin, I think he said—around 9 P.M., after it had been in progress about two hours. He and Caughey immediately notified General Yu Ta-wei, who promised to check. Yu called back in twenty minutes to say that General Chen Cheng had given the necessary orders and the demonstrators were being escorted to the hotel. Half an hour later the Communists informed him that the disturbance was still going on. A second call to Yu revealed that Chen had "given orders" only. The authorities thus dragged their heels interminably.

The consensus of correspondents is that the beatings were the work of either the CC clique, possibly through Tu Yueh-sheng, the gangster boss of Shanghai (opium, prostitution, river piracy, etc.), or the "Chen Cheng military clique."

From Ronald Stead, who came to lunch, I learned what may be an interesting fact, if true. He said that earlier in the week in Shanghai one Heng Chi-tao, president of a school for talented refugee children, had talked about the "national peace campaign" which was sponsoring the peace delegates, claiming it had a total membership of 100,000 and that it had no Communists in it and had nothing to do with the Communists. It favored U.S. withdrawal from China. The interesting fact was that a USIS man asked why the demand for U.S. withdrawal was spread on their English posters and not on the Chinese posters. Heng replied, he said, that the man must be mistaken, that the Chinese posters advocated postponement of American assistance until China was united.

At four-thirty I went with Peng to keep our weekly meeting with the Gimo. We were kept waiting, as Marshall's talk had lasted through the lunch hour and up to three o'clock, and the Gimo had not got around to his nap until after that. A clean-cut First Lieutenant Shah (Hsia) of the Chinese air force kept us occupied until he arrived, then retired and Peng did the translating again. The Gimo fanned himself with a palm-leaf fan. The decorative cross on the wall had been replaced since last week by three big maps: of the world, of Manchuria, and of Asia. No tea was served this time.

The ever polite Gimo opened by asking what I had been studying during the week. I replied: (1) the Hsiakwan station incident, the effect of which was totally bad in the U.S., and (2) the peace negotiations. He ignored comment on the former and said of the latter that the Communists were refusing to concede what it would take to reach agreement. I asked if they had not agreed to make withdrawals from Chahar and Jehol that would remove their military threat against Peking. He replied that this was not true; they refused to evacuate Chengteh, from which they have based guerrilla operations which constantly harass the railway to Mukden. Furthermore, they refused to evacuate northern Kiangsu, thus creating a refugee problem (three to five million) for the government and also maintaining a threat against Nanking and Shanghai. Moreover, in evacuating certain places they insisted that Nationalist troops remain out and leave the civilian administration to the Communists, and they insisted on control of the Tsingtao–Tsinan railway line. He went on: the government had offered to give them one Manchurian province to garrison and then had offered, in return for their evacuation of Chahar and Jehol, to give them two other provinces. But, he said, the Communists, accepting the first offer, refused to move from Chengteh or Kalgan.

I asked if the American field teams' additional power were not a step toward insuring that the Communists actually carry out what they agree to. He replied that it was better than nothing, but that full arbitration power actually was necessary.

I suggested the advisability of his holding a press conference in connection with the end of the truce period. I said the correspondents were in need of (1) a statement of what had been demanded; (2) what had been yielded; (3) what remained in dispute. He said he would think it over—possibly hold an off-the-record tea Monday.

Then he went into a long discussion with Peng, referring to a folder of papers he had, some of which he turned over to Peng, who told me later it was instructions for a statement after the end of the truce tomorrow. It would, said Peng, be subject to revision on the basis of the last-minute, hectic attempts to pull everybody into line; Marshall would see the Gimo again in the evening and possibly tomorrow morning.

NANKING, June 30—Charlotte Ebener of INS and Harold Milks of AP kept calling me at intervals during the morning to find out what was going to happen on the end of the truce. Peng finally came by at two forty-five, having been unable to reach me on the phone. He had a statement—English text—all ready, which I read while we drove down to the ministry. It added up to little of anything: no extension of the truce, but no fighting *if* the Communists refrained from attacking. He immediately gave the Chinese text to the Chinese press, and had I not called the Nanking Hotel the foreign press would not have had it before 4 P.M. As it was, Milks of AP was scooped because Logan of UP had his Chinese assistant, Chang Kuo-hsin, at the Chinese press conference. I talked to Peng about it afterward and he got rather annoyed, but ended saying he was doing the best he could, that the Chinese papers had pressured him on the basis of holding their afternoon editions, etc.

Apparently to mollify me he phoned around dinnertime and invited me over. Afterward we walked in his garden while he asked me questions about the American press and told of his plans for improving the twenty KMT papers under his jurisdiction, and for establishing a magazine on the order of *Time* for China, and later—when printing improves—a Chinese *Life*. The Communists claim he issued a directive to the KMT papers on the station riot saying: (1) deny government complicity; (2) blame northern Kiangsu refugees for the attack. Probably he did; he lacks the finesse of one of my old UP bosses who would have blandly informed his editors of "the facts" instead of issuing a directive.

NANKING, July 1—Kao Chi came to lunch. He is not clear on who he thinks beat him up. He says one man told him his beating was "a mistake"; also that Peng has instructed the managing editor of *Hsin Min Pao* to discharge the girl reporter who was beaten. The M.E. told the girl he would not fire her but would have to transfer her from the post she holds.

The vagueness of Peng's announcement about the status of affairs at the conclusion of the truce was so unsatisfactory to me that I thought the time had come to see if I could go over Peng's head to Madame Chiang to arrange something more revealing of what the situation was. I was a bit suspicious of the fact that Peng had appeared with an English text all prepared—generally that meant a document that Marshall had drafted and submitted to the Gimo as a suggestion for what he should say. Otherwise Peng usually drafted the English from a Chinese text in consultation with me. It suggested to me that Marshall was a party to the deliberate lack of clarity about the prospects for peace at the end of the truce.

The Generalissimo's doubts about the wisdom of leaving Communists in control of territory, with or without their troops, seem more reasonable today than they did then. By 1946 he had gone through twenty years of experience with their tactics, and we had not. Chiang was unwilling either to order fighting resumed or to extend the truce interminably without results, and he deliberately wanted to be obscure.

Acting on my own belief that the public deserved to know

what had been demanded, what had been conceded, and whether it meant peace or war, I resolved at least to make the attempt to put it on the record. To me the posture of saying, "We'll fight only if attacked," was one which lacked the ring of sincerity and one which could easily be twisted by the Communists to look like an excuse for resuming the war.

The Generalissimo had invited me to get in touch with him at any time through Madame Chiang and though I had considered it once I had not done so to date because of talks with various Chinese about her role.

The American impression was that Madame Chiang was a power in the government. During the war she had been a superb public relations figure for the Republic. She had addressed Congress, she charmed everyone she met. She talked fluent English and discussed with senators and representatives the substance of war and postwar problems in social conversation. To Americans she was a live, gracious, magnetic presence at a time when her husband was for them only a name who did not come to life out of the confusing accounts in the press and on the radio about his dispute with the Communists some eight or ten thousand miles away.

My talks with Chinese convinced me Madame Chiang's American reputation was entirely out of proportion in China, and in any event did not apply in the field of domestic politics.

She did, of course, have the kind of influence which any highly intelligent, activist wife would have on a husband. But in the political arena she was still a woman, and men were the officials who counted most heavily, particularly in China. I knew it was a case of getting her to persuade her husband.

I had argued with Chinese officials that part of the attention Communists got in the American media came from the "names make news" principle. Chou En-lai, their spokesman, was a familiar name in the U.S. To expect Peng Hsueh-pei, a newcomer, to compete in the spokesman's role was putting him under a handicap. T. V. Soong was a name well known in Washington, but his métier was economics. The best-known name, however, was Chiang Kai-shek, and my objective was to get him to do some speaking for the government—even off the record it would be effective, I felt. Through Pearl Chen, her secretary, I arranged an appointment with Madame Chiang for 5 P.M.

July 1 (continued)—She took me to the dining room of the residence and ordered Coca-Cola and chocolate ice cream, both welcome in view of the hot day. She wore a Chinese-style dress, a blue polka dot high about the neck with slits up each side of the skirt.

I began immediately with a lecture on what a lousy press China was getting, from two standpoints: (1) the administrative side and (2) the peace negotiations side. I cited Chou En-lai's press conference of last night at which he picked holes in Peng's statement and gave the correspondents a hard-hitting, persuasive account of the Communist arguments.

She agreed that in publicity the government was getting the short end. "I know what you want me to do," she said. "You want me to be there [at the Gimo's meeting with the press] and interpret. I did that during the war, and I'm tired of it, and I'm not going to do it any more." She went off in such a rush it rather surprised me, especially since I hadn't been thinking of that role for her, though it would have been a good touch. "Peng should do it. That's what a Minister of Information is for, and if he can't do it, somebody else should do it." I explained why I thought that, while Peng was capable of doing it, a more familiar name should be used.

She raised objections to the Gimo's involvement, stating that he was President of all China, above politics, and to hold a public press conference would put him on a level with Chou En-lai. I brought up the name of Yu Ta-wei, who had been one of the actual negotiators, and she immediately said he could and would do it. First I would go over the situation with him, sort of warm him up. Should Peng be there? I said I thought it would be good

—I foresaw trouble if he thought I was freezing him out—although with Yu I judge no translator will be necessary. Madame Chiang agreed to discuss it with the Gimo and see that it was set up. Later on, she said, it would be a good idea to bring in the press for tea and an off-the-record chat with the Gimo.

She said the Encyclopaedia Britannica wanted her to do a modern history of China, 1937 to 1946 inclusive, in 5500 words, apart from the war. I was fearful she was going to ask me to ghost it—the research job for me would have been impossible—but she only brought up what they might want, and asked me to read it over after she had it finished. She seemed distressed by the short length assigned. I gave Pearl Chen a lift home and came home to dinner. Chang Wen-chin had called earlier to offer me an appointment with Chou at 5 P.M. but I had to decline in view of my meeting with Madame Chiang. He promised to call back with another date tomorrow.

NANKING, July 2—During the morning I got a call from Madame Chiang saying she had discussed our business with the Gimo and that while he thought Peng, rather than Yu Ta-wei, should hold a press conference, Yu had been instructed to get in touch with me and to tell me the whole story of the negotiations. Accordingly it was no surprise to receive a call from Peng's assistant saying the minister would like me to go with him to see General Yu at 3 P.M.

Yu, a jolly little fellow whose English struck me as being from Harvard, where he was educated, with an oddly Southern accent to it, came in practically quivering with anxiety that what he was about to tell us would be published. Nevertheless he proceeded to recount what had happened during the truce, interspersing his account with periodic digressions to say he thought it unwise to reveal anything at present.

His story on the communications agreement, which he was assigned to negotiate and which is about agreed on, is that he (Yu) approached Chou on this basis: we want communications restored; we assume you do too. We have no demands; what do you want? Chou had three demands: (1) that all fortifications be demolished; (2) that Communists be given representation in the Communications Ministry at all levels—joint control; (3) that there be no railway police.

Yu said that on the first point General Marshall worked out a compromise under which fortifications should be permitted at important stations—something like 1000 meters around Class 1 stations, 500 meters around Class 2, etc.—and this was agreed to. On the second, Yu maintained it was a political question outside the scope of his authority. On either this point or in connection with another, a committee will be set up to discuss the problem. On the third point Yu conceded: there need be no railroad police in Communist areas.

I don't recall that he went into the talks about reporting authority of the American members of the field teams. On the military side, Yu produced a map marked to show what the government had proposed and what the Communists counterproposed on troop dispositions. Since the place names were in Chinese it did not mean too much to me, but in effect it showed that the Communists controlled just about all the area north of the Yellow River—dominated it by holding the railways and key cities—except for the corridor extending into Manchuria from Peking to Changchun. While they were willing to withdraw from the Kiangsu and Shansi-Shensi areas, they insisted on garrisoning three spots in the latter which Yu said threatened the key rail and city centers. Furthermore they insisted that government troops not go in, but that "peace prevention corps" maintain order and the civilian administrations be kept. Yu's story was that the Communists were willing to withdraw in southern Jehol and Chahar, but not to give up Chengteh or Kalgan; and that government control of these cities was a quid pro quo for a government offer to let the Communists garrison three provinces in the extreme northwest of Manchuria. The Communists, he said, will always accept a new offer but balk at giving the quid.

Someone had given Peng a talk about the futility of his propaganda to the effect that "the government is sincere but the Communists are not"—it sounded to me like a replay of what I had been telling Madame Chiang—and he kept telling Yu about it and asking what could be published out of what he told us. Yu kept objecting that it was unwise to reveal any of it lest it give the impression everything had been agreed on and that, regardless of what the Communists did, the government intended to observe its promise of silence as to what went on in the Committee of Three. We left promising not to betray any information that shouldn't be betrayed.

In talking it over afterward, Peng saw objections to every suggestion I made as to what could be used to give correspondents some news on what the twenty-two-day truce had accomplished. I went to the Nanking Hotel to check up on the extent to which my information, now collected from Marshall's office, the Gimo, and from Yu, was ahead of the correspondents'. Logan's account indicated he had printed piecemeal about 90 per cent of what had happened; and from Yu's recital I must say the only parts I had not already read in the papers was the map-marked, Communist-proposed deployment of their troops in North China. From Charlotte Ebener I learned why Logan was so uninterested in hearing anything more: Marshall had held an off-the-record session for the correspondents yesterday afternoon. He was angry, she said, because Chou had talked so freely Sunday night.

I took Ronald Stead home to dinner. He had not known about Marshall's session. To bring him up with the rest of the correspondents I told him most of the story, on the same off-the-record basis. When I concluded he remarked: "I have printed all of that, piecemeal. The fact that I have seems to me to be a tribute to two persons, myself and Chou En-lai." Then he said that immediately after Peng's press conference on Sunday he and Lieberman had gone over to see Chou, who had given them a complete fill-in. He showed me the story he had written Monday, and it had the situation down to a T, except that he kept out the off-record information. Stead himself had not become an instrument of Communist propaganda—he impresses me as being one of the most objective reporters operating in China—but there were one or two points where the presence of Communist argument issuing from Chou, and the lack of any presentation of government argument, had that effect, subtly, even though Stead observed the rules of impartial interpretive reporting. I end the day frustrated by the futility of trying to loosen up the government to put out its own news, and with Marshall, who apparently prefers to bottle it up if he can and seems to be using me as an instrument to bring pressure on the people I am working for.

NANKING, July 3—Although Peng had asked me to meet him at the ministry at ten-thirty he did not show up until nearly three, and then with interesting news. The National Defense Council decided this morning to summon the National Assembly, postponed from May 5 because of Communist refusal to name delegates, for November 12. "I had the honor to propose it," said Peng. I asked him what it meant: was it to bring pressure on the Communists to come in? He said yes. Details were to be worked out at a meeting tonight at Dr. Sun Fo's, with Foreign Minister Wang Shih-chieh and others.

When I got home, Lieutenant Hickey was there with an envelope from Marshall marked "priority, secret." It was an extract from minutes of a meeting between Marshall and Chou at ten-thirty this morning in which Chou suggested that "the four documents, three of which have already been passed by the Committee of Three," be published. He referred to (1) the understanding on restoration of communications; (2) the reporting authority of the field teams; (3) on committees to study the political questions. The fourth is Marshall's compromise proposal for military agreement "in principle" plus further negotiation of the question of civilian administrations. The minutes showed that Chou was also worried about Peng's end-of-truce statement Sunday; he could not make out whether it threatened hostilities or not.

This only increases my feeling of being misused by Marshall. If he himself edited or amended the English text of the statement Peng put out, what is he suggesting that I do? Get some documents published that he so far has persuaded both sides to bottle up? I phoned for a date to see him and Colonel Hutchin replied through Hickey I could have 9:40 A.M. tomorrow. I had to beg off on the ground that I was dated at nine with Wang Shih-chieh and since I have had to ask Wang twice to postpone dates he had set up, I did not feel I could do it again. So it was left in the air.

NANKING, July 4—The talk with Wang Shih-chieh was very pleasant. Like most Chinese, he is short. His English is not too fluent but it covers the shadings of political expression required. He is gray-haired and wears glasses. He received me at the *Waichiapou*, the Foreign Ministry.

I sounded him out on the National Assembly announcement. He indicated that the government was determined to go ahead in any case, but hoped the Communists would come in. The government did not yet know, he said, what it would do in case of Communist refusal, but tended to think that most minor party people would participate in any case. He asked about U.S. reaction: did Americans feel that Communist participation in the government would improve it? I said I thought it was true of a large segment of U.S. opinion, leftist or liberal in thought. Like Carson Chang and Sun Fo, Dr. Wang seems a mild, reasonable man who could do the KMT a lot of good if it did not have the CC clique like a millstone around its neck.

Almost as soon as I returned I got a call from Chang Wen-chin asking if I could see Chou at eleven-fifteen. This time Chou was more relaxed than before, when he had seemed to have his guard up, and we had a free, informal talk of about forty-five minutes.

I told him of the situation on the suppressed Communist papers and led into a discussion of the move on the National Assembly—what did he think it meant? He said he had not been consulted, although when it was originally called for May 5 the government had consulted all parties. He said he favored reconvoking the PCC also.

Then into the negotiations: did he feel any real progress had been made, or was the military situation hopeless? He said no, agreement could have been had on the basis of Marshall's proposal, which he said was to agree on troop dispositions (he noted there were some minor disputes still outstanding on that) and negotiate further on the retention of Communist civilian administrations.

I tried to explore this angle. The government, I suggested, feared that in agreeing to this it was in effect consenting to a separate Communist state, more or less, north of the Yellow River, which printed its own currency, kept its own troops, had its own postage, etc., and then laid itself open, also, to taking the Communists into the National Government. Chou's reply was to go back to the PCC resolutions and to point out that eventually there would have to be elections and the structure of the *hsien* [county] and district governments in relation to the National Government would be worked out. The idea, he said, was to settle the whole business in the political coalition. Refugees (in the case of Kiangsu) would be permitted to go back and vote, would be afforded protection, would be given some land—enough to make a living—etc. It sounded very ideal and democratic and I refrained from going into the proposition that the existing Communist governments had in the first place been set up by force of arms, and that there remained some suspicion as to the guarantees of life and limb.

Chou noted that a Shanghai Chinese paper had reported the granting of licenses to a number of newspapers—fifty-two—and over a hundred magazines, but not to the Communist weekly, *Masses*, which was about ten years old in Chungking and which they now wanted to establish in Shanghai. Could I do anything? I promised to inquire.

NANKING, July 5—Had an hour's talk with General Marshall this morning, and I do him an injustice. As if he had read my thoughts, he addressed himself to them.

First, he thought I should know Chou's feeling of alarm over

Peng's statement of Sunday—its ambiguity and veiled threats. I
said I understood he (Marshall) had read and edited the English
text before it was put out. Marshall said he had, but he saw two
English versions, quite different. I don't know what version he referred to, but it may have been one independently translated
from the Chinese, for I have seen how differently two translators
can turn into English the same Chinese text.

Second, he emphasized that he did not want to use me to put
pressure on the government for which I was working. This was in
connection with Chou's request that the four documents be published. I said I did not consider it against the interests of my em-
ployers to do anything I thought would further his (Marshall's)
efforts, regardless of what the KMT thought of it, but that I did
understand why the government was against publicity at present.
It was because of unwillingness to give Chou any excuse for claiming that any of it had been agreed on.

I told Marshall about seeing Yu Ta-wei. I said I had felt that
possibly the whole thing had been "talked out" in secret and
needed some public opinion brought in, though I could understand the government's reluctance.

Marshall went inside to get a map (we were on the veranda)
and showed me where things stood now, militarily. Chahar is no
problem. The Communists have agreed to withdraw to the outer
wall, and the Gimo has agreed to let them hold Kalgan although
it is just inside the outer wall. Jehol is no problem; the Communists have agreed to withdraw to Chengteh. For my ears only,
Marshall said the Gimo had agreed to let them hold Chengteh although he was withholding this information from the Communists for the present. North China is the problem, and for
political rather than military reasons. The Communists agree to
withdraw all through the Shantung peninsula, subject to the conditions already made public: namely, that their troops be replaced
by peace preservation corps and they retain the civilian administrations where, said Marshall, they have been for years. Likewise
in northern Kiangsu they agree to withdraw—they are within

miles of Nanking now—to a triangle. The Gimo wants them to withdraw to the other side of the railroad, the north side.

In this connection, Marshall said it was Communist violation of the June 7 truce order—when they moved along the east-west rail line taking towns—that provoked the KMT into war preparations. The KMT moved three divisions by sea to Tsingtao and three divisions by air to the rail junction to the west. This was in violation of the January 10 agreement, but Marshall told Chou he could not object to it because of the Communist violations that provoked it.

At any rate, the government—meaning the army and CC clique, and possibly but not necessarily Chiang Kai-shek—was hell-bent on licking the tar out of the Communists last Saturday morning, the antepenultimate day of the truce, some thirty hours before the expiration of the extension, when Marshall called on the Gimo at 9 A.M. for a conference that stretched until after two o'clock. Marshall's argument to him was this: regardless of your claim that you want peace, your military commanders talk war. If they start one, the world will say that what happened here is just what happened in Japan—the army decreed war. If the people (he told the Gimo) could voice their opinion it would be overwhelmingly for peace, and therefore it would be the army decreeing war against the will of the people. This is what happened in Japan, and look at Japan today.

This argument, he said, had a tremendous effect on the Gimo. Marshall said he quoted the Bible and almost wept during the lengthy interview. Remembering that I saw the Gimo about two hours after this session, I recalled that already (as Peng disclosed to me on the way back that day) he had made up his mind the truce would not end in attack.

Then, going back to the political deadlock, Marshall said he told Chou he must think of something to propose; he could not just let it stand there because the KMT was ready for war. For example, said Marshall, why not negotiate that point—the retention of civilian administrations—with a committee of, say, Wang Shih-chieh and Chen Cheng? Chou added the name of Shao Li-tze. Marshall then put the proposition up to the Gimo, who was persuaded to accept and to see Chou personally [I am not aware that this meeting ever came off], and went back to Chou to tell him: now you have a committee you yourself named, in effect; you named the government's negotiators; it's up to you to work it out.

This is really dramatic, imaginative, and bold action. My admiration for Marshall increases each time I get a good close-up of him.

Then Marshall explained the origin of the U.S. stories that General Albert C. Wedemeyer would be appointed U.S. ambassador. He had mentioned it in an off-record session with the press. This raised doubt in Chinese minds that Marshall would stay, thus weakening his hand in the negotiations, and drew reaction from the Communists because Wedemeyer had been Chiang's Chief of Staff during the war. Marshall said Washington had cabled to inquire whether he wanted Wedemeyer's orders canceled to counteract the effect of premature disclosure of his assignment, but that he had not yet answered the cable, which was two days old. He foresaw that impending Congressional adjournment would make it unlikely there would be time to pass legislation permitting the general to become ambassador and stay in the army, and he mentioned that Congress did not take kindly, in any case, to having military men in civilian posts.

So, said Marshall, his idea was to send General Gillem to Peking as head of EHQ to succeed Walter S. Robertson (whose resignation had, in fact, already been turned in before Marshall came out in December), since Gillem was current on the situation and Wedemeyer was not; have Wedemeyer made commanding general of the theater, replacing Gillem. He then went on to say that, having racked his brain for a man of stature to be ambassador (he said he had thought of Stassen), the only suitable name he could think of was Leighton Stuart. He asked my opinion.

Remembering the high praise of Stuart from my friend in San Francisco, I said I thought he would be excellent. Although I did not know him, I was told he was the one man in all China who had the complete confidence of all shades of political thought from Chen Li-fu on the right to Mao Tse-tung on the left. We discussed the reaction of public opinion back home and agreed there would be no trouble about it.

[My notes for February 22, 1947, reported that Dr. Stuart told *Time* correspondent Fred Gruin that Marshall had offered him the job the previous day, July 4.]

When I got back I found a nice letter from Senator Arthur Vandenberg, written June 3 in response to mine. Alluding to his own recent dealings with Byrnes vis-à-vis Russia, he says: "I am surer than ever that appeasement only multiplies the hazard from which it seeks escape." Ironic that Wallace, the foremost prewar opponent of appeasing Japan and Germany, now reverses with respect to Russia, and Vandenberg, a prewar isolationist, now condemns appeasement.

CHAPTER SEVEN

Generalissimo wonders if Marshall and Washington realize that U.S. policy promoting truce and coalition "plays into Communist hands." Marshall feels his job is "eight or nine tenths solved." Assassination of two Chinese liberals in Kunming arouses U.S. indignation. In face of government determination to oust Communists from positions threatening Nanking and Shanghai, Marshall abandons further efforts to restore constantly ruptured truce.

My entry for July 6 began with the statement: "This day has been notable for two things." One was having had Nathaniel Peffer to lunch. The other was a session with the Generalissimo from which I drew the impression he had begun to realize he had to "do something"—be a bit less stubborn with Marhall—to get American support.

Peffer I had met at General Marshall's Fourth of July reception in the pleasant courtyard of his house. I was not aware Peffer was in China, nor did I know him by sight; until someone introduced as I thought I was looking at a dead ringer for Lou Stark, the short, quiet, gray-haired labor news expert for the New York *Times* in Washington. With the awed respect of a fan for an author I immediately invited him to lunch on his first free day. "We talked until three-thirty," I noted. "Peffer in conversation exhibits the same fair-mindedness as appears in his book."

As for my impression of Chiang that day—that he was beginning to realize he would have to bend a bit more to Marshall's will—it was, I think, superficial. While I had my self-reporter's nose close on the scent of what was happening in China, Chiang's thinking embraced events taking place elsewhere. He was seeking to gauge the trend of relations between the United States and Russia.

In Paris the Big Four Council of Foreign Ministers was at work seeking to bring some political order into the post-war world. After weeks of deadlock they had "settled" the dispute between Italy and Yugoslavia over Trieste—only to have Italy promptly reject it and to have riots break out in Trieste.

The Council also decided to invite twenty-one nations to meet in Paris July 29 for the first postwar peace conference, but no sooner had this been announced than Russia's Molotov blocked the issuance of bids, objecting that China should not be one of the inviting powers. He also demanded that Germany pay $10 billion in reparations to Russia. Chiang was wondering whether the U.S. was going to be firm in dealing with the Soviet Union.

Chiang had had some twenty years' experience in dealing with Communists. Byrnes, and the American public, were just beginning the experience. It made for different assessments of tactics, one by a man convinced to the core, through personal experience, that Communists were tricky and untrustworthy, one by a people uneasy over Russian intransigence but unwilling to believe it would be permanent. Chiang and Marshall, looking at the China situation in different frames of mind, thought they understood each other's viewpoint but did not really understand or mutually accept the difference. I shared Marshall's underlying disbelief in the correctness of Chiang's outlook.

NANKING, July 6—Today's interview with the Gimo was the most interesting to date. It lasted about an hour. During the conversation we had tea and Chinese meat-filled cakes and cupcakes.

Somehow the Gimo phrases his questions in a way that seems disconcerting to me. He started off by asking what the reaction was in America to the announcement of last Sunday. I said it was taken to be a truce extension but the ambiguous phrasing led to uncertainty about what would happen in the way of war or peace. But the editorial expression in America? he persisted. I said that from what little I had seen there was relief that war did not resume and hope that some settlement could be reached.

Then he went into a long discussion of Russian relations: what did I think of the Foreign Ministers' meeting in Paris? I said it appeared that Russia was conceding a bit in reaching an agreement on Trieste and fixing a date for the peace conference. Chiang agreed, and said he thought a firmness of American opinion had brought it about. What would Russia's attitude be in the Far East? I said that behind Russia's iron wall it was hard to know what shape the country was in and therefore hard to forecast, but there were some signs indicating she was weak internally, comparatively speaking, and therefore one might expect a similar grudging yielding by Russia of what she had to concede in the Far East.

This brought the Gimo to the point he had in the back of his mind, apparently, from the start: did America realize that the aim of the Chinese Communists was delay until China collapses so that they could take over? Did America realize that President Truman's policy—of (1) cease hostilities, (2) coalition, and (3) finally U.S. aid—did Truman realize he was playing into the hands of the Communists? That the Communist Party, by delaying the end of hostilities, by refusing to enter coalition, was delaying American aid and making it harder for the National Government to exist?

This was all spread out in rather lengthy argument, during the course of which I had the opportunity to put in that National Government prestige in the U.S. had slipped tremendously because of corruption in the government, and because of incidents like the Peking newspaper suppression and the railway station riot. What corruption? he wanted to know. In the takeover from the Japanese, and in Formosa, etc. Indulgently he informed me there was no corruption in Formosa; he knew the governor and he was a good man. Very thoughtlessly I cited Peffer's statement to me earlier that he had heard of it from several sources in the few days since his arrival. During the interchange we also discussed the attitude of America toward the Chinese Communists, and Peng was dumbfounded when I ventured that I regarded them as the genuine Communist article rather than simple agrarian reformers, but thought they were first Chinese. "You mean they are patriots?" Peng shot at me, unbelieving. I have picked up enough Chinese to detect—or fancied I detected—some considerable ad-libbing by Peng in his translation. I sketched in briefly my visit with Chou En-lai during the week.

At any rate, the Gimo ended up saying that he wanted us to study by what way this theme—that America was playing into the hands of the Communists—could be got across; how the U.S. could be shown that the order of items in her policy needed to be reversed.

Nanking, July 7—Central News told of the arrival of eight members of the U. S. Congress in China. I noted that Senator Owen Brewster of Maine was among them and phoned Till Durdin to see whether they were coming here. He said they were due in at eleven-thirty, would lunch with Marshall, and leave immediately. I said that since Brewster was the one I knew best, ever since the time he entered the House, I would go to the airport and bring him to Marshall's in my car. Later Hutchin phoned to say that if it didn't compromise me with the Chinese—an idea that hadn't even occurred to me and certainly doesn't bother me—I could ride back from the airport in one of Marshall's cars and stay for lunch. Which I did. Besides Brewster and Senator Allen Ellender of Louisiana, whom I knew well, there were Senator Butler and several House members with whom I was less well acquainted.

The group had just come from Japan on one of those Congressional travel junkets ostensibly to study how the U.S. was getting along in the world. Brewster said he had seen the President just before they left Washington, and Truman said he could tell General MacArthur he was backing him 100 per cent, and if he wanted his (Truman's) job, he could have it. Owen said he had reported this conversation to MacArthur, who asked him to carry back the following word: You'll never have to worry about me, Eisenhower is the man to watch. I take Truman's backing of MacArthur as another indication of his determination to be firm with Russia, since that is MacArthur's attitude.

I sat next to Brewster at lunch. He reads the political signs as indicating that the Republicans are a cinch to capture the House this year. Butler was renominated 2 to 1 over Griswold in Nebraska, despite Stassen's active speech-making support for Griswold. This is a blow to Stassen, who will be lost unless he can put Ed Thye across as senator from Minnesota. Brewster interprets a Republican victory as forecasting a return toward isolationism, but not as much with respect to China as elsewhere. He sees Claude Pepper of Florida as thinking in presidential terms for 1952 and regarding Henry Wallace as his rival.

Brewster said that last night in Shanghai Chinese police had killed General Gillem's mess sergeant, and found it an alarming indication of the extent of anti-American sentiment; also, he said, the Jews in Shanghai are passing the word that Nazi advisers have strong influence in the Chinese government. I said I knew of none whatever in Nanking, though there might be some in the administrative setup in Shanghai of whom I might not be aware.

The Congressional crowd was fascinated by Chinese currency so I peeled off a $1000 bill for Brewster. He asked me to sign it so he could show it to the boys in the press gallery in Washington.

Auerbach got back from the trip to Yenan he finally wangled. He said that while he was there a KMT B-24 landed and surrendered to the Communists; the pilot said he would rather do that than fight a civil war. The Communists, however, refused to let Auerbach talk to the crew. He thinks the Communists do not want to fight but were ready to fight last weekend.

I got hold of Peffer and told him I had incautiously let his name slip in talking to the Gimo, and I felt I had made a mistake. He decided that if it came up in conversations he had, he would say he had read reports of corruption in the newspapers, rather than say he learned of it from KMT members.

NANKING, July 8—Peffer and I lunched with Wang Shih-chieh at his home. This reminds me of Peffer's call from the SSU house the day he came to lunch, to ask for an appointment. The man at the other end quizzed him at great length on who he was, what he was doing in China, how long he had been here, how long he intended to stay, etc., and finally reported that Dr. Wang was not home. How very Chinese, Peffer had commented.

At Dr. Wang's luncheon, in addition to Madame Wang, who spoke no English, there was a Mr. Li, ambassador to Cuba, and a Mr. and Mrs. Chen of the Ministry of Education. Wang said China would favor abolition of the UN veto and asked if we thought the U.S. would. I thought not at present, though a government campaign to build popular support for it might put it across; Peffer thought it could be sold to the public. Incidentally, Peffer said he thought the Communists were wrong in demanding fourteen seats on the forty-member State Council which will be set up under the new constitution to be considered by the National Assembly—it would give them a veto and create the same kind of problems as the veto in the UN.

Wang was very discouraging about the negotiations. When a reasonable, balanced fellow like him shows such complete mistrust of the Communists as he does, it makes me feel the case is hopeless.

I worked on a lengthy memo for the Gimo on how to get attention in the U.S., but held it for further consideration. The Communists are out with a new four-point demand which is disgusting, an example of propaganda and vituperation rather than anything seriously designed for negotiation. The points are: (1) immediate cease-fire (okay); (2) resumption of PCC (questionable), broadening of government into coalition, "reorganization" of Ministries of National Defense, Foreign Affairs, Finance, Economics, Interior, Communications, and Education—i.e., inferring these are the ones they want; (3) military demobilization, oust

MAGIC, give back lend-lease, advise the U.S. that the Chinese people will not be responsible for any loans; (4) U.S. stop aggravating Chinese civil war.

Mr. and Mrs. Turner of the U. S. Embassy came over for dinner. Turner says his last trip to Shanghai concerned repatriation of German nationals. He said that, out of a list of about 500 in Shanghai (exclusive of lists in other cities), 184 were exempted. He said American hell-raising had got the exemptions reduced to 39. Ten of the list they were told could not be touched, and that T.V. had personally put a dozen on exemption. He said $60,000 U.S. was paid to keep one man from being repatriated.

Continued lack of action on providing me with a house was beginning to get me down. I was comfortably enough fixed personally in the relatively spacious SSU establishment, which had long since been furnished, but my wife and three children were waiting in Washington for word from me that living quarters were all set and they could come ahead. David Lu, my friend in Washington whom Dr. Soong had mentioned the first day as one who could work with me as "a team," had not yet arrived, and I was looking forward to his coming. Central News carried an item saying he had landed in Shanghai, but I had not heard from him. These things put me into extreme depression. There was no relaxation available from the endless talks about politics and war, except the army movies and crossword puzzles in the Shanghai English papers. One night the USO put on a show at the Officers' Club, which I attended with Auerbach and some visiting SSU personnel. The entertainment was excellent, but the affair as a whole was Kipling, 1946: the white man's burden. The white man was enjoying himself in exotic surroundings, with lanterns strung between the willow trees in the compound of the Wang Ching-wei palace, while the moon came in and out of the fleecy-clouded sky—and outside it seemed that China was about to commit hara-kiri.

NANKING, July 10—Dave Lu arrived today, and his coming pepped me up a great deal. Like myself, he came out rather uncertain as to what he is to do, although he talked to T.V. in Shanghai.

Franklin Ray, of UNRRA's China office in Shanghai, has charged CNRRA, the Chinese counterpart relief organization, with mismanagement, and Harold Milks of AP asked me if I could get comment from Dr. Soong. I went over to No. 1 House to see him, since I also had a query from Lieberman as to the status of the freight airline Claire Chennault is trying to get started. T.V. said that the head of CNRRA, T. F. Tsiang, would be answering the charges about his agency at a press conference Friday. On Chennault, he said the airline would be approved if the project was cleared with UNRRA and CNRRA, but only for the duration of the relief problem.

On my own I broached the tip from Brewster that T.V. had been personally responsible for taking a dozen Germans off the repatriation list. T.V. readily admitted it. "No one is willing to take responsibility here," he said. "We needed those men." He said they were four dye experts, three brewers, three doctors, and a tannery expert, eleven in all. "I walked into it with my eyes open. I knew I would be criticized." We walked back to his office in the Executive Yuan, where he wrote out a statement and asked me if I could get a question asked about it at Peng's press conference this afternoon. Henry Lieberman asked an appropriate question and Peng read him T.V.'s reply, but didn't know quite what to say when he was asked if the Germans were "obnoxious."

NANKING, July 11—As soon as I got to work T.V. phoned me to come right on down. Bill Youngman, one of Tommy Corcoran's partners from Washington, had arrived on a trip and convinced him that the Chinese government—and T.V. personally—cannot escape blame for CNRRA maladministration just because T. F. Tsiang, the man in charge, is a man he dislikes; that he cannot wash his hands of it and leave it to Tsiang to speak for the Chinese government. So in three or four drafts worked on by T.V.,

Bill, and myself, we got a statement ready by around 4 P.M. which was given to Peng to put out.

Ronald Stead took me to dinner at the Chungking Restaurant where Jimmy Wong and his trio hold forth, assisted by three Chinese girl crooners. With night clubs officially closed, it is the closest approach to one in Nanking. The trio makes up in enthusiasm what it lacks in music, but the nasal-voiced girl singers were cute and it was an amusing experience. We had a martini to start and glass of excellent port after a Chinese-Western meal.

NANKING, July 12—Last night's dinner must have affected me. Auerbach took me to see a German doctor named Schroeder, who claims my spleen is enlarged and a blood test indicates I have or have had malaria. I already was aware I had dysentery, but the question is: bacillus or amoebic? I had to skip a party Peng was giving for the press.

NANKING, July 13—Schroeder gave me a shot of emetine and various other drugs to take for my other ailments.

Auerbach had Chou En-lai and some of the Communist delegation to dinner. In my condition I could not attend. I went over and talked to Peng but came back before the guests left, for a brief visit.

Peng did not see the Gimo today because I could not make it. I found this a most interesting fact.

For several days I lay around trying to recuperate from my various ailments, glad of a chance to talk things over with Dave Lu.

I had now been in China approximately three months. It was taking strenuous effort just to keep up with developments. General Marshall was candid as well as generous in supplying information whenever I asked for it, but he was under no obligation to do it regularly.

Unquestionably Peng was better informed than I with

respect to Kuomintang policies and plans and knew a lot of
detail that it would have been helpful to me to possess. He
was not uncommunicative, but I judged he believed Kuomintang plans had best be kept secret; perhaps he was fearful I
would "leak" embarrassing information to the American correspondents, who were in the main hostile to the government
and almost uniformly so in Shanghai.

My impression of Peng's relationship to the Generalissimo was that Chiang looked on him as a spokesman to be
called in and informed what the press should be told. This
was not a relationship which could be of much value, in my
belief. I remembered the case of a public relations officer in
Washington who had been told by one of his superiors:
"Come in after the meeting and we'll tell you what to tell the
press." His reply was: "Tell me what the facts are and I'll decide what to tell the press." This was an attitude I applauded.
I had no intention of being a spokesman for the Chinese or
any other government, including my own, but it seemed
elemental that if my advice as a man supposed to know
American official and public thinking was to be any good, it
would have to be based on intimate knowledge of what the
facts were.

The Generalissimo was asking me, in effect, to devise ways
of convincing Truman, Marshall, and the American people
that the U.S. policy of truce and coalition was helping prolong the economic deterioration of China and was helping
the Communists. I did not really believe it, partly because of
gaps in my knowledge of all the factors involved, but more
because in theory the agreements engineered by Marshall in
Chungking seemed to offer a real solution: let both sides lay
down their arms and gradually merge their armies into one
which would serve the whole nation, not a political party;
let the Communists take part in the government and replace
the Kuomintang's "political tutelage" with more democratic
government. I did not believe that putting U.S. aid to the
government first on the list would solve China's problem.

It is hard now to understand how American policy makers clung stubbornly to the hope that the Communists would in fact accept the theory and give up their private army. Hope persisted in Marshall because the only alternative was a military solution.

How much of this did America grasp? Practically none, said Dave. The U.S. was aware that General Marshall was trying to end the fighting, but in a "let George do it" sort of way while it pursued its own domestic interests. My own reading of the daily pouch of U.S. press information confirmed this.

Dave said he thought he could open up one additional pipeline of information for us through Ambassador Stuart. He had been a pupil of Dr. Stuart's at Yenching University, and the traditional Chinese teacher-pupil bond remained strong in both of them.

NANKING, July 18—Dave has heard, among other things, that T. V. Soong is burned up by the appointment of Dr. Stuart, on the ground that he is not a big enough man.

This morning, feeling some slight rise in health and spirits, I went over to see Marshall. He was about to leave for Kuling, where the Gimo flew on Sunday, to accompany Stuart when he presented his credentials, but he plans to return immediately. We sat on the veranda and talked while he awaited a visit from Yu Ta-wei. One thing about working over here (I'm reminded every time I see Yu) is the morale-building effect on a comparatively short man of suddenly becoming taller than the men with whom you deal.

Marshall was plainly annoyed with the Gimo for leaving for Kuling. His departure stopped the negotiations cold, and Marshall interpreted it as an attempt to do just that and to force the Communists into coming to terms.

He said that the last remaining problem—that involved in the military settlement—is eight or nine tenths solved. The (1) cessation of hostilities order, (2) field team agreement, and (3) communications agreement are all in the bag, including assimilation of Communist railway workers into the civil administration, as far as anything can be in the bag with the opposing armies straining to get at each other. The straining, with negotiations suspended, is very strong and threatens to become really widespread civil war.

The critical military points are northern Kiangsu and central Hopei. In both it appeared probable that the fighting was the result of spontaneous combustion, coming to a head on both sides at the same time, rather than attack by one side or the other. The government had retaken the Tsingtao–Tsinan railway line and got itself out of a hole there, but the result was to spur Communist retaliation at Tatung. The Communists have the force to take Tatung and will do so, said Marshall.

Then, going into the spots where the retention of Communist civilian administration is still in dispute, Marshall named the northern tip of Kiangsu and Antung in Manchuria. That is the way things stand now, though there are a thousand little complexities involved in everything. For example, the engineer on the Yellow River dikes wanted to divert half the water into the old channel and retain half in the present channel. The Communists feared to have the new channel split their forces in half, which it would do for some three hundred miles, without some means of communication. It was proposed to build eight barges, each capable of carrying two or three hundred persons, and station them at eight points to provide ferries. But Chou told Marshall he would agree only if the Nationalists would refrain from using one bridge on their half of the river for military transportation. This the Nationalists refused to do, but Marshall thinks he can persuade them.

NANKING, July 19—I went over to the Executive Yuan intending to do nothing more than ask T.V. to name a date and time when he would be likely to be in a relaxed frame of mind, unhurried by callers, so that we could have a long discussion. I found him in conference with T. F. Tsiang and an American whom I judged, from newspaper photographs, to be Benjamin Kizer, UNRRA's departing China head. T.V. greeted me, told them, "I want to talk to Mr. Beal," and led me to the little anteroom. His snub to his callers was embarrassing to me and I told him the very simple purpose of my call. "Let's talk now," he said. I demurred, saying I did not want to interrupt his conference. "No," he said, "I like to talk to you." I know he despises Tsiang as "a politician," a term he uses contemptuously, and suspects him of trying to build himself influence through CNRRA, but it was scarcely conducive of relaxed talk to have T.V. insist on seeing me while Tsiang and the other man cooled their heels.

So, making the best of it, I brought up the first thing I could think of. I said the UNRRA situation had not come out too badly because Mayor La Guardia of New York, UNRRA administrator, in his Senate testimony, had said his cutting off of further shipments to China except for food was not political in motive, and had publicly spanked the UNRRA China employees for making their charges to the newspapers instead of coming to him first; also that a Colonel Harrington had cleared CNRRA of discriminating against Communists in relief.

But, I went on, it was necessary to do more than issue dignified statements after a situation had developed. It was necessary to have someone constantly following the situation as it developed so as to be able to advise how to head off reactions that might reflect unfavorably against China. I added that the most difficult part of my job was reporting for myself—finding out what the government was doing, so that I would know what to suggest. It was like pulling teeth to drag it out of the people.

T.V.'s reaction was: "You had better come to see me every day. We can talk it over—anything that comes up." He suggested 4 P.M. as an hour when he was usually free.

I mentioned having heard (I was careful not to say where) that he was peeved by the Leighton Stuart appointment. He said no, not particularly, though he thought a man of greater international prestige might have been picked. What annoyed him, he said, was seeing Stuart quoted as saying that (1) Bill Gray's now famous *Time* article on the Chinese economy was right, and (2) the KMT should love the people more. His point was that Stuart as a university president had every right to say that, but not as the accredited representative of a major power to the government of China.

I said my understanding was that Stuart was somewhat temporary, named for the express purpose of helping Marshall's peace efforts, and I thought that in time Wedemeyer would succeed him. Wedemeyer would be better, said T.V.; he was "very cautious" and would not speak as Stuart had. We discussed also Marshall's efforts, and though Soong said he thought Marshall lost sight of the political and particularly the economic implications of his negotiations, he praised Marshall as "a fine Christian gentleman" who "bends over backward to be fair" and avoid offending either side. Soong always speaks with genuine admiration about Marshall. "I didn't get along with him in Washington," he said. "We fought over Stilwell."

And so we broke it up. "Come back tomorrow," he said.

NANKING, July 20—The MOI's housing man has advised me that the occupants of the house they had found for me refused either to move to other quarters the ministry had found, or to accept a money payment to move. I felt it was high time to have a showdown and after lunch I went to see Peng and laid it on the line: I had cabled my family to come ahead, and now I had no prospect of a house. I could probably countermand my cable, but I would have to do so quickly. Was I being unreasonable? I said I realized the Nanking housing situation was tough. He said he did not think I was unreasonable, but the occupant of the house in question was a section chief in the National Defense Ministry and he didn't know who was "behind" him. I asked if it would help if I talked to T.V. and Peng seemed mightily relieved.

So at four o'clock I went to the Executive Yuan. T.V. was not feeling well and had spent the day at home, but had left word I was to come over to No. 1 House. He came to the big oak-beamed, blue-tapestried living room in a summer lounging suit with short sleeves and open neck; the heat was affecting him, he said, and on his neck and arms was evidence of the use of some salve against prickly heat.

I broached my housing situation, explaining my quandary about the family. Before I got more than a couple of sentences out he interrupted: "Tell them to come along. I will personally guarantee that you will have a house." He laughed rather bitterly and added: "At least I can do that much. Tell Peng to come and see me— tomorrow morning."

While we talked the first edition of Central News was delivered —the English edition; he works and thinks in English. He hurriedly looked through it, paused over a Kuling dateline, and read it aloud in a sarcastic tone. It quoted Stuart as saying he could not talk for publication because of his position as ambassador.

He was tense, preoccupied. The plain fact was that, aside from the subject of the house, I had nothing to take up. But we did talk for some forty minutes; some reminiscing on his part, some discussion of the current situation. He recalled his trip to Moscow to negotiate the Sino-Soviet Treaty of August 1945. "Stalin, at first, tried to convince me that China should cooperate with Russia," he said. "He said there would not be war between the United States and Russia because America did not want war and Russia did not, but that the way to deal with the Americans was to scratch their faces and take everything you could."

Driving around a bit on the way back, I was impressed by the amount of building that is going on around town. Whether they are being financed by the government, by banks, or by individuals, a lot of houses and other structures are going up out of materials put together on the spot. Logs are assembled, a couple of workmen using a wooden horse saw them into planks, and up goes a frame; next they saw smaller planks and soon the structure has walls and roof. Raw bricks seem to materialize from nowhere. I noted one "factory" consisting of four big tentlike matting roofs on a big frame of bamboo poles (no sides) under which at least fifty truck chassis were being fitted with stake bodies made of wood being cut on the spot.

NANKING, July 21—John Blandford, one of T.V.'s economic advisers on relief problems, called me to say that an UNRRA source had told him that two Communist students had been denied passports out of thirty-seven students selected by a CNRRA-UNRRA-Ministry of Education committee to go to the United States. When I mentioned this to Dave Lu he said he had heard that three persons invited by the U.S. from Communist territory in the cultural relations program, which is under the direction here of John K. Fairbank's wife, Wilma, also had been denied passports. I took this information over to the Foreign Ministry, where I saw Vice-Minister Liu Chieh. He said the matter had not come to his attention, and I left the names Blandford had given me for him to look into. Liu told me that Bill Gray, who had gone back to the U.S. recently, had applied for a visa to return and he had recommended approval.

Yesterday T.V. had suggested changing our meeting hour to 6 P.M., and I found him at the Executive Yuan, relaxed at the end of the day and not nervous as he was yesterday. I mentioned the passport business. He said it was relatively unimportant and that the unfavorable publicity didn't matter much. But when I casually mentioned Bill Gray he said instantly: "By all means he must come in." He called the Foreign Minister and got a vice-minister, Kan, on the phone and asked to see that Bill got his Chinese visa "quickly."

T.V. said Peng had failed to come to see him, "but I'll see him Monday." We talked about the Gimo's trip and I said some of the correspondents were writing that he went to Kuling to halt the negotiations. I took T.V.'s failure to comment on that as tacit admission it was true.

For the umpteenth time I went over my argument about what it takes to get U.S. attention, applying it specifically to the Gimo: if he wanted to present his views he himself had to voice them, say in a speech. "We'll write a speech for the Gimo," said T.V. I suggested that August 14, the anniversary of V-J Day, might be a good occasion. T.V. said that would give enough time and he would have someone start to draw up a preliminary draft immediately.

We left the building separately but as I was looking for a phone to summon my car I encountered him again. "I'll send you home in my car," he said. "Transportation is bad here. Even I have to use this measly Lincoln. But I've got a Cadillac coming from the U.S." I have ridden in the Lincoln before, but had not noticed it was a bulletproof job. The glass windows were fully an inch thick and as he dropped me off at the house the door swung shut with the heft of a bank vault's.

There was a tendency, on Marshall's part as well as among the correspondents, to suspect the Generalissimo of wanting to "halt the negotiations" every time he left town, and the newsmen were always a bit annoyed that they learned of his trips only after he left. Foreigners in the capital, including myself, tended to forget that China was in effect at war, that the Prime Minister felt obliged to go armed with a pistol even in his office. As shown in entries below, Communist armies were very close to Nanking at the time. The need for security was very real to Chinese officials, and it would have been folly for the government to announce the Generalissimo's movements in advance, as President Nixon can announce plans to fly to Miami for the weekend.

Hindsight makes me realize, however, that Chiang may well have wanted a temporary halt in negotiations. He had two reasons for wanting to get away briefly from Marshall's unrelenting pressure, despite his feeling that delay was only helping the Communists. The government was determined not to tolerate the Communist threat so near to the capital, no matter what cease-fires might be arranged elsewhere. Its troops were deployed to strike the enemy in North Kiangsu as they subsequently did. Beside possible fear that Marshall would be demanding another truce, Chiang may well have feared his ability to control the military, which were straining at the leash to get going.

The Nationalists were just at the beginning of a series of successful military campaigns which lasted through the rest of 1946, despite a cutting off of arms supplies by the United States. The tide began to turn against the government in 1947. The ambiguously extended June truce just petered out as a truce.

NANKING, July 22—Shao Li-tze, the graying, round-headed little fellow who was once Chinese ambassador to Russia, was a most charming dinner guest last night. He encouraged me to try out my Chinese on him, the first time I've tried it in polite conversation, since his English is as limited as my Chinese. I did all right as far as I went, but without my notes handy my range of vocabulary was extremely limited. He says the Communists have been offered nine seats on the States Council, which with the Democratic League's four would give them thirteen, one short of veto power. They are still holding out for fourteen.

Lunched at the American Embassy with the SSU trio, Dave Lu, and George Silk, who came up here yesterday to do a picture story for *Life* on the new ambassador. Mr. and Mrs. Smyth and Philip Fugh, the adopted Chinese son of Dr. Stuart, were there. Dr. Stuart, a kindly old character, remembered my friend Larry Sears as one of his teachers at Yenching. He reminisced at lunch of the Japanese attempts to get him to negotiate peace with Chiang, on any terms, and how the Japs gave up on it after the Potsdam declaration. Afterward he told me he had had two intimate conversations with Chiang in which he felt the Gimo was being completely sincere. The Gimo said he really preferred settling the Communist problem by peaceful, political means rather than by military force, and wanted a Communist opposition in the government but not while they had an army. Stuart said he had asked the Gimo three things: (1) to disavow government connection with the Kunming assassinations and make it utterly clear to the world; (2) to withdraw the suppression of publications; (3) to reopen the PCC. He said the Gimo was already doing the first, apparently referring to the dispatch of the central police head to

Kunming to conduct the investigation; agreed to the second with the exception of Communist publications while the Communists were fighting him—"and I agreed with him," said Stuart. He said of the third request that Chiang indicated it would be done along toward September or October.

He said he had told the Gimo the Communists had invited him to Yenan. "Why don't you go?" Chiang asked. Stuart replied that the time was not ripe, but that if he did he wanted certain commitments from the Gimo.

The reference to the Kunming assassinations was to the recent slaying in that city of two prominent members of the Democratic League, one of them a university professor, by unknown persons. Later it was revealed that the assassins were members of the secret police attached to the Kunming garrison headquarters. The State Department's White Paper noted that "there were indications that KMT secret police were intimidating leading Democratic League members and Chinese liberals in other parts of the country." It also told of Communist activities during this period, in line with the Yenan attack on U.S. China policy. "In mid-July the first serious incident involving the Communists and U.S. marines occurred—the kidnapping of seven marines in East Hopei and their detention by the Communists for several days before being released. This was followed at the end of the month by a deliberate Communist ambush of a U.S. marine-escorted motor convoy bound from Tientsin to Peking, during which three Americans were killed and 12 wounded."

July 22 (continued)—At my evening appointment, T.V. said the situation in northern Kiangsu had been critical recently—had really threatened Nanking and Shanghai—but was now thoroughly under control. He spoke of the economic necessity of getting coal from Shantung and the need of northern Kiangsu in the process. I gather that he, like the Gimo, thoroughly condones the army's idea that the Communist *must* be driven from this proximity to the political and economic capitals. The Gimo's attitude, I gather, is like his attitude prior to the capture of Changchun in Manchuria—he would not negotiate short of that.

I can see some point to the economic argument, if you accept the KMT view that the Communists cannot be trusted to carry out the PCC resolutions which (in the fullness of time) contemplate merging the local and district administrations—KMT and Communist—into coalition governments as on the national scale. I can understand how Chiang may, from his viewpoint, consider it essential to the economy to have North and South China one unit instead of two as they now are, and that on this point could feel it necessary to fight rather than compromise; like Lincoln's decision that the U.S. could not exist half slave and half free. But I can scarcely work up the same kind of conviction about it as over Lincoln's position.

Dave Lu came back from a dinner with General Chen Cheng to say that this determination with respect to northern Kiangsu is written all over the military. They will not tolerate so close a threat to the capital, and the government must have Shantung coal and needs both regions to get it. Fighting has been heavy and there have been heavy casualties. T.V. says the Communists have 500,000 men in northern Kiangsu.

NANKING–SHANGHAI, July 23—Dr. Soong called me over to the Executive Yuan at eleven. He showed me a dispatch from a Chinese consul in the U.S. saying that the New York tabloid *PM* had a story saying that air conditioning units intended by UNRRA for skin disease wards in Chinese hospitals were being used in Soong's home and office. T.V. had a report from T. F. Tsiang, who was present, that they were part of a purchase of U.S. surplus stocks, not part of UNRRA shipments, and had not been destined for skin disease wards. [Soong denied he was using any of them. I learned later, but not from him, that one unit had been put in General Marshall's residence.] What the government did not have use for had been sold commercially. We got to talking about UNRRA and I expressed the desire to talk to Donald Gilpatrick, State Department man in the Shanghai consulate, who keeps an eye on UNRRA and CNRRA for Will Clayton, the Assistant Secretary of State for economic affairs. T.V. said okay, go down and see him. Tsiang said I could travel with him on the five-thirty plane. I asked Tsiang about a story (Charlotte Ebener's) that CNRRA was paying 20 per cent interest. He said it was not true; CNRRA's rate was 9.6 per cent per year.

We also discussed a statement by Madame Sun Yat-sen, issued in Shanghai last night, urging the U.S. to withdraw its forces from China to prevent spread of civil war. Madame Sun, as the widow of the Republic's founder, is bound to get widespread attention in the U.S., proving my point about the news value of prominent names. Although she is also, incidentally, the sister of T.V. and Madame Chiang, T.V. had not known about her statement, nor had I until Peng called me to say he had suppressed it in Central News and asked what he could say in reply. I told him nothing; her criticism of the government had been implied rather than direct, and an official reply would only be putting on the shoe in public. I did not mention that he had reacted already by suppressing it in Central News.

When I got to the airport I learned that CNAC's Capital Express, Dr. Tsiang's flight, was sold out, but that another plane would be going down at 6 P.M. During my wait Francis Chang, head mechanic for CNAC in Nanking, told me a long story about his work in aviation for sixteen years—since he was twenty—and how hard it was for a Chinese employee to support himself and his family under inflation. He gets around 300,000 CNC a month, or something less than $150 U.S. at the official rate, which is unrealistic. American pilots and maintenance men get from $600 to $1200 a month U.S., with a $300 U.S. living allowance if married. He told about a recent strike by the Chinese employees and how they had to give in, also how the Chinese Army Air Force had failed utterly to carry out its boast of being able to keep the line running. No wonder there is anti-American feeling here.

The 6 P.M. flight from Chungking for which I was waiting did not get in until seven-thirty, coming in out of the west ahead of a huge thunderhead formation, a big-bellied C-47. It taxied to the little clot of vehicles and people waiting on the open field, and what seemed to be a small army of Chinese got out, carrying all sorts of miscellaneous parcels—bundles of bedding, bunches of oranges, cardboard boxes, a few battered suitcases. This was the day's influx of minor government employees arriving in the new capital. Others, still lower in rank, have been coming down the Yangtze by junk.

I was impressed by the somewhat casual way in which flying in China is conducted. Earlier, when the five-thirty flight left, the plane started to taxi across the grass. I thought it was taking a short cut to the head of the runway, but when I looked again it was airborne and climbing fast. It had just splashed through a few mud puddles and lifted itself into the lowering sky against the stiff breeze. Now, to service the C-47, half a dozen coolies in tattered clothes came out carrying 50-gallon drums of 100-octane gasoline suspended from the inevitable shoulder-to-shoulder bamboo poles, and another pair carried a gasoline motor pump. The crew ran a hose from the drum to the wing tank and pumped in the gasoline with the put-put, then repeated it on the other side. Meanwhile, other workers, so nondescript in appearance that one would expect them to know a left- from a right-hand monkey wrench, checked the oil and the landing gear.

Finally Francis Chang put me aboard. It was a bucket-seat job, flying deadhead to Shanghai as I discovered, since the only passengers besides myself were Chang's cousin and his son, who looked to be about ten years old and got sick just before we landed, probably because of nervousness on a first flight. We reached Shanghai after dark. Tsiang, by prearrangement, had sent his car to pick me up. On George Silk's invitation I put up in the *Time* penthouse suite at Broadway Mansions, where Dick Johnston is the only current occupant. Rather than have their servant, Wong, get me dinner so late, I looked up Till Durdin and we ate in the Aero Club downstairs. It's easy to understand why the correspondents prefer Shanghai. One lives comfortably at the Broadway Mansions, miserably at the Nanking Hotel.

SHANGHAI, July 24—By appointment I met Donald Gilpatrick at his office. He is balding, reddish-brown-haired, and gives the impression of a well-balanced, keen fellow. He recounted the background of the UNRRA-CNRRA squabble more clearly than I have heard it to date. CNRRA suffers, he said, from (1) lack of funds, since what the government appropriates goes to the agencies which get the CNRRA goods, and (2) inefficient management. He thinks, however, that the reorganization of the last two weeks will improve things a lot.

There were several journalistic guests for dinner in the *Time* suite, including an American photographer and a man from the London *Daily Telegraph* who had just arrived from Harbin, Changchun, Mukden, and Peking. This pair reported that the Russians have stripped Manchuria of everything—but everything; even the Communists are sore at them. The newsmen devoted the dinner conversation to damning the Nationalists, criticizing U.S. policy, ridiculing China's World War effort, and echoing each other until I thought: maybe China is living in an incestuous economy as Bill Gray reported, but it isn't half as incestuous as the journalism. The boys sit around talking to each other and working up a fever.

SHANGHAI–NANKING, July 25—Wong got me up at 4:30 A.M., gave me toast and coffee, and sent me off at five in the *Time* car for what I thought was a 6 A.M. flight, but which proved to be seven. Half of flying is waiting at airports. While I waited for the car I watched the sampan fleet on Soochow Creek just in front of Broadway Mansions, a fleet which is home for Chinese families who make their living I know not how. It was still dark; here and there a light showed among the boats as evidence of some matutinal stirring, and on one of them a rooster crowed. Ah, China.

At the airport some Indians, one in a sari, were awaiting the six-thirty for Kunming and, presumably, Calcutta. A man in pith helmet and shorts, looking like a German repatriate awaiting repatriation, sat with a flaxen-haired German woman. Hundreds of Chinese jammed the terminal.

My flight got away more or less on time—a sleek C-54 with a cute Chinese stewardess. It was a smooth trip. As we circled Nanking and came down over the Yangtze, the copilot pointed out some gunboats, newly acquired from the U.S. "They have their guns pointed at that village over there, where the Communists are," he said.

I called on T.V. and asked when the CNRRA reorganization would be complete. It's all done, he said, showing me the draft. Well, I said, let's tell the press about it. He asked me to draft a release. He said he was going to see the British movie, *Henry* V, at his home tonight and invited me to attend.

NANKING–SHANGHAI, July 26—Marshall's Cadillac was parked outside when I got to T.V.'s home on the hill last night, as well as that of the British chargé d'affaires, Wallinger, who came with his wife. The road winds up the hill, which is not very high but does give a splendid view over the city and Lotus Lake. The house is on the order of an English manor house with big ceiling beams, a huge fireplace surmounted by an enormous moose head, and doors leading to terraces. The main room is huge. T.V. said that upstairs there were only two big bedrooms and bathrooms.

Madame Soong and their two daughters, one named Katherine, were there. No drinks were offered, but the girls passed around a tin of hard candies. The big, comfortable leather divans and chairs were arranged and the movie began. T.V. remarked that he had wanted to see it ever since he read the review in *Time*; said he got to see movies only about twice a year. The film did not live up to my expectations, I think because I was exhausted from lack of sleep and it was torture keeping awake through sixteen ten-minute reels, especially as there was only one projector and the operator had to stop and turn on the lights to change reels, thus breaking into the dramatic buildup. But it was an enjoyable evening. There were light refreshments after the show, and in a couple of minutes Marshall led the exodus. He was wearing a light tan summer suit rather than the uniform I usually see him in.

This morning Dr. Peng asked Dave and me to go to Shanghai with him, where he wants to have a press conference tomorrow. He had a release prepared which he wanted me to work on, one designed to develop the theme the Gimo wanted to put across: (1) the Communist demand for unconditional cessation of hostilities means unconditional disruption of communications and unconditional economic chaos, unless it is accompanied by solid agreements on these quid pro quo items; (2) American policy of forcing coalition was being defeated by the Communists through delaying tactics, in the hope that chaos would promote revolution, and in the fear that American aid to a coalition government would only strengthen the KMT; (3) delineation of the economic reasons why the government is insistent on clearing the Communists from northern Kiangsu and Shantung.

I called T.V. to ask if the trip would interfere with getting out the release of the CNRRA reorganization. "I'll talk to you about it when you get back," he said.

The Communists appear to be badly alarmed over the Nationalist military pressure in northern Kiangsu. Wang Ping-nan came to see Auerbach and conferred with him privately. After he left Auerbach gave me a harangue: what the hell was the government trying to do—wipe out the Communists? It occurs to me that the situation just now—the mood on both sides—is very similar to that at the time of Changchun. Again the Communists, having grabbed territory and extended themselves when the opportunity presented, are faced by a government determination to deal with them by force in certain specific places. But if the government gains its point—and if retaliation elsewhere doesn't add a new complication—my hunch is that the Gimo will be in a more generous frame of mind and possibly the final gaps can be bridged by Marshall.

The MOI party had a good flight down to Shanghai on the five-thirty plane. It was the first time visibility was good, and we kept the Yangtze in sight all the way. As we circled Shanghai for the landing we could see ships anchored for miles in the Whangpoo. It was a graphic picture of the port congestion. Dave and I put up at Broadway Mansions in the apartment of his friend, "Newsreel" Wong, who is not occupying it just now. [Newsreel was Chinese representative of *News of the Day*, an American newsfilm service. He had become famous early in the Sino-Japanese War for his picture of a Chinese baby, dirty-faced and crying, sitting upright in a rubbled street which had been under bombardment.]

SHANGHAI, July 27—Determined to get some rest this trip, I lounged all morning and didn't dress until noon, but did get some letters off to the States.

Peng's press conference, for the Chinese at four and the foreign correspondents at five, did not impress me as having much effect. Although he had the typed statement in front of him he did not distribute copies, or read it. He did work in the ideas toward the end, but I couldn't see that anyone understood what he was trying to get across. "He talked like a spokesman of defeat," Ronald Stead commented to me afterward.

SHANGHAI, July 28—Breakfasted with Bill Costello of CBS, who says CGRA is still unable to get a satisfactory radio signal to the U.S. CBS is shifting its Far East headquarters to Tokyo for the next year because of lack of facilities here.

Peng asked me about reaction to his press conference and seemed surprised when I told him the correspondents did not seem to understand what he was trying to say and I doubted that much, if any, got cabled abroad.

One of the correspondents yesterday invited me to go to a Chinese theater with him last night, but because of feeling tired I declined. This morning he told me about the play, a satire on corruption, which sounded so intriguing that I got hold of a couple of tickets and arranged with Dick Johnston to borrow George Silk's interpreter, a chap named T. W. Tsui, to accompany me.

The play was in a medium-sized theater on the Avenue Foch called the Spreading Brightness. Its title might be freely translated as *How Officials Get Promoted,* or alternatively *A Picture of Parvenu Officialdom.* There were racks in the back of the seats to hold the inevitable glasses of tea, and between acts a girl came through the rows of seats carrying a kettle, filling the glasses with hot water. The heat, of course, was terrific and most of the audience was using palm-leaf or folding fans. I was the only foreigner present, as far as I could make out. The curtain went up on the dot; the spotlighting and other mechanics of production were professionally sharp.

As Tsui explained it to me, the authors had protected themselves by using titles more than fifty years old—dynasty titles—for the characters, and by presenting it as the dream of two of the characters involved. Yet, he said, there was no mistaking the sly allusions to H. H. Kung, Chungking's wartime Minister of Finance (and brother-in-law of Madame Chiang and T.V.), in the "Minister of Finance" on the stage, and to the Generalissimo as the "governor" who developed headaches which could only be cured by the application of gold bars to his head. Tsui also thought he could discern touches of Madame Chiang and Chen Li-fu in it.

The plot: two robbers enter a deserted house, tended only by a watchman, threaten him against revealing their presence to police, and then fall asleep. This is by way of prologue.

The play itself opens with the robber's dream. A mob storms into the house and leaves two men apparently dead. Examination of the bodies reveals that one is the magistrate of the *hsien* or county and the other the secretary-general. Thief No. 2, it develops, is a double for the magistrate and has donned his clothes and badge of office. Then the chief of police arrives, full of apology for having been playing mahjong and arriving too late to protect the magistrate from the mob. Thief No. 1 palms off No. 2 as the magistrate, and himself as an old friend of the magistrate who had just arrived on a visit only to encounter the mob at work. He orders the two dead men buried. The "dead" magistrate turns out to be still alive, but Thief No. 1 orders him buried anyway.

Next come members of the magistrate's cabinet: the Ministers of Health, Education, Construction (a homosexual), Finance (in a gown made of a bank note and carrying a bag labeled 80 per cent), and finally the ex-magistrate's concubine, wearing a foxtail as symbol of her status. The concubine is first to discover the hoax, but agrees to cooperate for a share of the loot the new "officials" expect to gather in. Others begin to catch on, but they also cover up. A cabinet meeting is held, presided over by the concubine, and it is decided to penalize the community $200 million, half for burial expenses of the deceased, and half to cover medical treatment for the magistrate's injuries at the hands of the mob.

Then they learn the governor of the province is coming on an inspection trip (here the authors apparently borrowed their plot from Gogol's *The Inspector General*). The concubine is turned over to the governor, and the police chief provides his sister for the magistrate. The setting of the whole thing, incidentally, is a frame cut from a huge bank note, with one door representing an old-style Chinese coin with a square hole in the middle, and another in the style of a safe door. The governor makes the officials cough up gold bars for his headache. He criticizes them for having paid $500,000 for a rug. When they tell him they paid only $50, he says he would like to buy one that cheap. Etc.

The climax: the Finance Minister organizes the mob and produces the real, unburied magistrate. Gold bars, however, have convinced the governor that the resurrected man is a phony. He starts to denounce the Finance Minister, but when he notes that the man is slipping more gold bars to his page, the governor ends up praising him. Then the mob turns on everybody.

The epilogue: the thieves wake up, are captured and led away. The old watchman hears a cock crow. "A new day comes," he says.

The ridicule of the principal characters is at times subtle, at times bitter, and there is more farce than subtlety in the whole. The audience lost none of the satire, laughing throughout, but not applauding particularly. I came away wondering if popular revolt based on an attitude of "a plague on both your houses" would come before the KMT-Communist question could be settled.

SHANGHAI–NANKING, July 29—Dave and I arose at five to catch the 7 A.M. plane to Nanking. I looked up Peffer to tell him about the play. He was as amazed as I. He has, incidentally, thoroughly convinced himself there is no hope for political settlement and the only hope for the U.S. is a truce.

When I saw T.V. he said T. F. Tsiang had urged against putting out any release on CNRRA reorganization on the ground that things were quieting down. I said this was the attitude that killed off constructive government news, time after time; but I did not argue the point.

NANKING, July 30—Today's session with T.V. was devoted to studying what should go into the Gimo's speech of August 14, assuming he agrees to it. The consensus was he should talk about (1) domestic reconstruction; (2) political progress; (3) the economic situation. T.V. asked me to sell the Gimo on the idea when I go to Kuling Thursday, and to tell him he (Soong) approved. I said I thought the Gimo had fixed ideas and it was hard to sell him. "If you write him a good speech he will use it," said T.V. "I once wrote him a speech and he changed only one word."

NANKING, July 31—A long talk with Marshall.

He says the military situation has become minor in the sense that the KMT is hell-bent to come to a decision in Shantung and Kiangsu by force of arms. What's more important now is the feeling that the government's prestige—and the Gimo's personal prestige—is being destroyed abroad, because of the terrorism represented by incidents like the Kunming assassinations. Marshall agreed with me when I said perhaps it was a question whether the government's prestige was not already irretrievably lost and I could picture him thinking how his own influence for good in the situation was going down with it.

He said the ambushing of the marine convoy near Peking was

definitely the work of the Communists. He is withdrawing the marines from Tsingtao, now that the Nationalists are in there with an army. Probably it will be misinterpreted by the Communists as another evidence of aid to the KMT, like the recent arrival of gunboats for the navy, though this was something put in motion two years ago.

Fighting threatens in Jehol. The Communists are out of hand.

I had slowly become so frustrated by the blowing up of the truce and uncertainty about housing the family that I had gone over intending to ask Marshall if he would mind if I cashed in my chips and went home. I never got to it, partly because he kept talking and partly because I felt that if he was still in there pitching I should stay too. Then, after lunch, I got a cable from Betty voicing discouragement about the delay on housing and the difficulty of getting shipping accommodations. It renewed my feeling of utter frustration. I considered asking T.V. to release me, and going home with Dave as soon as we could arrange it.

When I saw T.V. I put it up to him. "Please," he said, "have Mrs. Beal come. I will see that you get a house and furniture—whatever you need." It wasn't cajolery, it was sincere. "What we are doing here is right," he went on. "History will judge us, years from now, as having done the right thing." He spoke of the need for holding Asia against Communism. "I'll keep at it until I collapse," he said.

I wasn't kidding myself that my presence was essential to anything, but here is Marshall, who could pull out but is sticking, and Soong, wearing himself out in a backbreaking economic job, although I suppose he could resign. It made me feel I could stick it out a while longer. I doubted that Betty had received my air mail letter written after T.V. had personally taken an interest in finding a house, so I cabled her that she could cancel plans to come out with the family but that a letter was on its way.

CHAPTER EIGHT

Generalissimo goes to mountain resort of Kuling to prepare statement marking first anniversary of V-J Day, in which he begins political maneuver designed to split third parties and independents from their association with Communists.

Kuling, a mountain resort some four or five hundred miles up the Yangtze from Shanghai, was the temporary capital of China at the beginning of August 1946, since it was where Generalissimo Chiang Kai-shek was escaping the oppressive, humid heat of midsummer in Nanking. CNAC extended its Shanghai–Nanking Capital Express flight to Kiukiang, the airport for Kuling, to accommodate the government officials who needed to see him on policy questions. Dr. Peng said he would be making the trip August 1 and, having been present when the Gimo gave me a personal invitation to go up there, invited Dave Lu and me to go along. Even though I expected to talk to the Gimo about making a speech, I somehow neglected to pack a business suit, which turned out to be a minor embarrassment. Dave said it would be cool and I took slacks and sweaters out of the slim wardrobe I had on hand, for I was still living out of the flight bag with which I had flown the Pacific, pending the family's arrival. I was thinking of it more in terms of a vacation, which in effect it was, than as a business trip. Four of us started out; Peng had his personal assistant, Henry Tseng, along.

NANKING–KULING, August 1—We were at the airport at 8 A.M., just as the Shanghai flight came in. There was a long wait, however, and we were informed that the plane's radio transmitter was out of order. When we finally boarded we were told we would have to fly back to Shanghai first to get it repaired. But after we were aloft I noticed we were flying west rather than east. Francis Chang, the chief mechanic, was aboard, and I asked him about it. "Oh," he said, "it's a clear day and we are going to follow the Yangtze." He said he had come along in case of trouble.

We landed without mishap, in the middle of a grass field on the bank of the Yangtze at Kiukiang—no runways. The airline had a thatched hut for headquarters, and the U. S. Army had communications equipment housed in a big tent, with its antennae strung on tall bamboo poles, to service Marshall's flights in and out and provide him with a message channel.

Kiukiang means Nine Rivers, said Dr. Peng, a native of the province, but not because of the presence of nine streams. It was so named because here the river winds somewhat in the shape of the Chinese character for 9. Getting to Kiukiang corresponds to getting as far into the interior as to Pittsburgh from New York, or rather to one of those Ohio pottery towns like East Liverpool, since Kiukiang is a small town and the center of a famous Chinese porcelain industry that is just being revived, if one can compare the delicate Chinese output with the heavy ware turned out in Ohio. With our luggage we boarded a small river steamer, loading it to what must have been twice its capacity, and chugged across the calm and muddy Yangtze to the town, where an American LST and a Chinese freighter were docked.

Some local official was on hand to meet Peng, and we all drove by jeep to a local restaurant, the usual rambling sort of riverside Chinese eating place where, on a balcony overlooking some Yangtze backwater, we had lunch. It was an excellent meal. First the waiter brought a steaming bowl of water which he put on the table, in which everyone sterilized his dishes and chopsticks. Among the dishes were chicken and the locally abundant Yangtze carp, washed down with a locally produced *huangjiu* or yellow wine, with tea before and after the meal.

From the village we had fourteen miles to go to the foot of

Lushan, or Lu's Mountain, on the top of which Kuling is perched. As an American colonel so dryly remarked, in China they have only ten- and fifteen-passenger cars. What with our greeter, the driver, and a *Central Daily News* man who had attached himself to the party, we were seven, with baggage, for the jeep. I rode in the front with Peng and the driver, resting my weight on my left elbow and right buttock; at the end I felt somewhat asymmetrical.

The road was gravel and dirt, about like some fourth-grade road in back-country Maryland, and we careened along at twenty-five miles an hour, scattering pigs, chickens, and peasants from our path. Surprisingly it was marked with traffic signs as to curves and sharp corners, which in addition to the Chinese characters had on them a big exclamation point and the English word "alarming." The road was so narrow that whenever the driver saw another car approaching he drew up to the right and stopped to let it pass.

Sentries began to appear soon after we left Kiukiang, and at the mountain's foot, where OMEA had an information booth, passes had to be shown to the soldiers. With great walla-walla, five sedan chairs were selected, for the only way up the mountain was by path. The coolies wore conical straw hats, rope sandals, shorts, and a thin cotton cloth, used as a shawl over their shoulders to prevent chafing from the weight of the chair on its bamboo poles.

Finally the convoy started off. There must have been forty in all, with four to six coolies per chair and others carrying luggage. It was all reminiscent of my boyhood in India, when I made the ascent to Mussoorie in the Himalayas by chair.

It was a steaming, tropic day when we started, well over ninety degrees. Butterflies fluttered around, alighting on the stone steps of the path and flapping their wings tentatively; dragonflies buzzed overhead. The steps rose steeply along the mountain's side and as soon as we got high enough it was astonishing to see how abruptly the whole mountain rose from the flat flood plain of the Yangtze, as from the ocean. The average grade of the ascent must be thirty degrees, and there is one stretch called the "heroic slope" (because it takes a hero to climb) which surely must be forty-five degrees.

Momentarily I kept expecting the coolies to stop and rest, but they kept pushing up, spurting into a run occasionally to surmount some especially steep incline. They finally stopped at the one-third mark, where they wrung the sweat out of their shoulder cloths like water out of a saturated towel. There were sentries to be convinced the party was friendly. After a rest we started on the second leg. Pint-sized Dave rested his head against the back of his wicker chair, but I strained my neck muscles trying to keep my head vertical and trying to apply body English to helping the coolies.

The motion of the chair was something like riding a camel, or a small boat. Every so often the coolies would fall in step and the chair would bob, bob, bob like a skiff taking the wake of a cruiser. The coolies' idea of a joke was to spurt forward and crowd the men carrying the chair ahead. As we rose, the view of the Yangtze was magnificent, and the air became fresher and cooler. We passed coolies carrying bags of UNRRA-CNRRA flour and all manner of goods. Most of the time the mountain dropped almost sheer from the unguarded right side of the narrow path, hundreds or even thousands of feet. There was the constant gurgle of watercourses when we entered a ravine, and the constant background noise of the cicada.

At the second resting place we had tea. Again the cups were sterilized in boiling water, and there were more sentries. One Chinese, who was walking up, was carrying his coat and wore around his waist a bullet-filled holster with pistols on each hip. My coolies laughed over some joke one of them had made, and I asked Dave what they found amusing. "They are complimenting you on your weight," he said. I took the hint and put my portable typewriter in his chair, to equalize things just a bit. In the end my six coolies (to Dave's four) wanted a little extra because the foreigner was so heavy, so Henry Tseng gave them an extra 1000 CNC, and with the bonus it came to only $9.00 U.S. for six men. The coolies are a stouthearted and cheerful lot whose working life span as chair-bearers is only five years. After that they retire to carrying luggage and goods up the mountain.

We sighted Kuling as we rounded a little ridge near the top. It looked almost exactly like Mussoorie, in the Himalayas, hung on the side of the mountain. The Fairy Glen Hotel, where we had reservations, was a pleasant surprise. It consisted of a group of neat buildings and room pavilions in well-kept grounds. I was shown to a room containing a white iron bed with springs, bureau, dresser, desk, and wicker chairs—all spotless white as was the linen. A screen door gave on a small balcony with something of a view. There was a bathroom with china washbowl and pitcher, a china commode in a wooden chair, and a tin cradle-like tub in one corner; everything immaculate.

Some thirty Chinese newsmen are up here covering the Gimo. They invited our party to dinner with them tomorrow night.

KULING, August 2—Took a walk in the morning and it was like being back in the Himalayas—narrow paths, wonderful vistas, and swift watercourses tumbling over huge stones in every ravine. Our party made a tour by sedan chair in the afternoon to a couple of old temples perched magnificently on the edge of the mountain. One, called Fairies' Cave, was Taoist. It featured a "drop by drop" spring which comes through the rock of the cave and keeps a pool at constant level. The other, known as the Yellow Dragon, is Buddhist. It had some "dragon fish"—small, red-bellied fish with four legs and a long tail, combining the looks of a tadpole, miniature crocodile, and goldfish. Moth-eaten priests begged donations at each. Along the way there were boys who had locusts tied to a string—live locusts the size of small mice. We tried a short cut coming back, descending perhaps a thousand feet and crossing a stream by jumping from rock to rock, until the path became so steep and lost in vegetation, which came up shoulder high on the coolies, that we gave up and made for the regular path. "Like Stilwell's retreat through Burma," said Dave, and it was wild indeed.

During our absence Shen Chang-huan, the Gimo's English secretary, had been around to invite Peng and me to dinner at the Gimo's at eight-thirty. We had accepted the correspondents' invitation to dine with them at six-thirty, so there was nothing to do but go there first, still by sedan chair. There was one girl among them, Madeleine Hsieh, alert and smart-looking, who spoke good English. Peng made a brief speech saying in effect that China could not be judged by American standards for speed and we must trust the Generalissimo to work out a political settlement just as he had solved the problem of the war lords and the Japanese. To me he said: did I understand the background of his mention that "our two American friends" (Marshall and Stuart) were "impatient"? It was commentary on the fact that on his last visit to Kuling Marshall had refused to see the Gimo.

Peng was horrified when he discovered I proposed to go to the Gimo's in khaki slacks and a jacket I hoped to borrow from some appropriately sized correspondent. He insisted I wear one of his summer suits. It fitted well, but I felt self-conscious in it because it was a light greenish tan with a heavy white vertical stripe. Just before we were ready to leave there was a terrific downpour of rain, and we went off in sedan chairs with front and side curtains hung from the canopy. We were first to arrive.

The Gimo's residence appeared to be a rambling lodge-type house. The living room, with a big fireplace and a fire crackling, was well furnished. The upholstery had a green and white horizontal stripe and was part modern, part Chinese. There was a painting of the Gimo—not very good—over the fireplace. Chiang and his wife were playing Chinese checkers in one corner, he in plain khaki uniform of the type known as Chung Shan, she in a black Chinese-style dress with a tan sweater-like top. She said he had been playing the game for only five days but was already very good. She said Mrs. Marshall had taught him to play and given him the set. She finished her game and then insisted that I play him. I thought she eyed my suit as something familiar, but it may have been my imagination. The Gimo nullified my usual strategy and beat me handily. While we played, the other guests arrived: Admiral and Mrs. Cooke, their twenty-one-year-old daughter and sixteen-year-old son, and Mrs. Marshall.

The dinner was Chinese style. Mrs. Marshall sat on the Gimo's right, Mrs. Cooke on his left; Admiral Cooke on Madame Chiang's right, I on her left. General Huang, the huge man who heads OMEA, was the only other Chinese beside Peng. The Gimo, as the only one at the table who did not speak English, was kept cued into the conversation by Huang. I developed unbounded admiration for the way Huang managed this, keeping it all very jolly without really being obtrusive about what he was doing—it was superbly adroit. The drink was watermelon juice, but there was also the usual *huangjiu* in which I drank to Madame Chiang and the Gimo.

It was a pleasant affair. After dinner the Gimo played Chinese checkers with Miss Cooke while Madame Chiang and Charlie Cook played bridge with the Admiral and his wife. Mrs. Marshall, Peng, and I played three-cornered checkers. We broke up about ten-thirty. The Gimo drew Peng and me aside to say he would see us in a couple of days and would let us know when. It was still raining when we left. Our wet and shivering coolies brought us back to the hotel in the dark.

KULING, August 3—George Silk, who is still pursuing his picture story for *Life* on Ambassador Stuart, informed us at tea that the Communists had announced in Nanking that Yenan had been bombed. If the government is responsible, it was a stupid move, since there is nothing there of a military nature that justifies such action. But the Communists have made false claims of this sort before—like the one at the time of my arrival, which Marshall called them on, that their troops had been bombed by American planes. After tea our party went over to call on Dr. Stuart, who had no official information on the incident. He said Marshall was coming up about 6 P.M. with Dr. Soong. Marshall did get in, but T.V. was not with him. Central News has it T.V. will arrive tomorrow with Chen Cheng and Pai Chung-hsi.

KULING, August 4—After breakfast I drafted a brief memorandum for the Gimo about the speech I proposed for him. Then to church, with Dave Lu, to a little union chapel where a clean-cut young missionary named Kepler preached. Madame Chiang, Dr. Stuart, and General and Mrs. Marshall all attended, and after the service Mrs. Marshall invited me to lunch.

Marshall and I had old-fashioneds in wicker chairs on the lawn before the meal. He was still very concerned about the Kunming assassinations, but not as much about the bombing of Yenan. He said the Nationalists sent him word that they had done it to destroy the B-24 that had surrendered to the Communists, and the message reached him just as Chou En-lai was protesting about it. He said Chou also claimed they had strafed Mao Tse-tung's house and General Chu Teh's headquarters.

At lunch Marshall reminisced, as he is fond of doing. He told one anecdote about visiting the Paris opera with the first Mrs. Marshall, when he was a young officer in 1910, and to avoid losing her in a milling crowd as the audience was leaving got her attention (and everyone else's) with a loud, shrill whistle through his fingers. He told of a conversation he had with Senator Tom Connally, a favorite of mine in Washington, when the senator opposed a bill he wanted, just after he became Chief of Staff, to create the rank of lieutenant general.

During the afternoon our MOI group took a walk of seven *li* to a spot from which we could see Po Yang Hu, the second largest lake in China, miles away on the plain. The Chiangs and the Cookes had picnicked there last night and their sandwich wrappers and melon rinds were lying about untidily.

Peng got word that our date with the Gimo is eleven-thirty tomorrow.

KULING, August 5—Chiang received us in a small office at the Kuling summer training camp, with his English secretary, Shen Chang-huan, doing the translating. The Gimo first read the Chinese translation of my memo, said he agreed with it and would make the speech. But there was then that inevitable question about The Situation—what did I think of it? I said I saw two dangers in the present drive to throw the Communists out of northern Kiangsu and Shantung: (1) Communist retaliation elsewhere that would create full-scale civil war; (2) the economic strain this would produce. Chiang replied that there was practically a civil war going on now, and it would come in any case because the Communists never ceased attacking and the government had to defend itself. Then he turned to the speech, suggesting I draft an outline. Peng interposed that we would consult Chen Pu-lei about the actual writing.

Later, with Dave Lu, we called on Chen Pu-lei, a frail, soft-spoken little man, obviously possessed of a keen mind. Peng says he has been intimately associated with the Gimo for some fifteen years and writes his speeches, but has always refused any government post. Chen asked me about U.S. reaction to the Kunming assassinations, and I told him it was bad. I had told Peng the same, and quoted the New York *Post* editorial to him. Chen seemed distressed about the killings in a way I had not noticed among other government people.

T.V. had got in and we went by the house where he was staying. Peng had a talk with him while he was being massaged by his Chinese-Australian masseur, but I did not, for he left immediately for the Gimo's.

KULING, August 6—Peng, Dave, and I breakfasted with T.V. this morning. T.V. has a big appetite. The breakfast consisted of porridge, steak, (the tenderest I've had in China), ham and eggs (T.V. had four), coffee, toast, and peaches. I asked T.V. if he minded if I stayed in Kuling for a while, since the Gimo had invited me. He said no, and to make sure the Gimo kept his speech short, for he tended to be very long-winded.

T.V. lunched with the Gimo and we with his secretaries, Chinese style. Dave, who knows about so many of these people, told me later one of them used to be No. 3 man in Manchuria, a lieutenant general under the old war lord, Marshal Chang Tso-lin.

Dave also said Stuart had told him one of the reasons why the Gimo came up to Kuling when he did was a belief that Nanking was not safe. I did not realize that the Communist threat was that critical, despite T.V.'s guarded reference to it in Nanking the other day.

We saw T.V. and Peng off down the hill and then Dave went with me as I delivered to Chen Pu-lei a proposed outline for the Gimo's speech. I asked Chen to propose to the Gimo that when the Kunming assassins were arrested he (the Gimo) personally make the announcement. This would show, I said, how important he regarded the case to be. Chen said he would make the recommendation, though he thought the details should come from Kunming.

Dave Lu found an item in today's *Ho Ping Pao* from Nanking which amused me. It quoted me as telling their reporter I was much impressed by the fact that their paper got up here the same day it was published, that I liked the scenery, and that I was grateful to the Gimo for inviting me up. I did remember having some leading questions asked me to that effect by someone while the reporters were talking to Peng after our visit to the Gimo.

KULING, August 9—This loafing is restful. I stopped by the desk this morning to make sure what day it was. Tao Hsi-sheng says the Gimo may go to Shanghai or Nanking tomorrow, for what purpose he doesn't know. The first draft of the speech has been approved. And English translation is supposed to be upcoming tomorrow. Mail from Nanking: SSU is closing down its Nanking mission and the MOI has arranged to take over the house and furnish it. A most happy solution of the problem—I don't even have to move.

KULING, August 10—Peaceful as it is in this beautiful, cool, bucolic spot, one soon realizes that even here the tension that exists in China today pervades the atmosphere. The subtle air of off-stage menace may have been put into my mind by the arrival of Fred Gruin of *Time*, who was rather cryptic about the story he was working on but set his researcher to finding out how many steps there were in the path up the mountain to Kuling, one of those precise statistics with which *Time* likes to lard its stories. It popped into my head that it might be appropriate to the mood if it turned out there were—not 39, of course, but 39,000, bearing some faint allusion to John Buchan's thriller. The researcher never did find out, however.

Then Eric Chou of *Ta Kung Pao* came to lunch, and with him a girl reporter for *Ta Kang Pao* of Nanking. The girl, a Miss Wang, supplied a scrap of information when she remarked that *Ta Kang Pao's* editor was a man without newspaper experience, put in by Chen Li-fu, chairman of its board of directors. This was more confirmation that *Ta Kang Pao*, which means *Strength Daily*, is a CC paper, and that it was exhumed from the provincial town where it formerly existed and moved to Nanking as an effort to confuse the reading public with *Ta Kung Pao*, the neutrally liberal *L'Impartial*.

We got to talking about *Ta Kung Pao's* editorial of the day before yesterday, about which Dave had told me. It dealt with the political situation. It said, in the free oral translation Dave supplied: We oppose continued fighting while people talk peace; we favor cessation of hostilities and a withdrawal of troops before the peace talks are resumed; the reorganization of the government should follow the spirit of the PCC resolutions, and after reorganization the National Assembly should be held to reorganize the army. Regarding the constitution, we favor redistribution of administrative power to prevent the trend toward dictatorship; we favor the equalization of power in various areas; governors should be elected, provinces should have self-government and thus be able to supervise the central government and prevent the dangers of dictatorship. And the National Assembly should be held to institute constitutional government.

This was more specific than the average Chinese editorial, though still a bit vague in the Chinese fashion. Here was the impartial paper, speaking the voice of non-Communist people of

China who in my conviction are in the vast majority, and who are plain weary of war in a way and to an extent I find it hard to believe that the rulers of the government recognize. It aroused a rather caustic, sneering answer in the government mouthpiece, the *Central Daily News*, which said in effect: "Down with fence sitters." It argued that this is not the time for a coalition government—this is a time to strengthen the government. This was a reply echoing the Chen Li-fu philosophy.

Eric said that after a recent similarly forthright editorial he had written his boss agreeing with the thought expressed but warning him it would come under attack. Sure enough, it did, and significantly in the little local paper of this community, and with greater significance when this obscure paper's editorial was picked up and reprinted widely by government papers in China. Eric said his editor replied that he knew he would be attacked but was determined to stick to his line. So, in a way, *Ta Kung Pao* represents a sort of quiet determination by the people to resist the CC campaign to "strengthen" the party.

And what a gathering there is up here just now of the CC clan. The head of the Farmers' Bank, the publisher of *Shun Pao*, Cheng Tien-fong, former head of the Central Institute of Political Sciences, which is the KMT's training school for government work, and Miachen S. Shaw, chairman of the Cooperative League of China (not to be confused with the Chinese Industrial Cooperatives). Chen Li-fu himself is due up here Monday. Yet Marshall and Stuart have been so emphatic about the Kunming assassinations that almost everyone I talked to kept asking: what is the reaction to the assassinations? Tonight, in the cool of this mountain retreat, away from the steaming plain on which Shanghai, Nanking, and Hankow were reported sweltering in 110-degree heat, I get the feeling of a slowly mounting psychological tension within the KMT that bodes ill for the government.

Played tennis today with a young fellow named Li, son of a former war lord and governor of Kwangtung Province. The young Li is hoping to go to the U.S. soon to study chemical engineering.

KULING, August 11—The Chinese text of the Gimo's speech was delivered to Dave, together with a Chinese summary, around noon. He had it translated in first draft by around 6 P.M. After dinner Shen Chang-huan and Tao Hsi-sheng joined us and we worked over the English text, clearing up the meaning of ambiguous parts and taking out of the Chinese text some of the old clichés about never fighting unless attacked. Dave's impression, and mine too, was that it was not a bad speech. It followed rather closely the outline I had turned in. There was more of a tendency to blame the Communists, and a sort of stubbornness underlying it, but it did pledge the government anew to carry out the PCC resolutions, which the Communists have been charging it will not do, and it definitely committed the government to go ahead with the National Assembly on November 12. We worked until the lights began to flicker at 11 P.M. I was most anxious that the English text be a faithful translation of the Chinese text, so that no one could accuse the Gimo of saying one thing to China and another to the U.S.; also that the summary was a faithful reflection of the whole text.

KULING, August 12—Shen, Tao, Dave, and I had another session on the English text of the Gimo's speech. We finished by one o'clock and sent it by courier down the mountain to a waiting army liaison plane which was to rush it to Nanking to be mimeographed and distributed to the foreign correspondents tomorrow. Most of the changes we asked were okayed by Chen Pu-lei.

At 5 P.M. Dave, rather nervous and excited about it, went to keep an appointment with the Gimo which Dr. Stuart had urged Chiang to make. Dave's account of the interview was very interesting. What nonplused him was the fact that the Gimo raised the issue of his party membership. At the MOI he has been given blanks to fill out asking for data on when he joined the KMT, who introduced him, etc. He has ignored them, and has had one inquiry as to when he will turn them in. He says he will not join, will quit his MOI job and even Central News if necessary, and appeal to T. V. Soong. He told the Gimo, under questioning, he was not a KMT member and was, in fact, a U.S. citizen. The Gimo replied that he should join the San Min Chu I Youth Corps —"no, you're too old"—or the party. Recounting it afterward, Dave thought there might be another explanation beside pressure: the Gimo could be genuinely anxious to get good men into the party. He figures he has one out. When the Gimo wanted to marry Soong Mei-ling, her mother refused to sanction it unless he became a Christian, but he refused to do it until he had studied the Bible. He did, taking two years at it. Dave figures it will take him quite a while to study KMT party doctrines and principles.

Dave said the Gimo inquired about the English copy of his speech and, on learning that it had gone to Nanking, gave orders that either Dr. Peng or Yu Ta-wei take a copy to Marshall as soon as it was ready. This apparently was a touch inspired by the fact that Marshall and Stuart had issued a joint statement in Nanking which wounded the Gimo, not only because of its content but because, as Shen told me confidentially, no advance copy had been supplied the government, as was usually the case. The statement warned of the economic strain that would accompany full-scale civil war, which already was spreading and threatening to get out of hand, and suggested that the government could not stand it. It concluded by saying the military problems could be solved but not the problem of district and local civilian administrations.

Shen interpreted this (or maybe reflected the Gimo) as either paving the way for an end to Marshall's mission, or an attempt to put pressure on the government by lessening its prestige. He said he inclined toward the latter view. I asked how a statement of the facts as to the economic danger of civil war could lessen the prestige of the government. He replied that for Marshall to state them gave support to those who argued that way and made it harder for government supporters to argue against it. I said it was a sad commentary on something if a statement of facts lessened the prestige of the government.

KULING, August 14—It has been raining steadily for two days. Lina Wang, the girl from *Ta Kang Pao*, had asked me if I could arrange an interview for her with Mrs. Marshall and I had said I would try. I started over through the pouring rain, having resolved not to use sedan chairs again, and by the time I got to the Marshall house my trouser legs were soaked from the knees down and my shoes and socks were wet through. Mrs. Marshall insisted that I put on one of General Marshall's bathrobes and a pair of khaki socks and straw slippers while my clothes were dried out. She also had me drink some tea, into which she put two teaspoons of medicinal rye to ward off a cold.

We had quite a chat while I was waiting. She said first of all that she had adopted a policy of not giving interviews of any kind, and had undergone several unfortunate experiences after her arrival. She said when she went to Shanghai it was printed somewhere that she and the general had quarreled; and when he went down to bring her back to Nanking it was printed he had to beg her to come back. This led her to recount an incident of the previous day. Madame Chiang had come over, almost in tears; some friend had sent her a clipping from a New York newspaper (she didn't identify it) quoting some unidentified WAC major as asking: what happened to the $2 million Madame Chiang had raised in the U.S. for Chinese war orphans? Madame Chiang said she had turned every penny over to a committee, of which she was not a member, and its books were open to public inspection. She was wondering whether to issue a denial; the Gimo told her to ignore it.

Mrs. Marshall was sewing on a child's dress as she talked, and she went on to describe the account she had heard from Madame Chiang about the Gimo's kidnaping at Sian in 1936—this apropos of a remark I made about there being a stubborn streak in the Gimo. From that she got to discussing Marshall's mission, and expressed bitterness that he should be assigned, just at the moment of retirement, "to be a messenger boy between the Generalissimo and the Communists, because that's all it is." She was moved to tell me about the summons [at the moment of their arrival in Leesburg, which she described in her book, as mentioned in the first chapter] and after a pause she said: "I've written a book." It was about her life with General Marshall, and she wrote it in the three months he was away on his first trip to Chungking. She wrote from 3 A.M. to eleven or twelve o'clock each morning, sitting propped up in bed. Marshall had wanted her to have something to do and suggested she occupy her time straightening out the voluminous clippings and memorabilia she had kept, and the book was the result. It was simply written, she said, since she had never written anything before, but it had to come out. It was entirely about the family side of his life, but still it illustrated the strain he was under during the war years. Marshall refuses to have a biography written, but approved this. It was being published by a New York firm that had enough paper to print 100,000 copies and would come out in November. She had turned down an offer from the *Saturday Evening Post* to serialize 25,000 of the 75,000 words.

I think she enjoyed telling me about it, as any writer does, and it led her to reminisce about her own life. Her book begins with her marriage to Marshall and ends with the scene at Leesburg she described to me. Her title is *I Married a Colonel* [but the publishers put it out as *Together: Annals of an Army Wife*].

I stayed for lunch. It was a pleasant visit.

Eric Chou and a colleague came in around five o'clock and we had tea. Eric thought the Gimo's statement would satisfy the Youth Party (which is really an appendage of the KMT and whose leader is here right now) and possibly the Democratic League, but that the Communists would require much more. He thought the Gimo was taking a crack at *Ta Kung Pao* in his exhortation to the people to distinguish right from wrong, etc.— a passage which I had taken to be excusable only as the kind of fatherly inspiration for a largely illiterate people.

But Eric's impression was confirmed later when Tao dropped in; that's what the Gimo had in mind. Huang Yen-pei, the charming pantomimist who had told me about government corruption at dinner, is a Kiangsu man, and many of his followers are among

the three to five million refugees driven from their homes by the
Communists. The Gimo would not have overlooked the fact that
he had protested this expulsion a month or so ago by letter to
Chou En-lai and by wire to Mao Tse-tung. Another Democratic
League leader, Carson Chang, head of a group which previously
was a separate party known as the National Socialists (but no kin
to the Nazis), would be attracted by the Gimo's offer to accept
"sound improvements" in the draft constitution. It begins to look
as if the Gimo's efforts are now being bent toward splitting off
as much of the opposition as possible and then going ahead with
the November 12 National Assembly.

Dr. Stuart has gone to Peking. Central News quotes him as
saying he thought the Gimo's statement would help the peace
talks.

KULING, August 15—A request I had put in long ago and forgotten, for an interview with General Chen Cheng, the Chief of
Staff, came through just as Dave and I were about to start off for
a walk. I went to the house where Chen is staying but no one
there could speak English, so a hurry-up call was put in for Dave.

Chen is a little fellow, with gray pompadour and some of the
Gimo's mannerisms, such as looking at his nails while he thinks
of phrases. There's a touch of red in his cheeks and the tip of
his nose and one assumes it's the sign of stomach ulcers. Chen
wore his uniform with five rows of battle ribbons and when I
apologized for coming tieless as soon as I got his note, he lifted
his small feet to show me he was wearing Chinese shoes of blue
cloth with felt soles. At a summer resort one doesn't worry about
such things, he remarked.

He thought the Gimo's speech was a suitable comment on
Marshall's efforts, which he praised with apparent sincerity. In
considerable detail he gave me the usual government story about
places where the government sought to keep its commitments
to Marshall, only to come under Communist attack, and with
a bit of a grin commented that it was a hell of a poor way to fight
a war. I think the year's record probably bears out the fact that

in the fighting that has taken place the government has always
felt under the restraint of Marshall's displeasure—and world displeasure, too—while the Communists have not. Chen noted that
since August 7, when Mao Tse-tung sounded off on an anti-
American line which has been consistent since then, the Communists are in his opinion being "pushed" by Russia. I was glad
for the interview and the contact. Chen impresses me as not devi-
ous, a bluff and forthright soldier.

KULING, August 16—T.V. came up here last night, with General Marshall, and phoned to say he would like me to go to Shanghai with him tomorrow as he has work for me, also to ask me to
come over at 9 A.M. When I got to the house he was having breakfast with Chen Cheng. He came out of the dining room, handed
me a statement he proposed to issue Monday. It announced (1)
a new exchange rate, with the rate left blank; (2) abolition of
export duties; and (3) creation of a Port of Shanghai Authority.
He said it was secret and asked me to "polish it up." Like most
government statements, it was not entirely clear.

I returned to the Fairy Glen to keep an appointment with
Chen Li-fu, who has the room next to mine, and whom I
encountered last night. Chen came to my room and started once
again to give me the standard argument that the Communists
are not trustworthy. Mixed in was a recounting of Chinese history from 1926 on, which of course I have read and heard before,
but which it is interesting to hear from one who has participated
in it, with due regard for his strong bias. Each time I talk with
him I get a little better understanding of how to read the minds
of the government.

The nuggets this time were sidelights on Chiang Kai-shek, illustrating his tendency to try to appease (conciliate) his opposition beyond the patience of people like Chen, and at the same
time his basic stubbornness. I think these two qualities are showing up in Chiang's present approach to the Communist problem.

Chen told how, under Borodin's influence, Dr. Sun Yat-sen
gave Communists positions of influence in the cabinet during

the time Communists were members of the KMT. Wang Ching-
wei, Chiang's long-time rival, was at this time the tool of the
Communists; Chiang was considered "pink," but the Communists
could not be sure of him, and so, according to Chen, planned to
kill him by seizing control of China's best gunboat, which was
to bombard the Whampoa Military Academy, where he resided,
and by arming 4000 laborers. This plot, said Chen, was discovered a few hours before it was to be executed on March
20, 1926, and forestalled by retaking the gunboat and disarming
the coolies. He said Chiang refused to avenge it, preferring to
"let bygones be bygones," and hoped to retain Communist backing for his Northern Expedition against the war lords.

Chen, who was educated in the United States in engineering,
was talking without an interpreter, and in describing Chiang as
"pink" he threw in the parenthetical explanation, "a little left
of eccentric."

But the Communists failed to support the expedition, Chen
went on, and after the government was moved from Canton to
Hankow they dismissed Chiang as Generalissimo. That was when
he set up a government at Nanking. After this Chiang called on
Chen to crush the Communists politically and oust them from
the KMT Party posts they held. This he did by "conversion"—
he mentioned again the 23,500 he had personally converted and
said they included, in round numbers, about a thousand district
and a hundred provincial leaders, plus the head of the Communist secret police. He pictured it as a triumph for American scien-
tific and engineering-trained minds over the Russian-trained
Communists. For the CC clique, he explained, is nothing but a
"brain trust" of young American-trained scientists and engineers.
This, I think, was what Chen wanted mainly to convince me of.

At any rate, over a ten-year period to 1936, Chen said without
any trace of false modesty, he and his brother crushed the Communist influence within the KMT. By this time, he said, Chiang
was convinced that war with the Japanese was inevitable, and
rather than have the Communists on his flank—even though
they had retreated to Yenan, their numbers greatly diminished—

he wanted Chen to negotiate with them, to come to terms if possible. This Chen proceeded to do. Chou En-lai came to Shanghai for the talks, which were going on when the Gimo was kidnaped at Sian.

Chen said he also was negotiating with a representative of the Third International, whom he named but whose name did not register with me. He said he forced this individual to cable Moscow that Chiang should not be killed because chaos would result in China, and the Japanese, whom Russia feared on her Siberian border, would have an easy time taking over. Back from Moscow came the cable that this view was right. Chen apparently forgot —at least he omitted—the detail of his first account to me that he had threatened Moscow's man with a pistol and said his life would be a forfeit for the Gimo's.

I asked why Chiang Hsüeh-liang kidnaped the Gimo. His explanation was that the Manchurian war lord had acquired the nickname "Non-resister" by giving up Manchuria to the Japanese without a fight and wanted to regain face by getting the Gimo to agree to fight Japan. Chiang Kai-shek, said Chen, felt at that time that China was not ready.

Coming down to more recent history, he said that Mao Tse-tung, after his October 10 conversations with Chiang last year, had been attacked by his leading followers in Yenan for selling out the Communist army. His defense to the Politburo, said Chen, was to remind his critics that the New Fourth Route Army and the Red Army once had been declared illegal by the government but nevertheless had continued to exist and to grow in power.

Chen was interrupted by a luncheon date from finishing his account, but he insisted on coming back at 9 P.M. to complete it. What he said then was that the "incidents" of which the Communists have made such good use—he mentioned the Nanking station riot—are spontaneous things growing out of popular hatred of the Communists, based on this long experience with them as untrustworthy. Obviously he was hoping I would pass this line along to Marshall. He asked me to tell Marshall he

(Chen) was here, and commented that Marshall "does not understand" this history, nor that these demonstrations cannot be suppressed by him (Chen), though he claimed he was doing his best.

Eric Chou dropped in during the afternoon and said Chou En-lai had told his *Ta Kung Pao* colleague exclusively that the Gimo's speech was an "ultimatum" because it left out the Communists. This seems to me to be a panicky reaction. I have seen the Communists in apparent panic three times now: before the recapture of Changchun, and when the government made up its mind to drive them out of northern Kiangsu, and over this speech. The first two reactions were to military threat. This, if I am correct in interpreting Chou, is to a political threat. Maybe they see, as I do, a move by the Gimo to win cooperation by the other parties and go ahead with coalition in the hope and belief that the U.S. and world opinion will recognize that it is Communist intransigence, and not KMT resistance, that is holding up constitutional government. Since Chou knows much better than I how strong or how tenuous is his hold on the Democratic League, it may well be panic. But I still think Chiang is holding the door open for Communist participation. This is based on his long record of reluctance before he engages in an outright military test of strength. But I also feel that Chiang's basic stubbornness is that he feels he has paid as high a price as he can afford in the PCC agreements and that, like Lincoln, civil war is preferable to paying a higher price, which would mean dividing China. Oddly enough, when Tao came in with a monitored report of editorial comment on the Gimo's speech, this same thought—comparison with Lincoln's decision—had occurred to the New York *Times* editorial writer, as Dave translated the Chinese version to me.

At four-fifteen I saw Marshall, who was to see the Gimo at five. I asked if the Gimo's speech had harmed the negotiations in any way. He said no, he didn't think it made any difference one way or the other. He said his own joint statement with Stuart in Nanking was Stuart's idea. Stuart had thought some report on the difficulties should be put out, but Stuart's draft was "innocuous," and since he wasn't going to sign any innocuous statements he had put in the final part to the effect that' the fundamental issue was the character of local governments in the regions from which troops would be shifted.

"The next statement I put out will be my last," he said. "And that will mean the end of Executive Headquarters, everything." This answered a question I had been wanting to ask but did not feel like putting point-blank.

Marshall wore khaki slacks and a blue coat and we sat on wicker chairs on the veranda with an old-fashioned apiece. He had several for-my-ears-only items. One was that Truman's cabinet had been discussing the China situation and was hell-bent to redefine China policy. They originally intended to issue a statement on Wednesday, August 7. Marshall had called this off— said it would come at a most inopportune moment. Instead, Truman apparently had sent Chiang a personal message, through the Chinese ambassador in Washington, about which his only knowledge at the moment was from Madame Chiang via Mrs. Marshall. Madame Chiang had been hurt because it was "strongly worded." This explains the queer Washington stories of last week: a hint of redefined China policy, followed by Undersecretary of State Dean Acheson's denial. Marshall commented that cabinet meetings are "like a sieve." He said the message had "something to do with terrorism" such as the Kunming assassinations and was delayed in transit because of the telegraph strike in the U.S. Chiang did not get it until Monday. Marshall expected, of course, to find out all about it when he saw Chiang.

I outlined my hunch as to what the government was up to. That, he said, was precisely Chou's reaction, and he was taking Chou's statement to the Gimo. I went on to say that the conviction was constantly firming in the government that the Communists could not be reasoned with, and that I myself, despite the constant self-reminder that I was closer to government sources and thinking than any other, wondered on the basis of the Communist propaganda line and action from about June 9 on-

ward whether the Communists were not actually using his mediation efforts as a delaying effect to give them time to gain
strength.

Marshall reacted rather sharply to this—not in a personal way,
but so quickly and positively—that it made me think perhaps he
has been wondering himself. He said, however, that on the contrary it was the government that was stalling for time, for the
Gimo had told him many times that the fruit had to ripen before
it could drop. Reflecting on this point since our talk, I think Marshall confuses Communist pressure for immediate truce with the
desire to settle things peacefully.

I said the government was more than ever convinced that Russia was pushing the Communists. This Marshall confirmed in
another totally off-the-record remark: he had access to Moscow's
secret propaganda orders to the Chinese Communists in Shanghai. Then—and there may have been significance in the juxta-
position of thought—he said that what was making his job
impossible were things like the Anping incident. [This was a
reference to the ambush of a marine convoy near Peking, in which
three marines were killed and twelve wounded; two investigations
established that it was entirely the work of Communists and the
Nationalists were not involved.] He said he had threatened to
withdraw from the negotiations but Chou implored him not to.
He refused at first to let an EHQ field team investigate, because
it would just play into the hands of the Nationalists, for whom
the incident was ready-made. The field team inevitably would
line up two to one, U.S.-Nationalist vs. Communist. But he finally
agreed on certain conditions. [The State Department's White
Paper later pictured him as feeling that "it would play directly
into the hands of the small group in the Kuomintang which was
blocking his efforts to terminate the fighting."]

Marshall went off to the Gimo's and I met Dave Lu, for we
had an appointment with the Gimo later. We saw him in the
living room of the lodge and he had tea served, with Chinese
meat cakes and small pieces of chocolate pie. It was little more
than social. It may be he knew more than I did about editorial

reaction to his speech, for all I knew was that it beat the telegraph strike into the U.S. and got good play in the New York *Times*, with text.

He did ask, however, what effect I thought it would have. I said I thought it would be good in the U.S. and in China, but I could not gauge how it would affect the negotiations. Any Communist reaction? Only what a newspaperman had told me of Chou's, which I thought panicky.

We dropped it there. I asked permission to go to Shanghai with T.V. He said Soong had raised the point with him and he had consented, but wanted me to come back. He asked what places of interest I had seen, and named several I should see on my return. In addition to these local sights, he said, there was Nanchang, four hours by train from Kiukiang, and he would assign someone to accompany me. (Dave said later he was just being polite and that I need not feel compelled to return, though I certainly would not mind coming back to this delightful spot.) Dave threw in the information that my family was coming and the Gimo said I must take them to Peking in October.

He referred briefly to the Paris peace conference, commenting that only firmness by the U.S. would curb Russia. We left after about forty minutes. Dave felt a lot better about his own situation than after his private interview.

CHAPTER NINE

Visit to Shanghai shows economic problems mounting. U.S. stops shipment of ammunition to Nationalists. John Leighton Stuart, new U.S. ambassador, tries to revive political negotiations.

Going to Shanghai with T.V. was obviously going to involve work connected with the economic situation; this was clear from the secret draft he had asked me to "polish up." It was a welcome prospect to get away, at least temporarily, from the frustrating political-military negotiations which sometimes seemed on the verge of getting somewhere but never did.

The interlude at Kuling had been bracing, and the knowledge that I was assured of a house removed my worries about my family's arrival. I had no firm word from my wife on sailing dates, but I assumed some of my air mail letters had got through to relieve her of the uncertainty and depression I had reflected earlier. I was aware that a U.S. shipping strike would delay her departure, but at least everything was lined up for her arrival with the three children.

The SSU house which I had unexpectedly acquired was a gray stucco structure, amply spacious even if it had the appearance of having been planned as a doctor's or dentist's residence *cum* office. This I deduced from the fact that the large upstairs room I expected to use as a master bedroom had a tiled floor and the tiles ran halfway up the walls. It had a large living room, a small room just off that which I was using as my private office, a dining room large enough to entertain eight or ten, and four additional bedrooms as well as two baths. The retreating Japanese—or somebody—had decamped with the radiators, but there would be time enough to remedy that.

With the house I had inherited the SSU servants. The cook and No. 1 boy were known to me as Chang and Wong, but David had discovered their real names were Chiao and Hsia; presumably they felt American soldiers needed simpler common names to handle. After Dave talked to them we renamed them properly: Lao Hsia, a term which he said implied respect somewhat in the connotation of "Old Hsia." The cook, a jolly, roly-poly fellow, became Chiao Ssu-fu, equally respectful of his culinary skill. He was good at any type of cooking, Chinese or Western. He performed wonders in his inadequate kitchen just behind the house. I remember Peffer exclaiming over the Indian curry Chiao had cooked for our lunch and how I felt a suburban matron's type of pride over having pleased a distinguished guest. One night Hank Lieberman had come to dinner and we were sitting in the living room afterward when the lights went out, as they often did in Nanking. We continued talking and in a moment Lao Hsia came in noiselessly with candles. "Boy," said Hank, "you've got your servants well trained." But it was not my training.

KULING–SHANGHAI, August 18—Arising before the Fairy Glen had its electricity turned on for the day, Dave and I dressed by candlelight and breakfasted practically by flashlight in order to be at T.V.'s by 7 A.M. Soong emerged from the dining room fully dressed but wearing a blue knit stocking cap, which apparently he uses to keep his pompadour trained. He said the Gimo had just summoned him, so we would have to postpone our departure.

As it turned out, he stayed until twelve-thirty. We got periodic bulletins from General J. L. Huang, the huge man from OMEA who seemed to be in charge of the house: "He is in conference with the Gimo. . . . He is writing something. . . . He has gone

to see General Marshall. . . . He has gone back to the Gimo's."
Feeling sure the Gimo would have him stay for lunch, we had
our meal, an excellent steak lunch. When Soong got back he had
Chinese chow, but while he was eating that Huang rustled him
up another steak, which he ate also. Quite an appetite. After
lunch Dave and I started out ahead. I walked one third of the
way down, to the first stop, but rode the rest of the way because
of the need for speed and the fact my pace was not equal to that
of the coolies. We had scarcely reached the bottom before T.V.
caught up with us.

We boarded a Lincoln seven-passenger convertible and at forty
miles an hour covered the fourteen miles to Kiukiang. En route,
T.V. commented that Marshall was exercised about the Kunming
assassinations and had cited the fact that a group of Harvard professors had passed a resolution deploring it. "Those professors live
in an ivory tower," said T.V. "They do not know about conditions in China." I told him how Chen Li-fu had tried to sell me
on the idea such incidents were caused by anti-Communist hatred
and that he could not control them. T.V. said that Chen was "a
millstone around the neck of the KMT" chiefly because his Western education had not changed his Chinese mind. He ridiculed
the idea that the CC is only a brains trust. "But those fellows
have no influence," he said rather surprisingly. "If the Gimo
threw them in the water they'd stay in the water."

At Kiukiang Chen Cheng was waiting, with a Chinese navy
tug, and he and T.V. were piped aboard to the salutes of a line
of officers. Our party was given wicker chairs on the quarter-deck
and as we crossed the Yangtze I could not help reflecting that if,
on February 18, someone had told me that in six months I
would be aboard a Chinese navy tug four hundred miles upriver
in the interior of China, I would have thought him crazy.

At the primitive airfield there was a special CNAC plane waiting. We headed for Nanking at low altitude to keep under a cloud
ceiling. We stopped there to drop Chen Cheng and his party and
pick up Madame Soong and their daughters, and T.V.'s secretariat, and Dr. Peng Hsueh-pei. My chauffeur met me with what

mail had accumulated, an unexpected bit of alertness on the part of the servants. At Shanghai there was a Central Bank man with a jeep to take me to the Metropole, where a room had been booked for me.

SHANGHAI, August 19—T.V. had called his meeting on the exchange rate statement for 9 A.M. at the Bank of China. There were about twelve around the table in the wood-paneled directors' room and the meeting had already started, early. John Blandford was there, and K. C. Wu, mayor of Shanghai, and Pei Tsu-i, of the Bank of China, and Peng Hsueh-pei, and several others whose Chinese names I cannot remember. The discussion went on with the amount of the new rate left blank.

I lunched with John Blandford, who is pessimistic about the situation and who thinks that if Marshall leaves he will have to go too, since what he is doing to help reorganize the government will be meaningless. Blandford is annoyed by an interview Jim Brennan gave the AP in Garden City, Kansas, printed in this morning's *China Press*, expressing the personal opinion that all-out war was the only solution in China and would involve Russia and the U.S. T.V. issued a brief statement disavowing such views himself. I was struck by one point Jim made: that China now has the best government it ever had, judged by Chinese standards. It got me to wondering if, against all the previous governments about which I knew nothing, this might actually be true.

Auerbach had once suggested that when in Shanghai I meet Colonel Amos Moscrip, head of SSU. I telephoned and he invited me out for a drink, but somehow I failed to make connections with the car he sent for me. Auerbach, he said, had left by air for the U.S. on August 11.

At Peng's press conference Tang, from the ministry in Nanking, asked if I had received the cable from Betty which he airmailed me in Kuling. I didn't. What did it say? He said he couldn't remember exactly—he knew it was signed Betty and the last word was "love" but the rest was dim. Something about being delayed. Only Tang would be capable of this.

SHANGHAI, August 20—The new official exchange rate, announced at 10 A.M., is 3350 to $1.00 U.S. At eleven the market appeared to have quieted down at around 3800. I talked to Donald Gilpatrick, who was pleased with the government's action. He suggested an export-import clearance system, similar to what he had worked out for France when the franc was at the arbitrary official rate of 100 to the dollar. Import licenses required buying dollars at 250 francs, export licenses at 300. It was helpful at balancing trade at no cost to the government. He also was encouraged by the Port of Shanghai Authority which was created yesterday. Gilpatrick had one additional idea: General Glen Edgerton would arrive Saturday to head UNRRA's China office, and it would be a good opportunity to review the constructive steps the government has taken, both with CNRRA and in connection with the financial picture.

I saw T.V. at the Bank of China and passed these ideas along. He was interested in the export-import clearance system and said he would get in touch with Gilpatrick. He threw cold water on the idea of any special welcome to Edgerton on the ground that he did not like to go in for "we are being good boys" publicity after being spanked.

SHANGHAI–NANKING, August 21—Up early to catch T. V. Soong's special plane back to Nanking. Dave is staying over one day. The chauffeur met my plane and when I reached the house the servants greeted me with flattering enthusiasm.

The press hostel is operating. The Nanking correspondents are well set up but still grumbling despite the fact that the government is subsidizing them to the extent of $12,000 to $15,000 U.S. a year.

NANKING, August 22—Dave came in on the morning plane. He, too, felt pleased with the household arrangements. We called in Chiao and Hsia to discuss the household routine and warned them that, unlike their former master, the U. S. Government, I did not have limitless resources behind me. After dinner Dave and I dropped in on Peng Hsueh-pei for a talk. Although we are in the "autumn tiger" by Chinese reckoning and the days are very hot, it was cool under the stars on Peng's spacious lawn. We had a very interesting discussion in which he found some fault, some failing, with almost every minister of the government, and concluded that inefficiency, rather than corruption, is the besetting sin of this government. He refused to concede that this is the best government China ever had, in comment on Jim Brennan's interview. He foresees no further negotiations with the Communists until the government has thrown them back north of the Lunghai Railway, which should take about two weeks. The Nationalists are engaging crack Communist troops in this fight, and a Communist defeat or withdrawal would be as important a victory strategically as was Szepingkai in the advance on Changchun. The government is confident it can win. But at the same time Tatung is about to fall to the Communists, and Peng admitted that damage would have to be repaired too.

And so it goes—there is always some loose end to tie up before negotiations can begin again. But, surprisingly, Peng did not reflect total recalcitrance about letting the Communists retain civilian administrations. He said it was a question chiefly of northern Kiangsu and Shantung, for reasons of assuring a supply of coal for Nationalist China. Elsewhere, I gathered, the government will be willing to leave the areas to the Communists.

NANKING, August 23—Dave Lu called on Ambassador Stuart, who told him that General Marshall has gone back to Kuling and that he (Stuart) expects a break within two or three days on the further broadening of the Nationalist Government. He did not explain, but it seems unduly optimistic to me. However, there is another unexplained incident. T. V. Soong saw Chou En-lai yesterday. Soong told Peng to publicize that fact but did not give any hint of what it was about.

Stuart's account to Dave of the Marshall-Stuart statement of August 11 jibed with what Marshall told me. Stuart said Marshall had added the part at the end saying that the question of civilian administrations was impossible of solution. This seems to rule out Shen Chang-huan's interpretation that the purpose of the statement was to impair the prestige of the National Government.

Canadian Ambassador Victor Odlum, according to Charlotte Ebener, has been advocating U.S. or UN trusteeship over the "disputed" areas, apparently as a way to break the deadlock over civilian administration. Odlum saw Chiang in Kuling this week and Stuart here today. I suspect he is acting on his own, since he has very little to do, rather than intervening on behalf of his government. What he proposes sounds very much like benevolent occupation, similar to MacArthur's in Japan. Nevertheless the correspondents wrote stories about it today, pinning it on a "non-American diplomatic source," and said the government is seriously considering it, which I doubt.

Rumors of personal enrichment in the exchange rate adjustment are already starting. Peng said he heard criticism at a party gathering based on three lines of questioning: (1) why was it announced in advance? (2) why now, when everyone was more or less settling down? (3) why wasn't it submitted to the Supreme National Defense Council?

The answers are relatively simple: (1) it was announced Sunday because no markets or banks were then open; (2) the old rate of 2020 to $1.00 was getting more and more unrealistic, not "settling down"; (3) the National Defense Council had in fact given blanket authority some time previously for the Executive Yuan to act as necessary to stabilize the financial situation. My own banker, the manager of the National City Bank, told me the rate was an extremely well-kept secret.

NANKING, August 25—Bill O'Neill, Far East manager of Reuters, and Doon Campbell, the local correspondent, joined Dave and me for a picnic in the country Peng had planned. We drove to Niu Shou Shan (Cow's Head Mountain) over a rutty road and took a path to an old ruined temple, where the picnic fare consisted of water with lime juice, tea, and some Chinese cakes. While we ate, Peng told us that the story of the Kunming assassinations was being put out by Central News today. The story, as he told it, was that at the funeral of one of the two victims, a man named Li, the second victim, named Wen, made a speech bitterly attacking the government "gestapo." He said there must be "gestapo" present at the funeral and defied them to shoot him on the spot. An army corporal, present in plain clothes, started to get out his pistol but was restrained by his captain, also in plain clothes. Afterward they followed Wen and shot him on his way home. Peng said the two assassins have been sentenced to death, the garrison commander under whom they served put under house arrest, and other commanders given various degrees of punishment.

NANKING, August 28—A long telegram came in to Peng today from Chen Pu-lei in Kuling. It took a long time to get it decoded and more to translate it in preparation for Peng's weekly press conference for the foreign correspondents. It was, of course, from the Generalissimo, who wanted to combat the Communist-inspired impression that the government did not want to cease hostilities, and saying among other things that the PCC will not be reconvened. The news to me was the refusal to call the PCC back into being, though I should have anticipated it last week when Peng told Dave and me that there was a question as to the legal status of the PCC, which had adjourned without any provision for its recall after it worked out the key political agreements in Chungking.

I dropped in to see T. V. Soong and found him tired and depressed at the end of his day. I asked him about his conference with Chou En-lai. He said he had done it unofficially, just to see what possibilities there were in the situation. They had got nowhere, he said, and agreed neither would talk about it, but T.V. had noticed in yesterday's Chinese papers stories quoting Chou as saying that T.V. had represented nobody but himself, and that the talks came to nothing.

I asked what was meant, if there was more than appeared on the surface, of the refusal to call the PCC. He started to say,

"Something is . . ." and paused so long I suggested: "Something's cooking?" He said, "Between the U.S. and Russia, but in Europe." I agreed that things seemed very tense as a result of the argument at the Paris peace conference, but said that I could not foresee war. The U.S., I ventured, was merely determined to thrash out the Russian issue in the UN. He considered this moodily but said nothing.

NANKING, August 29—T.V. was even more tense and fidgety than yesterday. But I knew that as long as he wants this daily schedule continued I had better insist on talking to him. As an opening gambit I asked whether the U. S. Army had asked for all of Broadway Mansions—something the foreign correspondents in Shanghai have been worrying about. My mind was not on that question, however, and I let his reply escape me; I think it was that the U.S. had not yet made the formal request but was going to, in which case the correspondents would be taken care of, since (it may have been irony) the U.S. was as interested as China in a good press in China.

With a brush he squiggled notes and orders on official documents as he talked. When he finished he stood up and started putting papers into his briefcase. He said an American Congressional delegation was coming to Shanghai and would it be a good idea for him to have them to dinner? He did not know what group, or the names, but it must be the House Military Affairs subcommittee, which is on tour under the chairmanship of Ewing Thomason. I said a dinner would be good, and he asked if I would like to attend. I told him I would be delighted, and since he is leaving tomorrow for the weekend, that I would fly down Monday for it.

I mentioned that Sun Fo, in a public speech at a reception for Norman Corwin, said he thought the Communists, as well as the government, wanted peace. This did not jibe with the attitude Sun had expressed to me privately, which surprised me at the time as I understood Sun to be very pro-Communist. I said to T.V. that it looked as if Sun was maneuvering for some bigger job in a coalition that included the Communists.

"He wants this job, obviously," said T.V. "There's no question about it." I suggested there was little possibility of a coalition government just now, and asked T.V.'s opinion of Sun. "I wish I could let him have this job," he said. He paced the straw summer carpet to the coat rack and put on his jacket.

Somehow it is stimulating to watch T.V. at work. He is not happy when he is in power because of the near-impossible job he has in the face of criticism from all quarters. I can imagine he feels the insecurity of Sun's maneuverings, and can well calculate the possibility that Sun would be a Prime Minister acceptable to the Communists in a coalition. Yet, as Dave says, I can believe that T.V. cannot be happy out of power, either. Even so, to me there is not discernible any of the pussyfooting in T.V. that a smaller-caliber individual might display under the circumstances. It's possible his interview with Chou En-lai was to make a personal assessment of his remaining in the job under a coalition, but I frankly doubt he would be so unsubtle. I think he wants to keep the job but would take it calmly if politics threw him out, and would, as he has mentioned to me, take his family on a trip around the world. He would be relieved, at first, to get rid of all his problems, but would fret toward the end to get his hands on the job again. Even if the politicians manage to get him ousted, he is too able a man to be kept down.

NANKING, August 30—Central News carries announcement of the Committee of Five which Dr. Stuart has been promoting, more or less as a compromise between the Communist demand for reconvening the PCC and the KMT refusal to call it back. It will deal with organization of the State Council, the forty-member group which will replace the present Supreme National Defense Council under the plans for the coalition government. The committee cannot deal with reorganization of the cabinet or military problems, but only with the division of State Council membership among the parties, since that is the present stumbling block. The KMT members are General Wu Tieh-cheng, secretary-general of the party, and little-known Chang Li-sheng, Minister of Interior. The Communists are Chou En-lai and Tung Pi-wu. Stuart, of course, is the fifth member. This is something Dave's pipeline to Stuart has informed us about in advance.

My sinus has been acting up and I resolved to stay in bed to-day, but a request I put in for an appointment with Marshall, whom I felt I must see again, came through for 11 A.M. and naturally I kept it. He seemed relaxed and as I had been told he had no other appointment before lunch, we stretched it out until twelve-forty, sitting on the veranda.

There is, he said, a new element in the situation, and it is secret. He has got Chou and Mao Tse-tung to consider issuing, entirely independent of the KMT, a cease-fire order four or five days in advance of the effective date, with the understanding that Marshall would try to get the Gimo to reciprocate. This was his purpose in making his sixth trip to Kuling, on which he left later today. Marshall figures that unilateral Communist action of this sort, calling Chiang on his claim that if the Communists would just stop fighting things could be settled, would embarrass the KMT enough to pressure them into similar action and thus permit negotiations while the fighting was stopped. It's the reverse of the proposition he was trying to win the Gimo to at the time he went to Mukden, which Marshall believes would have succeeded if it had not been for the Nationalist military leaders. Marshall said the men who are crossing him up are the CC clique, General Tu Li-ming and the military leaders in general, exclusive of Chen Cheng.

I told him my reading of the government mood was that the Nationalists were currently stalling and would not be willing to do any business until they won the substantial military victories Chiang was insisting on, driving the Communists from northern Kiangsu and from the Lunghai Railway. "And from Chengteh in Jehol," Marshall added, remarking that Yu Ta-wei, who had called on him just before I arrived, had given him a memorandum saying Nationalist troops had entered Chengteh, from which the

Communists had withdrawn. Marshall said the impression of stalling was precisely his own conclusion, as well as of Till Durdin and A. T. Steele, to whom he had recently been talking. Mention of Steele, the seasoned correspondent of the New York *Herald Tribune*, led Marshall to say he found it surprising that Steele, regarded as pro-KMT, had found it widely evident that KMT liberals were being alienated from the party by its terroristic excesses.

Marshall said his discussion of the terrorism with Chiang had led to some pretty strained relations between them. He said he had told him the only thing holding China together was the Gimo's prestige, and that was rapidly deteriorating to the vanishing point. Referring to an incident of terrorism in Shanghai, he told Chiang: "You claim these people are being followed to guard them, but I'm not so naïve as to believe that. They are being pursued. Substitute the name of Himmler for Chen Li-fu and you have the same thing Germany had." Marshall said the only thing that kept him on reasonable terms with Chiang was the great shine the Gimo has taken to Mrs. Marshall, who has introduced him to the game of Chinese checkers. At their last luncheon together, outdoors on the grounds at Kuling, the Gimo insisted on having a board brought out and playing a game with Mrs. Marshall during the meal.

Marshall produced a transcript of a talk he had last night with Chou En-lai in which he chided Chou for the Communist propaganda campaign claiming that the U.S. was creating the civil war by arming the KMT. He also thought the time had come to let Chou know he (Marshall) had access, once a week, to the propaganda orders from Moscow to Shanghai, and Shanghai's replies, "even at the risk of losing that source, because we know it anyway."

Marshall told me he had stopped a lot of aid to the KMT from coming through, and that no more ammunition would be shipped. One purchase which had been approved by the U.S. and through the higher official echelons had been finally stopped by denial of an export license. He was surprised when I told him Dean

Acheson had announced publicly that no more war weapons, including ammunition, would go to China until it formed a coalition government. He said he had wanted to keep that information from the Communists, since he felt it would only inflame them in their campaign to cut off American aid. On the other hand, he added, the KMT is encouraged by feeling dead certain the U.S. has no choice but to supply them because of our clash here with Russia.

This led me to ask why Russia, which is never bashful about demanding what she wants, had failed so far to insist on having a hand in mediating the dispute in China. "She could do it easily," said Marshall. "She could demand that the U.S. representative on EHQ in Changchun be one of her men, since that is in their sphere of influence." Was it that Russia was too involved in Europe, or was she waiting for the U.S. to fail in China?

Marshall dismissed the idea that Russia was too busy in Europe. She has plenty of strength out here, he said, and knows that the U.S. is not going to go to war or send troops. She could move from Siberia or North Korea. Russia's propaganda attack on him here, he supposed, was one means of bringing pressure on the U.S. in Europe. No, Russia's restraint was probably based on the belief that the U.S. was going to get the limb sawed off. Marshall's calm recital of it in those terms made me realize why he sticks at this job past the point where an ordinary man would give up. He doesn't want to let his country down.

He commented that he is getting awfully tired of bawling out both sides in China, and that reminded him of another thing he had said that irritated the Gimo: that the Harvard professors who protested the Kunming assassinations were more right than a "bunch of military high school graduates"—meaning Whampoa Academy men, of whom the Gimo is one, an allusion which he said was not lost on the Gimo.

Tonight's Central News announces the occupation of Chengteh.

In the privately circulated portion (to editors) of which David gets a copy, there was report of much criticism of the government's fiscal policy at this morning's meeting of the Legislative Yuan, headed by Sun Fo. Complaints were made because the Legislative Yuan wasn't consulted, in fact did not know about it before it was announced, and it was stated also that Minister of Finance O. K. Yui was kept in the dark too.

NANKING–SHANGHAI, September 7—In view of the prickly heat that has afflicted me on top of my other ailments, Peng has dreamed up a means of giving me a change of scene by asking Dave to go to Hong Kong to transact some MOI business for him, and having me go along. It will take clearance with T.V. so Dave and I decided to go down to Shanghai for the weekend, primarily to see his younger brother off for Yenching, and continue on to Hong Kong if T.V. approves.

On the flight down Dave told me about his talk this morning with Ambassador Stuart. The Communists have asked Yenan for instructions about participating in the Committee of Five. So far they have stalled, blocked, refused to participate. If they refuse to come in, Marshall and Stuart have no choice but to issue a statement giving the facts of the case and quitting. This will be followed, Stuart said, by American withdrawal from China. To what extent, he did not elaborate with Dave.

I would judge it would involve (1) immediate closing of EHQ, which Marshall has told me personally would happen; (2) withdrawal of MAGIC, which is something of a long-range program anyway and would take a millstone of present expense off China's neck; (3) no U.S. loan, which in turn might cause T.V.'s replacement as Prime Minister—by whom? Certainly not by Sun Fo; possibly by Chang Chun. I presume it would mean no difference in the ordinary sort of government-to-government support, for certainly we would continue to recognize Chiang Kai-shek's government. Yet, having a background, off-the-record knowledge of Truman's long-standing, stubborn determination not to appease Russia, it is hard for me to believe he would abandon China to Russian acquisition, for I think that is the way he would look at it.

Stuart also told Dave the Communists were extremely jumpy, afraid of their own shadow. He said Chou had told him that if the U.S. withdrew Russia would not come in. I don't see how that can be relied on. U.S. withdrawal is what Chou devoutly desires but because Russia is advocating it; Chou must know that if Russia were not in the picture the KMT would feel no restraint at all in mopping up on the Communists. Also it would seem naïve to believe this in view of Russia's actions since the war and in view of Marshall's comment as to how easy it would be for them to move in troops from Siberia or Korea.

I dined with Ronald Stead, and talked afterward to John Dowling about the Chicago *Sun*'s failure to print a letter of correction about its story stating that T. V. Soong was using an air conditioning unit intended for a skin disease ward of a hospital. The head of CNRRA's Washington office had sent a letter reciting the facts to the *Sun* but it had been ignored. Dowling showed me his original copy, which mentioned also that Marshall and the Canadian ambassador, Victor Odlum, also got units and that probably none of the recipients knew the origin or intended destination of the units. The *Sun*, apparently, edited out this part. Dowling, admitting he probably was wrong on the skin disease angle—which happens to be the poisonous part of the story—was reluctant to concede there was anything else wrong with his story but finally agreed to recommend to the *Sun* that it print the CNRRA letter. It is, of course, an outrageous breach of ordinary practice for any decent newspaper to deny someone accused the right of reply.

SHANGHAI, September 8—Went with Dave and his brother Sam to the Community (American) Church and afterward to Newsreel Wong's for a good Chinese meal. Today, for the first time since arrival, I feel a strong desire to close up shop and go home—not on the grounds of a psychological insecurity, which I felt at the outset, but because I'm tired of the whole thing. But I can't define precisely why, especially with my family on the way over. The morning paper says the U.S. maritime strike may delay the

departure of their ship beyond September 11. I'd like to wire them
to wait for me in San Francisco, fly over to join them, and motor
back across the country to Washington.

SHANGHAI, September 9—I saw T.V. at his Bank of China office and broached the Hong Kong trip. He inquired how long
it would take and seemed interested in Peng's idea that Dave
should explore the possibility of an English-language paper there,
but did not comment on it. Finally he said, sure, go ahead.

I told him I thought the Communists would boycott Stuart's
Committee of Five and that the result would be the end of Marshall's mission. I emphasized that I was voicing my own judgment
only, since I had not seen Marshall after his return from the latest
trip to Kuling. I outlined what I thought a U.S. withdrawal would
mean, as well as my guess as to how Truman would react.

"Russia won't go beyond Manchuria," T.V. said easily, as if
he were sure of it. "But China needs Manchuria," I suggested. He
sort of winced and agreed this was true. But, he added, Russia
was too involved in Europe and the Near East just now to take
on more than Manchuria in the Far East. Of the U.S. loan he
commented: "We can get along without it. It would be nice to
get it, but we don't absolutely need it." I said that must mean
the new exchange rate and other economic steps were working
out satisfactorily. He nodded. I ventured that the chief trouble
with the ordinary kind of government-to-government aid, in
event of a break with the Communists, is that it usually is too
little and too late. "Halfhearted," T.V. commented. "Russia is
never halfhearted when she decides to act."

I said that, if Marshall left, someone should see Truman, presumably Ambassador Wellington Koo. "You draft some ideas for
him while you are in Hong Kong," said T.V. He added that in
last Monday's dinner for the visiting congressman, which I had
been forced to skip on account of my bad sinus, he had been
asked about the Communists. Remembering my injunction that
the U.S. congressman needs no education on that score, he had
stressed the economic strains of the continued fighting.

He inquired about the family, and when I mentioned the possible delay in the maritime strike he asked: "Are these labor troubles symptoms of social unrest?" I told him I thought they were no more than the inevitable postwar readjustment in which prices and wages jockeyed for position; that the U.S. tradition for settling issues by majority vote was by now too deep-rooted to permit any suspicion of violent political action.

He said not to stay in Hong Kong too long, and if Marshall left, to come back immediately. He arranged priorities for Dave and me on tomorrow's plane.

SHANGHAI–HONG KONG, September 10—After some effort I got hold of Nathaniel Peffer last night and we dined at the Metropole: martinis, an excellent Chateaubriand, baked Alaska. He launched into a bitter condemnation of the KMT and so overdid the "they can't fool me" theme that it took some of the sheen off my veneration of him as a pundit. He has spent a month in western China: Chungking, Kunming, Chengtu; he is convinced the KMT has no support anywhere, even among the businessmen who might be expected to be its last-ditch supporters. Chiang remains in power only because of the army, he said. At a discussion Sunday night with a group of editors they agreed—the way he put it was "I got them to admit"—their only defense of the Kuomintang was the negative attitude that "if you don't back us you'll get the Communists" and the government's prestige was sinking lower and lower. Where in the past people have always excused Chiang Kai-shek personally, said Peffer, and blamed the crowd he had around him, now they have no use for Chiang himself.

The reason for all this, he said, is the universal corruption and inefficiency, the carpetbaggers sent in to take over from the Japanese, the terrorism of things like the Kunming assassinations. Of the latter incident he said he did not think Chiang knew in advance it would take place, but that Chen Li-fu or someone close to him did, for Chen Li-fu, whom he repeatedly described as a thoroughgoing fascist, is heading up all the secret police activi-

ties now. Peffer was extremely vehement about all this. He predicted there would be a wave of student riots in the near future.

I told him what I thought was going to happen soon in China,
and asked him what he thought U.S. policy should be in event
of Marshall's withdrawal. "Withdraw the marines, withdraw the
army, withdraw everything but the diplomatic and consular personnel, the military attaché and his staff, etc.," he said. But would
this not leave China to Russia? "We would be backing a losing
horse even if we won. Even if we aided the KMT outright in
fighting the Communists, there would be an uprising inside of
five years." As for Russia, he remarked: "With Russia, it is a question of timing." He doubted that Russia would extend itself south
of Manchuria even if she did enter China. But in any case, he
insisted that the U.S. could not challenge Russia in Asia because
the Chinese government was too weak an ally. In Europe we have
a sound basis for our position on issues like the Dardanelles, and
thus can oppose Russia there.

He wound up by saying he may be at the low point of the
pendulum, and I told him I thought he did take too dim a view
of the situation. I agreed with his judgment on parts of it, but in
any case I was glad to hear his views since I see KMT sources so
much.

CHAPTER TEN

Visit to Hong Kong during Moon Festival brings more tales of venality of army commanders on mainland.

To visit Hong Kong for six days was to learn about air travel in China during the immediate postwar era, to sample the life of wealthy Chinese expatriates, and to hear tales of what happened in neighboring Kwangtung Province when the task of taking the country from the defeated Japanese filtered down to local areas through the echelons of the Chinese army command.

The Shanghai airport at six o'clock of that September morning in 1946 was a busy place as travelers of various races prepared to scatter to destinations all over the Far East. Customs clearance was in effect even between major Chinese cities at the time. Some months later, on a flight from Peking, a chap just ahead of me in the line boarding a Shanghai-bound plane was discovered to have a false bottom in his suitcase, concealing what apparently was several pounds of heroin. Besides customs, there was an inspection of inoculation certificates. There was a desk in the main waiting room at Shanghai where a Chinese medical officer was administering cholera shots to those who lacked them, and assisting was a nurse who presided over a kit which included an alcohol lamp to keep a small pan of water boiling for the sterilization of needles.

Our plane, a bucket-seat C-47, was a bit late getting off and in good weather we skirted the very flat coastal plain created by the Yangtze delta, within sight of the sea. Soon, however, we were over a range of stark, treeless, dark gray mountains. Dave remarked that, over the thousands of years of Chinese history, in the populated areas every tree within reach had been chopped down for firewood. As we approached our first stop, Foochow, although it was barely midmorning, the navigator handed out box lunches. There was no hostess. The boxes held two sandwiches, one of jelly and one of peanut butter, a cookie, and some potato salad.

At Foochow the airport was a grass field circled by high mountains. During the stop two local passengers got aboard but were asked to leave because they had no cholera shots. A terrific argument ensued in Chinese which lasted for twenty minutes and involved three policemen, two airline officials, and the navigator. The couple finally got off, under a bit of shoving, and the woman was weeping when she left. We landed again at Amoy—also an undeveloped field—and it was a refueling stop, with gasoline being pumped into the wing tanks from big steel drums by means of a small motor. There was a final stop at Canton, where the field had runways and a control tower, for it had been a busy airport during the Japanese occupation.

Then, in a few minutes, we were circling the archipelago that makes up Hong Kong. The American pilot said it was his first landing at the Kai Tak Airport and he wanted to look it over before alighting. Victoria Island, with its famed "Peak," was reminiscent of St. Thomas in the Virgin Islands, and the airport, near Kowloon on the mainland side, was rather tricky to approach. Some years later my friend Peng Hsueh-pei was killed there when his plane crashed on an attempted landing.

The arrival was a bit of a letdown. For one seeking escape from the heat of the Yangtze Valley, it was ninety-seven degrees and the humidity was 95 per cent. There was another customs inspection and passport forms to fill out. But the discomfort was overcome as we took the ferry from Kowloon and taxied from the ferry landing at Victoria over a pass to skirt a couple of inlets en route to the Repulse Bay Hotel, where a friend of David Lu had booked us rooms. Here, amid typically British colonial luxury, we had rooms facing the bay and the breeze was cool. As we prepared for an afternoon nap I noticed workmen digging in the lawn in front of the hotel; later I read in the paper that the bodies of two British soldiers killed during the Japanese occupation had been dug up to be buried in a military cemetery.

It was the time of the Moon Festival in China, and Dave's friend, Eddie Eu, had invited us to a party at his home on one of the cliffs near the hotel. Dave had made some remark about Eddie's "shack" on Repulse Bay to which I had paid no attention, and I was not prepared for the actuality. The Eu mansion was a baronial castle perched on an eminence of rocky splendor, a huge edifice with an elaborate entrance driveway leading from a stone-pillared, iron-grilled gateway into a courtyard. Coats of armor in the entrance hall were typical of the décor. The rooms were spacious and high-ceilinged; there was a big stone terrace on the bay side, as well as a tennis court and a big swimming pool lighted from under water for evening dips.

About twenty or twenty-five guests were on hand, including some of the British officials of the colony. We had gimlets—the typical British colonial drink of the tropics—and a Chinese buffet on the terrace, danced under the brilliant moon, and in midevening a swim in the pool through which the clear ocean water flowed constantly. At midnight we supped on "moon cakes" and fruit.

During the evening I had been introduced to what seemed like about ten of Eddie's brothers and sisters, and there was mention of others who had been unable to come from places like Singapore and Bangkok for the party. As we walked back to the hotel Dave explained that Eddie's father, then dead, was the "tin king" of Southeast Asia and a gay old dog with numerous concubines; some of the numerous family members were half brothers and sisters. Each, said Dave, had inherited the equivalent of around $10 million U.S. in the old man's will.

Standing in ghostly magnificence just across the bay, its broken windows and torn roof visible in the bright moonlight, was another mansion apparently built on the same scale as Eddie's. Dave said it belonged to T. V. Soong but had been ruined during the Japanese capture of the colony. Recalling that Eddie had pointed out a few chips in the stone of the mansion and grounds as evidence of Japanese bullets, I wondered how the one structure had emerged from the fighting relatively unharmed. Dave said he was wondering too.

Reading the newspapers the next day, I reflected that everybody—British colonialists and wealthy Chinese—was taking up life again pretty much where he left off before the war. The impression came chiefly from a story in the *China Mail* containing an account of all the lavish parties in celebration of the annual autumn festival and noting that nothing had been done for the street waifs. "The one discordant note in the festivities," said the *Mail*, "was the fact that nothing was done to make the occasion a happy one for the children of the streets. It was thought that the years of hardship and suffering through which all had passed would have taught those more blessed with material wealth to show a little more kindness to their more unfortunate brethren. Evidently the war has not taught our wealthy playboys, who squander huge sums at cabarets and gaming tables every night, anything at all. It would have been a fine gesture on their part to have got together and made some effort to give the little waifs a small measure of enjoyment on such a festive occasion."

Nor could the festival erase the brooding presence of the struggle in progress on the mainland. The *South China Morning Post* reported that Tan Kah-kee, leader of Malayan Chinese in Singapore, had cabled President Truman urging that all American aid to Chiang Kai-shek be cut off. For

twenty years, his cable charged, "corruption, despotism, de-
ceit, bad faith and ascendancy of reactionary characters have
been the outstanding feature of the regime in China."

The nearest major Chinese city to Hong Kong is Canton,
birthplace of Sun Yat-sen's revolution and capital of a province whose people were by far the most energetic of all
Chinese in spreading their entrepreneurial genius throughout
the rest of the world. Before the war on the mainland increased the proportion of refugees from other provinces, the
great majority of Overseas Chinese were Cantonese. Most of
the Chinese restaurants one can find in any foreign city
feature Cantonese dishes; I have encountered Chinese chefs
in communities all the way from Berlin to Inuvik, a new
Eskimo-Indian administrative settlement in Canada's remote
Arctic near where the Mackenzie River empties into the Be-
ring Sea. The Cantonese have a reputation among other
Chinese of being overfond of girls, gambling, and graft.

One day when Dave was going about his business for Peng
Hsueh-pei there were repeated telephone calls for him from a
man who refused to leave his name. When they finally connected the man came out to see us, accompanied by his son,
an English-speaking secretary, and a man from the *South
China Morning Post.* The visitor, a Chinese named Shum,
said he had been in hiding since July, was afraid to travel
about alone, and did not dare use his own car, the license
number of which was known to "certain persons." Shum had
published a Chinese paper, *Wah Kiu Yat Po,* without inter-
ruption during the Japanese occupation. A small, slight, neat-
appearing man who spoke good English, he told Dave he had
done it under duress and claimed he helped maintain the
morale of the Chinese community with between-the-lines
material. It was the typical excuse of a collaborator, for
naturally the performance had got him listed by the Chinese
among Japanese collaborators from the Canton area.

The point of Shum's story, however, was not to sell his
excuse; it was that he had been told he could get his name

removed from the list in return for certain considerations. The offer came from representatives of Chinese army headquarters in Canton and of certain Hong Kong and Canton KMT party figures. The considerations were that he appoint ten party faithfuls to the staff of his paper. This he did, at a cost of $6000 HK a month, in July. The new staffers remained in Canton, drew their pay, and did no work for the paper. Yet somehow his name did not come off the collaborator's list. Instead, he was one of twelve for whom warrants of arrest were issued, and the Chinese government requested his extradition. So far the Crown Colony had ignored the request. Meanwhile the price for removing his name had gone up. Now they wanted 51 per cent of the stock of the paper, which he was unable to deliver. One of the go-betweens had told him: "Tell us just how much you can pay. As for myself, I want no money; all I want is a modern house."

Shum had lived forty years in the Colony but retained his Chinese citizenship. He could have acquired British citizenship but claimed he wanted to remain Chinese. He told his story to Dave in private while I talked to the *Post* man, S. Y. Leung, who was Chinese editor of the English-language paper. Leung said his judgment was that about 90 per cent of the local Chinese, who comprised about 95 per cent of the Colony's population, favored Chiang Kai-shek, and he discounted Tan Kah-kee's blast by saying, "Maybe he has some ax to grind." He said the British showed some signs of learning from the war, having announced that a municipal council would be formed to give the Colony some slight measure of self-government, and having permitted Chinese to live on the Peak, from which they were barred before the war, as well as opening more posts to them in the colonial government.

The privilege of living on the Peak was of course a symbolic concession to the Chinese postwar, but scarcely a sociological benefit to them. This I learned as a dinner guest, with Dave, at Eddie Eu's other home, a mansion on the Peak which made the Repulse Bay home seem like something of a shack after all. The opulence was positively overpowering: suits of armor, marble floors, huge stone fireplaces big enough to roast an ox, push-button elevator artfully concealed amid the English castle-like surroundings, a billiard room, and a baronial dining room two stories high with room to fete fifty guests.

Most of our stay in Hong Kong was plagued by bad weather on the fringes of a typhoon which was in progress near Hainan; rain and high winds marooned us indoors and promoted conversation with Dave's numerous friends and old classmates. From the papers I followed the progress of the U.S. maritime strike and deduced that my family was still delayed in San Francisco. There was one other conversation I found interesting. It was with Harry Ching, an Australian Chinese who had lived in Hong Kong thirty years and undergone the Japanese occupation. He was one of the editors of the *South China Morning Post & Hong Kong Telegraph.*

Ching recalled that on Christmas Day, 1941, confined to his home because Japanese shelling of intervening territory made it dangerous to go to his office, he had written a leader for the next day's paper saying Hong Kong would never give up. Someone phoned from the office to say, "It's all over." His editorial was scrapped and someone else wrote a substitute urging everyone to be calm.

Ching and his wife were jailed and for a long period they had nothing to eat but a bowl of rice, a small salt fish, and some spinach each day. They eked out their rations by selling some canned beer at three hundred yen a can, enough to give them three days' extra food per can.

On V-J Day, said Ching, Chinese flags blossomed out all over the Colony, and had a plebiscite been held the vote would have been 90 per cent to give Hong Kong back to China. The population was gripped by victory hysteria and by the fact that it had been agreed that China was to take over from the Japanese occupiers—the Chinese are great believers in getting on the side of the authorities. But the

Chinese failed to arrive in sufficient numbers. They had no troops handy and while they were making the effort the Royal Navy nipped in—Ching said because the British had got wind of a Chiang Kai-shek "plot" to keep Hong Kong—just to make sure the Colony stayed British.

In the two months following the local population saw so much corruption going on at Canton and other nearby Chinese areas in the taking over that they were perfectly content to remain under British rule. Ching felt that within two months of V-J Day a plebiscite would have revealed "110 per cent" sentiment for Britain. He said a small contingent of Communists present in Kwangtung Province, later transported to join their northern comrades under agreement with the U.S. and the Nationalists, did some taking over in their area and turned in a bang-up job of it, reforming land rents and providing fair administration. He conceded it was done for a purpose, to sell Communist administration to the Chinese and the British in the hope of future control, but was nevertheless a stark contrast to the performance of the army.

CHAPTER ELEVEN

Chou goes to Shanghai to mend fences with third parties and independents. Marshall uses threat of withdrawal to edit contents of Chiang statements.

There was a Philippine airline operating from Hong Kong to Shanghai, and since it offered non-stop service David Lu and I elected to fly back that way, continuing on to Nanking via CNAC.

Returning to the capital was returning to another world, the world of political negotiation. I could not escape the reflection that China was adjusting to the business of carrying on its existence at different levels, each seemingly disembodied from the whole.

At the local level it was a case of human cupidity. For thousands of years in China the man with power over his fellow man had used the power to take what he could. So it had been with the war lords, exacting tribute of one kind or another from their subordinates, who ground it out of their subordinates, and so on down until it reached the peasant. In return—and to protect his own base—the war lord guarded his subordinates against squeeze from outsiders; Peng, for example, had hesitated to move in my behalf against an army official occupying a house he wanted because he did not know who was "behind" the man. Now the army had power, theoretically under central authority, but it was an authority that existed more on paper than in fact.

Chiang Kai-shek was Generalissimo, the Commander-in-Chief, by popular Western belief a dictator able to order an execution on the spot; but by no means did he have as much power to issue orders that were obeyed without question as did Harry Truman as Commander-in-Chief of the United States. The regional generals were responsible to Chiang, sure enough. But his mastery was based on a highly developed sense of how far he could go in making them comply with his wishes. Garrison commanders were in a position to use the share of power which filtered down to their level to line their pockets with little fear that word of their venality would reach Nanking, or that if it did it would be capable of proof.

At the national level, the motivation was political, a struggle for power. Unquestionably at the bottom of the Kuomintang Party hierarchy the motive was the same uncomplicated venality as at the local level in the army. If political considerations were involved, as in the case of the Hong Kong publisher, they were incidental. His political liability merely served to make him a convenient target for financial exploitation. Undoubtedly, down the line, party members moved against "Communists" to cloak instances of personal avarice.

But at the top of the party structure were the brothers Chen, who did not exercise majority control but were in effect the largest stockholders' bloc. It was not possible to prove they did not benefit from corruption on the part of their subordinates, but neither was it possible to prove they did. My own belief was that their motivation was an uncomplicated conviction that Communism was poison, of which they had convinced themselves through personal experience. They were identifiable as an evil force by opponents because the party structure was clear-cut in its lines of authority, instead of consisting of a number of pyramids of power as in the army, independent of each other and only tenuously under command of Nanking. Thus Peffer, plumbing the situation for himself, could conclude that it was "the army" which held Chiang in power, and carry that over to believe that Chen Li-fu "must have known" about the Kunming assassinations.

On the neutral plane of U.S. mediation the motivation was a mixture of self-interest and missionary altruism. We undertook to promote unity in China in the interest of world stability, which was in our own interest. At the same time we believed the solution to both corruption and political intrigue was to seek establishment of a unified China, in which the army would be divorced from politics and devote itself to defending the country; a China in which KMT and Communists alike would compete democratically within a reorganized governmental structure for support by the people, exchanging power as often as they won such support. Given the climate of the times in the Western world, given the fostered belief that the Chinese Communists were really honest agrarians and not the undemocratic Russian type, this was not unsound as a concept on which to base the mediation effort.

The difficulties of convincing others we knew better than they what would solve their problems was quickly reimpressed on me, however, as I returned to the scene of the negotiations.

NANKING, September 20—I dropped in at General Marshall's to see what had been going on. Colonel Hutchin showed me a report (I judged from SSU) claiming that Wang Ping-nan was beginning to regret the anti-Communist reaction to the Anping incident [a Communist attack on U.S. marines] and inclined to believe that the Communist propaganda line should switch from complaints against U.S. military aid to the KMT and concentrate instead on preventing a U.S. loan. Before I finished reading it General Marshall happened to enter the room and invited me out on the veranda for a brief chat before his first interview of the day.

In rapid fire he gave me a quick fill-in. Chou En-lai has gone to Shanghai. The Gimo is insisting that the Communists nominate their members to the State Council before he issues a cease-fire order. Marshall said that "of course" Chou En-lai thought the government was trying to move in on him—I was puzzled by the "of course" since it seems like a reasonable request to me. Through Wang Ping-nan last night—Marshall commented it was the first time he had received Wang—Chou insisted on getting something in writing. I was about to ask what when his first visitor showed up. He remarked that his chief job at present was to avoid the appearance of putting any block in the way of negotiations. He said the most disturbing element was a report he had received only half an hour previously indicating the government intended to launch an attack on Harbin in Manchuria. "Of course if that happens the fat's in the fire all over," he said.

But why should it be? I've seen him worried, time after time, about the danger that an impending attack—first Changchun, then Chengteh—was the signal for a complete outbreak of warfare everywhere; but these fears proved unfounded, though it is true that fighting has increased, gradually, over the last two months. Also, he was wrong in predicting that Tatung would surely fall to the Communists as retaliation for the Chengteh offensive—at least up to now, and it looks as though the city is about to be relieved by the joint attack by General Fu Tso-yi from the west and General Yen Hsi-shan from the south. I still think the Communists are talking a good war, still overbluffing on their true military strength.

Marshall's mention of the State Council led me to inquire what kind of veto the Communists were insisting on. Was it that they wanted enough votes, together with the Democratic League, to veto changes of a constitutional nature in the government structure, or to veto statutory changes? It was, he replied, to veto any changes in the PCC agreements. Later I looked up the PCC resolutions on this point and found that the provision is for carrying State Council decisions "on general matters" by majority vote, and for a two-thirds vote of members present on decisions "affecting a change in the administrative program," with the proviso that "where doubt arises as to whether a certain decision affects a change in the administrative program, a ruling on the point shall be made with the agreement of more than 50 per cent of the members present." In view of the Communist insistence on a firm veto, it is hard to understand how they happened to agree to this proposition in Chungking.

One thing Marshall said I found of great interest: Chou was having trouble with the Democratic League, now that Carson Chang had split off. I had missed, during the Hong Kong trip, this bit of news, which seems to indicate that the political bait in the Gimo's speech from Kuling is being taken, at least in part. Marshall said Chou had to be careful not to alienate Lo Lung-chi by what he did, in view of Carson Chang's departure from the coalition; heretofore he has been able to dictate to the League.

At the MOI Peng told me that Chen Pu-lei had brought up with him a point mentioned in one of my memos to the Gimo: that criticism of Chiang for taking the advice of "reactionary advisers" failed to take into account that his prime administrative adviser is T. V. Soong and his prime military adviser is Chen Cheng. The Gimo wanted this brought out and the question, said Peng, was how to do it specifically.

I replied that the point was, who are the Men Around Chiang with respect to strictly political decisions? My impression was that on this plane the Gimo really took no one's advice but acted on his own. Peng said this was true to a degree, but that certain men had ready access to him and he listened to their advice. These included Chen Li-fu, Chang Chun, leader of the Political Science clique, and T. V. Soong. But Soong, he added, is not primarily interested in politics and never makes a political recommendation to the Gimo unless he is sure in advance it will carry. On strictly economic matters the Gimo has complete confidence in him and leaves great power in his hands.

So, Peng continued, it boiled down to a question of whose advice most influenced the Gimo. He said he thought Chen Li-fu was fairly persuasive with him, and that in general it was the officials of the party organization, rather than the ministers of the government, who wielded most influence. And when it comes to the party, the CC clique has the largest voice in the central executive committee, with about 30 per cent of the members, and thus controls the machinery and the execution of party decisions. He said he did not know offhand what the statistics were on the division of the KMT standing committee, but thought it was in the same proportion. Thus, while Peng is not the ultimate authority on this subject, it boils down to about what I expected. As to specific measures calling attention to what liberal advisers the Gimo has, all I could do was to say I would give it study.

Moe Votaw of the MOI is back from a trip to Peking with a tale of stupid KMT publicity in connection with EHQ. There is no liaison between the government's portion of the headquarters and the MOI representative, or for that matter with the Gimo's local headquarters or the garrison commander. EHQ's reports go of course both to the Communists and to the government, but the government man gives MOI only about one in ten of them, whereas the Communists get all of them and put them out continually. The result, he said, is illustrated in the following incident:

On August 31 the Communists put out a story about the strafing of Field Team No. 11 by KMT planes, asserting that four Communist members had been killed. Not until September 12 was the true story told—a story on which the American members checked on all points with the KMT members. The facts were that when it became necessary for the Communists to flee Chengteh they arrested the field team and forced it, at bayonet point, to retreat with the troops. When Nationalist planes strafed the troop columns the field team members left their vehicles and took cover in the fields; several got flesh wounds but no one was killed. The story finally came out at a joint press conference at which each of the three colonels told their stories. It took Walter Robertson, the EHQ chairman, all day to get the Communists to agree to the conference. Twelve days is, of course, a trifle late for the facts to catch up with the propaganda.

One item in today's issue of the bulletin put out by the MOI's international department I found sardonically amusing. It quoted *Ta Kung Pao* as slyly turning the tables on America's editorial advice to the rival Chinese factions by suggesting editorially that the U.S. and Russia should get together and make mutual concessions to achieve mutual understanding.

NANKING, September 22—During the morning, going over some Communist handouts, I discovered one in which was reproduced what purported to be the official statement of the incident involving Field Team No. 11 at Chengteh, signed by all three members. It varied considerably from the account I had heard, and I dropped by Marshall's to check it with Hutchin. He showed me their own report from the American member and there were important variations, but I could not be sure of the full extent to which the Communists deliberately distorted the story since he did not have the official three-man text.

Hutch said General Marshall wanted me to come to lunch, so around twelve-fifteen I went back. Caughey, Hutch, General Marshall, and I sat on the veranda and had old-fashioneds and then adjourned to the dining room. Marshall exclaimed when he noted that the table was set for a Chinese meal. He noted that Mrs. Marshall had put a stop to them after her arrival, though they had been frequent before that. There was sweet and sour pork, Cantonese style, chicken, etc., ending with a Western dessert—some cake and soufflé arrangement—and tea.

As usual, Marshall's directed talk at the table was reminiscent. He recalled a conversation he had had with John L. Lewis, the CIO president, at a state dinner at the White House in 1938. He had asked Lewis how he felt about the personal criticism directed at him in connection with the labor disturbances of the time. The question was never fully answered by Lewis, except in a casual way indicating he didn't pay much attention to it, but it led to a long discussion which revealed to Lewis that Marshall, as the officer in charge of the Civilian Conservation Corps program then in effect, was "a familiar of union hiring halls." Marshall then told how he promoted jobs for CCC boys by writing letters to their officers extolling their performance when it met certain rigid qualifications he had set. He gave an example: "It has been brought to my attention that John Smith has driven trucks 75,000 miles under the CCC program without any accident, even to a dented fender; that he has graduated from motor mechanic school; that his character is good; etc." Boys armed with his letters could get a job anywhere, but Marshall found unions blocking the hiring, even when the lad had an offer of a job, the money to join the union, and the willingness to join. Lewis, he said, kissed it off on the basis that labor had the most votes.

I mentioned that I had been aboard the British cruiser *Belfast* in the Yangtze Friday for Admiral Boyd's cocktail party and commented that inevitably I compared it mentally with ships of the U. S. Navy, and that I had been on the shakedown cruise last January of the new aircraft carrier *Franklin D. Roosevelt*. That cruise, I said, had caused me to wonder about the wisdom of merging the armed forces as currently proposed; I knew this would sound treasonable to him, as a strong advocate of merger.

He was interested. He asked why. I said the army was having G.I. demobilization riots at the time, while the navy, though also bothered with some demobilization trouble, had a complicated machine to run and was already shaking down to peacetime strength in workaday fashion. The navy had morale: 90 per cent of the *FDR*'s officers were regular navy and in the wardroom discussions they spent their time arguing whether they could safely use jet planes on carriers. Was it wise, I asked, to endanger navy morale at a time when the U.S. was supreme on the seas by merging the organization with an army suffering from low morale?

Marshall said that of course what I was talking about would not be affected by merger. What it would do, he said, would be to eliminate all the unnecessary duplication that adds to the cost of maintaining a military establishment, which makes taxpayers reluctant to retain adequate forces. He said the most striking example of duplication he had noticed during the war was when he visited the tiny Pacific Island of Espiritu Santo where he found an army base hospital and right beside it a navy base hospital. Competition between the services for permanent bases often resulted in matching installations where operations did not justify it, merely to save the morale of troops who otherwise might feel they were discriminated against. He deplored how service rivalry often bogged down in debate over inconsequential points, and cited the fact that the navy had insisted on having its own mission to China as well as the army's MAGIC outfit. This small question, he said, had to be fought through to the Joint Chiefs of Staff before it was resolved in favor of one mission.

I was reluctant to let the meal pass without some discussion of U.S. foreign policy and the Chinese situation, so I broached the Wallace controversy [which had broken out as a result of a pro-Russian speech by Wallace and Truman's dismissal of him as Secretary of Commerce]. Marshall said the thing to watch for now was how much opposition Wallace stirred up. From this it was easy to slide into the Chinese situation. He invited me out on the veranda and we finished our talk alone.

Wang Ping-nan had called on him during the morning with a memorandum from Chou En-lai. He sent for it and let me read it. In two and a half single-spaced pages it merely reiterated the demand that the Committee of Three, headed by Marshall, meet before the Communists agreed to take part in Stuart's Committee of Five; and it also named as a condition the issuance of an order by the Gimo stopping hostilities. Marshall commented that it was useless to convene the Committee of Three unless everything was prepared beforehand. During the June truce there had been only three meetings, but it took six weeks of advance spadework to make them productive—up to the final sticking point, that is, of Chiang's refusal to discuss the Communist demand for retaining the civilian administration in northern Kiangsu. It is the minutes of these meetings, showing the agreements reached, that Chou is now threatening to publish—minutes that Marshall himself furnished to Chou. I remarked that I failed to see how publication would hurt either the U.S. or the National Government, and Marshall agreed with a gesture indicating it was of no consequence.

If the Committee of Five got going, he said, it would give him a chance to introduce several compromise plans he had in mind. He had this bit of news: Chiang had caved in on the issue of discussing the northern Kiangsu civilian administration issue. On his trip before last to Kuling Marshall had persuaded the Gimo with this argument: "You have no right, on this small issue in northern Kiangsu, to endanger the peace of the whole world." Again I got a glimpse of why he clings so tenaciously to a seemingly hopeless job, and I suspect I have been wrong in thinking he could not stay much longer.

He added that in talking to Wang he had "taken a bit of a risk" by giving him a stern lecture. He told Wang that the Communist propaganda contained personal attacks on his integrity, questioning his good faith as a mediator—like one release sneering at him for taking walks in the woods at Kuling while people fought in the valley. While the Communists are saying things like that in public, he told Wang, in private they are relying on him to argue their case with the Gimo. He said he was not personally resentful, and that in the U.S. they probably helped him rather than hurt him. But, he said—and his blue eyes lit with fire as he told me about it—Wang must understand that he was not going to countenance such duplicity. If it continued, he was through.

Marshall said that on his return from his next to last trip to Kuling he had carried to Chou a carefully phrased, three-part list of (1) things to which the Gimo had agreed; (2) "statements" of the Gimo—i.e., more cautious than agreements; and (3) Marshall's "impressions" of the Gimo's attitude, being points that Chiang wanted conveyed to the Communists without personally taking responsibility for them. The Kiangsu point was one of the latter: he is willing to have it discussed by the Committee of Five. Of course this still gives him ultimate veto on it.

He said he had also taken Wang to task for some of the Communist violations of the original agreements, particularly for their offensive in Shantung Province, and upbraided him for their utter failure to provide their lists for military demobilization, as the Nationalists had done. "I don't see how that possibly could have hurt you," Marshall told him.

I told the general about my attempts to find out who exercises the most influence on Chiang; about efforts to get the government to be more constructive in its propaganda than to fall back on the line that "if you don't back us you'll get the Communists"; and about the Hong Kong publisher. When I rose to go he asked me how I liked my job, and seemed pleased when I said I found it intensely absorbing but did not want to extend it beyond the year. I guess he feels the same way.

At this time it was apparent that Ambassador Stuart would be more prominent in the negotiations if they continued. When General Marshall discussed Stuart's appointment with me on July 5, my enthusiasm for it was based entirely on what my friend in San Francisco had told me about him. When I subsequently met Dr. Stuart he seemed to bear out the picture of a gentle, calm, fair-minded man as sensitive to Chinese customs and culture as one could expect in any Westerner. What sources Marshall had for deciding to recommend the appointment—which he had offered Stuart the night before our talk, as Stuart recorded in his autobiography, *Fifty Years in China*—I did not know. I did know that General Albert C. Wedemeyer, who had been wartime Chief of Staff to Chiang Kai-shek after removal of General Joseph (Vinegar Joe) Stilwell, had been under consideration. I agreed with Marshall's feeling that in the current situation the Communists would be suspicious of the neutrality of a man who had served the Gimo, but I did not know until I read it in Wedemeyer's autobiography, *Wedemeyer Reports!* that his appointment had been definitely set when it was canceled. Wedemeyer resented the fact that the Chinese Communists were able, in effect, to veto an American appointment.

Until Stuart was named the post had been vacant since the unexpected resignation of Patrick Hurley, who had charged that U.S. foreign service officers were sabotaging his and U.S. policy. Marshall, though he held the rank of ambassador, was Truman's personal representative for a specific mission. He lived apart from the diplomatic setup and had a small headquarters staff of his own operating from his house. When Stuart came to stay in Nanking he occupied the ambassador's residence and was under the observation of the career officers in a way that Marshall was not.

I became aware that these officers had a suspicious attitude toward Stuart, apparently because he had an adopted Chinese son, Philip Fugh, as his confidential secretary. Fugh, a man in his forties, was actually of Manchu stock, son of a duke in the last dynasty. For many years he had been Stuart's trusted companion, but embassy officers thought it unfitting that a Chinese national should have access to all the confidential information that came to an ambassador. One day I invited Fugh to lunch. Fred Gruin, *Time*'s Nanking bureau chief, who had been living with me temporarily while he looked for a house, was also present.

NANKING, September 23—Fugh recalled that as a boy of eleven he paid a formal call on the old Empress Dowager, during which the only sound in the room was the rustle of his Manchu gown, for a ceremony at which he was presented with a blood-red porcelain bowl to hold the red ink paste one uses to stamp one's "chop." He still has it. He said that for three months he had been the representative of the Executive Yuan in Manchuria, but had resigned because he saw that if he stayed further during the "taking over" process he would have become involved in some army deals. I remarked that most of the corruption in China—the big stuff—could be traced to the army, and he remarked: "The army is a privileged class."

He told about a visit of Soviet Ambassador Petrov to Ambassador Stuart. Fugh and Stuart plotted beforehand on some plan to break up the visit if the conversation got beyond control, but it didn't. Fugh recounted the conversation: Petrov asked if the U.S. would ever get out of China. Yes, sincerely, said Dr. Stuart. Why was the U.S. finding it so difficult to bring the two sides together? It was the two sides which were finding it difficult to get together. Why didn't the U.S. follow the decisions of the Moscow Big Three Foreign Ministers' conference? Fugh's narrative trailed off without indicating the answer to this question.

We got to discussing the Gimo's position and what effect his sudden removal from the scene would have if it came about for any reason. Fugh said there would be chaos but that Chen Cheng and Pai Chung-hsi, if they could get together, would control the army. Chen and Pai are rivals, he said, and do not get along. Pai is a former Kwangsi war lord who once considered himself a rival of Chiang Kai-shek, but who has now given that up. Fugh seemed to think of him as fairly enlightened as ex-war lords go. Pai is nearly sixty, older than Chen, but Chen is the more modern-minded, more technically skilled.

If Fugh is a reflection of Stuart (and he has the reputation of a mystery man who practically does Stuart's thinking for him), Stuart seems to have finally acquired a fraction of the same suspicion of Communist motives as the Communists have indoctrinated the government with, by their actions over the last twenty years. He said he had advised Marshall and Stuart not to write any more letters to the Communists, since they use them only for propaganda. He commented on Chou's "threat" to publish the minutes of the Committee of Three meetings, saying it was a strange threat because, aside from the fact that nobody cared, it wasn't a Chinese thing to do—it wasn't cricket in the Chinese sense.

NANKING, September 26—Dave Lu came back from his trip to Shanghai for a medical checkup. His X rays indicate a touch of TB sometime in the past, and at present a quiescent pleurisy. He thinks he had better go back to the U.S., and I think so too. His help here in keeping me current on Chinese news and gossip is extremely useful, but it also would be helpful to get regular reports from him about U.S. thinking about China from Washington.

Philip Fugh had fixed me up with a nine-thirty date with Dr. Stuart. The car failed to arrive and I had to go by rickshaw. Stuart invited me into his office and during the visit General Marshall called to say he was coming over, but we covered quite a bit of ground before he arrived. Marshall obviously had something on his mind but gave no indication to me what it was.

I was interested in sounding out Stuart's feeling about the corruption of which one heard so much, vaguely, concerning the top people. I said I believed that if the National Government was to win support from the U.S. it would have to do so on the basis of good administration and economic reform, and one of the things that troubled me was the continual circulation of stories of venality. I added that, in close observation of T. V. Soong, I could see no evidence of this, only of a man working hard to keep the country together, though of course I was not aware of everything he did, and even less in a position to judge the Gimo and Madame Chiang.

Stuart replied that in his early days Chiang had made money from "a lot of rackets," but that was before Sun Yat-sen had "fired his imagination." He said he was sure that the Generalissimo and Madame Chiang were "clean" and sincerely working for the good of China. On the basis of what he had heard he expected the Gimo, when he returned to Nanking, to make some changes in government policy and personnel. Stuart said he knew something personally about the situations in Peking and Tientsin, which were bad, and he had told the Gimo so. "If we could get more mayors like K. C. Wu in Shanghai," he said.

As for Soong, he said T.V. was, in his opinion, scrupulously honest as a government official within his lights, which probably were not as strict as we are accustomed to in the U.S. But Soong, he went on, has good plans for China, involving land and taxation reform, highway building, etc., which also may be in the offing once the Gimo gets back.

Stuart touched briefly on his conversation with Petrov. He said Petrov had expressed the opinion that the U.S. presence here was aiding one side. Commenting to me, Stuart said this was in effect correct, and it was a position the U.S. could not defend. He said that if the negotiations finally came to nothing he favored U.S. withdrawal but continued U.S. support of China—rather than the KMT—with pressure on the government to reform, applied in such a way as not to offend the Chinese. Chiang, he said, is capable of being very stubborn when he feels he is being forced into something arrogantly; he will stand on his dignity and take the consequences. Stuart said he thought an important element in U.S. policy should be always to keep the door open for Communist participation in the government—never let them be frozen out.

There was a lunch at the International Club for some performers of the Chinese Cultural Theater Group who were putting on tonight's presentation of *An Evening in Cathay*. They are about to open a tour in the United States. Their director-producer is a Miss Averil Tam, who impressed me as a sort of Chinese Greer Garson. Each member of the troupe was "the foremost" something in China: foremost Mandarin speaker, foremost movie actress, foremost *p'i p'a* soloist, etc. Conversation at the seven-course lunch with Miss Tam made me think the performance would be very interesting and entertaining, and so it turned out to be. The affair was held at the OMEA auditorium, with Lee Wei-kuo, who is just back from six weeks in Manchuria, acting as master of ceremonies. It was worth going through the rain (whip end of a typhoon that hit the Fukien coast) to attend. The dances and the music, though completely Chinese, were good. Excellence in an art, however strange the forms may be to an alien, generally shows through in the performer. They are all amateurs, most of them with non-artistic ways of making a living. Sung Yue-teh, the *p'i p'a* soloist, works for the Shanghai Power Company.

NANKING, September 27—One scrap I left out of yesterday's entry. After seeing Stuart, on the embassy grounds I encountered Bradley Connors of USIS. He asked for my phone number; said Marshall had told him I would like to be kept informed. I asked if he would stay here awhile; he said about a month. He had come up from Shanghai "to keep Stuart out of trouble." Was Stuart in trouble? Well, he had been talking a lot recently to newspapermen, and Philip Fugh had been doing a lot of talking too. I mentally filed this information away. Perhaps Marshall has concluded that Stuart is too naïve and is keeping a check on him; perhaps embassy underlings are watching Stuart; one cannot rule out the possibility that the "sabotage" that Hurley complained of—if it existed—is still going on, potentially.

For lunch I had arranged through Chiang Kang-chen, my new translator-assistant, for an invitation sight unseen to Liang Shu-ming, secretary-general of the Democratic League. Also present: Fred Gruin and his interpreter, Colin Ho; Chiang Kang-chen; David Lu; Liang's interpreter, also named Lu; and John A. Bottorf, SSU, who dropped in on me Wednesday, bearing two bottles of Johnny Walker Red Label, a gift from Moscrip in Shanghai.

I called for Liang at his house. He is an elderly, thin, tall Chinese with a grizzled, close-cropped head. He wore a mandarin gown as did his interpreter, Lu, who graduated from Yenching in 1938 and has visited England. Liang spoke no English, but Lu's was good. Liang turned out to be a vegetarian, and I was sorry I had not calculated that a non-English-speaker would prefer Chinese food. But Lu explained that he was not strict, taking to vegetarianism only because he was a student of Hindu philosophy, and could eat vegetables that were cooked with meat; so he was able to eat everything in Chiao's usual excellent meal except the beef.

The conversation before, during, and after the lunch was interesting for several things. One was Liang's denial that the KMT was a party of landlords. Having heard Lo Lung-chi and others parrot this Communist claim, I was intrigued. China, said Liang, is not divided on a class basis. He said the parties are fluid, in effect "floating on water." Fred Gruin's attempt to get him to state the basis of support for each ended in nothing more than this.

He echoed the Communist line that a cessation of hostilities was the first requisite. When Fred suggested there already had been two cease-fires and that each time fighting had continued, Liang said things were different now. Certain agreements had been reached during the June truce. I asked if it were not true that the Communist attack on the Lunghai Railway and in Shantung, June 9, two days after the truce started, had not caused the present military situation. Again he ducked; said the government had attacked first, but in any case it wasn't important now who attacked whom.

I attempted without success to get him to say why the Democratic League should refuse to participate in the National Assembly when that offered them a chance to shape the government to their liking, a chance they would not have if they stayed out. Why not pull out afterward if they failed to get things set up as they wished? Lu, the interpreter, did some arguing of his own on this point. Liang argued that the delegates were not democratically elected, were Kuomintang appointees; the KMT draft constitution was bad. He had no answer when I pointed out that the KMT's delegates had nothing to do with those of the Democratic League, which they could name by any method they chose; and that the constitution was there to be worked on.

Fred asked: if the Communists, as they threaten, held their own National Assembly, would the Democratic League participate in that? Liang said it hadn't been decided; there would be a consultation soon. He seemed to see no inconsistency in being against a KMT-called Assembly on the principle that it was a one-party affair, and being willing to consider joining in a Communist Assembly which obviously would be a one-party affair.

There was nothing in the discussion to bear out Peng's statement to me that the League was a bunch of opportunists. Liang seemed willing to stick to the Communists, albeit with a nondiscriminating acceptance of what seem specious arguments to me. Peng may be thinking of Carson Chang.

A cable from Betty reports a good trip by the family to San Francisco and that "the strike still continues." The legend indicated it was sent either the seventeenth or twenty-first, not later—six or ten days to reach me. Ta Kung Pao says the four hundred missionaries (who are on the same ship) are boarding ship "immediately" so I suppose the family is now on its way.

NANKING, September 30—Dave got a call from the Executive Yuan for us to come over at eleven to see Dr. Soong. He came back to town Saturday but did not go to the office as he was not feeling well. We waited in the conference room until Fugh was through.

T.V. was, as usual, busy with documents but was cordial to us both. He seemed in good health, although he complained that he still was not feeling well and planned to get away soon for a real rest. I inquired about a report in two Shanghai English papers that he was going to the U.S. to attend the International Monetary Fund conference. He said he was not going and hadn't intended to. He hoped to go to Tsingtao to "lie on the beach for a couple of weeks."

Since I had not seen him since before my Hong Kong trip I had prepared a list of things I wanted to talk about. Second item was the monetary situation: the Shanghai papers were speculating about another devaluation and claimed that China was required by the IMF to declare a parity for its currency before the end of the year. T.V. said China was exempted from that provision under an arrangement which gave wider latitude to countries which had been under enemy occupation. I suggested that point needed clearing up. He had a yellow legal-size pad in front of him. He folded the top sheet in half, cut it off with a letter opener, and wrote out a two-paragraph statement (1) denying he was going to the U.S. and (2) pointing out the exemption on a foreign exchange declaration. Perhaps, I said, the order might be reversed so as not to overemphasize the former. "Put it in journalese," he said, waving his hand.

Dave seemed hesitant to mention his own business—his desire to go back home for medical reasons—so I brought it up. T.V. said that of course Dave's health came first and he should be guided by that. Dave said the best time would be right after my family arrived.

No. 5 on my list was the political situation. I said my current impression was that U.S. withdrawal was not as imminent as I had thought last time I saw him. Marshall did not want to pull out while there was any hope of success or do anything that would block negotiations. I said I considered the period between now and the National Assembly's work crucial to relations with the U.S. The papers had stories of arrests being made in the government's investigation of corruption in Canton during the "takeover" period. Whatever could be done to show that the government was determined to root out corruption should be done, I said, adding that I had heard the Gimo had some administrative changes planned involving mayors and provincial governors, and some moves on land and tax reform. T.V. confirmed it but offered no details. As to the investigation in Canton, he said that when the report came in something could be done to show that the Executive Yuan was not involved in any of it. T.V. still tends to overlook the point that even though his own skirts may be clean corruption anywhere in the government has a damaging effect on China. But I did not press the point since it can await the report.

He asked me what I thought of the general situation. I said it looked better: the Communist military threat had been pretty well broken and their propaganda had defeated its own purpose since early in July. He agreed with this estimate, and went into reasons why, looking back from this vantage point. American officers overrated the Communist military strength because they knew the KMT weaknesses but not the Communist weaknesses. He had seen it happen time and again in China, even under the war lords. A general might have one division of crack troops, but whenever he tried to expand it into an army or several armies the thing disintegrated and fell of its own weight and inefficiency. The answer, he said, was training. The Communists had relatively few trained troops. They had expanded from a few thousand before the war to probably 800,000 of the 1,200,000 they claim now, and the same thing has happened to them. Besides, they have no air force. He said the government's experience during the war was that guerrilla operations are effective only from bases, and then only for a short distance around those bases. The thing to do, therefore, was to smash the Communist bases—not Yenan, since that was too far away, but places like Kalgan.

He said recapture of Communist territory had turned KMT troops fanatically against the Communists because of the killings of villagers they uncovered. "The Communists rule by terrorism," he said. He emphasized that his estimate of the situation and its needs was in retrospect and confidential.

Just before we saw T.V., one of his aides, C. P. Kiang, had mentioned to me the problem of the press hostel in Broadway Mansions. I knew I was borrowing trouble if I raised it, but I did. I suggested that the correspondents should by rights pay for their housing now that the war was over, but if they were going to be evicted from part or all of their space in Broadway Mansions they would need equivalent space elsewhere. T.V. rang a buzzer summoning Kiang and told him that when S. Y. Liu, the Shanghai alien property administrator, arrived Wednesday he was to get in touch with me.

During the afternoon Chris Rand of the New York *Herald Tribune* dropped in and I gave him a hint of impending action on Broadway Mansions to carry back to Shanghai so that the correspondents would be partially softened up to expect the worst. I know, of course, that no matter what the final solution is it won't satisfy them; even leaving them totally undisturbed will give them only temporary satisfaction. They have families here now, or on the way over, and want to expand.

Chris had heard that the Gimo was about to issue a statement. I made inquiries of Lee Wei-kuo, who said the rumor had been around town all day, and Peng, who said he knew nothing about it—though he had just come back from the Gimo's and seemed distraught. Peng quickly okayed T.V.'s brief statement for release, and agreed with Dave that he had to go back to Washington for reasons of health.

After dinner, when Dave came back from a visit to see Stuart and call at Central News, he had the explanation of the rumor. Marshall and Stuart had suggested to the Gimo that he issue a very conciliatory, polite open letter to the Communists, offering them every inducement to come back into negotiation. It proposed simultaneous efforts on military and political questions by the Committee of Three and by Stuart's five-member group, and a cease-fire order thereafter. The Gimo had agreed to put it out not later than tonight. But at the last moment he had added a final sentence which in the Americans' opinion destroyed the entire effect, something saying that all the above conditions had to be met before a cease-fire would be issued. Marshall had called on Chiang again and had said that if the statement went out that way he would withdraw. Hence no statement tonight. Somehow this story depresses me.

CHAPTER TWELVE

Biggest U.S.-Chiang crisis occurs when Marshall urges General-issimo to delay government drive on Communist-held city of Kalgan. Generalissimo finally offers ten-day truce but Communists reject it. Marshall and Stuart issue joint statement reciting facts which tend in net to blame Communists. Government takes Kalgan.

Marshall was rather overdoing his threats to quit. The perspective of time suggests his repetition of this threat tended to depreciate its effectiveness. Yet in the atmosphere of Shakespearean tragedy which enveloped Nanking at the time it seemed—at least to me—that his departure was all it would take to let slip the sleeping dogs of war. And as the Bard remarked in another place, there's nothing either good or bad but thinking makes it so. Marshall thought the government's determination to drive the Communists from Kalgan was bad; to me Marshall's departure from the scene would be bad; ergo, either was bad and both were bad. My feeling of impending doom came at the start of a ten-day period that proved in fact to be critical in terms of my personal mission to "keep the Chinese out of trouble with the United States." The importance of the crisis was clearer after it was over, as often happens, since the distraction of other, more routine events dulled the immediate perception that a turning point had passed.

NANKING, October 1—Tonight the Chiang Kai-shek government appears to be at the crossroads. It looks like the payoff. But

I hedge that by remembering there have been several times before when I thought the final showdown had come, only to discover that life went on about as usual and tension drained away.

The day has, however, had a note of urgency. I started by feeling depressed and tried to study a memorandum T.V. had asked me to look over, proposing a two-year program of adult education for democracy suggested by an Old China Hand, Frank W. Price of Richmond, Virginia. There was word of meetings going on: Marshall, Stuart, Wang Ping-nan, T.V., the Gimo—everybody seeing everybody else. Word came that Wang had handed Chou En-lai's reply to Marshall, responding to the three-part list Marshall had brought back from Kuling. Gerald Samson of the MOI's London office, who is here on a tour of China for the British Liberals, came in to say that he was with Ambassador Stuart when the latter got a phone call from T.V. and had to leave, inviting him to lunch to finish the conversation later.

After lunch Samson reported the crisis was here. He quoted Stuart: "We will have very good news, or very bad news, within forty-eight hours." I received the daily Communist release containing the text of Chou's letter. A distracted reading of it indicated Chou was only repeating his blanket demand for a cease-fire, but there did appear to be a different and urgent tone in that he also demanded that the government immediately halt its advance on Kalgan or take the blame for splitting China in two.

Figuring that when I saw T.V. he would probably be very rushed, I prepared a brief memo boiling down my feeling of urgency about the situation in one page. I put no special effort in it, but stressed the importance of not forcing Marshall to leave, lest the government be blamed by the U.S. for rejecting peace. Then I went to the Executive Yuan.

Daylight saving ended last night and it was dusk by the time I climbed the two flights of the spacious, Chinese-style building. T.V. was still at work, and I waited in Jim Brennan's old office until it was quite dark—six-fifty or thereabouts—before the connecting door opened and Soong's bodyguard beckoned me in.

Soong's black felt hat was laid out on the divan and he had his black lacquer cane in his hand, and a gracious smile on his face. I got the message, but I handed him the memo and said it was terribly important. He started to read it and because the light was bad he walked over to his desk and switched on the small green-shaded desk light. He read it over, slowly, and then remarked that he had not seen Chou's statement. I had anticipated that, though I was sure he must know its contents, and handed it to him. He read it through, sneering at some of the propaganda in the first part of it. "Well," he said, "I'll think this over." I said if he wanted to talk about it to give me a ring, at any hour. "It won't be to-night," he said. "Maybe tomorrow." There was a suggestion, I thought, that he disagreed with my argument and was merely smoothing it over, but I could not be sure.

We walked downstairs to where his Lincoln was waiting. He said, "By the way, I fired T. F. Tsiang today. It was getting impossible to get along with him. P. H. Ho will replace him as head of CNRRA." When I got home Fred Gruin told me his interpreter, Colin Ho, had come in with a report, apparently straight, that the Gimo was going to call off the Kalgan attack. I wondered if it were true and whether T.V. already knew it when I saw him.

Then I saw Dave, who was typing in our office. He shut the door and announced dramatically: "China is at the crossroads of its history tonight." He had received a call from Stuart and had gone over to the embassy to see him. Marshall had informed the Gimo today that unless he ordered a halt to the Kalgan offensive he would pull out and the U.S. would end all its aid—everything. Dave went on, obviously quoting the sequence of Stuart's remarks: "Marshall has been here ten months now." I felt Dave's excitement, and had to remind myself that after all I had told T.V. on September 8 that this moment was coming. The Communist desperation over Kalgan doesn't alter the military facts as they existed yesterday. I got out a carbon of my memo to T.V. and asked Dave to read it.

Fred Gruin had invited the Communists to dinner, and around

seven-thirty they arrived: Wang Ping-nan, a Mr. Wu, a Miss Wu, and a Miss Chiang. They all had beers while Fred and I had scotch and water, and we sat in the living room and discussed the weather and other non-political topics somewhat self-consciously and rather pleasantly. It turned out that Wu and the two girls were all Yenching graduates. The two girls were plainly dressed and not beautiful, but attractive. Even Wang, when you see him often enough, loses some of his sinister, bulletheaded, slant-eyed appearance. We continued inconsequential talk at the dinner table. Chiao, my cook, as usual had a wonderfully good meal: mushroom soup, roast chicken with browned whole potatoes, tomatoes, and Jello and peaches.

We finally took a cautious venture into politics when I remarked that Chen Li-fu had told me the story of his contacts with Chou En-lai over some twenty years and I would like to hear Chou's account of the same period. Wang thought Chou would be happy to tell me sometime.

Then Fred began asking some questions. Wang filled him in on the fact that Chou had replied to Marshall, that the Communists had rejected the government's invitation to attend the National Assembly, and casually—so casually I missed it and learned of it only later when Fred remarked on it after they left—that Marshall had told the Gimo today that he must call off the Kalgan offensive. I suppose I missed it because I already knew it from Dave, and Fred did not. But the Communists seem to know as much about Marshall as Stuart does.

Wang spoke mostly in English but lapsed occasionally into Chinese and Miss Wu did the translating. He spoke with finality about Communist attitudes, not as one who had to think over what his group might have to say. He said that if the Gimo called off the Kalgan offensive and agreed to discuss military and political questions concurrently it would bring the Communists back into the negotiations. He claimed the Communists did not know officially the Gimo had agreed to the latter. Fred pointed out that this was not the same as a general cease-fire order, as set forth as a condition in their propaganda, and Wang blandly agreed. He also explained why the Communists rejected participation in the National Assembly: (1) they could not talk peace while fighting is going on; (2) the order fixing November 12 for the National Assembly was taken unilaterally by Chiang. There is some merit to his first point, but the second is more an excuse than a reason.

Wang and Miss Wu asked questions about U.S. reaction to Wallace and about election prospects. Wang noted that Ickes had backed Wallace, and when we turned to a discussion of the State Department, he knew who was head of Far Eastern affairs, who was his assistant, who was head of the China desk, and who was his assistant. I wonder if Foreign Minister Wang Shih-chieh could name them all.

NANKING, October 2—It looks as though the break will come tomorrow.

Central Daily News came out with an editorial that was distinctly not conciliatory, ending with a warning to the people to be prepared for worse things to come. To me it was the tip-off.

Henry Tseng brought word that Peng wanted me to stand by at the MOI, but noon came and went without Peng's return from the Gimo's, where he had been summoned at 7 A.M. The wait was broken by lunch with Eric Chou and one of *Ta Kung Pao*'s editorial writers, Hsiao Chien, recently returned from England, and his very attractive half-English, half-Chinese wife. I left early to get back to the MOI by two o'clock. Although the weekly press conference was scheduled for three-thirty, it was not until three-twenty that Charlie Wan came in with some material to be typed out.

It was the government's letter to Marshall, imposing two conditions: (1) upping the Communist-Democratic League strength on the State Council from twelve to thirteen seats by providing that one of the four non-partisan members be nominated by the Communists and agreed to by the government, in return for which the Communists should nominate their candidates for the State Council as well as for the National Assembly; (2) working out a concrete program, with timetable, for allocating Communist troop locations. These two accomplished, a truce would follow.

It was obviously not what the Communists would accept. My only thought was that perhaps it held the door open just a day or so more, for instead of a yes or no on the vital question, there came the usual ambiguous words.

After a few minutes Charlie Wan came in with a more provocative precede statement. He had been working on it all day. It was, of course, something translated directly out of the Gimo's own Chinese, and therefore past doing anything with. Polishing up the English, however, kept the press conference waiting until four-forty. Peng had given orders earlier in the day to make it a joint Chinese-foreign affair, and had arranged for the *Central Daily News* auditorium to accommodate the crowd. At least fifty were on hand, and the foreign correspondents were practically lost among them. It was, of course, a bilingual affair. Chinese and English texts were distributed. Peng read first the Chinese version, then the English. To subsequent questions he was very evasive. He had to be; he had to avoid any mention of Kalgan, under instructions, and to stick to his text. One pertinent question from a Chinese correspondent was: how could the government "give" a non-partisan seat to the Communists? Peng's answer: the government was doing its utmost to make concessions and this was the best that could be done. This was verbally translated for me by Chiang Kang-chen.

I was expected at the Executive Yuan to see S. Y. Liu. We discussed the Broadway Mansions housing problem for the foreign correspondents and decided it would have to be worked out in Shanghai. General J. L. Huang was to represent the interests of the U. S. Army, which wanted twelve floors, and I the interests of the foreign correspondents; we would try to work out a mutually satisfactory agreement and then take it to Liu for approval.

By this time it was 6 P.M. and I debated whether, in view of last night's experience with T.V., when he obviously didn't want to be bothered, to wait to see him or let it slide for tonight. I decided that since I had submitted a memo I owed it to myself to follow through, and at least find out what had happened to it.

I did not have to wait long and found T.V. in an affable mood. A sudden heat wave took the temperature up to ninety today and he was dressed in a lightweight blue slack suit and was closing a window, complaining of lumbago, when I entered. He said he had passed along the memo—"showed it," he said—to the Gimo, who remarked he was bearing it in mind, among many other considerations he had to weigh. I told him the current status of the Broadway Mansions business, remarking that I was approaching the job with the knowledge that no matter what the outcome was the correspondents would not be satisfied. He laughed and said, "Of course this is a bad time to get them stirred up. The money involved is of little consequence, but it's the principle of the thing." We also discussed Price's memo on education, which I had thought was good, involving visual education and radio, both neglected in China, but that of course it was long-range.

T.V. stretched out in his chair with the air of a man who had passed the point of decision with respect to the negotiations. Yet he kept returning to them. He asked about the arrival of my family. Was my house okay? Was there anything he could do? This was all under the heading, "Let's talk about more pleasant things." But then he came back to Topic A.

"If the Americans pull out, it becomes a fight for survival of the state," he said. "It will be all out—Democratic League and everything." I said surely the Communists could not regain any military threat if the Kalgan offensive were called off, but he said they could. I said that if they came into the government they would cause him trouble and raise a lot of hell, but I honestly thought it would be good for China.

"If they come into the Executive Yuan I would feel that I must get out," he said. I ventured with a "come, now" air that secretly, while he hated being Premier, he would hate not being Premier more.

"No," he said, "you don't know my background. I am fond of comfort. I am pleasure-loving. I only took this job out of patriotism. I don't like the constant criticism, the attacks on me." Returning to Kalgan, he remarked that while the Nationalists held off their attack the economic situation "gets worse every day."

Depressing as it was to contemplate the war threat and its economic consequences, there was a man-to-man feeling about the conversation that warmed me to T.V. as a man who, I had grown to feel, was doing his honest and able best for his country.

At dinner—no guests tonight—Dave, Fred, and I discussed the harping of the liberals on the idea that the U.S. should get out of China, and the frame of mind which prompted them to indignation that a coolie had been killed by a marine, which was understandable enough, but at the same time to ignore it completely when the navy assigned seven planes to fly vaccine to a Communist epidemic area. I reflected bitterly that the same Chinese liberals who professed to believe it was the U.S. fomenting civil war who would be first to be clapped in jail if the U.S. withdrew and it became a question of "survival of the state."

Peng had asked me to stop by General Marshall's to explain a change in the last paragraph of the English text of the letter to Marshall—something I had suggested because the original text made no sense to me. After dinner I went over, intending to tell Hutchin that it was nothing sinister and let him pass the information along to Marshall. But Marshall was there and he motioned me to a chair. The furniture had been arranged for a movie. Marshall read over the sentence and agreed that it made no difference. The important thing, Hutch commented, was whether it made a difference to Chou En-lai.

Marshall told me, in substance, what I had already learned second hand from Stuart via Dave and from Wang Ping-nan. I handed him a carbon of my memo to T.V. to let him know I was putting in my two bits' worth for what I thought would help keep the negotiations open. He questioned me about the wording of one paragraph, and I realized I had worded it a bit ambiguously, but I assured him T.V. understood my point, which was that if the Marshall Mission had to break up at this point, for the sake of U.S. relations it must not be the government which caused the break. It was a phrase adding "let the Communists do it" which had caught his attention. He seemed satisfied.

He seemed under great strain, as well he might. He said that in June the Gimo had agreed to let the Communists keep Kalgan —it was virtually the only concession the government made—but he now was admitting openly he was out to take Kalgan. What the Gimo proposed would take time to work out; thus he (Marshall) was putting the U.S. in the position of aiding the KMT in the use of prolonged negotiations as a cloak for crushing the Communists. This he would not do, and had so told the Gimo.

But despite his strain, he brushed it clear from his mind and in a seemingly serene mood he ordered the movie to start. There first was a War Department short, *Seeds of Destiny*, containing a depressing series of shots of the kids left in Europe—maimed, sightless, starving. In view of the tension I felt reflected from him, it was nerve-racking. It was followed by a fairly good murder mystery, *Deadline for Murder*, I think it was titled. Hutch drove me home afterward.

NANKING, October 3—Last night, after writing down the experiences of yesterday, I got to thinking—chiefly because of the intense strain I had seen Marshall under—that I owed it to him not to let my own effort end where it stood. I drafted a memo to the Gimo, very brief, less than a page, putting in simplest terms my feeling about the danger to the government in Chou's maneuver. This morning I sent it off by messenger. I told no one about it, neither Peng, nor Soong, nor Marshall.

I waited all morning, reading clippings, without hearing anything of my request for an interview—today—with the Gimo. Gerald Samson came in and told me two interesting things: (1) in talking to Madame Chiang yesterday he raised the question of Kalgan; why couldn't the government hold off that drive in the interests of peace? Madame Chiang said that after all Kalgan was on the railway line to Peking, and therefore must be considered a threat to Peking. (2) Sun Fo, this morning, told him he thought the Kalgan drive should be called off, and also spoke very definitely of the Communist problem as being part and parcel of the world Communist problem.

The first item I found interesting because of General Marshall's mention last night that in June the government had agreed to let the Communists keep Kalgan. Now to have Madame Chiang, who up to now has shown complete sympathy with and understanding for the American point of view, argue for going ahead and taking Kalgan was indication to me that the temptation is too great and has infected the whole government, not only the army. It was a more definite statement of the same attitude T.V. had indicated yesterday.

The second item was interesting because I have been wondering about Sun Fo, and this seemed a sound viewpoint. I feel the drive on Kalgan should be called off, but at the same time I think we are just kidding ourselves if we fail to recognize that the Chinese Communists are regular Comintern Communists.

Immediately after lunch I got a call saying the minister wanted me to meet him in his office to go to see the Gimo at four o'clock. I phoned Hutchin just to let him know I was going. Peng did not seem offended at my having acted without consulting him. From what he said I gathered that my letter had gone to the National Government instead of the Gimo's headquarters, and had been sent back to the ministry for translation. He advised me to send such things direct to Shen Chang-huan, particularly if they were confidential.

We waited at the headquarters until Pei Tsu-i came out. Liu Chieh had arrived meanwhile, and the three of us went in together, with Shen and the Gimo's other secretary, Tsao, who took notes in a little book during the conversation. T.V. was just leaving. The Gimo was in the civilian version of uniform, with the inevitable Parker pen in his breast pocket. His usually close-cropped hair had been cut recently, so that he seemed bald. He did not seem under particular strain.

He gave me a more attentive reception, however, than any time so far. It showed in his eyes, in long pauses when he said nothing but thought it over, fingering his mustache, or holding his nose in his fist, or examining his nails, or crossing his legs and jiggling the free foot. Shen Chang-huan did the translating, for which I was glad, and for the first time I felt I had done a good job of getting my ideas across, because I had thought out an outline in advance and I presented it in short takes.

He said he had read my memo and wanted me to elaborate on it. I reiterated the main points: the present period is crucial; the Communist demands amount to a propaganda trap; if it was to be countered the action must be molded into the present situation, and not superimposed later on whatever comes out. The important point—the crux—was that under no circumstances should the government take the action that brought the Marshall Mission to an end. If there was no choice but that, let the Communists be the ones to do it. Therefore: why not call off the drive to Kalgan, giving the Communists until October 12 (which I understood was the deadline for sending out the National Assembly notification) to nominate their candidates and participate in the Committee of Three, which, after all, they themselves had demanded. Attach no other conditions. Would this not put the Communists on the spot? I added that I did not entertain the illusion that this would solve everything, for the Communists were clever and resourceful, but I did think it would put the onus on them.

I knew I was putting it on a completely cynical basis, but I felt the Gimo was forced to look at the situation cynically and he could best be approached on that basis. I even went so far as to say I personally was convinced that the Communists did not honestly want to join the government—which was not quite true, although my doubts about their intentions are damn few by this time—and they should be given a chance to prove it through such a maneuver.

I fancied Liu Chieh's jaw rather dropped as I stuck my two bits into the negotiations and that Peng was also agog, though I could not see his face. I knew there was danger that my proposal would be interpreted as having come from Marshall—when as a matter of fact he may actually be sore when he learns about it—but thought that to protest to the contrary would only create that impression if it was not in his mind.

The Gimo remarked in passing that October 12 was not a deadline for the National Assembly, but he mentioned it only as a correction of fact and not as something that made the scheme impossible. He wanted to know just how this plan could be accomplished. I said that if I were doing it I would make a very terse announcement stating very simply that the government was unilaterally halting the drive on Kalgan, and asking the Communists to respond by making their nominations for the State Council and National Assembly. Chiang replied that cease-fires could not be ordered unilaterally; the way he put it was, what if the government stopped fighting and the Communists did not? It had been tried twice before. I said I knew that truce had to be a bilateral act, but I wondered if it would not be actually possible with the government apparently in such complete military control. The Gimo thought this over but gave me no argument.

His next thought was that in any case the government must await the next move of the Communists. I said I felt the same way but what I was fearful of was that there might not be time— Marshall might act too soon. I was careful to add, without belaboring the point, that I had avoided asking Marshall how long he would stay because I wanted to give the government my independent judgment on it.

The Gimo said he would consider my proposal. He conversed with Peng and Liu in turn. I picked up enough of the latter conversation to realize that Liu's presence was purely coincidental, he apparently having shown up to bid the Gimo good-by before leaving for the UN meeting in the U.S. The Gimo brought the interview to an end—it was businesslike throughout, without the customary tea—by saying he wanted me to come in oftener.

I drove immediately to the Executive Yuan to meet General Huang and S. Y. Liu on the Broadway Mansions problem. We decided to meet in Shanghai Saturday to look the situation over on the ground. T.V. had gone home early and I did not see him.

Chen Li-fu came to dinner. I had thought I could, under the

guise of having him meet Fred Gruin, work in a bit of feeling-out
on the possibility of converting him to a halt-the-drive-on-Kalgan
campaign, but after a few minutes gave up the idea completely.
He told Fred the same story I've heard so often. I did manage
during the evening to confirm, I think without overemphasis,
that he is board chairman of *Ta Kang Pao*. He said it was something in name only, which does not seem reasonable to me.

Dave came in late to say that Stuart had asked his opinion
on the advisability of resigning if Marshall pulled out. Dave said
he had counseled resigning, on the ground that he had no political support in the U.S., and why hang around until he is eased
out?

NANKING, October 6—On my return from Shanghai Dave
filled me in on his information from Stuart: the peace negotiations have taken a sudden turn for the better. The Gimo has
agreed to a ten-day Kalgan truce, with a few minor conditions
such as Communist nomination of candidates for the State Council and National Assembly. Marshall and Stuart may announce
it jointly today. It will give the Communists a chance to prove
whether they really want to keep negotiating.

NANKING, October 7—General Marshall held an off-the-record
press conference this afternoon for the American correspondents.
According to the account that I received, he told them of the
weekend developments. The Gimo has agreed to a ten-day truce
on Kalgan, with certain conditions relating to the National Assembly and the nomination of candidates, and also conditions
relating to Communist removal from certain areas which are
mostly academic now anyhow because the government has retaken most of the territory involved. Now it is up to the Communists to reply, and they have been reminded they had better
do it quickly or the government would beat them to the goal by
taking Kalgan.

Marshall also said a misunderstanding had taken place between
himself and the Gimo and explained how it happened. After the

Gimo got back from Kuling he had presented the Gimo with the draft of a proposed open letter containing seven points (which he did not list for the correspondents). He told the Gimo that he could accept the seven-point program as a Marshall proposal if he took it all, but could not pick out individual parts of it and call it a Marshall proposal. The Gimo studied the letter a couple of days, then agreed to it with one change, a final sentence which according to Marshall vitiated the whole meaning of it. Marshall told him that if that was his attitude the government was just using the negotiations as a cloak for its operations against Kalgan, and since the U.S. could not be put in such a position as mediator, he had no choice but to cable President Truman recommending his recall.

At this point (and Marshall did not relate this, which came to Dave from Stuart) he actually drafted and dispatched a message to Truman. But here Stuart stepped in. Then in Chinese face-saving fashion (by means of a third party) he let the Gimo know. Chiang held up the offending sentence and Marshall's message was caught in the nick of time. Two hours later it would have been in Truman's hands.

Then (back to Marshall's account) the misunderstanding arose when Central News referred to one of the seven points by itself, asserting that the government had agreed to Marshall's proposal that concurrent military-political negotiations be held in the Committee of Three and Stuart's five-member committee. This led to an official denial of sponsorship by Marshall and an oblique retraction in Central News. Peng had told me at the time about Marshall's protest but he did not explain it, and its significance therefore escaped me.

Sunday, when Marshall and Stuart spent four hours with Chiang, the two generals had a man-to-man talk and discovered that it was not dirty work by Chiang but a misunderstanding that was eating them both. Central News had made a mistake. That led to the Gimo's agreement to Marshall's proposal and the dispatch of the offer to the Communists.

Dave left tonight en route to the U.S. He seemed pretty much cheered up by the prospect. He has no passage yet but will arrange it in Shanghai and will be there in any case when the family arrives.

NANKING, October 8—Toward evening I got a call from C. P. Kiang of T.V.'s office inquiring about the Broadway Mansions deal. I went on over. While I was talking to him about it, it developed that Stuart and Marshall had put out a joint statement. Unable to get Hutchin on the phone, I called Hank Lieberman, who described it to me. It was a terse recital of the facts, occasioned by the Communist rejection of the Gimo's offer of a ten-day Kalgan truce, and it left the blame pointing strongly at the Communists.

When I notified the receptionist I wanted to see Dr. Soong it turned out he had sent a car to try to find me. The Gimo had called a meeting of his advisers after the statement (which was issued without notification to the government). With Soong were General Yu Ta-wei, the Gimo's negotiator in the Committee of Three, and Peng. T.V. said there was some difference of opinion whether the government should issue a statement. He was inclined to favor one, a terse statement reciting the facts and putting the government's position on record. I agreed, and we drafted one forthwith. It sought (1) to emphasize the repeated Communist rejections at each stage of the current efforts to end the deadlock, and (2) hold the door open for further negotiations and Communist participation.

While we waited for it to be typed T.V. remarked: "I thought I was going to get a week's rest, but now it doesn't look that way." He was worried about rising commodity prices. I told him I had bought two tons of coal at the bargain rate of 290,000 CNC a ton, but would have to pay $350,000 next time. He said it should not cost that much; surely I could get it for 150,000 a ton. "If it were not for this Communist imbroglio," he said, "China would be sitting pretty right now."

NANKING, October 9—T.V. went back to the Gimo's for dinner last night and C. P. Kiang informed me today he will be leaving in the morning for a week in Tsingtao, after all.

Nathaniel Peffer came to dinner, nursing a bad cold. He was as bearish about China as when I last saw him in Shanghai. The country, he said, is ruled by garrison commanders, with repression everywhere. He said at one place he was told they didn't have to kill more than five or six a day. He said the Wen I-to assassination in Kunming had made a deep impression in educational and liberal circles, and he expected that after the colleges opened there was likely to be a big memorial meeting somewhere—Peking or Shanghai, but not Kunming because the repression there is harsh—touching off a spark that will run like electricity through the country. He plans to confine himself to writing magazine articles, because one cannot predict far enough into the future to make a book worth while. He spoke in the bitterest terms about the Gimo, T.V., and Madame Chiang.

Marshall flew to Shanghai and back today to confer with Chou En-lai—the first such call. I don't know what it means.

NANKING, October 10—Today was a holiday—the Double Tenth. I had a lousy night, unable to sleep, worrying whether the radiators will be installed in the house before it turns cold, convinced I was suffering from some disease I couldn't recognize, annoyed because the house was too cold to get up and read. Finally I wrapped the quilt around me and read in bed.

Peng had planned a picnic for the foreign correspondents at a spot twenty miles out in the country known as the Rock of the Thousand Buddhas. But when I got to the MOI I found him at work on a statement. Chiang Kai-shek's presidential term was up and the KMT's Standing Committee, meeting at 9 A.M., had extended it until the new executive elected under the constitution takes office. This held up proceedings an hour and a half, but we finally got off. The road was rough and dusty, but the temple and rock were rather worth it. We had a picnic lunch of sandwiches, cakes, chestnuts, bananas, etc., and then climbed part way up the hill but gave it up because it was getting late.

Peng asked me to go with him to the reception being given by the Chiangs at the National Government headquarters. I had not wanted to go but agreed to do so and was glad I had. It was strictly an official diplomatic affair. Peng had two guests, a Mr. and Mrs. Yung, he a cotton magnate who was kidnaped in Shanghai a couple of months ago for $2 million U.S. ransom. Peng wore a tux, Yung a blue Chinese gown with a black jacket. We arrived about half an hour late, at five. The U. S. Embassy and MAGIC officers were out in force. Around five-fifteen the Gimo and Madame Chiang arrived, walking down a center aisle cleared through the guests to the big head table of sandwiches and other hors d'oeuvre, behind which they took up their posts. About fifty persons passed by to shake hands, after which, with hundreds more milling around the huge room, the Chiangs invited everyone to have tea. He wore civilian uniform without ornaments except for four rows of service ribbons. She was in a Chinese flowered dress with a black jacket. He seemed in good health, unworried, at ease; I thought she was forcing her smile a bit.

Peng drew me away, with his guests, to see the building, which he said could seldom be seen by outsiders. It turned out to be a very elaborate affair, with Chinese-style courtyards and covered walks extending a long distance back to the presidential office building itself, a yellow brick structure erected during the presidency of Lin Sen.

It was about four stories high. We rode a small Otis elevator up to the third floor and saw the big council room with tables in the form of an elongated E where the Standing Committee of the KMT's Central Executive Committee holds session; where it had met this morning, with Chiang absent, to re-elect him to his third (not consecutive) term, and where the Supreme National Defense Council meets each week. Peng, although not a member, attends as Minister of Information.

We also saw the President's office on the second floor. It is a small room, smaller than my dining room, with wood-paneled walls and a blue décor in rug and chairs. The President's desk, of some light wood, lacquered, modernistic with a glass top, is placed obliquely near a window, with only a few desk gadgets on it, including a row of writing brushes in holders. Three telephones are on a small table to his left, just in front of the window. There are small reception rooms on each side of the office, one in blue and one in green. The atmosphere of the suite is one of quiet, unostentatious neatness and dignity.

NANKING, October 11—A visit to Colonel J. Hart Caughey filled me in on the current status of negotiations. Marshall is coasting for the time being; everything is up to Stuart. Stuart is hobnobbing with the leaders of the Youth Party and the Democratic League on a plan to entice Chou En-lai back to Nanking from Shanghai so that negotiations may be resumed. Marshall's visit to Chou in Shanghai was an attempt to put him on the spot. It was against protocol and therefore should increase the pressure to get him back. Caughey's personal opinion is that Chou went down to mend some fences with the Democratic League.

Kalgan fell to the government at 2 P.M., according to Central News from Kweisui, although Nanking military sources do not yet have confirmation. If the report is correct, the Nationalists did take it within their ten- to fifteen-day prediction.

The Communist release for today carried the text of Chou's letter to Marshall. His first reason for turning down Chiang's terms was that, "according to the principles of the previous agreements, the Chinese Communist Party and the Democratic League must hold fourteen of the forty seats in the State Council, that is a little over one third of the total vote, in order to ensure that the Peaceful Reconstruction Program would not be revised unilaterally." I asked Lee Wei-kuo about it. This, he said, was agreed on, not at the PCC, but informally at a meeting between the Communist and KMT representatives. At the KMT's CEC meeting in March (says Wei-kuo, who was there) the government men were questioned about reports to this effect. Sun Fo and

Shao Li-tze evaded, but Wu Tieh-cheng said: "Since we did agree to this, why shouldn't we admit it?" So Chou is right on that one, but he doesn't have it in writing.

Chou also claimed that "the list of National Assembly delegates can be produced only to the reorganized government and even so not until the draft constitution has been revised by the PCC, acknowledged as the only draft to be presented to the National Assembly, and the distribution of membership of the National Assembly has been finally agreed upon." Wei-kuo says all these points were in dispute and Chou is merely stating the Communist position.

CHAPTER THIRTEEN

Amid its far larger problems, government's attempt to pare down subsidy to foreign press hostel in Shanghai is stymied by resistance of correspondents.

The Generalissimo's painfully reached decision to offer a truce as his armies were advancing on Kalgan, and the Communists' rejection of it, were indeed a turning point, the most critical of the 1946 negotiations. I felt that for once I really *had* kept the Chinese "out of trouble with the United States." I was under no delusion that my memo and argument had been decisive; the pressure on Chiang was strong from Marshall and Stuart, with all that represented in terms of what he needed in terms of support from the United States. I confined myself to one point: that if Marshall pulled out of China because the government refused to stop fighting it was the end for sure of American support for his government. I might not have felt impelled to insist on seeing Chiang personally if I had not been so utterly convinced from observing Marshall's tension the night before that, in spite of previous unfulfilled threats to leave, this time he really meant it.

Possibly the Generalissimo was gambling on a personal conviction that the Communists would reject the truce. If Marshall was looking for an excuse to withdraw his official mediation, he could have taken the Communist refusal as an equally good reason. But in the psychology of the period that occurred to no one.

Fortunately I had the distraction of the problems of Broadway Mansions as a press hostel to keep me from brooding too much about politics during this sequence of events. This involved a weekend trip to Shanghai which confirmed in me an opinion I had developed as a newsman: that journalists *en bloc* are unreasonable people. To be candid, the trip also afforded me some amusement.

The press hostel in Chungking during the war had become famous as the shelter from which China's story got out to the world at a time when she was fighting alone against Japan. The hostel was created by Hollington Tong, then Vice-Minister of Information, who was China's first American-trained newspaperman, a graduate of the University of Missouri and the Pulitzer School of Journalism at Columbia. Tong, a gentle soul and living embodiment of the Lincolnian precept of malice toward none, told part of its story in his book, *China and the World Press.*

"I founded it," he said, "as a place where foreign press representatives, both men and women, and foreign members of my own staff might live. It has been considered one of my more notorious deeds by some members of the Kuomintang. They argue that had there never been a press hostel in Chungking, the criticism of the government would not have been so thoroughly diffused through the entire foreign press group. I considered it one of my happier brainstorms, for I felt that comparatively comfortable correspondents would be more sympathetic to China's cause than extremely uncomfortable ones. Perhaps the whole difficulty was that I didn't make the press hostel comfortable enough!"

How the foreign press had parlayed the necessarily spartan accommodations of Chungking into possession of the top floors of Broadway Mansions in Shanghai at the war's end I did not know. They could not complain about its comfort, even luxury. It towered over Soochow Creek at one end of the Bund and included several penthouse suites. As Japanese property, the building had been taken over by the Alien Property Administration, and the space not used by the correspondents was allocated to U.S. officers of MAGIC and their families. Since the Chinese were assuming the expenses of MAGIC, the question of rent from the officers did not arise, but the government wanted to move them to other space. As for the foreign press, it did seem unreasonable that more than a year after the end of the war the correspondents got quarters rent free from the Chinese government.

It was true that housing was short in Shanghai, as everywhere at that time, and that private owners in the city took advantage of the shortage to charge exorbitant prices and to demand "key money," amounting to payment for the privilege of renting, which in one case I knew of amounted to $5000 U.S.

I flew from Nanking on a Friday afternoon and put up in one of the hostel apartments temporarily unoccupied. I went first to the seventeenth-floor penthouse club to get information on the number of individuals involved and the space they occupied. By chance Walt Rundle, UP bureau manager and president of the Foreign Correspondents' Association, happened to be in. He took a very truculent attitude toward the government's intentions. Why, he asked, couldn't the Executive Yuan get space somewhere else? If the government asked the correspondents to move it meant only one thing: it wanted to get them out of China. This followed, he reasoned, from the fact that exorbitant key money and rents were being charged in Shanghai.

When I got back to my room I got a call from Peggy Durdin, wife of Till Durdin, inviting me to have dinner with them and some other guests. But this was shortly followed by a call from Rundle. He had spread the alarm through the building and had summoned the corps to an emergency meeting at 6 P.M., as though the correspondents were about to be deprived of their beds that very night. He informed me with an air of "or else" that they wanted me present. I readily agreed.

The meeting seethed with indignation. Rundle dwelt on

the impossibility of finding space elsewhere, and others chimed in. What had happened, someone asked, to the Generalissimo's assurance they could stay? This was something I did not know about. The belligerence turned to threats: okay, if the government wanted them to leave China, they would pull out. This implied they were doing the country a favor by their presence. One suggested that perhaps Randall Gould, editor of the Shanghai *Evening Post & Mercury*, would like to hear about this foul plot and carry a story. I found it hard to conceal my amusement; I could not, by any stretch of imagination, picture their indignation spreading as far as Randall Gould, let alone arousing protest by his readers.

One wife suggested that perhaps they could go so far as to pay a "reasonable" rental, to which Dixie Tighe of International News Service promptly commented: "I don't think we should budge an inch." She asked, "What brings it up now, just at this time?" I replied that it was simply the lapse of time.

At that point I felt it appropriate to say that if the question was decided in favor of letting the correspondents stay, it was contemplated they would be charged rent, but it would be nominal. It was the principle of not subsidizing the foreign press, rather than rental income, which was involved. This was a point to which no self-respecting correspondent could object, but since they were operating under a full head of steam they reverted to outraged talk about the price of rents in Shanghai.

It was Miss Tighe who deflated the pressure by remarking: "Well, I suppose we can at least pay what we have been charging our offices." It was hard for anyone present to act very outraged after that sally, which everyone present understood. No reader, surely, is ignorant of the fact that foreign correspondents live abroad under generous expense accounts, and some of them are very ingenious practitioners of the art. I once heard a newsman complain about being transferred from Japan to Washington. "I don't want to be a millionaire," he said. "I just want to be a foreign correspondent and live like one."

Miss Tighe's remark, in fact, broke up the meeting after a three-man committee had been instructed to telegraph protests to Chiang Kai-shek, T. V. Soong, General Marshall, and Ambassador Stuart; also to phone immediately to Marshall and Soong. "What," I asked, "you're not going to telephone the Generalissimo?" "No," said the humorless Rundle, "he doesn't speak English."

Next day I met with General Huang and the Alien Property Administrator, S. Y. Liu. Huang reported that the army had been even tougher in resisting the prospect of moving. Liu seemed encouraged when I said I thought the correspondents had conceded they should pay rent if it was more or less nominal. No decision was reached, but General Huang thought the Executive Yuan might obtain one floor for its Shanghai offices by finding other space for some of the MAGIC personnel, leaving the newsmen undisturbed.

I was not further involved in the matter. I did, however, take the precaution of telling the whole story to Randall Gould when he and his wife Dorothy took me to lunch at the American Club. Gould agreed that, with housing conditions what they were, it was in the government's interest to provide quarters, but that the correspondents should be willing to yield the point of paying nominal rent without making such a fuss about it.

I was glad of a chance to visit with Gould, who was writing dispatches from the Far East years before, when I was a wire editor for the United Press in New York. During our conversation about things Chinese I asked him about Tai Li, a general who had built up an enigmatic reputation during the war. The U. S. Navy, with whom he cooperated, considered him a stout and effective fighter against the Japanese; as mentioned earlier, the navy insisted on awarding him a medal posthumously, to Marshall's chagrin. To others he was the embodiment of Kuomintang evil, the kind of commander who, suspecting a soldier of spying for the Japanese, would execute him on the spot. Supposedly Tai Li had been killed in an air crash during the Christmas season prior to my arrival in China, but I had heard the theory expressed that he was not on the crashed airplane. Instead, he was supposed to have made use of the accident to go underground on some mysterious KMT plot against the Communists.

I was asking Gould his opinion of this story when Fred Hampson of AP happened to pass the table in the company of a Chinese. Gould stopped them and introduced me. The Chinese was Tommy Chao, a reporter for *Shun Pao*. Gould asked: "Tommy, is Tai Li dead?" Chao replied: "Yes." Gould commented that if anyone could judge the truth of the rumor it was Chao, prompting Chao to elaborate that there was so much frantic telephoning between Nanking and Shanghai the day of the crash that no doubt was left in his mind that Tai Li was on the downed plane.

After they left, Gould told me about Tommy Chao. He had been Chungking manager for Reuters, and a resident, with his wife, in the press hostel. He wrote a book published only in Chinese, commenting unfavorably on the conduct of a number of the American and British correspondents in the hostel. The denizens of the establishment felt that his reporting of their sophomoric antics exposed them to "maximum public shame and contempt," according to a resolution they adopted. They accused him of distorting gossip he had picked up, but chiefly vented their spleen on the ground their "privacy" had been invaded. An attempt to expel him from the press hostel ended when he resigned from Reuters and thus automatically lost his right to live there. Since then, said Gould, he had been able to get work only with Chinese papers.

That afternoon I spent some time watching the sampan fleet on Soochow Creek, a spectacle that had fascinated me since my first arrival in China. Hundreds of small boats bobbed in the filthy harbor water, providing homes for Chinese families presumably connected in some way with traffic up the creek, though I could never determine what. The small craft paved the water from bank to bank, and when an occasional small vessel came along to be rowed laboriously up the channel the hard-working coolie crews had literally to push them aside to clear the way. There were always children hopping sure-footedly among the boats. Beneath their bamboo mat canopies the families lived; rice was cooked over small fire pots aboard; the creek itself provided all the bathroom facilities they needed.

On this particular afternoon I noted a small boy, about two years old, standing in a partly waterlogged skiff just out of reach of the sea wall and the sampan to which it was tied. He seemed uncertain what to do as he stood in water reaching over his ankles. Then a girl about six, possibly his sister, noticed his predicament and in seamanlike fashion pulled the skiff close to shore and helped him up a ladder to the sidewalk.

A candy vendor came along the embankment and soon half a dozen youngsters had come flocking off the sampans as if responding to the call of a Good Humor man. None of them could have been over eight, and the candy vendor seemed about ten or twelve. The bright-eyed little kids looked over his sweetmeats and cookies and asked the price, but none bought. I assumed none of them had any money. They seemed to accept quite matter-of-factly that luxuries of this kind were out of their reach, but took pleasure from the knowledge that such delights existed.

I had some change in my pocket, 600 CNC in two bills, and offered it. The eldest girl grabbed it out of my hand and refused the others when they crowded around demanding a share. But when I made it clear in sign language it was for all, a little reluctantly she handed the vendor the $500 bill and got change. Then she doled out the grimy $100 bills to the others. Two of the kids bought cookies, after the usual childish hesitation, picking up first one and then another before deciding. The others folded up their bills and when the vendor moved along they went back to their sampans.

The brave acceptance of life's hardship among the Chinese poor always moved me when I got such glimpses of it, and I was still feeling unsettled as I mounted by elevator to the seventeenth-floor Press Club to eat with a number of correspondents. Their mood had changed since their indignant meeting and they refused to let me pay my bill. I was, they said, the guest of the club.

Since I had traveled by plane exclusively since leaving Washington, I resolved to return to Nanking by train. There was one at 7 A.M., and I was glad to have Sidney Quong of Central News as a traveling companion. A cold drizzle was falling as we walked down the unroofed platform at Pei Chan station and found our first-class car, part of an eleven-car train. The car was equipped like a Pullman without berths: plush seats facing each other, two to a seat, with a narrow, built-in table between them. Eight such setups on each side of the aisle provided sixty-four seats and every one was occupied as we pulled out. I was the only foreigner in the car. The fare was only 17,000 CNC compared to 45,000 CNC on the airplane.

First order of business was the distribution of covered glasses for tea, which came in little individual packets at $700. As far as I could make out, every passenger bought tea. Sid and I had breakfast: four eggs, some bread, and a brown liquid masquerading as coffee. But the tea was hot and throughout the trip trainmen came through with a long-spouted brass teakettle, refilling the glasses with steaming water.

I could not help comparing the scenery and the trip to the Pennsylvania's New York–Washington run which I had made so often. On a train which would compare with the Congressional it took twice as long. Soochow, a town famous for beautiful girls with beautiful teeth, and Wusih, home of

Wusih Cement, looked fairly industrial, like West Chester, Pennsylvania, seen from the tracks.

Yet there were constant reminders of China's troubles. Soldiers were everywhere, including armed railway police aboard the train. At each station there were cement block-houses, and pillboxes at all bridges over the numerous canals and waterways along the flat countryside. Occasionally an armored train, in camouflage paint, stood on a siding, as well as individual armored cars, gasoline-powered and fitted with railway wheels, for emergency use.

At Changchow we passed a fourth-class train consisting of cars crammed with men, women, children, and bundles. Some passengers were sitting on the floor and others standing because there was no room to sit. As we pulled out, we passed one car where a mother was holding her son while he stuck his bare bottom out the door. Even the boxcar roofs had passengers. Yet the children were bright-eyed and lively. Some of the cars had Arabic lettering, presumably rolling stock of the U. S. Army used around Cairo or in Iran and supplied to China via UNRRA. At a village north of Chinkiang a cow was lying dead in the road, and about twenty villagers were standing around while it was being skinned and cut up on the spot.

We pulled into Nanking's Hsiakwan station almost on schedule, at 1:35 P.M.

CHAPTER FOURTEEN

*Marshall sidelights on his dealings with Chiang. Soong backs
agricultural reform plan. Henry Luce pays visit to China.*

Shanghai drew me back within a few days because the family
was arriving October 15 aboard the President liner *Marine
Lynx*. I lunched at the Press Club that day so that I could
watch the Whangpoo River for its arrival at the Bund.

It was six months to the day since I had left them in
Washington. At 2 P.M. I went to the wharf and waited while
the ship was warped into her berth. The rail was crowded
with passengers and it was a long time before I spotted John,
my elder son, and got his attention. He disappeared and came
back in a moment with Carolyn, the youngest, going on four,
who started screaming, "Daddy," and tried to climb over the
rail. Then he fetched Bill, and finally Betty, who had been
standing in line for the customs officers. There was an even
longer wait until all the customs and immigration officials
had completed their work and we were finally reunited.

At times, as I waited, it seemed very unreal that we were all
in China, and I was overcome by a sense of what a tremendous
undertaking it had been for Betty. For me it was simple
enough to take off with a flight bag, a briefcase, and a portable
typewriter; for her it meant closing the house and packing
enough to re-establish us in a China where, we had been mis-
takenly informed, we would be unable to find much of even
the ordinary necessities to buy. There was also our 1939
Pontiac to ship, and seventeen days to keep the children

amused in San Francisco while the maritime strike held up the ship's departure.

The hardships of the trip came out in short bursts of information as Betty and the kids competed with each other to tell me about it. The ship had not been converted from carrying troops and the males and females slept in segregated forty-bunk cabins; the railings were wide-open affairs and Betty had to keep watch on the children every minute they were on deck; some crew member had conned Johnny into believing he could catch fish by trailing a basket in the wake; the passengers had rechristened the ship *Marine Stinks*. By 8 P.M. I finally got the family installed at the Metropole Hotel. It took another day to clear the trunks through customs, and I coughed up $1 million CNC—something like $250 U.S.—to get my car transported across the Whangpoo River, where it had been sitting for a couple of weeks since its unloading from another ship.

While in Shanghai, in anticipation that shipping would still be tight by the time my contract expired in March, I visited Thos. Cook & Sons with the idea of going home by way of India. They were too discouraging; they said they probably could get us all as far as Bombay, but that facilities beyond there were booked solid and they could promise nothing. So I abandoned that idea and applied to the American President Lines for passage home.

We took the night train to Nanking. The family had a surprisingly neat, clean four-bunk compartment, and I had a lower berth two cars ahead. The children were intrigued by being served tea immediately, in glasses. From what little she saw by morning light before we pulled into Nanking, Betty was astonished at the number of ponds and waterways that laced the flat countryside, and shocked by the signs of poverty.

For several days I relaxed, taking the family for drives to see the sights of Nanking. I edged back into the accustomed rounds when I was invited to a tea party the Generalissimo and Madame Chiang gave for Walter S. Robertson, the head of Marshall's Executive Headquarters in Peking, who was returning to the United States on being replaced by General Gillem, as Marshall had mentioned earlier.

Peng was one of those attending the ceremony, at which Chiang presented Robertson with a Chinese decoration, and afterward the Generalissimo conferred with him briefly. Peng told me on the way back that, contrary to what Chou En-lai said in his formal reply to Marshall rejecting the ten-day Kalgan truce, the government had not promised fourteen State Council seats to the Communists and Democratic League. This I knew, but I mentally recalled Lee Wei-Kuo's account of the meeting he had attended at which the three government negotiators had evaded questioning on the subject and one finally said they might as well admit they had— informally. I had complete faith in Lee Wei-kuo's reliability. It meant, of course, that the three had gone beyond what Chiang would permit. Also, said Peng, there seemed to be some dispute between Chiang and Marshall over government troop disposition. Assuming the January 13 truce was reinvoked, Chiang felt the Nationalist troops should not be restricted in movement because it was the government's duty to "protect the country." Apparently Marshall, like the Communists, believed they should be spotted in their own areas.

Dr. Soong came back from his brief vacation looking tanned and rested. He said he had visited Admiral Cooke's flagship, done some fishing, absorbed some sun, and felt a lot better. He gave me a capsule account of the capture of Kalgan: the Communists rejected the truce, he said, because they thought they could stop and defeat the main Nationalist column from Peking. They did repulse this attack, but not as successfully as they had hoped, and while they were still engaged, General Fu Tso-yi marched in with his troops from the north.

One day Peng asked me if I knew anything about an invitation to Henry R. Luce to visit China. I said no. Peng said

T.V. had sent him word of a cable from Ambassador Wellington Koo in Washington stating that Luce, accepting an
"informal" invitation from the Generalissimo, was to arrive
in China October 24, accompanied by two of his editors, Roy
Alexander and Robert T. Elson. Alexander was managing
editor of *Time* and Elson was my chief in the Washington
bureau. T.V. had been unaware of the invitation; Luce was
an old friend of China and was of course welcome any time,
but did Peng know when it went out?

Then I recalled that in my first interview with the Generalissimo one of his disconcerting questions was: what had I
heard from Harry Luce? I hadn't been thinking that Luce
would be writing me, but I told the Gimo that before I came
to China I had talked to him and he had mentioned that
possibly he would be making a visit during the year. Chiang
replied that when I wrote him to be sure to say he was welcome, and so was Mrs. Luce. This I did. When I saw T.V., I
told him this story and asked whether this might have been
the "informal invitation." Soong replied it was quite likely;
Luce tended to take such things literally, but in any event the
government was delighted to have him.

This was a story I should have kept strictly to myself, but
I could not resist telling one of the *Time* correspondents in
Shanghai, with the result that it reached the ears of Donald
Starr of the Chicago *Tribune* in garbled form. Starr's story
about the visit was based chiefly on criticism of the fact that
Luce had flown over in an air force plane with General
Frederic H. Smith, Chief of Staff of the strategic air force.
But he included a paragraph on the "unofficial story behind
the visit" which, in addition to being inaccurate, credited
me with a great deal more enterprise than I possessed.

Starr's story said: "Jack Bell, American supernumerary who
moves about in high quarters of the Nanking government, is
said to have mentioned casually an intention to write a letter
to Luce while in a conversation with Chiang. The latter, according to this account, just as casually suggested that his

regards be sent to the publisher and that the latter should come out and see him sometime. Energetic Bell wrote the Chinese Embassy in Washington and the invitation went on from there to Luce, who hastily accepted."

I made a call on General Marshall ostensibly to let him know about Luce's impending arrival, but I chiefly wanted to find out what his post-Kalgan mood was.

To me the Communist rejection of the Kalgan truce had been the final proof that they had no intention of settling peaceably. I had not then heard the saying attributed to Mao Tse-tung that "political power flows from the barrel of a gun," but my observation had been that at every stage of the negotiations which I knew about the Communists dragged their heels when they believed they had a chance to score militarily, and every time the fighting went against them they ran to Marshall with the argument: "How can we talk peace when fighting is going on?"

There was nothing especially significant about Marshall's going to bat for them when they did, as some right-wing critics and historians have implied. His motive, the mission's motive, was the honest motive of wanting all fighting stopped. He had been repeatedly frustrated in his efforts to do it by moral suasion, but he had one other weapon and that was the Nationalists' reliance on the United States for their arms and ammunition. This very practical restraint was invoked. Since June, U.S. arms supplies had been cut off. It was, of course, restraint on one side only, since the Communists had possession of vast Japanese war stocks and no one knew what help they were receiving from the Russians.

My own conclusion at the time was that it now behooved the United States to decide, for the sake of its future in the Far East, whether peaceful settlement was impossible and, if so, whether it would support the legal government of China, which it recognized. Conclusions of this nature are reached only gradually, and even after the net balance seems to be in one direction the conclusion does not harden all at

once; there was still the possibility of a coalition government
in the National Assembly, but the chances seemed so dim
that foresight required the U.S. to begin thinking about alternatives.

In talking to Marshall I did not presume to outline what I
thought U.S. policy should be. I broached the idea indirectly
by saying that in connection with Luce's visit I suspected he
would arrive with his mind thoroughly made up that the
Chiang Kai-shek government must be supported, but I
judged he would be strong for making it clean house and
might be helpful toward that end. I return to my journal:

NANKING, October 19—"If you let this bunch know you are for
them, you can't do anything with them," said Marshall, referring
to the KMT. He recalled that in the critical period of week before
last, in his tensest session yet with the Gimo, when in effect he
threatened him with withdrawal from China, the Gimo went into
a long speech in which he quoted the Bible and indulged in generalities but did not budge an inch on concessions. He said it was
not until Stuart tipped off the Gimo that Marshall had actually
radioed Washington his request for recall that the concessions
came. His story differed from Stuart's account, that Marshall did
not know about it until after it happened.

Marshall was started on a topic and he went on. He said the
eight-point program the government came out with was, as I
suspected, essentially the program he had suggested after that trip
to Kuling, the editing of which by Chiang had caused all the
trouble in the first place. He said Madame Chiang had come over
one night, at nine o'clock or so, with the proposed statement. I
gathered this was Monday or Tuesday night. Marshall read it over.
"It was terrible," he said. Madame Chiang invited him to change
it. He told her it wasn't the kind of statement that could be
edited, that it was hopeless as it stood. "Finally," he said, "I cut
out a page and a half of the Gimo's generalities—just cut it right
out." He said Chiang held four meetings with his advisers the next
day, thrashing it out, before the thing finally was accepted in the

manner Marshall desired. "The Madame sold it," he commented.

This led him to several parenthetical comments about Madame Chiang. He said that Chiang always insisted that she be present for interviews with Marshall, persisting even when she was sick, or tired, or tried to beg off. He said she had once remarked to him, in discussing the Gimo's lack of understanding of Western democracy, that in all her years with him she felt she had made only a "two per cent impression" on him with respect to this point. Another sidelight was that Madame Chiang once related to Mrs. Marshall how she had found the Gimo, on the roof of their residence where they take sun baths, with his head in his hands, moaning that he could not give an order to his generals and make them obey. "He can be of help in some things, though," said Marshall. "He can persuade people. Pai Chung-hsi used to hate him, but now he is devoted to him."

He said the fact that Sun Fo was popularly believed to be the author of the government program was probably a help in the eyes of the third-party people whose present activity was encouraging. But Marshall himself is staying out of things and letting Stuart handle the political maneuvering. "That was what I told Chou in Shanghai," he said. "You have questioned my integrity and now I am through!"

I said Yenan had issued a statement yesterday which I thought was very interesting because, while it used the same tough language the Communists have been using for several months, its tone was distinctly different from the recent tirades. "It's the most encouraging thing I've seen," said Marshall.

He made a brief allusion to the position he was in during the first week of October: first at the point of issuing a withdrawal statement which would destroy the government's case before the American public, and then in the position of actually issuing a statement unfavorable to the Communists. I derived some satisfaction from the fact that it was on this precise point I had made my argument to the Gimo.

Marshall told me he thought the best way of dealing with the Gimo was by specific illustration, and he launched into several

examples of how he had belabored the Gimo over incidents such
as the Kunming assassinations and the newspaper suppressions.
He worked himself into quite a bit of anger in telling how, when
inquiring of Peng why some liberal publications were suppressed,
he had been told it was because they had not registered. "I told
the Generalissimo—and I asked Madame Chiang if she could translate it accurately—'Why, that would make a dog laugh.'" Mrs.
Marshall came into the room and we broke off our conversation.

Later in the day I dropped in at the MOI, where Peng said he
had a document he wanted me to look at. It turned out to be a
very sketchy and hard-to-understand summary of a program for
areas recaptured from the Communists. The sensational part to
me was a statement that land rents were to be limited to one
third of the harvest of the main crop. If this was a step toward
agrarian reform, which has been the big selling point of the Communists, it deserved something more than an obscurely worded
statement tossed casually at the correspondents on a Saturday
evening.

I questioned Peng about it. His story was that in China the
customary land rent has been 50 per cent: i.e., 50 per cent of the
main crop goes to the landlord; the other 50 per cent, and the
minor crops, to the tenant. Out of his share the landlord pays
the taxes, some 10 to 12 per cent to the Central Government,
but often much higher locally. The KMT has had a program of
reducing the rent one quarter, leaving the landlord 37.5 per cent
out of which he had to pay taxes. But in effect, said Peng, because
of peasant illiteracy and the comparative difficulty for them of
computing a percentage of a percentage, the rent reduction has
not been enforced or practiced and remains little more than a
slogan. Peng said that in a discussion of land rents in retaken
areas at the Supreme National Defense Council on Wednesday he
himself had argued that the whole thing could be made very
much simpler by cutting the landlord to one third: the peasant
could understand dividing a crop into three piles and giving the
landlord one of them. I asked if this meant that the areas re-

captured from the Communists would be better off with respect to land rents than the rest of China. Peng said it was true.

This was a story, I suggested, which to be used effectively needed to meet two conditions: (1) the correspondents had to be convinced it was on the up and up, a genuine improvement of conditions, and not a window-dressing scheme labeled agrarian reform; (2) it should be released at a time when it would get good display, and not casually tossed out as a mimeographed handout. I suggested a full-dress press conference tomorrow evening, to hit the Monday morning U.S. papers, with a complete text of the program available in addition to the summary, and a Q. and A. session to explain anything the newsmen didn't understand. Peng said he would phone Dr. Soong to see if he was free, and that if he considered it important he would hold a press conference. Soong told him to come over right away.

We went, a bit to my surprise, to Soong's house on the hill where he rarely likes to discuss business. When T.V. came into the big beamed room he was wearing a checked sport coat and gray slacks and seemed in a good mood. He slouched comfortably in one of the big leather chairs, throwing both legs over an arm.

I said that as specific action toward reform the program was infinitely more effective than statements of government opinion. Was it really a genuine move? Soong said it was. He said his own idea was to take the land from the landlords and give it to the tillers, but he proposed compensating the landlords. The system he outlined was that the landowners, unless they tilled the soil themselves, would get bonds from the Farmers' Bank of China which would be amortized over a period of ten to fifteen years. The bank would hold a mortgage on the land which would be paid off by the tenant in yearly installments over the same period. In effect the landlord would be forced to sell to the tenant at a nominal figure—approximately what he would collect in rent for the period involved—unless he farmed the land himself and hired people, for wages, to work it for him.

This was different from Peng's summary, and even more beneficial to the peasant. Peng explained that at Wednesday's meeting (held while T.V. was flying down from Tsingtao) a "slight" change had been made—the system was to apply only to land requisitioned by the government which, for physical reasons such as the destruction of boundaries, could not be returned to the owners.

T.V. asked whether the story had been put out at all. Peng said no. "Then tell them not to publish it," said T.V. "I want to have it changed. I want to protest at the next meeting. I think the time has come for bold action."

He elaborated: the government had to compete with the Communists in their own field. After all, it was only being tried in a limited way—60 to 80 *hsien* of China's 3000? Peng thought more —so that errors could be eliminated before it was extended to the rest of China, or it could be dropped if it didn't work. T.V. asked me: didn't I think bold action was called for? I agreed.

Having dealt with that, T.V. instructed Peng to see that Luce and his editors were put up at No. 1 House when they were in Nanking, and at the Park Hotel when in Shanghai. He added, with the injunction that it was not to be repeated, that the Gimo is going to take a trip to Formosa very soon. Luce might want to go along, in which case a special plane should be provided. He asked me to go to Shanghai to meet Luce.

A. T. Steele of the New York *Herald Tribune* came to dinner. He wants help in getting a trip to Sinkiang. He has just spent ten days in Yenan and ranks the Communist hierarchy thus: 1. Mao Tse-tung; 2. Chu Teh; 3. Liu Shau-chi; 4. Lin Piao. Liu Shau-chi was a name I had not heard before. Steele said he is a man of forty-eight, thoroughly trained as a Communist, and the probable successor to Mao Tse-tung. He said talk of dissension among the Communists is absurd. Lin Piao, a Mao man, is No. 1 in Manchuria. Rumors of rivalry cannot be anything more than that Manchuria and Yenan are now geographically split and may be pursuing more autonomous courses. Steele is flatly convinced that the Communists are ideologically, spiritually, politically, and geographically tied to Russia, and while they would like to make use of the U.S. capitalist system to develop industrially at a time when Russia cannot give them that sort of help, they are first and last Communists, without quotes. They cannot be "weaned away" by the U.S.

NANKING, October 21—When I talked to Peng about Steele's request for permission to go to Sinkiang, he said, "Very confidentially, and we must not tell the correspondents this because sooner or later they will write it, the situation in Sinkiang is very delicate. The Russians have told us: 'If you want our cooperation, you must not let too many British and Americans come up here.' We need materials from Russia, and it is easier to get them from Russia than from the U.S. and Britain, and so we have to be careful not to send too many Americans and British there." This meant, he said, that he had to ask permission of the governor in each case, and it was also what had prevented a visit to the province by the British General Carton de Wiart.

Fred Gruin reported having a very satisfactory talk with T.V., who invited him to lunch at his home on the hill. He said T.V. shared the Chen brothers' theory that the Communists could be reduced to military impotence and could even be liquidated. But he was bearish on any improvement of the economic situation until the political dispute was settled, although he seemed to believe the Communists would come to terms.

NANKING, October 22—In midmorning I suddenly got a call from C. P. Kiang asking if I could come over right away to see Dr. Soong. It turned out to be nothing more than that he wanted me to make sure Fred Gruin did not quote him on his interview of yesterday. Betty and I lunched with Peng at his home, together with several members of the Academia Sinica attending the current council session. Among them was Hu Shih, Lo Chia-lun, and a university president and library head or two. Betty did well with the chopsticks until she tried to cope with a dish of jellied fish balls. Peng told her it was quite polite to spear them.

After lunch I went to see Ambassador Stuart, who had been talking to Democratic Leaguers in the morning. We had a long, relaxed talk in the living room while he awaited the arrival of

Carson Chang. I was impressed by Stuart's sense of balance; although he may give the appearance of being politically naïve to someone like Marshall, he is capable of taking part in the negotiations without the same strain. He is more philosophical about it, and I think that is necessary in dealing with the Chinese. There's a bit more fatalism to him, which God knows is a help when you've got to take things as they come and can apply little more than body-English to the political situation.

I was more direct with Stuart in outlining my own feeling that political coalition is next to hopeless, and it has become a question of working out a China policy that the U.S. could support. In this connection I mentioned the agrarian reform program outlined by T.V. Stuart agreed that the changes made before its adoption by the Supreme National Defense Council made the plan of little value, but he thought it was a good plan and very important as T.V. conceived of it. "I understand that Chen Li-fu helped work out that plan," said Stuart. "That's a curious thing about him. Although he has this obsession about the Communists, and although he heads the secret police, he has advanced social ideas. He is personally honest, he lives very simply, and he never has indulged in graft or squeeze. He is very sincere, both in his hatred of the Communists and in his leftest social tendencies." This was the first kind word I had heard spoken about Chen Li-fu by anyone.

Stuart thought the political situation was more hopeful than he had seen it for the past month. Actually, he said, it had come down to a question of non-essentials. Chou En-lai was in essential agreement with each of the eight points of the government statement but felt the manner in which they were presented constituted an "ultimatum" and he refused to accept an ultimatum. Chiang, on his part, had told Stuart personally that the Communists had to write a letter accepting all eight points before anything further could be done. Of course, there still remains the pathological distrust on both sides, each seeking for some solid guarantee that commitments will be carried out.

This is what the third-party people are now trying to provide, said Stuart. Potentially the balance of power is in their hands. They could offer each side protection against the abuse of authority by the other, though naturally it would operate chiefly for the Communist minority. He saw the turning over of the current phase of negotiations as having a double advantage: it gives the Chinese a chance to work out their own salvation, and it withdraws the U.S. from the position of being a target for all criticism. Most active at present, he said, is Hu Lin, of *Ta Kung Pao*, "who is as neutral as it is possible for a man to be." But in the present situation "face" has become more important to the opposing parties than even their own interest or the interest of the country.

This led to a discussion of several Democratic League personalities. Lo Lung-chi, he said, is disliked by practically everyone but his colleagues are trying to save his face. Carson Chang is a man of unquestioned integrity, but a doctrinaire. Apparently he is about to take most of the Democratic League out of its position as tools of the Communists with his newly formed Democratic Social League. I was reminded of the bait Chiang Kai-shek put in his August 14 speech for Carson Chang, promising to consider "sound" inprovements in the draft constitution—a phrase I had wanted to eliminate since who was to decide what "sound" improvements were? Stuart said that, while to some extent the KMT's feeling that the League comprises a bunch of "opportunists" is true, it's more that they are "practical."

He had an interesting bit about the Youth Party. He said its leader, Tseng Chi, was so harassed by the Japanese during the war that he was forced into actions that could be interpreted as collaborationist. The Chen Li-fu crowd, he said, has "pointed a bayonet at his heart" since then and forced him to go along with the KMT. It's one form of blackmail. Of Sun Fo, Stuart commented that he lives on the reputation of his father, Sun Yat-sen, and is personally colorless. Our talk was broken off by the arrival of Carson Chang.

NANKING, October 23—Lee Wei-kuo points out two specious points in the formal Communist reply to Chiang's last offer of a truce. First, if the Communists demand the government give them back all cities they held January 13, the government with equal logic could demand that they turn over all of Manchuria, since the Communists held none of it on January 13. I said they would argue that, since the Russians held it, both the Communists and the KMT should take it over. "But they agreed that the government was entitled to take over Manchuria," he said; which of course is true.

Second, they distorted the actual agreement on military dispositions (which he helped work on) by claiming the government had more armies in Manchuria than permitted. This agreement provided that in the first stage of deployment the government would be limited to five armies, and in the second stage to five divisions, but did not limit their strength in the takeover. Moreover, the preliminary step toward any redeployment—submission of the list of units to be retained—was never taken by the Communists.

I took the 11 P.M. train to Shanghai.

SHANGHAI, October 26—Luce, Roy Alexander, and Bob Elson arrived around 7 P.M. in the special plane of Assistant Secretary for Air Stuart Symington, accompanied by General Smith. Mayor K. C. Wu and I took them all to the hotel and later to dinner at the mayor's. It was a Western meal and K.C. was his usual bouncy self; everybody seemed to enjoy it.

SHANGHAI–NANKING, October 27—Luce had turned down T.V.'s invitation to fly with him to Nanking, and I had planned to fly up with the Luce party tomorrow. But during the night I reflected that Luce would be seeing people all day and I might as well take advantage of the additional time with my family by going with T.V. So I had shaved and was beginning to pack when I got a call at eight-thirty from C. P. Kiang asking if Luce could come over for breakfast. I phoned Luce—apparently woke him up

—and he said yes. I said I'd drop by and pick him up. But hitches developed. The car the city had assigned me was not there and I had to send for a taxi. I wasted more time while the hotel totted up my bill, $392,000, almost all I had with me. As a result when I got to the Park Hotel Luce had already gone. I finally arrived at Soong's at nine-thirty. Luce and T.V. were seated, alone, on his glassed-in veranda. Surprised at my own nonchalance, I said I had already had breakfast but would have coffee with them. I never did find out whether Luce actually got there for breakfast, but I suppose he did.

Luce was interested in two things in this conversation. Why, he asked, had not the correspondents written that the military situation had changed things? He was not too coherent as to what he meant, but I gathered that his point was that the KMT's military victories had more or less settled the political situation. T.V. told him yesterday's capture of Antung was another very severe blow to the Communists. Kalgan cut off their land route between Yenan and Manchuria, and Antung cut off their sea route. Now they are bottled up in Shantung. Luce's other question was: why so much prominence to the Democratic League when politically it was so insignificant? I said it was because they could wield the balance of power in a coalition.

Luce left shortly after ten to go to church and T.V. told me I had the run of the house and garden while he held some conferences. I sat on the veranda reading the paper but finally went out in the sun on the spacious garden lawn and, wandering about, began to appreciate it for the first time. The red-painted Chinese tea house, glassed in, was picturesquely set near one corner, and the paths wound among the rocks and plants that bordered the whole thing. Around eleven o'clock T.V. and Madame Soong came out to give the garden a final inspection before we left for Lungwha airfield. Madame Soong said that with only a couple of days in Shanghai in two weeks she had a lot of work to do on the garden each time.

The trip was very pleasant. We climbed over a cloud bank at around five thousand feet and then flew out of it into a slightly hazy blue sky such as China has in autumn, with a clear view to the horizon. I was glad to get home in time for lunch and to spend the day with the family.

NANKING, October 28—It was another day of meeting Luce. Fred Gruin got word that he would be in at ten-thirty and that Roy Alexander and Bob Elson were going right on to Peking. I went to the airport with Lee Wei-kuo and numerous others. Wei-kuo and I took Luce immediately to the Executive Yuan for a talk with T.V. which lasted about forty-five minutes. Then Luce went to lunch with Ambassador Stuart, and at 3 P.M. had an appointment with General Marshall. Meantime T.V. had set up a dinner at his house on the hill for tonight: Luce, General and Mrs. Marshall, Ambassador Stuart, Betty and I being the guests. The Marshalls could not come, since they were entertaining Jim Farley, and Stuart had to decline because of laryngitis, so John and Ruth Blandford were substituted.

It was the best Chinese banquet meal I've ever had in China. Sharks' fins and crab, shrimp, abalone, crushed bamboo and chicken, mushrooms, sweet ham and pigeon eggs, cabbage heart and mushrooms, chicken and rice, yellow watermelon from Formosa, and chocolate and candied apricots. Dr. and Madame Soong were very genial hosts. It was informal dress. Madame Soong wore a stunning Chinese-style black velvet dress with a matching jacket, and a jade dinner ring on each hand, a jade bracelet on one arm and a gold bracelet on the other, pearl cluster earrings, a pearl necklace, and a pin that looked as if it were carved from jade, with a border of diamonds. She carried a black chiffon handkerchief with which she dabbed at her mouth and eyes. Even in company she refers to T.V. as "Daddy."

We had coffee in the huge wood-beamed living room. Madame Soong played a game of Chinese checkers with Luce and beat him. Luce kept insisting that in America the game was called parcheesi. Then Dr. Chu, T.V.'s economic secretary, got to describing how to play "Russian poker" and Luce finally called for a demonstration. We gathered around the dining-room table and played. T.V. was lucky; I got in toward the end and had good luck. Before dinner one scotch and water was served the men, one tomato juice the ladies. No drinks afterward, though T.V. offered a final round as Luce started to go. The dinner conversation was mostly about America: Luce was quizzed on the Republicans. He thought the GOP a cinch to take the House, a bare possibility for the Senate. He said the Republicans have a lot of good candidates for 1948, but I got no hint from what he said as to his own leanings. It was a very enjoyable evening.

NANKING, October 29—Through Shen Chang-huan I received an invitation from Generalissimo and Madame Chiang to attend their dinner for Luce, with T.V. and Shen the only other guests. But around five-thirty I came down with a bad attack of diarrhea and had to beg off. Some sulphadiazine pills quelled it during the night, but I was sorry to miss the dinner.

NANKING, October 30—Attended Peng's dinner for Luce. Most interesting person there was Archbishop Paul Yu Pin, a big man (six feet two) who strikes one immediately as having personality.

Fred Gruin is leaving tomorrow on a correspondents' junket to Kalgan to see what a city recaptured from the Communists looks like.

NANKING, October 31—The other day, chancing on a copy of Wendell Willkie's *One World*, I found a reference in it to Lee Wei-kuo as one who was "wise beyond his years." I was reminded of it this morning while driving down to work. Wei-kuo's jeep had been seized by the garrison troops because of some minor infraction of regulations and he came over to the house to ride with me. It was a chance to have him meet the family. He brought Betty a box of tea from Formosa.

En route downtown he gave me a fill-in on the current effort of the third-party figures. His sources are excellent, wider and more personal than Peng's because of his long service—nearly seven years—as secretary to the Gimo. He said that Tuesday morning the Gimo had called in the third-party leaders and urged them (as the papers said) to do their utmost to bring about a peaceful settlement. He offered to order a cease-fire if the Communists would at least announce the list of their delegates to the National Assembly; in fact he would make that offer if only the Democratic League would name their delegates. According to Wei-kuo, this was received with considerable elation by the Democratic Leaguers.

This strikes me as a consummately clever political move. I suppose it does represent a degree of "concession" in the jockeying back and forth, but as a gambit for beating the Communists politically it is masterful, and is in keeping with the plan which obviously has been in his mind for weaning support away from the Communists and enabling the holding of a multiparty assembly. It puts the Democratic Leaguers very much on the spot. If they really want to promote peace they can do it by a very simple act. They cannot defend refusal on any very reasonable grounds. And if the Leaguers and non-partisans come in, the Communists would have to do so too unless they were willing to have their own Assembly more one-party, less democratic, than the KMT's.

Wei-kuo had some personal background on the Gimo's frame of mind, throwing light on the sincerity of his desire for constitutional government, as a result of his recent six weeks in Manchuria and his contacts with Chen Cheng. The general made three trips to Peking. The first involved military arrangements designed to defeat the Communist siege of Tatung.

The second was to deploy government troops into favorable defense positions in event of a cease-fire, which might be ordered "at any time." Chen had shown Wei-kuo a letter he had received from the Gimo, nineteen pages long, and though the characters were large it ran to about a thousand words, which was long for the Gimo. In this letter Chiang repeatedly stressed one theme: get into positions capable of defense if a cease-fire is ordered and the Communists violate it; make sure that the government troops will scrupulously observe the cease-fire. This would indicate that

for at least six weeks Chiang has been willing to stop fighting if
he felt his military strength permitted, always remembering his
utter lack of faith in Communist observance of truces.

Chen's third visit to Peking was heralded in the press as a final
massing of strength and strategy to take Kalgan. But Wei-kuo
had this story: at the Double Tenth celebration (which I had attended), Chen had asked him to go along, and they left next
morning. When they arrived at approximately 1 P.M. Chen asked
the local garrison commander for a report on the Kalgan fighting.
While he was waiting for a reply, around 2 P.M. a reconnaissance
plane in the area radioed back word that Kalgan had fallen to the
government. Chen's first word was from the air force, and it was
he who informed the garrison commander.

Wei-kuo says the Communists rejected Chiang's offer of truce
because they were dead sure that with numerical superiority of
three or four to one over the Nationalist column pushing up from
Peking they could stop that drive and, with an unexpected sneak
through a pass southeast of Kalgan, menace Peking itself. The
pass stratagem was discovered in time to rush a regiment to its
defense. This regiment was decimated in the fighting, but it did
hold the pass. Meanwhile General Fu Tso-yi's troops got into
Kalgan from the north, and the setback given the main column
at Hwailai was recovered. It was a decisive military defeat for the
Communists.

Wei-kuo also called my attention to a Central News dispatch
from London October 29 reporting on a broadcast by a "Mr.
Maslennikov" over Radio Moscow. Maslennikov said that three
factors had changed China's international position: (1) China
took an active part in the defeat of Japan; (2) the unequal
treaties with Britain, America, and other countries have been
outlawed; (3) China had signed a treaty of alliance and friendship
with Russia which "expressed the mutual interests of the two
peoples."

Wei-kuo went on to say that Russian Ambassador Petrov, in
recent conversations with Foreign Minister Wang Shih-chieh, had
complained about attacks on Russia in the Chinese press, includ-

ing one cartoon uncomplimentary to Stalin which had been reprinted from some American publication in the official *Central
Daily News*. Wang had told him this was only natural reaction to
the bitter attacks in the Russian press on China. Petrov asked him
to note that these attacks were always against Chinese "reactionaries" and never against Chiang Kai-shek or the Chinese government. Wei-kuo interpreted the Maslennikov commentary as a gesture intended to follow up this propaganda situation.

Along the same line, Wei-kuo learned last night that when the
Nationalists took Antung the Russians had moved troops across
the Yalu River bridge and stationed them on the Manchurian
side. Nationalist commanders sent word to the Russian commander: this end of the bridge is Chinese soil and you have no
business here. It was a tense situation briefly, but the Russians
withdrew to the North Korean side of the bridge.

Wei-kuo interprets all this, I think correctly, as an attempt by
Russia to show support of the Chinese Communists but at the
same time an unwillingness to tangle with the Nationalists now
that they have established military superiority over the Communists.

A call from Brad Connors at ten-thirty informed me that Bob
Elson and Roy Alexander, the two editors accompanying Luce,
were coming in from Peking around 1 P.M. and I could get a better ETA at noon. When I called base operations at noon, surprisingly I got Bob on the phone. In my rickety ministry car I went
out and picked them up. I was glad to be able to furnish them
with a drink, of which they claimed to be in need, and a steak
lunch on which Chiao did fairly well.

Ambassador Stuart gave a dinner for Luce tonight. I arrived
shortly before eight and found Bill Gray, Bob, and Roy there
with Philip Fugh, Peng, Wang Shih-chieh, John Melby of the
embassy staff, and General Yu Ta-wei. Luce was absent. Today
was the Gimo's birthday and he had gone off with Madame
Chiang, modestly in the Chinese custom, to hide from the cele-
brations of it. Luce went with them, and so did General and Mrs.
Marshall. They went by train to Wusih. Luce arrived at Stuart's

about nine, after we had eaten, and said they had picnicked at noon on an island in the lake and had a very relaxed day.

Stuart's dinner was very correct and well served in the spacious embassy. The gentle old missionary educator was a perfect host. There were martinis before dinner, sauterne with the fish, burgundy with the ham, brandy afterward, and later on, in the living room, scotch. Melby said Teddy White's book, *Thunder Out of China*, was very favorably reviewed in Sunday's New York *Times* and *Herald Tribune*. I remembered the news digest I had been reading earlier this week reporting on a speech he and Owen Lattimore had made somewhere, in which Teddy repeated the old saw that U.S. policy in China was driving the Communists into the arms of Russia. My own view is that Chinese Communists policy is driving the U.S. into the hands of the KMT. Certainly since July the Communists have been snarlingly suspicious of their best friends, the Americans, and have made it impossible for the U.S. to do for them what they would never be able to do for themselves—worm peacefully into the government of China and have a chance to influence it toward the social reforms they claim to advocate.

Luce dominated the conversation after dinner, as he has at all these Chinese functions I have attended with him. He said there was only a smattering of recognition, when they arrived at Wusih, that it was the Gimo and Madame Chiang; but word got around and when they went back to the train in the afternoon the whole town was out and there was literally barely room for the car to pass through. He recalled General Marshall's commentary on the cheering throngs: "They want so much to be happy." After a bit of this Luce decided he wanted to have "my talk with Stuart" and the rest of us all were thus dismissed.

NANKING–SHANGHAI, November 1—I went to the office full of work to do, only to find a telegram from Shanghai saying my car was still on the other side of the river, there was no crane to put it on a barge, etc. I was so frustrated by the long delay in getting action on it that I decided that if I could get aboard the U.S. plane taking Luce and his party to Shanghai this afternoon I would go and stay until I got the problem cleared up. Bill Gray was able to arrange the passage quickly.

There was, however, the luncheon given by Dr. Wang Shih-chieh at the Foreign Ministry. Luce, Bill Gray, myself, George Yeh, a couple of Foreign Ministry officials, and a General Chu, head of the Chinese mission to SCAP in Tokyo, were present. Luce was chiefly interested in Chu's ideas—on how Japan should be dealt with. Chu demurred on the ground that he could not begin to outline them in less than several hours of exposition. But he was quite critical of MacArthur: said the SCAP commander took no advice from anyone, was extremely sensitive to criticism, and was not following the kind of policy which would instill democracy in Japan.

I made the plane at three-thirty, though it was a wrench to leave the family so soon again. By way of clearance I dropped in on T.V. I took a minute to outline my current view of the situation: in the immediate period China had a chance to win stronger support from the U.S., building on the turn of events that have followed the last Marshall-Stuart statement. I told him I intended to prepare a very careful memorandum for the Gimo on the agrarian problem. "Please do it before you go," he said. "It comes up next Wednesday." I knew I could not do it before I left, but I also knew I could get it to the Gimo by Monday morning, which would be time enough.

The air trip to Shanghai was smooth and pleasant. It was, I think, General Lucas' plane, fitted for staff work. On arrival at Shanghai I inherited, luckily, a room at the Cathay which had been reserved for Elson and Alex, a spacious, well-appointed double room at $44,000 CNC a day. After a call home I settled down to await word about the car, and started reading a book Luce wanted me to give to Foreign Minister Wang, Harold Nicolson's *The Congress of Vienna*.

SHANGHAI, November 2—With the help of Bennett Yuan of the MOI I got the China Travel Service to take over the shipment of my car to Nanking. I cashed a U.S. check at the Chase Bank and picked up a bit of Shanghai gossip from the manager. He says T.V. is currently gunning for his brother, T.L., in a financial way; says that when T.V.'s companies need exchange it's easy to get, and when they don't, it's tight. I said I had heard horrendous tales about all the high-ups in China but never found anyone who could substantiate any of it. "You can't put your finger on that sort of stuff," he said. Spent the afternoon working on my memo to the Gimo.

Tonight it was a dinner at Mayor Wu's, for Luce again. In addition to the *Time* people there were some Chinese politicians, some American China Hands, and Consul General Monnett Davis. The dinner was good, Chinese but served Western style, with the inevitable sharks' fins included. K.C. stood up well under the *kan peis*. In the hotel I ran into Ed Bayne, who is an economic adviser of some sort to T.V., who wanted me to suggest to Luce that *Fortune* do an article on Central Trust, which he described as an octopus-like enterprise combining the functions of U. S. Commercial Corp., a banking business, and insurance including life and maritime and land shipping. It is run by S. Y. Liu, the alien property man. Ed also said T.V. this week got the Gimo to approve an order compelling the government ministries to keep all their deposits in the Central Bank, instead of scattered through four banks. It will reduce the deposits of H. H. Kung's Bank of China to about 30 per cent, and the others even more, and will have a strong deflationary effect. The move, he said, was based on the ground that the government needed tighter control of its funds, and Ed thought T.V. had "real guts" to take this move just ahead of the National Assembly. He said T.V. has managed to avoid any new note issue for the last sixty days.

What impressions of China Luce and his editors took back with them was not clear to me. The various dinners were chiefly social and it was a case of the visitors asking questions rather than expressing opinions. In Shanghai Luce grilled Mayor Wu at considerable length on the military situation, which I thought a bit odd since K.C. was up to his ears in municipal problems and only peripherally aware of what was going on in the fighting. But I learned some years later that Luce, who also sought answers from the most competent sources wherever he traveled, also pursued information and opinion—and explanation of opinion—from whatever source available when a question was on his mind. During the Asiatic conference in Geneva in 1954 I took him to a dinner with Walter S. Robertson when he spent the entire evening arguing with him the issue of Trieste. Robertson was by then Assistant Secretary of State for the Far East, and Trieste was a current State Department problem though not in Robertson's bailiwick.

My only clues came from his breakfast with T.V., when Luce wanted to know if the Nationalist tide of victories had not "changed things," had not in effect settled the KMT-Communist dispute militarily, or at least brought it in sight. Similarly he found it puzzling that so much attention was being paid to the Democratic League, which everyone admitted was without any real influence.

Both these questions reflected a practical man's view of the current situation from the standpoint of American interest, untouched by the psychology which had come to affect those in China who were steeped in it. His first question implied there was nothing to be ashamed of in military victory. Almost a year's striving for truces continually broken had built up a feeling locally that it was wicked to fight. This applied to both sides, of course, but somehow it was more wicked for the Nationalists because in their case it was being done by "reactionaries" and "militarists." Even now the Communists—Russian and Chinese—benefit from this subconscious acceptance that they are expected to be aggressive, an acceptance based on fear of opposing them. Luce convinced himself, I think, that the basis of the Marshall Mission was obsolete long before American policy makers were ready to admit it.

SHANGHAI, November 3—By pedicab I went to the Community Church for the morning service. The ride back through the streets of "Frenchtown" was interesting: Russian-language signs giving evidence of the White Russians who had once found haven in the foreign-dominated Chinese city. I noted a corset shop, I think on Bubbling Well Road, appropriately named "Madame Fanny."

I invited Norman Soong and Mrs. Newsreel Wong to dine with me at the Cathay. (Norman Soong was a Honolulu-born Chinese who covered Tokyo for Central News Service, the government agency.) We got to talking about the fabulous and often feuding Soong family which had produced the Prime Minister, Madame Chiang, Madame H. H. Kung, and Madame Sun Yat-sen. This was Norman's account of the feuds that go on among them: Madame Kung, the eldest daughter, always felt it her duty to take care of the youngest sister, Madame Chiang, and there was a relationship between these two that tended to put Madame Sun, the middle sister, apart. Since the death of her husband Madame Sun has devoted herself to a sort of one-woman crusade for his "Three People's Principles," the *San Min Chu I,* while the others have been mixed up with politicians running the government. T.V., in alternating at running Chinese finance with his brother-in-law, H. H. Kung (whose wife, said Norman, is the guiding genius in that family), naturally drifted into rivalry with him which was fostered and promoted by their respective underlings.

With respect to T.V. and the Gimo, Norman commented that their present relationship is almost identical to that existing twenty years ago when T.V. was financing Chiang's Northern Expedition. T.V. is the financier, Chiang the soldier. Two decades ago T.V. was Finance Minister of the provisional government at Canton. Chiang asked for money as he needed it, and T.V. saw that he got it.

After the government was established at Nanking T.V. began thinking in terms of budgets, while Chiang was not. This led to T.V.'s ouster in favor of H. H. Kung, who didn't bother about budgets and from whom Chiang could get all the money he wanted. But that couldn't last and Chiang had to go back to T.V.

Afterward I dispatched my memo to the Gimo and returned to *The Congress of Vienna*, absorbingly interesting as a story of the influences that created a united nations front against Napoleon and those that caused the front to disintegrate once peace came. The parallels with the world today are obvious.

SHANGHAI, November 4—I got the household goods through customs by showing up personally and opening a barrel of china. It hurt me to see that beautiful packing disturbed, with the stuff still to go to Nanking. I was told I would have to open two other cases, when it was discovered I worked for the Chinese government, and the whole shipment was passed.

At the local MOI office I got a secondhand account of what Waldo Drake of the Los Angeles *Times* learned on a trip to Sinkiang. The provincial governor told him he had asked the Gimo for winter uniforms for 100,000 troops, together with food and some trench mortars. The Gimo refused on the ground that the material was more needed elsewhere. He also told Drake that the Russian-dominated "independent" Mongolians had cut one of two roads from Lanchow to Tihua, and the other was in danger of being cut. A third and much longer route has been cut by Russian-dominated Turks of Sinkiang Province. The garrison troops on the remaining stretch have had to beg for their food. Russia is apparently aiming to cut off the northern point of the province, north of the Altai range, to push China back from its present border, which is only some five hundred miles from the Kuznetsk Basin area where the Soviet Union set up an industrial complex during the war in an attempt to escape enemy attack. If this is accomplished it will push the northern border of Sinkiang back to about the latitude of the southern border of Outer Mongolia. At the governor's request Drake is writing none of this but is going to tell Marshall the whole story.

Just after 5 P.M. I remembered that I had not received my ticket back to Nanking which I had asked the MOI to get for me. In some panic, figuring the Gimo might possibly want to see me about my agricultural memo in the morning, I phoned the MOI only to learn the request had been forgotten. I figured the only thing to do was to go down to the station and take my chances for getting aboard the 11 P.M. train.

Till Durdin gave me a lift to the station. I got in line at the ticket window, but it suddenly decided to close. A policeman spotted me and asked if I had a passport. I told him yes, and handed him my card. He handed it back. Another window opened, but after taking care of a couple of customers it closed too. I found a man wandering about the station with a ticket. I took him to the China Travel Service desk and established that it was genuine, was first class, and was for the 11 P.M. night express. So I bought it for $27,000—it turned out that fares had gone up 50 per cent that day. The CTS man suggested I ask the stationmaster about a berth. I found a very languid-mannered though apparently intelligent young man who took my card and listened while I explained I was in great need of a berth on the Nanking train. He spoke Chinese to the others in the room and they all found it very funny. He suggested I try again tomorrow, since the train was all sold out. He was not interested in my idea that what I was looking for was a possible cancellation. No, he said, the train was sold out.

I was determined to get aboard and stand up all night if necessary. I tried the inquiry window; I was told it was no use waiting. But I did. At ten-forty one of the men who had waved me away asked to see my card. I gave it to him, with my ticket, and he came back with a berth—$15,000. I handed him $20,000 in my relief, but he indignantly handed the change back. Later I saw him on the platform. He gave me his card—he was a railway official—and was very polite. The berth turned out to be an upper in an American-type Pullman, which was fair enough. Despite the loud talk and the incessant smoking in a little-ventilated space, I managed to get about as much rest as I ever get on an overnight train trip.

NANKING, November 6—One of the questions submitted for Peng's press conference asked the truth of reports that T. V.

Soong was about to be replaced as Premier by Chang Chun. I decided I should see T.V., though I knew Peng would be asking him what to say. While waiting—the National Defense Council meeting was lasting longer than usual—I discussed it with C. P. Kiang, who said he thought Chang Chun was a better bet for Secretary-General of the National Government and that in any case T.V. had no intention of resigning. Then with the air of a man asking me something confidential he said he had heard indirectly that I had applied for passage home. I replied that my contract would run out in March and I was trying to be foresighted in view of the extremely heavy demand for transportation. He said "we" wanted me to stay.

When T.V. got in I asked him about his resignation and got the answer I expected: no intention to get out. I asked what the NDC had decided on the agrarian problem. He said it had been put over a week, and asked me to send him a copy of my memo to the Gimo. He said he was leaving for Shanghai immediately and would be back Sunday.

NANKING, November 7—Had another talk with Lee Wei-kuo this morning. He told me in greatest confidence that he had urged the Gimo to issue a cease-fire, not as a quid pro quo for Communist acceptance of the first seven points of his current offer, but to rob them of their main current argument: that they could not name their National Assembly delegates or talk peace while there was fighting still going on. He said the Gimo is considering it and probably will do it on the eve of the Assembly. His argument was that it no longer matters whether the Communists take part; what matters is bringing in the Democratic League. This of course is the struggle both sides are making at present; the government to pull them in, the Communists to keep them out. If they don't come in, Chiang may as well postpone the Assembly again.

From this we got into a discussion of what the government had to do to compete with the Communists: clean out corruption. Wei-kuo said that after all the National Government had few corrupt men. He ran down the list of ministers, describing them as "clean" with two or three questionable. He said the Chen brothers were "personally" clean, and had an angle on the "renovationist" movement which differs from my previous information that it is an attempt to purge non-CC elements from the KMT. Wei-kuo says the younger elements in the party have, in the last three or four years, become resentful of the regimented loyalty the Chens have imposed as a result of their early indoctrination in Russian organizational methods under Borodin, and restless also because the Chens have failed to clean out corruption among their followers. This discontent reached the stage where the Chens decided the smart thing to do was to try to lead in the same direction, and the "renovationist" movement was started and put in charge of two of their vice-ministers.

The corruption, he summarized, is not in the National Government, generally speaking. It is in the army, among the garrison commanders; in the provinces; among the mayors. And there has been a wholesale ousting of mayors recently. In Canton, of course, the corruption is terrible.

Somehow he got around to a little anecdote about the Gimo. Madame Chiang had called Mrs. Marshall on the telephone. The Gimo insisted that he wanted to speak to her, too, which he proceeded to do, in English: "How do you do? You come back? Good-by." It is only in the last year or so, he said, that the Gimo has been picking up a few phrases of this sort.

The Republican sweep in the U.S. has been really sensational, with the Senate going GOP as well as the House. Central News is totally inadequate and I'm awaiting some newspapers impatiently.

CHAPTER FIFTEEN

Chiang in decisive political move summons National Assembly and announces he will delay reorganization of cabinet until after new constitution is adopted. Assembly opens despite Communist boycott.

Political tension began to build up in November as the date approached for the meeting of the National Assembly. There was no sudden drama in it, as on a football field when an end suddenly intercepts a pass and races eighty yards for a touchdown; rather it was like the slowly building tension of baseball, created by a slow development of advantage for one side which a homer or a major error could destroy. Slowly Chiang Kai-shek was winning his immediate political goal of splitting off the splinter personalities from the Communists in his attempt to make the Assembly more than a Kuomintang convention.

The military situation was relatively quiet since the Communists were in defeat with their forces in Manchuria physically cut off from the political headquarters in Yenan. Nationalist troops were not yet feeling the effects of having had their U.S. sources of ammunition and supply cut off in midsummer.

Economically the country was continuing to deteriorate, but only the men laboring under the responsibility of keeping it solvent—T. V. Soong and his officials—seemed to be dealing with it. The pressure on the CNC bank note rate was relentless; I attended one session at which a new rate of 5000 to $1.00 was considered but put aside when the Generalissimo decided it would be inopportune to change the rate just as the Assembly was meeting.

From Marshall I heard the first direct hint of realization that his mission was failing, though the thought had obviously been growing in his mind for some time, when he mentioned that Truman had said some kind words about him as a means of saving his face.

I was equally convinced that there would be no Communist-KMT coalition, but without personal despondency about it. My own mission now consisted, as I interpreted it for myself, of seeking to help the Chinese create the kind of government the U.S. would feel justified in supporting. The presence of the family had been a great restorer of morale, but I was also fascinated by the political maneuvering. I considered the Generalissimo to be a master tactician within the framework of the customs and traditions in which the country operated.

Nanking, November 8—Today was one of climax in the mounting pressure to get something done before the meeting of the National Assembly. Chiang Kai-shek issued a statement: (1) announcing he had ordered a cease-fire; (2) stating positively that the National Assembly would be held November 12 as scheduled; (3) asserting that the Executive Yuan would not be reorganized until after the National Assembly. He holds open a quota for the Communists and other parties any time they want to come in. The whole tone of the thing is patient but firm: we still want you guys in, but if you won't play we're going to go ahead anyway.

It is a consummate maneuver and I think I detect the hand of Marshall and Stuart in it. If it brings in the Youth Party, it's something; if it brings in the Democratic League, the Communists are licked in the game of political maneuver.

Peng read the Gimo's statement at a six-thirty press conference in the *Central Daily News* auditorium with all the Hollywood trimmings—floodlights, newsreel cameras, flash bulbs, and an air of excitement. One of the afternoon papers had a tip and the foreign correspondents were all sure it was going to be a cease-fire, yet not quite sure enough. Till and Peggy Durdin, Hank Lieberman, and Pepper Martin talked to Peng after the conference, and Peng, off the record, admitted that the government did not expect for a minute that the Communists would take the offer to take part in the National Assembly. An odd quirk was that the MOI was prevented from sending the text of the statement to the U.S. and Britain because last night the local gendarmerie closed down the Central Broadcasting Administration station on the ground that it was not properly registered. The director was so angry he made no effort to get it reopened. Such things could happen only in China.

I spent the morning writing an analysis of the American elections for Chiang, Soong, Wang Shih-chieh, and Peng. Toward noon I called on Dr. Wang to give him Luce's gift book, *The Congress of Vienna,* and we had a pleasant chat in which he showed a very intelligent understanding of the American political situation. Since my translator, Chiang Kang-chen, aspires to work for the ministry, I took him along to give him a chance to meet the Foreign Minister.

NANKING, November 9—Opened a CNC checking account in the Manufacturers' Bank of China and now I can write a check for a million dollars. What's more I'll probably write several, some of them bigger than that, before I'm through paying bills around here.

The Communists turned down the truce before it was a few hours old last night. Their reasons: (1) it was "unilateral"; (2) Chiang's order not to attack but "to defend against attack" would be used as a cloak for attacks; (3) the procedure violated the PCC resolutions. The first two reasons are specious; the logic of the first is positively insane, coming from a party which has been demanding an end to the fighting; the second is based on a "might happen" and has little more logic to it. The third is open to argument.

The Democratic League's position, articulated by Lo Lung-chi, who still seems to act as its spokesman, was that Chiang's announcement conflicts with the PCC because: (1) reserving quotas for non-participating parties is "unprecedented"; (2) the draft constitution, being submitted uncompleted, will lead to "numerous disputes"; (3) provision for amendment and revision six months later would make the constitution, fundamental law of the country, "uncertain to the people." These reasons, except as they reflect the Communists' currently panicky mentality, are just plain stupid and I can't believe that a constitutional authority like Carson Chang can seriously entertain them. Therefore I think the chances increase that Chang will pull out of the League and take most of it with him.

In midafternoon I got a telephone call from Ruth F. Bean, from the Shanghai SSU, looking for a place to stay. I invited her to stay with us, and she bore two bottles of Johnny Walker from Colonel Moscrip, which seems to be his standard present when he sends one of his people up here. She wanted a briefing on the political situation as it related to the National Assembly, and asked a lot of questions on details which I was unable to answer. Just as we were about to sit down to dinner Lieutenant Hickey called to say that General and Mrs. Marshall wanted Betty and me to come to dinner, but with a guest at our table I had to decline.

Fred Gruin got back from the Kalgan trip today. It was quite an adventure; the plane was put out of commission because of something wrong with the magneto; the weather was bad, bitter cold with little protection; they had to sleep on boards; they were aboard a train that was derailed by Communist action; at one point they were marooned in the middle of a river fording and had to be rescued piggy-back by a passing goatherd.

NANKING, November 10—The PCC steering committee met this afternoon, a most surprising development after the Communist and third-party rejections of Chiang's action—or protests, rather, since it is not something they can block by objection. Agence France Presse says that Marshall and Stuart want postponement of the National Assembly, which I am inclined to doubt. AFP also has a lengthy story on impending cabinet changes, including Chang Chun for Premier in place of T. V. Soong.

Doon Campbell of Reuters, writing in the Shanghai English papers, reports terrific destruction at Kalgan. Fred Gruin, in person, comes back with the impression that the Communists have suffered a political defeat, second only to their military defeat, in the antagonism engendered in the populace of the recaptured area.

NANKING, November 11—Newsreel Wong came up for the opening of the National Assembly and since he brought bedding with him I was glad to be able to put him up in view of his past kindnesses to me. As it turned out he needn't have brought his bedding, since our freight arrived today. The kids dug into it for their toys and the cook for kitchen utensils and dishes.

Politically it was a day of intense activity. T.V. was back, but had left the Executive Yuan by the time I arrived there and I did not go to see him. The Committee of Three—Marshall, Chou En-lai, Chen Cheng—met this morning, informally, but only to hear Chou go through all the old reasons why the Communists could not assent to joining the National Assembly. The Democratic League and other third parties petitioned the Generalissimo this morning to postpone the Assembly to December 1. He told them he would if they would produce their list of delegates. They promised to provide a partial list now and the rest before the Assembly met. I got a fill-in on all this when I called on Philip Fugh at five-thirty. He was in the midst of telling me about it when Ambassador Stuart returned from some affair at Ginling College and completed the story.

The question whether the Assembly would open tomorrow as scheduled was in doubt all day. Before I left the MOI I knew it had been decided officially to go ahead (the bulletin had been sent to delegates), but no announcement was to be made since it was merely proceeding according to schedule. After dinner I got a call from Harold Milks of AP, who said the Democratic League was claiming there would be a postponement. I called Peng at home, who confirmed it and said the delay was for "two or three days." He hung up in his eagerness to avoid telling me anything more.

Stuart confirmed that Marshall and he had written the Gimo's last statement. The Gimo had originally sent over one which he described as "repetitious and provocative" and invited them to edit it. Marshall, as usual, said he was too disgusted to do anything with it. The Gimo invited him to draft one, which he did, with Stuart helping. Stuart said the Gimo had previously promised him that before the Assembly met he would order a cease-fire. Chiang changed the Marshall-Stuart draft in several minor and unimportant phrases, and made one major change. Where the submitted draft proposed that another Assembly be called later—to give time for settlement of disputes in the meantime—he had evolved a compromise permitting revision within six months.

Stuart said the draft constitution, the coalition formula which the PCC had set up, was the basic issue and the Communists were intent on pursuing it. I said I thought the PCC pattern had remained for a long time, even though both sides deviated from it, but in the rejection of the Kalgan truce and in their apparent determination to keep out of a coalition under all terms but their own, the Communists had in effect destroyed that pattern, and that in any case it had been rendered more or less obsolete by the greatly changed military situation.

Stuart agreed, more or less, but said he still wavered between believing the Communists really wanted to come in and that they didn't. The Democratic League and the others still held hope, he said. He commented that the League is in bed with the Communists and finds it hard to get out, though most of the members would like to, and are trying to do it by taking the Communists with them. We concluded that a postponement would be smart: nothing to lose, and two points to gain: a better propaganda position and more chances of getting the others into the Assembly.

Fugh said the latest word about the Executive Yuan was that T. V. Soong would remain as Prime Minister. Chang Chun would be named Secretary-General of the National Government.

Till and Peggy Durdin came over for dinner, which we were able to put on with some style, being in possession of our china and having a couple of floor and table lamps to make the living room a little less bare. Chris Rand dropped in during the evening for some dope. I felt I could not pass on the details of what Stuart had told me, but gave him what background I could.

NANKING, November 12—The government took the day off because it was Sun Yat-sen's birthday. ("So *that* was why the Gimo picked today for the start of the Assembly.) I dropped in on T.V. around eleven to discuss the U.S. attitude toward policy just now. He said he saw no U.S. alternative to support of the government. It could not support the Communists, or pull out. I said that was undoubtedly true, but it might be halfhearted support. He argued that the way to do something is to do it all out, which is certainly his method of action. I agreed, but pointed out that America has done things halfheartedly before. The point is, I said, that the U.S. wants a strong moral basis for supporting the Chinese government.

T.V. confirmed what Philip Fugh had said: there would be no change in the prime ministry. "Chang Chun is not after the job himself," he said, "but some of his friends have been pushing him."

NANKING, November 14—Breakfast today was punctuated by a call from the China Travel Service saying my car had arrived. So I got Chiang Kang-chen and went out to the Hsiakwan station. It had to be towed back to the house, since it had not been serviced, but it came through the trip in fine shape. After lunch every chauffeur in the ministry was out at the house helping to put it together: replacing hubcaps, putting in oil, and polishing it. In comparison to the jalopies which abound in this city, I suppose it gives my chauffeur great face.

This morning there dropped in at the ministry one Alfred Kohlberg, treasurer of the American China Policy Association and leading figure in the so-called "China lobby." Short, bald with a laurel-wreath fringe of hair, he said he wanted to ask Marshall what lend-lease equipment had been given the Chinese Communists. When I said I thought none he quickly mentioned radio equipment. I presume he meant the radio sets Marshall gave them so that they could communicate with Yenan without having to go through KMT channels. He seems to be a manufacturer of linens at Amoy who has been coming out here for thirty years but has never lived here, also the kind of man who can spot a Communist at a thousand paces on a dark night. He said the ACPA was trying to get the State Department to reverse itself on the order stopping the sale of $75 million in munitions to China. He asked me to suggest the name of an American, not identified as anti-Communist, who might write a foreword to the authorized version of Chiang Kai-shek's book, *China's Destiny*, but I could not think of an appropriate name offhand. Peng had a lunch for him which he had to leave early to keep a 2 P.M. appointment with Chen Li-fu.

Shen Chang-huan telephoned to inquire, on the Gimo's behalf, the size of Tom Dewey's majority for governor of New York. Luce had told him that if it was more than 500,000 it would be very significant of a Republican trend. I passed along the information I had from USIS that it was between 700,000 and 800,000. Shen also said he had translated my memorandum on the agrarian situation and presented it to the Gimo with a brief saying he thought it was good business for China. The Gimo had ordered the Executive Yuan to study the problem and if it could be worked out during the National Assembly to promulgate it forthwith. I thought I would run over to see T.V. to find out what he had heard about it from the Gimo, but before I could leave I got a call from him saying he had been talking to J. Losing Buck (Pearl Buck's first husband) and Dean C. B. Hutchison of the University of California, head of a Sino-American agricultural commission which has been touring and studying conditions here. He said they both had interesting things to say about farm tenancy and that since Hutchison planned to hold a press conference Saturday morning he hoped I could get the correspondents to ask some penetrating questions. He asked me to breakfast with him at his house on the hill—("Be prompt as I have a meeting at nine o'clock")—to discuss it.

I signed off early to take the family for a ride around Nanking and Lotus Lake in the car. I still find myself amazed, periodically, that we have all transplanted ourselves out here, together with the car.

NANKING, November 15—At breakfast T.V. gave me some material out of the agricultural mission's forthcoming report for study, and outlined angles he hoped the questioning of Hutchison would bring out. I warned T.V. that it would be difficult to compete with more exciting political news with a quite important but much duller farm tenancy story, but said I would do what I could.

I picked out the five correspondents I considered the most thoughtful, interested in the constructive as well as the sensational, and gathered them at my house at two-thirty. They were Till Durdin, Chris Rand, Harold Milks, Ronald Stead, and Fred Gruin. The stony faces of these fellows as I waxed enthusiastic about what Hutchison's mission had found out about farm tenancy in China made me feel like a fool. Stead even went to sleep. But they did exhibit mild interest and promised to question Hutchison about his conclusions that tenancy is no greater here than in other countries, and less in fact than in the United States; and that landlordism is not an evil *per se*.

Then, by prearrangement, I went to see Hutchison, a tall, dignified, white-haired, pipe-smoking gentleman who takes a calm, judicious view of Chinese agriculture. He is willing to tell his story in answer to questions though he wants to avoid expressing opinions that might get him into the political controversy. I went back to report to T.V.

Then I learned that Marshall had called the Americans to an off-the-record press conference at 2 P.M. tomorrow, and that the Communists, on the eve of their departure for Yenan, had also scheduled one, time unfixed. I knew this knocked into a cocked hat any hope for even modest publicity on the Chinese farm tenancy situation, but it couldn't be helped.

All of this was interrupted by the opening at 10 A.M. (three days late) of the National Assembly, which Chiang Kai-shek described in his speech as the most important event in the history of the Chinese Republic. I suppose it is, but the pageant seemed to lack drama. Perhaps I have gone stale on political spectacles, or I just failed to sense any feeling of tension or import on the part of the delegates.

The hall was neat, brightly painted, bedecked with red, white, and blue Chinese banners—to my mind, rather tastefully. The inevitable portrait of Sun Yat-sen, heroic in size, was the backdrop of the stage. Long tables, with high-backed chairs, were on the platform, a few groupings of flowers about. The show was late getting under way. Delegates came in Western clothes, mainly, with some in Chinese gowns and some in the formal, old-style mandarin jackets.

Around ten-fifteen the temporary chairman walked in, a fat, bald old man in mandarin costume. He was Wu Chih-hui, about eighty-two, oldest delegate and a KMT member since the revolutionary days. The Gimo came in from the wings wearing a plain military uniform with the gold collar plates of a general. At my distance I could not tell whether his tunic carried a decoration, campaign ribbons, or just some delegate's badge. The foreign correspondents, occupying seats against the back and side walls, rose when he entered, but the delegates remained seated and gave him what seemed to me mild and scattered applause. The abstention of the Communists and other minority representatives naturally left many vacant seats on the floor. Ceremonies opened with the singing of the *San Min Chu I*. Then, under prompting, everyone faced the Sun portrait and bowed three times. The hall was utterly quiet except for the whirring of a newsreel camera set up in the center aisle. Old Wu recited something, still with his back to the audience; it gave the impression that Sun, not he, was presiding. This was followed by a mass swearing-in of the delegates, still directed at the Sun portrait.

Wu, who had a little fringe of hair around the back of his head, then gave the opening speech, followed by the Gimo's, which lasted twenty minutes and drew scattered applause. He read it from manuscript in what seemed a detached sort of way, pausing occasionally to sip water. Immediately afterward the meeting adjourned.

It was a commentary on the still confused political situation that the foreign correspondents were unable to find out whether the Assembly had adjourned until tomorrow, or to when; and whether the Young China (formerly Youth) Party had sent its delegates. The non-partisans did come in. In my second session of the day with T.V., I asked him about it. He said the Youth Party had definitely promised the government to take part but was still trying to bring others in; it was a question of face, as to when their participation would be announced. It still looks as though Carson Chang's Social Democratic Party will eventually join in, leaving the remainder of the Democratic League, and the Communists, out of it.

Reflecting on the fact that the Generalissimo was doing the best he could under the circumstances to go about his promised task of turning the government over to the people, I mentioned to T.V. that despite the unfairness—in fact untruthfulness—of the Communists' charge of a "one-party Assembly" that slant tended to creep into the newsmen's stories. I told him the correspondents were desperately in need of someone who knew what was going on and could give them straight answers to their questions. I suggested Lee Wei-kuo. "It's Peng's job," said T.V. "I'll tell him to be on the *qui vive*, to see that the correspondents get what they want." I said a daily briefing, say at 5 P.M., would help . . . and let my sentence trail off. T.V. burst out laughing. "So you get frustrated too," he said.

NANKING, November 16—After I sent a note to T.V. to let him know about Marshall's planned off-the-record conference I got a call asking me to come over right away. While I was waiting in his study, just off the big living room, I took note of some of the pictures. There was an excellent framed portrait of Madame Soong on his desk. In one corner was a three-quarter Karsh portrait of T.V., and on one wall a framed copy of Boris Chaliapin's portrait of him done for *Time* magazine's cover story. There was also a photograph of Roosevelt and Churchill at what must have been the Quebec conference, since Canada's Mackenzie King was in it. T.V. was standing just behind Roosevelt.

T.V. asked me what the Marshall conference was about. I didn't know, but I guessed it would be an updating on what had been happening politically that he had a hand in. I said I imagined he would tell them he had not attended the Assembly opening as a way of showing his displeasure, and possibly why he was displeased. Here I was fishing for confirmation of something Ed Bayne had told me to the effect that Marshall had made some proposal to Chiang to "split the KMT" which Chiang had turned down. Ed had quoted Marshall as saying: "If you don't do it, no U.S. loan." But T.V. volunteered nothing. He asked if I could report to him after the conference, and I said I would.

T.V. sent for me again, just after lunch, and after I told him it was too soon to learn what Marshall was telling the newsmen, probably at that moment, he ushered me into the dining room where a group was gathered around the table. There were Pei Tsu-i, John Blandford, Chu, T.V.'s economic secretary, F. Chang, the customs man, and a tall, lanky sandy-haired Englishman named Cyril Rogers.

T.V. explained: the government was considering two actions: (1) announcing a system of licensing all imports, and (2) readjusting the exchange rate. The question was, should they both be done at the same time, or should there be an interval between them? Two releases had been prepared. He asked me to read them and say which course I thought was better. He said the exchange readjustment would have to be made sometime in any case.

After reading them I said I thought that from the standpoint of public psychology the best thing to do was wrap it up in one package; the devaluation had to be done anyway and I thought it would be better to administer one nervous shock instead of two;

that anyway, with rumors always current that further devaluation would come, the public was prepared for another jump in the rate.

The opinions went around the table, the others discussing the economic effects. Li, T.V.'s man in charge of the present limited import license system, was sent for; later, T.V. summoned Minister of Finance O. K. Yui. (T.V. said: "Let's send for O. K. Yui. After all, he's got to know about this." And chuckled. Yui was not told in advance last time.) Chu argued a logical economic case for a one-package action; Blandford chimed in; Rogers opposed it, arguing for first imposing import licenses, then devaluation. Yui, when he arrived, was for separate action, and Li also, though he preferred an "import equalization fee" which he outlined, involving an export subsidy. Chang, the customs man, objected that it would have international angles that could be avoided by just charging a fee for import licenses. Pei weighed all the arguments and concluded it was wiser to take the two actions separately. "We are buying time," he said. "We need time." Out of the whole discussion I got the impression of men who felt the inevitability of collapse but were putting it out of their minds because there was no alternative but to keep on fighting against it.

It got to be three forty-five and T.V. was due at the Gimo's. Pei reminded him, but he said, "But we have come to no conclusion. I feel like a donkey with a bale of hay on one side and a bale of hay on the other side." We talked until three fifty-five, when T.V. collected several of the group and went off to see the Gimo.

When he started talking to Yui he had used Chinese, but lapsed into English and stayed there. Yesterday, with a copy of Teddy White's book in my possession for a few minutes, I ran quickly through all its references to T.V. (all very complimentary) and noted that he "thinks, talks, and acts in English." I rather think he does prefer English but that, like Dave Lu, he thinks bilingually. It struck me these Chinese men running the government are smart, whatever else they may be. Most of the conversation was in English, very fluent, very expressive in shades of meaning, very precise in expression of economic concepts. And we foreigners—Rogers, Blandford, and I—knew only a little kitchen variety Chinese. What other government in the world, major or minor, can work so readily in an alien language?

I went off to Hutchison's to find out about his press conference, only to learn that Marshall's had lasted until four and then the correspondents had trooped off to see Chou En-lai. While I was there Brad Connors showed up and told Hutchison he would arrange one for him late tonight somehow. I'm not sure it ever came off.

Without more than a faint prompting from me, Brad sketched in Marshall's remarks. He had expressed his displeasure by refusing to attend the National Assembly; if the government attacked Yenan, it was the end: full-scale civil war would break out and he would go home, EHQ would close, MAGIC would end. But he added that he had never heard any suggestion in the government that Yenan was a target and did not know whether it was just a Communist fear. Chou, said Marshall, had not told him what he told the correspondents. To the press Chou said this was the end; to Marshall he said he was going back to Yenan "for reorientation and new instructions." And Marshall said that even if full-scale civil war broke out, the U.S. would try to "pick up the pieces." One questioner asked if there was friction between him and the State Department, in view of a recent speech by John Carter Vincent which was critical of the government. Marshall's reply was: "My policy is the State Department policy." He added, however, that he had not seen the text of Vincent's speech, which I think means he feels that Vincent spoke out of turn, at least in his timing.

I went back to T.V.'s and gave him a report. He said Marshall had told several persons Vincent's speech meant nothing, and to pay no attention to it. What, I asked, had been the decision on the exchange rate? T.V. said the Gimo had made the decision for them: with the National Assembly on, it was best not to stir people up with an exchange devaluation. We returned to the dining room and after some more discussion drafted a statement announcing the import licensing system. Peng was sent for in the midst of it and instructed to put it out tomorrow.

I got home after 7 P.M. to learn that Shen Chang-huan had been after me all afternoon. The Gimo wanted to see me if I could come before six; since I missed that, make it tomorrow at three-thirty. He didn't say about what, but I suspect it is the farm program.

NANKING, November 17—Took the family on our first ride outside Nanking: out to Swallow Rock through the villages and countryside and then back along the Yangtze.

At three o'clock I got my chauffeur and rode to the National Defense compound. Guards stopped the car at the gate and also as I neared the Gimo's house, but in each case my card satisfied them.

Only the Gimo, Shen Chang-huan, and I were present on this occasion; Tsao, with his unobtrusive little notebook, was nowhere in evidence. The only change in the office was a high, angle-top desk against the wall to the left of the Gimo's desk—the kind of desk an accountant or draftsman might work at—with two green-shaded gooseneck lamps, just under the large wall map of the world. The Gimo was in good humor. He inquired about the family and then asked if I had any ideas about publicizing the National Assembly now that it was in session.

It was all the opening I needed—T.V. must have talked to him. I said it would be very helpful if someone could be appointed to meet with the press every day the Assembly was in session. Someone who could answer the correspondents' questions straightforwardly, someone who understood their psychology. He replied that this was a good idea. Did I think Peng would be a good man for it, or someone else—say Lee Wei-kuo? I said Lee would be a fine choice, since he understood Western psychology so well. I was careful to add that of course Peng could do it but after all he had his weekly press conference and this was more a service of answering questions, etc.

The Gimo said he agreed, and instructed Shen to telephone

Peng and ask him to assign Wei-kuo to this job. He asked me to attend every session of the Assembly (he qualified that to say it was not a must, but he would like me to do it) and keep in close touch with Lee and Peng throughout. I said I would be happy to do so, as I could not think of anything more important right now.

Chiang then outlined several policies he thought should be the aim of government publicity. First he wanted to combat the Communist propaganda that this was a one-party Assembly, for as a matter of fact beside the KMT there were the non-partisans, the Youth Party, and likelihood that the Social Democratic Party of Carson Chang would come in. This left only the remainder of the Democratic League and the Communists outside; and since the League was a coalition of men without any actual following except for the nucleus Social Democratic Party which, with the Communists, had been recognized in 1938 as a legal party, once the Carson Chang outfit pulled out there really was nothing left. I interrupted to say I had noted news stories saying this group had promised to join by December 1, and was this correct? He said it was true, but that since that promise was made conditions had changed and the Social Democrats were likely to come in within a few days.

Then he went into the history of the Democratic League, which I got Shen to repeat to me afterward so that I could take notes on it. There are four elements beside Carson Chang's: (1) the National Salvation Association, formed in 1931 to promote a war of defense against Japanese aggression, headed by an old-timer, Shen Chün-ju, a bearded old fellow over seventy-five; (2) the Rural Reformist Society, headed by Liang Shu-ming, the fellow who had once been to lunch; (3) the "Third Party," a group formed in 1931, when there were only two parties, the KMT and the Communists, by a man named Ting Yen-tai, out of certain KMT and Communist elements; when Ting died the party in effect dissolved since most of its followers returned to the KMT fold; (4) the Vocational Educational Institute, headed by the delightful Chinese opera character, Huang Yen-pei, whom I had met when Lieutenant Auerbach invited him to dinner.

All this took quite some time. The Gimo interrupted it to make a telephone call while Shen was interpreting one of his longer passages to me, and once to summon an orderly to have stopped some pounding outside the window which was interfering with the conversation. His voice carried a bit of annoyance when he gave this order, and it was the first time I have ever seen him indicate any trace of vexation.

Before I left he turned briefly to U.S. foreign policy to say he agreed with the estimate in my memo that it would remain unchanged for the time being but that the apparent defeat of Marshall's efforts would bring in a period of uncertainty.

Just before dinner Charlie Wan stopped by the house, on his way to the press hostel to deliver the statement on the import licensing system, with a message saying T.V. was interested in getting publicity on the farm tenancy problem and since Hutchison had gone to Shanghai on his way to the States, would I please go down to Shanghai and try to arrange it. After my experience with the Nanking group I could not picture the Broadway Mansions crowd working up the slightest bit of interest, and I resolved to visit T.V first thing tomorrow and talk him out of it.

NANKING, November 18—It was not hard to talk T.V. out of the Shanghai trip. I told him the Shanghai correspondents would not be interested in such a topic and I doubted I could evoke penetrating questions from them; I said I could give other reasons, but he waved them off. "I'll accept your judgment," he said.

Today's Assembly meeting I expected to find dull, but instead it was absorbing because of similarities and dissimilarities with procedure in the U. S. House of Representatives. The session began around ten-fifteen. I had a good vantage point in a box from which I could see the Gimo and Madame Chiang in aisle seats in the center section, first row, but I discovered I was in the delegates' section and had to retire to the back row downstairs. Of the correspondents, only Harold Milks, Ronald Stead, Doon Campbell, and Chris Rand were on hand, and they soon left. A delegate suggested that Sun Fo be named temporary chairman and the moon-faced, slick-haired Sun trundled from his seat at the back and up on the platform.

The meeting started with a reading of Sun Yat-sen's political will. One of the MOI's contact section men sat beside me and translated as we went along. A clerk read the regulations relating to the appointment of the presidium of fifty-five members, and the Assembly's secretary-general, Hung Lan-yu, explained them. Sun Fo then announced that Chen Kuo-fu would speak, but a delegate on the floor rose to advocate deletion of one word in the first article of the regulations. He got a good hand. What happened to Chen Kuo-fu I never learned, for this set off a succession of speeches advocating changes in the regulations. One speaker, a Miao tribesman from Kweichow, demanded representation on the presidium for the Miaos as Miaos, and threatened to bolt the Assembly if this were not granted. The dispute raged, with speeches charging the regulations were not democratic enough, that representation should be on a regional basis, that it should be on a vocational basis, etc. Delegates were just as windy and repetitious as at home. Sun Fo suggested that those who held the same views might cancel their speeches, only to provoke a protest from one man who said that was what he came here for, and he could not be shut up. This dragged on, with a recess, until twelve-thirty, when proceedings were adjourned for the day.

I hunted up Wei-kuo on the floor during the recess, but Peng had said nothing to him. I arranged to meet him in his office at four, saying I wanted to tell him about my talk with the Gimo yesterday. At four he still had not heard from Peng. We discussed the project for daily briefings and his views on the need for them fitted precisely with mine. I suggested that the Assembly might well borrow the five-minute rule from the House of Representatives in order to get down to business, but he said the killing of time was desirable now. For one thing, it was advisable to drag along until the Social Democrats announced their decision to join. For another, it provided a blowing off of steam, which had best be spent now rather than against the other parties. There is strong resentment among the delegates, he said, of CC tactics to get control of the Assembly.

He said that on the eve of last Friday's meeting the KMT delegates had met for an address by Chiang, who spoke for seventy minutes, urging the party to remember it was the host and urging members to treat the minorities with every consideration, tempering their language and avoiding bitterness. He said he had worked for the party for forty years or more and his goal was realization of Sun Yat-sen's program for turning the government over to the people. Wei-kuo said the Gimo also asked delegates to quit agitating for return to the 1936 draft constitution, saying the government had pledged its word in the PCC to a different draft and must keep its word. Wei-kuo commented: "There is far more division in the KMT than in the other parties, or among the parties." He said, however, that the atmosphere was better now than it had been on the opening day. Also, it has been decided within the last day or two that seats on the presidium will be kept open for the Communists, just in case they do want to join, as well as any other abstainers. All this, I felt, was precisely the kind of background information the correspondents need on which to base their judgment of what is going on.

NANKING, November 19—The third session of the Assembly opened at nine-twenty with the inevitable prayerlike reading of Sun Yat-sen's will. Yesterday's debate over revision carried on. There was considerable difficulty over the dialects being used, including poor Mandarin by Sun Fo and Hung, the secretary-general. Finally Sun Fo arbitrarily declared debate at an end and put the question: should the original regulations be approved, or should they be revised? There was a show of hands to open them for revision. One delegate asked why the electric voting machinery was not being used. Hung replied they would use it next time. Another inquired whether fraud was possible, with many delegates absent, since some could push nearby buttons as well as their own. If there was a reply to this, my translator did not let me know. But when the first electric vote was taken, lighting up the two boards on either side of the stage like an advertising sign, Hung invited two delegates—any two—to go back and look at the totals to make sure there was no mistake. As far as I could see, no one took him up on it. The vote was announced as 677 to revise the regulations out of 1297 present.

Then there was debate over the question of amending the regulations article by article. There was heckling and hissing from the floor, chiefly indicating impatience and a desire to quit talking and get to voting. Delegates got to interrupting each other, until Sun Fo announced no one might speak without his permission. Finally another vote showed 1001 out of 1311 delegates present in favor of amendment article by article.

There was a recess, during which I encountered Shen Changhuan, who asked me what progress was being made on our proposed news-background setup. I told him Peng had not spoken to Lee. Shen said he would give Peng until tomorrow morning and then inquire what was holding it up; he said it was his responsibility to see that the Gimo's instructions were carried out. Among the delegates I noted Chen Li-fu, Archbishop Paul Yu Pin, General Chen Cheng, and Chang Chun.

After recess there was more debating and more voting. At eleven thirty-five the session adjourned with no announcement of the next meeting. Later I learned that tomorrow the delegates will meet in units to elect their candidates for the presidium.

So far the Assembly has proceeded chaotically as parliamentary bodies go. Sun Fo has not the slightest conception of running a meeting and I suppose there is no such thing as a Chinese Robert's *Rules of Order*. I discussed this point with Lee Wei-kuo. He said Sun Yat-sen had written a book called *First Steps to Democracy* covering this very problem, intended as a textbook or reference in educating the Chinese to parliamentary discussion, and that Sun Fo certainly should have read and studied his father's book. I suggested a parliamentarian be appointed. He said Dr. Wu I-feng, woman president of Ginling College, is an expert and perhaps should be made deputy secretary-general for this purpose.

Another thing: only one half of a vote is taken; the affirmative total is subtracted from the number of delegates present. I suppose this is all right, but it handicaps the affirmative should there be any abstentions.

Betty and I dined with Lee Wei-kuo and his wife, heard his children play the piano, and had a very pleasant time. Lee is studying the three drafts of the constitution, article by article, to prepare himself for the job he is supposed to perform. He said, however, that after our talk last night Peng had told him and Hsu Hsiao-yen, the other vice-minister, in casual fashion about the Gimo's idea. It was, said Peng, a proposal of Mr. Beal's. How Beal happened to make it he didn't know—probably had asked to see the Gimo. He didn't think it wise to hold daily press conferences, but if Lee wanted to try . . . ? Wei-kuo, being Chinese, replied he did not think he was the right man for it. Peng indicated he was in a mood to skip it. Hsu, however, asked: but what if the Gimo inquired about it? Peng said Chiang probably would forget about it; probably he was just being polite to Mr. Beal and Mr. Beal did not understand about Chinese politeness.

Wei-kuo said he wished to make a motion at the next Assembly meeting proposing: (1) that a set of rules be adopted to govern debate; (2) that Sun Yat-sen's book be the set of rules; (3) that a parliamentarian be appointed as adviser to the chairman; and (4) that Dr. Wu I-feng be appointed parliamentarian. During the evening Wei-kuo got a call from Shen informing him he was down on the Gimo's calling list for eleven-thirty tomorrow. He promised to tell me the outcome.

NANKING, November 20—Having not seen General Marshall for some time, I was glad to draw a light day for a talk with him. I noticed on his schedule on the reception desk that after an appointment at ten and myself at eleven he had nothing listed until eight. We went into the living room where a fire was crackling faintly, a welcome sound on the cold day.

Most of what he said I imagine he had told the correspondents, but perhaps I have the background to draw more out of it. He confirmed what Stuart had told me, that they both had worked on the Gimo's last statement, but he said that certain portions he had put in had been deleted by the Gimo and that in its final form Marshall disavowed any endorsement of it. Therefore I was incorrect in suspecting that Marshall, having had his patience snapped by the Communists at the time of the taking of Kalgan, was now calling shots for the Gimo.

These were the points deleted by Chiang: after the sentence announcing a cease-fire "except to defend against attack," a clause offering immediate negotiations with the Communists for an unconditional cessation of hostilities. Apparently there is some distinction between that and a cease-fire issued unilaterally; at any rate the Communists, by reason of this omission, seized on the "only for self-defense" phrase as indicating a cloak for further attacks. Further along in the statement there was deleted a five-point proposal: postponement of the Assembly (without a time limit set, though Marshall was willing to set one and realized that without it the proposal was weakened); revision of the draft constitution on the PCC model, with subsequent approval by the PCC steering committee and its submission to the Assembly to be formally enacted; carrying out of the "platform"—a coalition interim government, reconstruction, military reorganization and integration, etc.; and working out of the unconditional cessation of hostilities.

Marshall commented that the Communists were clever and probably would have found grounds for objection in any case, and conceded that the statement as put out by Chiang was conciliatory and in no way objectionable. But he thought that under the original statement the Communists would have been "over a barrel."

What nullified the whole thing, however, was that simultaneously the Nationalist armies attacked Chefoo and made a landing. I interrupted to ask if this was really correct, since Peng had denied it categorically. "Oh, they made a landing," Marshall replied. I asked if he thought the Gimo was responsible. "He must have known about it," said Marshall. "It made a mockery of the statement. If it happened only once you might blame it on General Tu Li-ming, but it happens every time. The Communists did it in June, with their attack in Shantung, but this time it was the Nationalists. Every time there is a gesture for peace the army makes an attack that nullifies it. That's why the Communists have got so suspicious they don't trust anybody. Stuart thought they trusted him, but they don't even trust him. They don't trust anybody."

He grew very indignant of the "duplicity" of the government. "I'll not be a party to such maneuvering," he said. He criticized the Gimo for trying to win the support of the Democratic League (as he also criticized the Communists for the same effort) instead of letting them assume a balance of power to protect each side from the other. He said China needs an opposition party (something I have been telling Soong but which he obviously does not believe) and that he so advised some people last summer when he was approached to come out here as an adviser.

Marshall went on to say that now the government, according to Communist claims, is about to attack Yenan. If that happens, he said, he returns to Washington for good. He said Truman approved this stand, and had made a couple of adulatory references to him in recent speeches to "save my face" in the event of failure of the mission. He said his own observer in Yenan had reported that government planes fly over daily, and added that the government had no satisfactory explanation. "Every time Chou tells me there is going to be an attack it comes off," he said. Discussing the current state of Communist strength, he remarked: "The Communists exist every place the government ain't," and said that since he had withdrawn the marines from the railways in North China in an attempt to prevent the government from moving troops for an attack, the government's coal deliveries had been cut by 55 to 60 per cent because of Communist action.

Marshall said that at his last official meeting with Chou before he departed for Yenan he had made one request: Chou was to ask his committee to say yes or no to whether they want him to continue mediation. "If they say no that gives me an out," he said. "I can go home and Stuart can stay."

He also claimed the Gimo had said he could not carry out the PCC version of the constitution, which conflicts with Lee Wei-kuo's account of what the Gimo had told the KMT delegates on the eve of the meeting. Marshall said the draft constitution, as agreed on by the PCC and forced on the Assembly, is the only guarantee the Communists have against being crushed by the KMT majority.

Finally, Marshall turned to the loan situation. The government was putting great pressure on him for loans. The Economics Minister was asking for a $150 million cotton loan; they came in for other loans. Here Marshall really worked himself into a rage as he described his reply: "The army is draining 80 to 90 per cent of the budget and if you think the U.S. taxpayer is going to step into the vacuum this creates, you can go to hell." These were the words he asked to be conveyed to "the militarists."

Marshall read at length from a transcript of minutes of the various conversations he has had as he told me all this. He is obviously resigned to the failure of his policy, willing to call the shots for Chiang if Chiang will let him do it without interference, and smarting bitterly over what he feels is a diabolical bit of government duplicity.

At his press conference this afternoon Peng made a halting effort to reflect the Gimo's policy lines, but the result in my opinion was disastrous. Asked about the report that the government planned to attack Yenan, he said it was probably a Communist stratagem. As for the planes, they had to fly over Yenan to get to beleaguered Yulin; as for road repairs north of Sian, roads are being repaired everywhere. Doon Campbell persisted: "Do you categorically deny that the government is planning to attack Yenan?" Peng said he thought his previous reply answered the question in the negative. Did the Gimo say, as the UP quoted him, that he could take Yenan in five months and exterminate the Communists in five years? Peng replied with a non-responsive account of a meeting on pacification areas which was not attended by all the high military figures. Harold Milks made a final attempt to pin him down. Did he or did he not say it? Peng said the remarks attributed to the Generalissimo were so unintelligent as to need no denial.

Had I been writing an account of the press conference I most certainly would have written: (1) Peng today refused to deny categorically that the government intends to attack Yenan; (2) Peng today refused to deny that the Gimo had said, etc. If the government wanted to convey these two impressions, then Peng was only doing his routine duty; but if not, he is getting the government into trouble.

CHAPTER SIXTEEN

Assembly begins deliberations. Marshall still worried it will de-part from principles of all-party agreement at Chungking. Communists transmit final "no" to further U.S. mediation. Soong seeks to combat worsening economic situation with further currency devaluation and import licensing system.

David Lu wrote me from Washington that, judging from press and radio, there was little interest in the U.S. about what was happening in China. When China did intrude on the American consciousness the only question it seemed to raise was "When is Marshall coming home?"

In Nanking, winter was approaching. The Chinese capital lies in approximately the same latitude as Savannah, Georgia, with much the same climate. As the winter went on it seemed colder. Our radiators were never quite equal to the task of keeping the house at a comfortable level. Most Chinese were depending on their padded winter gowns and on charcoal braziers to keep them warm.

There was no letup in political activity. Now it was centered in the National Assembly. Chiang Kai-shek had succeeded in pulling all but the Communists and a small fragment of fellow travelers into the task of adopting a new constitution for China.

The Assembly's task was to adopt the constitution, a new draft based on the principles laid down by the Political Consultative Conference in Chungking the previous January—principles to which the Communists had subscribed at the time. The constitution was the instrument through which the Kuomintang was to end the era of "political tutelage" which Sun Yat-sen felt an illiterate people needed, and end the KMT's monopoly on running the government.

NANKING, November 21—Lee Wei-kuo told me today about his meeting yesterday with the Gimo. Peng was already there. Later, Wei-kuo learned that the Gimo had inquired that morning of Shen Chang-huan whether the National Assembly press arrangements had been set up and, on learning that Peng had spoken only casually to Lee, had sent for him. In Lee's presence he gave Peng a talking to, saying that providing translators for the correspondents was not enough; positive action was to be taken. Peng protested that daily press conferences were too frequent, that there wasn't something to tell the correspondents every day. The Gimo said he didn't insist on every single day, but the correspondents had to get more than they are getting.

Peng asked the Gimo how he should answer the question about Yenan submitted for his press conference. The Gimo said no, the government was not planning to attack Yenan, and as for the planes, not only were they flying to Yulin, but Yenan was Chinese territory and why shouldn't Chinese planes fly over Chinese territory? Which was certainly more forthright than what came out at the press conference. Wei-kuo kept mum, but to ease the tension brought up his proposal to introduce rules of order into the Assembly. The Gimo endorsed it, and later Wei-kuo handed in a motion which he will speak on at the next meeting.

After the session Peng asked Lee whether I had talked to him, and Lee evaded. Peng complained I had not talked to him; I am on weak grounds with respect to that. After considerable experience with him I have learned his reaction is invariably negative; I should, however, have let him know I was going over his head. Wei-kuo thought I should do something to assuage the hurt feelings.

I learned that T.V. had come back from Shanghai and went over to see him. He had a waiting room full of visitors, but in view of his eagerness to hear about Marshall he summoned me immediately. I told him my reading of Marshall's mood, including the fact that he felt he had been a victim of government duplicity.

"Marshall thinks I have opposed him," said T.V. "I haven't. I cannot spend hours talking in these negotiations. I'm too busy. My position is that I have to keep out of it." Although I have wondered, without anything on which I could base a judgment, what Marshall's attitude was toward Soong, I said I did not think Marshall considered him an opponent. "Oh yes, he does," said T.V. He paced the floor back of his desk. "Marshall's attitude is serious. If he goes back now he will be bitter and it could harm us. We must think about it." I told him Stuart would stay. "Yes," he said. "Of course. He is more understanding."

The Assembly met at 3 P.M. today to elect the fifty-five members of the presidium. Secretary General Hung Lan-yu droned through a reading of the names of the candidates, some 179 or so. It was announced that four presidium seats were being saved for the Democratic League and five for the Communists, a statement which was greeted by applause. My translator explained that it was "to show a spirit of peace and democracy."

Then there appeared at the microphone a wonderful figure, a bald, gray-bearded man in a loose maroon robe who stroked his beard with a preening motion and smiled in self-satisfaction as the floodlights were turned on and photographers took his picture. It turned out he was a Tibetan, and he thought two presidium seats should go to the aborigines—in short, he wanted to be a candidate. This of course was childish, since the issue had been debated for two days and the original regulations, slightly revised, had been adopted. Yet debate raged briefly on this point. It was settled in typical Chinese fashion when a candidate from Sikang withdrew his candidacy so that the speaker, Ma Ching-wang, might have it. This of course evaded the issue of representation for the aborigines as such, and was strictly unparliamentary, but it seemed to satisfy everybody, including Ma. The secretary-general arranged the whole business from the mike, and Sun Fo, the chairman, acted like a man who was just watching things go by. Hung seems a capable man. Then Hung requested the correspondents to leave. I never did get it clear just why, but apparently because they feared fraud in the voting if there were many in the hall beside delegates.

Fred and Violet Gruin came to dinner and Fred and I compared notes on Marshall. Fred got two impressions out of the last press session Marshall held: first, that as a man who up to now has been eminently successful he cannot accept the fact—or maybe is confused by the fact—that he has not been successful here; and that as a pre-eminent soldier his military judgment on the Chinese Communists' capacity for resistance has been wrong, and may still be wrong with respect to the effectiveness of their guerrilla strength.

NANKING, November 22—I looked up Peng and, as an initial move toward mollification, invited him to dinner tomorrow, then asked if I could make a suggestion about the National Assembly. I told him how the Gimo had sent for me, what I had suggested, but omitted mentioning Lee Wei-kuo as the man who should be spokesman. Peng's reaction was exactly what I expected. He had several reasons why it was not a good idea, among them the fact that he was in a delicate position and could not tell the correspondents everything he knew. I pursued it no further, and left him apparently mollified. Later, I talked to Lee Wei-kuo, who had seen Peng in the meantime and said he felt better. Wei-kuo had thought up a compromise: let Hung Lan-yu be spokesman for the Assembly as often as necessary, if not every day; let the two of us coach him as necessary. This had two advantages: Hung knew the Assembly, and it saved Peng's face. It should be reasonably effective.

My translator, in giving me the day's news items, listed the names of those elected to the presidium and noted that Shao Li-tze and Wang Shih-chieh had been defeated. To have two such prominent KMT liberals defeated made me suspicious at once. I asked Wei-kuo about it and he said a majority of the KMT presidium members were CC men but the clique had not gone about the election "gracefully." He started to explain but we were interrupted and I had to leave to keep an appointment with Ambassador Stuart, who was about to leave for Shanghai, and to whom I wanted to talk for a closer reading of Marshall's mood.

Stuart said he too was apprehensive that Marshall would go back to Washington embittered about China. He said he was sure the government did not intend an attack on Yenan short of the breaking out of full-scale war. He is convinced that Chiang Kai-shek earnestly wants to fulfill Sun Yat-sen's promise of a constitutional democracy for China and is making an honest effort to get the party to stick to the PCC principles in the draft constitution. The Gimo, he said, needs sympathy and encouragement rather than criticism.

This led him to mention that he had seen General Yeh Chien-yin the Communist member of EHQ (apparently during his trip to Peking), and had told him the Communists had it in their power to send Marshall home, or to come in and work for adoption of a constitution on the PCC principles with the U.S. "almost able" to guarantee that they would get it. They could do it, he told Yeh, if they were willing to take just a little risk. "And it's not much of a risk," I ventured, to which Dr. Stuart agreed. He said Yeh was quite stirred and wanted to go back to Yenan to take part in the discussions. Marshall had wired General Gillem to make every facility available to him.

He said Marshall was going to Tientsin for the weekend and there would be no further discussion of U.S. policy before the middle of next week, by which time some word should have been received from the Communists. As we walked to the door I mentioned that the CC clique seemed to be riding high in the Assembly but I understood they had aroused resentment by their tactics. He said that from what he knew he thought they would lose out, and promised to tell me about it when he returned.

At today's Assembly session a delegate got up to suggest that regulations be adopted governing procedure and controlling speeches. Sun Fo replied that the presidium intended to do so. Wei-kuo informed me that after receiving his motion to this effect the secretariat had drawn up a list of seventy-five procedural rules, the final one saying that any situation not covered by the above should be handled in accordance with Sun Yat-sen's book. So that should be satisfactory.

Then Hung read the results of the elections to the presidium. Chiang Kai-shek had received the most votes, 1371. Next was Sun Fo with 1246. Wu I-feng, the woman president of Ginling College, refused to accept her election, which I took to mean that her appointment as parliamentarian had been arranged for. Chen Cheng also declined election, which automatically elevated the next candidate in voting rank and thus gave Shao Li-tze a place.

Then the presidium members were called, one by one, to the stage. First was the Gimo, and he got a good hand. The floodlights were on. Yu Yu-jen, the Control Yuan president, was in his blue gown and long beard. Two members were in army uniform, one being General Pai Chung-hsi. Some wore mandarin jackets, some navy-blue uniforms, a few were in Western clothes. There was one woman, Liu Heng-ching, from Canton.

Sun Fo declared a recess and the delegates retired to the tea hall where long rows of tables and benches are always laid out with glasses of tea and plates of cakes, *chiaotzes*, and similar refreshment, all on the house for anyone with credentials which get him into the hall. As delegates milled about I ran into Chen Li-fu. He said he had resigned his presidium seat because he was too busy. Someone, he said, had to keep the party organization running. The Gimo had refused to let him resign but insisted on keeping the seat open for him. "They are treating you like the Communists and the Democratic League," I said, "keeping a seat open for you." "If the Communists come in I won't resign," he replied, and he went off chuckling.

NANKING, November 25—Chiang Kai-shek, as No. 1 on the presidium, presided at the first plenary session of the National Assembly today. Over the weekend the Chinese press had carried a letter of his written to Carson Chang, and a delegate popped up to ask Chiang to explain it. He said he had written it as Director-

General of the Kuomintang, not as head of government or as an official of the Assembly. Then, after some aimless discussion, voting began on adopting the regulations. One vote, taken over Chiang's objection, had the effect of requiring committee examination of the text before they were voted on by the Assembly. The voting took all morning, and when the session resumed at 3:20 P.M. it was with a speech by Hu Shih, who argued for having the Assembly act as a committee of the whole in examining the regulations. Approval of this in effect reversed the morning's vote.

With one recess, debate on the regulations took until six-fifteen. One speaker refused to be cut off by the Gimo. He finally gave up in the face of growing hissing and clapping. The first three chapters of the regulations had been approved without objection —Hung scarcely waited long enough to hear any objections—and the fourth was pending. The public address system was given to loud and impolite burps and spittings from time to time. The Gimo wore glasses for part of this session, the first time I've seen him wear them, and he got to fidgeting and looking at his watch before it ended. He was getting a good lesson in democratic procedure and was not quite used to it. Delegates were questioning and challenging their chief executive in a way never attempted before in China.

Wei-kuo said there were three undercurrents in the Assembly. Delegates are resentful of the fact that their jurisdiction has been limited to adoption of the constitution. They would like to enforce it as well. They resent the regimenting tactics of the CC clique. Finally they resent the great attention paid to Carson Chang and his Social Democratic Party, which despite its insignificant actual size is the fourth party in China, and is "making more noise than the whole Assembly."

Immediately after the session I attended a "strategy" meeting Peng had inaugurated at the Gimo's request. I proposed that the leading delegate of the Social Democrats be invited to take part in Peng's next press conference. Peng said he had been thinking about it but had decided to wait until next week.

NANKING, November 26—Today's session was stormy and disorderly, but the government was upheld narrowly—695 out of 1031—on the crucial point of limiting the Assembly to adopting the constitution. Had this limitation failed, one of the PCC principles would have been junked, for it was insisted on by the Communists as one of the safeguards they needed. They want another Assembly, with opportunity to select their own people, to put the constitution into effect. There are still other hurdles to overcome in the Gimo's effort to hew to the PCC line, but so far things are in control.

By the simple act of sitting in the same hall and hearing each other talk, delegates are beginning to get the feel of the convention. This does not lessen dispute; there seems an inability on the part of some to grasp the concept of majority rule, an incapacity to accept decisions that go against them. But there are signs that the liquid mass of opinion is beginning to congeal, in so far as establishing a pattern of parliamentary procedure for China, though the pattern still lacks sufficient definition.

Chairman for the day was old, bald-headed Yu Yu-jen, president of the Control Yuan, the most confused chairman so far, as he fingered the scraggly end of his long dirty-white beard. During the morning recess Chris Rand and I got to talking to Lee Wei-kuo. Lee pointed out the significance of the actions taken and said the opposition was coming from old-time KMT members who did not like the PCC decisions. But so far Chiang has kept the majority in line and Wei-kuo thinks the PCC principles will be upheld throughout. I asked Rand if this kind of daily guidance would be helpful; he said decidedly. So Wei-kuo offered to meet any correspondents who desired, on an informal basis, at the rear of the hall during each recess. This solution might have been fixed up without causing Peng anguish, but in any case now it is set up. I learned from Doon Campbell that the MOI's writing section has been making a daily running account of the proceedings which is very accurate and complete, and at the strategy meeting after the Assembly session I arranged to have this done at the hall itself each day and mimeographed for the use of correspondents.

During the afternoon session I went to see T.V. He had on his desk clippings of the farm tenancy story from the U.S. papers, and a New York *Times* editorial. He asked how the story got out. I told him it resulted from the release he had approved, even though Hutchison's press conference had not come off.

He seemed to be in a mood to talk. It was being planned, he said, to give as many as 50 per cent of the ministerial posts to non-KMT members in the reorganization that would follow adoption of the constitution. "Why not?" he commented. He asked if I had any further news on Marshall, and I told him of my conversation with Stuart. Had I heard anything further about him personally? I mentioned a piece I had seen in *Ta Kang Pao* (Chen Li-fu's paper) that the Gimo might head the Executive Yuan as the only person capable of harmonizing all factions, with Chang Chun as Vice-President. He shook his head and laughed. "No," he said, adding that Chang Chun was conciliatory, an able man, but vacillating in nature and not the kind of man needed in a crisis because he lacked drive. Continued mention of his name, he went on, is part of a CC clique campaign to give him prominence and bring him in for attack.

I told him I had heard comment around the Assembly on his own apparent lack of interest in the proceedings. "They probably don't understand why I am not fighting encroachments on the Executive Yuan," he said. He reiterated his indifference to the eventual political decisions and said he could not waste his time sitting around the convention while so much had to be done on the administrative front.

NANKING, November 27—Peng's press conference today was better than usual, more forceful in presenting the government's case. The best part, however, was the "guest speaker," Dr. John C. H. Wu, a constitutional expert who took part in the drafting of this and past constitutions, a former Methodist, now a Catholic, who has just been appointed Chinese representative to the Vatican. He explained the new draft and how it followed the PCC resolutions, and how it differed from previous drafts.

Dr. Wu, a tall, thin young man, spoke with good humor and effective sincerity. Lee Wei-kuo had insisted, at yesterday's "strategy" conference, that the correspondents must have such a briefing before the constitution was debated in the Assembly, and it was a good move.

While I could determine for myself by reading it that the PCC principles had been adopted I was glad to have an expert confirm it in view of Marshall's forebodings that the Gimo was going to welch on them. After Wu's presentation was over I asked him to say privately to me whether he felt (as Wei-kuo does) that the new draft actually compromises Sun Yat-sen's original theory of a five-power government. With typical Chinese indirection, and yet with great adroitness, he replied: "I think this draft is what Dr. Sun would be for if he were alive today." The CC diehards, of course, taking fundamentalist interpretations of Sun, do not recognize that Sun's mind was not static and that under the present circumstances—circumstances which the Gimo has to face in reality—he might indeed have been for the checks and balances introduced into his system.

NANKING, November 28—Thanksgiving Day, and we awoke to find a few big flakes of snow falling out of a gray, windy sky. It seemed incredible that we had reached the freezing point in the approach of winter in a house without any heat, without feeling the cold any more acutely than we had. It was only fifty degrees in the dining room at breakfast. As the day wore on the snow became heavier and stayed on the ground and clogged the windshield wipers. At night, with the dining room at forty-eight degrees for a boned canned turkey dinner, snow covered the ground several inches thick. The boys had built two snow men out in the yard. Sitting in the living room in coat and gloves after dinner, during a power failure which reduced us to candlelight, I learned that the workmen had finished the radiator installations today and turned water into the pipes. Tomorrow they will try out the new heating system. We are getting out of the woods. The kitchen stove still needs fixing, however.

Hu Shih presided at the Assembly today, looking very scholarly in his mandarin costume. The Gimo came in from the wings, in military uniform with his gold general's collar and one decoration, the Blue Sky and White Sun, carrying the official copy of the draft constitution in a bright red Chinese-style heavy paper folder. He took Hung Lan-yu's seat for a minute, then everybody stood up and he walked around the big desk to a spot directly in front of Hu, with his back to the audience. He bowed to Hu and presented him with the volume. It was a bit of pageantry and he got a good hand. Then he descended to the orchestra pit where there was a lectern and a microphone, and began a speech.

He spoke extemporaneously, holding the corners of the stand with his white-gloved hands as he began. As he warmed up he got to gesturing, and he drew frequent applause. Henry Tseng gave me a sketchy summary of it as he went along, which I jotted down as follows:

"He advised the National Assembly to consider the importance of the constitution, and how it was drafted. He told of the three periods in which the constitution was developed. The first was from 1933 when the Kuomintang asked the Legislative Yuan to organize a constitutional committee. This committee completed a draft on May 5, 1936. The second phase was during the war. In 1939 the People's Political Council organized a constitutional committee to examine the Double Five draft, and in 1940 it organized a promotion and execution committee. From the PCC to the present is the third period. He said the present draft was agreed on but not actually passed by the Communists, who withdrew from the discussions, but was passed by the other parties. Then he spoke of the tenor of the constitution. He said it was a Chinese constitution, different from others. The importance of the five-power government is that administration is separated from policy making. The President is powerful. Therefore if the constitution is not carefully executed this kind of constitution can result in great concentration of power. It is important for the people to know how to use their rights. Dr. Sun cannot come back to guarantee the rights of the people, but he said, 'I can and will carry out faithfully Dr. Sun's will in the guarantee of the people's rights. Although I am a soldier and the holder of executive power, I am a delegate representing the people and as such I think this constitution is better than the Double Fifth constitution.'

"Regarding its passage, it is important that the constitution be practicable. The best way to carry it out is for those who made it to do so. In conclusion he stressed its importance and he asked the delegates to think of their responsibility to the people they represent." Henry commented: "It was a very sincere speech—very frank and very sincere."

Hung Lan-yu then read the document from beginning to end, after which roly-poly little Sun Fo came up out of the audience to explain the draft. As I sat through this dull process the feeling came to me that despite all the suspicions and forebodings of its critics China was launched on the road to constitutional democracy. It won't be perfect, maybe not even good by our standards, but a multiparty government is in the making and the Communists are on the outside looking in. It will probably be less painful for China, during the next few years, if the Communists stay out; possibly it would be better in the long run if they accepted the situation and came in, for they would be a reforming influence and possibly their communism would be cured by constitutional democracy. But it's their own hard luck if they stay out.

Chris Rand came up and fished out of the pocket of his overcoat a statement just put out by the Russian ambassador, Petrov. It said the Soviet Embassy "deemed it necessary" to deny a Central News dispatch dated November 22 which "distorted the reason" why Soviet railway employees were being repatriated from Manchuria. It was not that they were in poor health or financial straits, as Central News said; it was because they were subjected to "beatings and other lawless acts" and the local Chinese civilian and military authorities did not give them protection. Furthermore, it was not true that two hundred of them would remain; all were being pulled out.

It was a toughly worded statement, and immediately suggested that Russia was laying groundwork for intervention in Manchuria on the ground of violation of her railway rights under the Sino-Soviet Treaty. Why Russia has held off this long is something that has puzzled me as well as American diplomats here, in view of the constant expectation that she would get into the situation on the side of the Communists.

It was too late to catch T.V. before lunch, but I went over afterward and showed him the handout, which I had borrowed from Rand. "A possible prelude to action," he said, sending it out to be copied.

I told him I thought the Assembly had made a good beginning and I intended to tell Marshall my opinion. "Tell Stuart too," he said. I said Stuart felt much as I did; that what China needed now was encouragement. "I think you should talk to him anyway," he said.

I left him after setting up a date for Gerald Samson, the London *Telegraph* man, at 10 A.M. tomorrow. Samson is just back from Yenan. I have not seen him but I understand he brought back word that the Communists are pulling out of Yenan for Kiamutze, their Manchurian base northwest of Harbin. "They'll never get up there," T.V. commented.

NANKING, November 29—Today the National Assembly began what in the House of Representatives would be "general debate" on the constitution with just about the same results. The two sessions were presided over by Tso Shun-sheng, Young China Party member of the presidium. The similarity with the House came in the fact that in this general airing of views the honors for noise went to the lame brains with irrelevant ideas who wanted to hear themselves talk. The men who could contribute intelligently kept still. Partly, I suppose, the disciplined section of the KMT is just waiting for the vote. The party whips in this operation are Chen Cheng and Chen Li-fu.

The point is that what might be called parliamentary human nature looks to me pretty much in China like what it is in the U.S. There is division within the KMT and the dissidents are not afraid to express themselves. Also the same sensitivity over the prestige of the body in which they have membership as in the House or Senate. The man who has emerged as "leader of the opposition" is Kung Keng, a goateed, stooped, frail old fellow who was a revolutionary comrade of Sun Yat-sen. He criticized the pending PCC draft as copying the U.S. and British constitutions; said that China had first copied the Japanese and now were copying Western instruments when what was needed was a Chinese constitution; the government was deserting Sun Yat-sen.

Peng told me during the afternoon I was to be summoned to the Gimo's tomorrow.

NANKING, November 30—The radiators are now in and slowly warming up—raised the dining room from forty-eight to fifty-two degrees—and the piano has been repaired, tuned, and painted. I changed some U.S. money at 4700 CNC to $1.00 for $940,000 and paid the servants.

Today's Assembly was more of the same. Archbishop Paul Yu Pin presided in the morning and Wu Tieh-cheng in the afternoon. The morning session was rather disorderly. When a Mongolian delegate spoke out of turn his fellows got quite angry and the cursing and shouting threatened to develop into a fight but didn't quite. The afternoon session was more decorous.

I went to the Gimo's at three-thirty, where I met Wu Ting-chang, the Secretary-General of the National Government, a heavy-set fellow who reminds me of one of the tally clerks in the House. We were joined by Foreign Minister Wang Shih-chieh, and to my surprise the MOI international department head, H. P. Tseng, rather than Peng. Wang was worried about all the news about China's domestic affairs carried by foreign news agencies, which he said has come to dominate the papers. I suggested that one explanation might be that these agencies are free while Central News is controlled. But our conversation was cut short by the Gimo's arrival.

Today he was wearing a mandarin costume: black jacket and blue gown, and from my angle I could see up his loose sleeves and note that he had got out his long underwear, as I had. Before we had really settled down Chen Pu-lei came in to join us. The Gimo asked my impressions of the Assembly and I listed the ways in which it resembled and differed from the parliamentary procedures I knew, and said it was heartening to see the beginning of a multi-party system.

He asked me about a dispatch by Pepper Martin to the effect that when the Gimo quieted some disorder at the Assembly the day he presided he did it by "intimidating" the delegates. I had not been aware of this story on which Shen gave me a brief résumé. I said it was part of what China had to put up with: tortured interpretation by immature or malicious reporters. I said I did not know Martin's journalistic background, but I knew some of the correspondents in China—one at least, and others in probably comparable circumstances—had been pulled off local assignments and made war correspondents by their papers to keep them out of the clutches of the draft.

Tea was served and the Gimo went into a long Chinese discussion with Wang, during which the latter suggested, apparently on his own, that Peng's weekly press conferences were not enough during the Assembly and that every few days someone like T.V. or Carson Chang should meet the foreign press. Let them say whatever they want to, even if they attack the government, said Wang, for it would demonstrate the beginning process of democracy. The Gimo agreed. The conversation, incidentally, brought out that Peng apparently had been omitted from the meeting by inadvertence, since the Gimo inquired where he was. Lee Wei-kuo also had been summoned but missed out because he had not returned to his office after lunch and did not get the notice.

I went back to the Assembly, where I sat next to Gerald Samson. He said he was quite impressed by what he had seen of the meetings during the last two days, and he judged from the dinner-table talk at the press hostel last night that the correspondents were also impressed. I was therefore rather surprised, on getting home, to find a USIS summary (to which was still attached Marshall's note to "send this to Mr. Beal today") which said the U.S. press

felt the Assembly had "fizzled." I phoned for an appointment with
Marshall and was given 5:30 P.M. Monday.

NANKING, December 1—Gerald Samson came to dinner. He said
the Communists are indeed evacuating Yenan for Kiamutze, and
the Nationalists certainly have given them cause to expect attack,
with planes buzzing the town as low as eight hundred feet. He
thinks it impossible to eliminate the Communists by military
force, and that the veto they want in the State Council is only in
the interim government. (Lee Wei-kuo says that with the divisions existing in the Assembly they would have a veto in effect if
they joined in.) Samson rather tempered my views on the Communists, making me think it might be worth one more effort to
bring them into the Assembly.

NANKING, December 2—Philip Fugh informed me that Ambassador Stuart, whom I wanted to talk to before seeing Marshall,
was free at eleven. Walton Butterworth, the embassy's minister-
counselor, sat in on the conversation, but midway Butterworth
was notified that a visitor had arrived to see him and he left.

I told Stuart I felt the National Assembly had made a start,
however inadequate, on constitutional democracy, and that in
this attempt the KMT Government involuntarily and subconsciously had purged itself of the sort of psychological extraterritoriality it had enjoyed. It would, I said, almost be in a position
to solve the problems for itself except for the need to have the
Communists in the national structure rather than as rebels, and
except for the transcendent consideration of the next to impossible
economic situation created by their continued belligerence. Marshall's advance forebodings that the government would repudiate
the PCC draft of the constitution had turned out to be unfounded.

Stuart said his own regular reports on the Assembly were encouraging and led him to much the same conclusion. Butterworth
commented that he had had the pending draft compared with
the PCC resolutions and it seemed to conform in all important

particulars, though the PCC was vague on many points. He said he didn't think the constitution particularly good, but at least it followed the PCC. Stuart encouraged me to tell Marshall my reaction to the Assembly, and suggested that I say he agreed with me. He said his understanding was that the Gimo could count on nine hundred delegates sticking by him, with about two hundred KMT members demanding return to the Double Fifth draft and some two hundred others likely to rally to them. The Gimo was exerting every pressure to keep his people in line, and with the help of the independents he probably could do it.

Peng had called a press conference at one-thirty. I was curious to see what kind of a house he drew, since he had named an hour rather inconvenient for the correspondents and one which conflicted with a press conference called by the Young China Party. But the conflict was solved by letting them have the same hall and have it first. Their spokesman was Chen Chi-tien, who claimed they had 400,000 members. He explained why the party had boycotted the oath-taking in the Assembly—I was not aware they had. It was, he said, that they took Chiang Kai-shek at his word when he said the period of political tutelage had ended, and they were independent of the doctrine of Sun Yat-sen, although they respected him. I thought the effect was good.

Lee Wei-kuo said that at this morning's weekly KMT meeting the Gimo for the fifth time had stressed the importance of the KMT sticking to its PCC pledges, and that he had uttered what many regarded as a threat; he said that if members went against the government's position they could do so on their own responsibility but that he might feel it necessary to take what measures he deemed wise. Did he mean, I inquired, that he might resign? No; that he might reorganize the party. Sun Yat-sen had done it several times.

Peng had two "guest stars" at his press conference. First—and quite irrelevantly at this moment—was Sun Yu-chi, an economics official from Manchuria, who with the aid of a map went into a historical review of the railroad situation there. Nobody took a note; he didn't even touch the current situation. But the second,

Sun Fo, was productive. He said the government was ready at all times to resume negotiations with the Communists, and he defended the PCC draft of the constitution against all critics. He also gave factual information about the Assembly and about its committees and said that, since twenty days was the anticipated length of the Assembly, in a day or two it probably would be extended.

This is close to what the correspondents need. One handicap is that mixing the Chinese and foreign press necessitates translation, drags out a press conference, and tends to limit questioning; but it would be presumptuous journalistic extraterritoriality to insist on a separate session for the foreign press. Nor is it good to mix in extraneous subjects. But it's progress.

At five I showed up at Marshall's. Colonel Caughey sat in at the start and took notes. Old-fashioneds were put before the three of us as we sat down. Marshall sent Caughey out for transcripts and minutes a couple of times and he finally drifted out to stay.

Marshall seemed genuinely interested in my impression of the Assembly. He conceded that the draft constitution followed the PCC guidelines, and commented only that he had told the Gimo at yesterday's three-hour session (also attended by Stuart) that it was now to be seen whether the thing would be amended to vitiate its intent. He had me read the transcript of his last official talk with Chou En-lai (part of which he had read aloud to me last time) and the minutes of his meeting yesterday with the Gimo, in which Chiang had said that because of the agrarian nature of China's economy he could last another two years fighting the Communists, and estimated the mopping-up job at eight to ten months. Marshall commented that he expressed the identical ideas when he (Marshall) first came out. His mind had not budged an inch in nearly a year.

When I mentioned the Chefoo landing as another foreboding that had proved wrong, he said the government had never denied it to him, and that the landing had taken place thirty miles away from the city itself. He was particularly annoyed at Yu Ta-wei, incidentally, because he had given Yu a transcript of Chou's last conversation, only to have it leak to Agence France Presse that Marshall had handed the government a 4000-word account of Communist views. He said he'd skin Yu alive next time he saw him.

I said I felt the Gimo was really in earnest in trying to put the PCC draft constitution across, to the extent of threatening to re-organize the KMT. "That's what we're trying to get him to do," Marshall commented.

Throughout the conversation Marshall harped at intervals on how blunt he was with the Gimo. ("His old foot went round and round and almost hit the ceiling," he said, referring to Chiang's habit of jiggling his foot.) He said he probably was the only person who spoke bluntly to his face. He dwelt on this to such an extent I got the idea he may feel subconsciously he has done too much bludgeoning. He said, judging from recent issues of *Time*, Luce had certainly been "taken for a ride" because he got all "mixed up in personal relationships."

This led him to mention that the Gimo, who has just received a new C-54, wanted Mrs. Marshall to use it to fly to Honolulu. Mrs. Marshall has developed a sinus condition, aggravated by their recent trip to Tientsin and Peking, which will require that she spend the winter in a warm climate. "If I go back I can pick her up there," said Marshall. "Pinehurst at the end of January would be just about right." But what he was illustrating was the Gimo's disregard of the desperate need of China for money, which led him back to a point he had mentioned previously, that the army's demands on the economy were creating a "vacuum" which the government was expecting the U.S. to fill with taxpayers' money, and he was damned if he would approve it. He said this was the way he replied when "they" sent word asking if he wasn't now ready to "forget the Communists."

NANKING, December 4—I dropped in at the National Assembly this afternoon for the first time this week. The Social Democrats, they told me, were in the forefront this morning, defending the draft constitution since it embodied what Carson Chang wanted. This afternoon Young China Party speakers spoke in favor of a bicameral, parliamentary government, and Sinkiang delegates advocated autonomy for their province.

T.V. came back from Shanghai. It is his fifty-second birthday. I told him briefly about my talks and said that while Marshall seemed satisfied with proceedings so far he still tended to be suspicious.

NANKING, December 5—Peng had Hu Shih at his press conference today. Hu was in his most good-humored, scholarly mood, completely at ease. He defended the PCC draft constitution as a "good, modern constitution" and predicted the Assembly would approve it without change. On the Hollywood theory that if one guest artist is good two must be better, Peng also produced a character who described the deepening of Tsingtao Harbor. The foreign correspondents got up and left.

NANKING, December 6—The *Central Daily News* carried an odd story today, as translated for me by Chiang Kang-chen: "A ray of hope is once more thrown upon resumption of peace negotiations as General Chou En-lai, in a personal letter to General Marshall, accepts continuance of the latter's mediation." I had just finished reading it when I got a call from T.V. asking me to come to the Executive Yuan.

I found him rather distraught. Had I seen Chou's letter? Just what the *Central Daily News* had carried. "You were right," I said, "in guessing that they would want Marshall to continue."

"No," he said, "they tell him they do not want him. They name impossible conditions. It's just a way of telling him they don't want him." He sent out for a copy of the Chou telegram. The text certainly belied the strange twist put on it by the newspaper. It said: "With the inauguration of the one-party manipulated National Assembly the PCC agreement has been utterly destroyed. There is short of a basis [sic] for the negotiation between the Kuomintang and the Chinese Communist Party. However, with a view to comply with the aspiration of the entire Chinese people for peace and democracy, the Communist Party takes the stand that if the Kuomintang would immediately dissolve the illegal National Assembly now in session, and restore the troop positions as of January 13, the negotiation between the two parties may still make a fresh start. Request the foregoing be transmitted to the government."

Both conditions were, of course, impossible, T.V. reiterated. He said Stuart interpreted it as a "no" to Marshall's mediation and has so informed Marshall.

After picking the children up at school it occurred to me I could drop in to see Stuart for a minute at the embassy as we drove by. Stuart confirmed that this reply was an end to Marshall's mediation and that Marshall also interpreted it that way. I learned the one thing I wanted to know—that they were planning no statement about it immediately—since it had a bearing on what the government should do. After lunch I sought one more bit of information: did the correspondents have the text, and how were they interpreting it? Doon Campbell said the Communists had just put it out, and that it seemed to bring things to an end; Harold Milks saw it the same way because the Communists named "impossible" conditions. I could not help reflecting that in six months or so there has been a change in the correspondents' reactions. I could think of at least one of the men who was here when I arrived whose reaction to this, as of then, would have been: now if Chiang will just dissolve this illegal Assembly and restore the January 13 military lines, we can start all over again.

In view of no plans by the embassy to make a statement and the fact that the correspondents had the text, I thought the best course for the government was to say it would not be deterred from the course toward constitutional government on which it had set, and argue in positive and dignified fashion the legality and multiparty nature of the Assembly. I thought it important that the government avoid interpreting the meaning of the telegram and avoid leaping all over the Communists.

T.V. returned late from a Supreme Defense Council meeting, appearing even more distraught than before. We went over a statement I had drafted and deleted one paragraph which reiterated that the government was pledged to adoption of the PCC draft, saying it would only stir up the KMT opposition. Then he said: "We'd better get Peng." But he learned that Peng was planning a conference at the ministry to discuss a government statement. He handed me the draft and said: "Please attend and use your own judgment. But leave me out of it. I don't want to involve myself."

Around six-forty I got a phone call from Peng. Did I know about the Chou telegram, and what was my reaction? I said I felt the government could well make a statement and outlined one along the lines of the one I had drafted. Peng said he thought the telegram spoke for itself and the government should say nothing. I offered to come on down but he said he was just leaving to see the Gimo and would call me afterward.

Later Charlie Wan telephoned to say that Peng had asked him to come to his house with me. I picked him up and we joined Peng. He said the Gimo thought the telegram spoke for itself and the government should just give out the text without any comment whatever. I said the only trouble with this was that the correspondents already had the text and that a dignified government statement would lead up to what the Americans would put out later. But I did not press the point because I knew he had instructions from the Gimo and lacked the initiative to change them or tell him they should be changed.

So a statement was typed out saying the government revealed the text as follows. Then I drove Charlie over to the press hostel but stayed outside myself, not wanting to be suspected of any connection with it. When Charlie emerged he said the correspondents had cursed him for alerting them for a handout the contents of which they already had, and had even refused to keep the copy he wanted to give them.

CHAPTER SEVENTEEN

Assembly adopts new constitution adhering to Chungking agreement. Major policy statement on China by Truman indicates uncertainty on what to do next.

Like someone just learning to ride a bicycle, the National Assembly wobbled down the road to adoption of the constitution, with Marshall watching to make sure it did not deviate from the PCC resolutions and rather suspecting the worst, and the Generalissimo occasionally nudging the handlebars to avoid a spill. The trip was completed on Christmas Day, purely by coincidence since the date was of no significance in the Chinese calendar.

It was a primitive step toward democracy, with much depending on performance in implementing the new order in the forthcoming administrative readjustment. But it was a step in the right direction; this Marshall conceded. Ambassador Stuart, with his long experience in dealing with the Chinese, thought it was a step worthy of encouragement and in secret he initiated plans designed to make the Nanking government more acceptable to Washington.

The steady deterioration in value of the Chinese dollar continued—I noted that on December 26 it reached a price of 7800 CNC to $1.00—but this went almost unnoticed in the wake of the sudden issuance by President Truman in mid-December of a new statement of U.S. policy. Although it stated that policy was unchanged, it was a document reflecting confusion and uncertainty about what to do next.

NANKING, December 9—Peng had Archbishop Paul Yu Pin at his press conference today. It was held at the Chungking Restaurant, and lasted two hours. The archbishop is a voluble fellow, loves to talk, and he handled himself well but produced nothing much in the way of news. Asked if it were true that the Generalissimo is interested in Catholicism, he replied: "I hope so. That's all the answer I can give."

George Yeh confirmed what the morning papers printed: that the government has under consideration sending someone to Yenan for negotiations, but has not decided yet, nor named an envoy. The papers mention Chang Chun, Wang Shih-chieh, and Shao Li-tze, but the latter has denied it.

NANKING, December 11—Lee Wei-kuo says the Gimo plans a high-sounding but empty gesture to placate the opposition in the National Assembly and assure passage of the PCC draft constitution with certain amendments agreed on with Carson Chang and the Young China Party. The gesture: extending the tenure of Assembly delegates, which would expire automatically when it adjourns, to continue until the new National Assembly, to be elected under the constitution, takes office. This should give the present Assembly a chance to keep an eye on the interim government and assuage its vanity. It probably will bring howls from the Communists.

NANKING, December 12—Peng had Tso Shun-sheng, a leader of the Young China Party (and a member of the Assembly presidium), at his press conference. He was fairly impressive; positive and sure of himself, patient with repeated "iffy" questions. His attitude in the net was friendly to the government. He bespoke his party for the PCC principles but he said it was not necessary that not a single word of the draft constitution be changed; however, he predicted there would be no major changes. Asked if his party would join the government if nothing came of the rumored negotiations at Yenan, he said it was best for all parties to join, and if his party was asked to join it would. He refused to comment on the Communist demand that the Assembly be dissolved.

When I saw T.V., I mentioned that the story still persisted that he was to be ousted as Prime Minister as a result of an alliance between Chen Li-fu and Chang Chun for that purpose. He laughed. "They can't do it," he said. "Nobody wants this job anyway. Who else can do it? I have the experience, the gray hairs— I'm getting new ones every day—and if they could oust me they would have done it long ago." I said that Chang Chun apparently was going to handle the Yenan assignment. He nodded. "That can cause a lot of trouble to whoever goes," I said. He agreed, but added: "He won't get into trouble—he's too slick. It's a useless trip."

NANKING, December 13—Johnny's birthday. The Butterworth children, Cynthia and Blair, came over for lunch. So did Ed Bayne, who mentioned casually that the government will be bankrupt in a month unless it gets production started. The unofficial exchange rate is up to 5500.

I called on Yu Ta-wei, who got to talking about U.S. reaction to China, noted *Time*'s complimentary story about him this week, and launched into an account of how he had improved the railroads. His idea is to consolidate the area south of the Yangtze, where there is no Communist interference, as a means of getting on a solid basis with what you have and giving China an object lesson on what can be done when you have peace and quiet. He also told how he broke the CNAC strike early this year. He ran the line from Shanghai to Nanking with the Chinese air force, refused to settle except on his own terms, and weeded out the "agitators" before he took the men back to work. He said the CNAC workers were the highest-paid transport workers in Shanghai, and that had he given in he would have had them back on his hands in a couple of months, plus strikes in all other transport departments. He did not seem to think this was harsh or repressive, indicating he was proud of his decisive action. "That's the way to deal with John L. Lewis," he said. I remembered Francis Chang's version from the standpoint of a chief mechanic.

NANKING, December 14—The Chinese papers reveal that one of the National Assembly committees has overturned one of the basic PCC agreements by voting to enlarge its powers. It proposed amending the draft to provide that the current Assembly elect the President and Vice-President of the Republic, the presidents and vice-presidents of four Yuans (exclusive of the Executive Yuan), as well as the members of the Legislative and Control Yuans; also to recall these officials; to initiate enactment of laws; and to amend the constitution "as far as it does not change the national structure," according to Chiang Kang-chen's translation.

I telephoned Lee Wei-kuo, who said Chen Li-fu, as the Gimo's whip, was alarmed. But the government has two chances to reverse the action. In case of dispute between two committees—and there is conflict with another committee which has approved the draft provisions for the Legislative Yuan—the steering committee decides. Failing that, there is still the plenary session of the Assembly itself. Wei-kuo thinks it will take the Gimo personally to beat the opposition.

NANKING, December 15—Having discussed the farm tenancy situation now with a number of experts and officials of the Agricultural Ministry in pursuance of T.V.'s wish to have a press conference on the subject, it occurs to me that one of the reasons why the Communist farm program may have looked so good in comparison with the KMT's is that what the foreign correspondents saw of the latter during the war was around Chungking, and Szechuan Province is one of the fester spots. In Szechuan about half the land is in the hands of ten or twelve persons, ex-war lords who invested their money in land when they ran out of war-lording to do. So that what the correspondents saw was the KMT at its worst.

In the afternoon I worked on personal accounts, fascinated by the discovery that I could work an abacus.

NANKING, December 16—Lee Wei-kuo was looking for me when I reached the office. In response to a request I had made some time back he had set up a date for me to meet Chang Chun at nine-thirty tomorrow. He said that at this morning's weekly KMT meeting the Gimo had once again lectured the party on sticking to the PCC principles in their voting on the draft constitution, and had invited those who did not submit to party discipline to withdraw. I reflected that it's a little odd that those who want democracy introduced to China are counting on dictatorial methods of bringing it about. They expect the Gimo to thrust it down the KMT's throat. Also, I wonder if Marshall, if he knows how the Gimo is verging on his suggestion of "reorganizing" the party, realizes that it would be the crackpots who would be purged, not the CC clique, which is the best disciplined. The crackpots can well be spared, but it still would leave the party with the CC people in a dominant position, perhaps even strengthened in a smaller KMT. And surely this is the acme of domestic interference on the part of the U.S., dictating to one party after beginning with a policy of keeping out of domestic affairs.

Peng had had a Socialist, King Hou-cheng, at his press conference. King said the Democratic Socialists had three major points (the Three People's Principles): (1) elimination of the phrase "San Min Chu I" from the first article of the constitution, though they had no objection to its presence in the preamble; (2) that nothing be added to the powers of the Assembly as provided in the agreed-on draft; (3) that the powers of the President to put certain decisions into effect "under emergency conditions" be eliminated and the draft returned to the original text. The party, he said, could compromise on other points but was firm on these. He put in a good word for the government. Remarking that adoption of a constitution was a historic step for China, he said it was the result of the "realistic and reasonable attitude of the Kuomintang."

The conference ended on a sour note. Chinese reporters hissed his refusal to discuss the party's internal affairs. This came after a question in Chinese—Samson Shen did not translate it—asking how many members of the party smoked white opium. It seems that one of the party members recently was arrested for this, and it was a snide question.

A CATC plane, a C-47, en route from Nanking to Shanghai in Saturday's bad weather, is missing, despite the fact that any plane on that run should be able to crash-land in a rice paddy; except for a few low hills, it's as flat as a carpet. Searches yesterday and today produce no results. Oddly enough, the plane was carrying thirty-six cases of bank notes. It could, easily enough, have detoured to Communist territory in northern Kiangsu, or even farther for that matter.

NANKING, December 17—I picked up Lee Wei-kuo and we went to see Chang Chun. He is of medium height, chubby to the point of being roly-poly, with high cheekbones which give him a Red Indian look, and a gray streak in his hair. He wore a well-pressed gray suit and spoke good English though he preferred to talk to me in Chinese, with Wei-kuo translating. He impressed me as a good-natured sort of fellow but, as T.V. says, not very decisive.

I said I was glad to see him before he left for Yenan. He wasn't sure whether I was kidding and replied half seriously that it was under consideration but had not been decided; perhaps he figured I was fishing for information, which I was.

Without anything else to talk about particularly, I was reminded of the farm tenancy situation by his identification with Szechuan Province as governor, and remarked that in my talks with officials it appeared the plight of China's farmers was not as bad as pictured by the Communists but was bad in his native province. He took this as his theme, and at considerable length, through Wei-kuo, he covered what I had learned already from Dean Hutchison and others: that the farmers, even in Szechuan, got more than half the crops (all the early crops, for example), and in poor years the landlords took the heaviest losses. Then he told how tough the tenants were in Kwanghsien, fifty-two kilometers north of Chengto, the provincial capital; when they felt like not paying rent, which was most of the time, the landlords were just out of luck. In China, he said, the government was on the side of the tenants, while in the U.S. it was on the side of the landlords—for didn't the consul general in New York have to move from hotel to hotel because his apartment lease was up? In Chinese, Wei-kuo threw in a reference to Marshall and I suspected (as I confirmed from him later) he was referring good-naturedly to Chiang's own status as landlord, for he owns the house on Ning Hai Road in which Marshall is living and Marshall probably does not know it. Chang described a land-for-the-tillers project at Kwanghsien which had been mentioned in the Sino-American Agricultural Commission's report and took credit for originating the scheme. Chang concluded by saying that on his recent trip to the U.S. he noted how little news there was about China: only civil fighting and Marshall's mediation. He hoped I would study this and offer suggestions. I replied that this was my field and I was working on it.

On our way back to the office Wei-kuo said Chris Rand had asked to see him and was coming in during the afternoon. I said Rand wanted to know what was going to happen to the MOI after coalition and how the KMT was going to support party activities when it was no longer the government. Wei-kuo volunteered the following confidential information about it: the Information Ministry was to have been transferred, with the Gimo's blessing (think he even said at his instigation), to the Executive Yuan and a set of regulations was drawn up. But the Legislative Yuan refused to pass them because Sun Fo held that MOI work was something nations used in wartime and had no need for in peacetime.

Now T.V. was making a second attempt to put it across and Peng was hesitating for two reasons. First, he feared he would be unjustly criticized as seeking to enlarge his own position as a government, rather than party, minister, and second, he was already in trouble with Chen Kuo-fu over the situation. T.V. had given him money to set up KMT party papers and Chen Kuo-fu complained that Peng, because of his closeness to T.V., was going around by the back door to get money when he should get it from the party.

This led us to wonder where the KMT was going to get party funds after coalition, since the membership dues are nominal, and many members do not pay, nor does the party dun them. The party hopes for three sources of revenue: a lump sum from the government (which Chen has asked T.V. for and T.V. has so far refused to provide) which it could invest for income purposes; putting the party papers on a business basis (Peng, he said, had a date to see Chen on this very subject today); and "manipulation" through the Farmers' Bank, of which Chen Kuo-fu is the head.

Shen Chang-huan called during the afternoon and asked me to come over for tea. He was interested in U.S. politics. He said that in my post-election memo to the Gimo I had named likely Republican presidential candidates, but how about the Democrats? I said Truman and Wallace; possibly Byrnes, but more likely not. How about Marshall, he asked. I said there would be pressure on him, but I knew he would resist it. I knew people who had heard Marshall say his attitude was the same as General Sherman's: if nominated he would not accept and if elected he would not serve. Yet that kind of draft—for President—was hard to resist. Shen asked about Byrnes. Was he likely to quit as Secretary of State, and if he did who would succeed him? I said Marshall, and wondered if Shen had a hint of something I didn't know. But it occurred to me that, looking at the U.S. political situation from the outside, it was easy for him to see Marshall as either Secretary of State or President, or even both. It struck me it is a distinct possibility, after all.

During the day Marshall's aide phoned Betty to invite us over to dine with Marshall tonight. The Blandfords were there, and Colonels Caughey and Underwood. We had old-fashioneds in the big living room beforehand, ice cream for dessert, and a movie afterward: It Shouldn't Happen to a Dog.

Marshall had just got word of Mrs. Marshall's arrival in Honolulu. He reminisced, as usual, about past events: about Newton D. Baker, a great man, who probably would miss out getting the place in history he deserved; about Henry L. Stimson, another great man. He recalled how in one of the pre-Pearl Harbor meetings with Stimson and Cordell Hull in Hull's always overheated office he (Marshall) had actually been put to sleep by Hull's droning voice, though it was really an important conference.

He recounted his first meeting with President Roosevelt, when he was Deputy Chief of Staff, in preparation for the message to Congress which announced the first big aviation program. Henry Woodring, Henry Morgenthau, Harry Hopkins, and a few others were present. FDR did all the talking, waving his cigarette in his holder, and ended up: "Isn't that so, George?" Marshall digressed to comment: "I distrust this first-name business." He continued: he had been studying the faces of the men present, some of whom he was seeing for the first time, and he replied to FDR, "I don't agree with you at all, Mr. President." He said he was nervously bid adieu by the others when the meeting broke up, and at the next White House reception Roosevelt "froze" him. But afterward Roosevelt appointed him Chief of Staff. He said FDR the politician, whom he distrusted, was different from FDR the statesman, and as the latter Roosevelt had backed him to the hilt in every crisis. He spoke glowingly of Roosevelt's steadfastness in that respect.

NANKING, December 18—T.V. was reading some personal mail when I called on him and I told him my efforts to publicize the farm program hinged on finding the right man to hold a press conference and finding a news peg. He said a news peg could be a forthcoming announcement of an increase in cotton and tobacco raising. China has been producing only 25 per cent of her cotton needs, he said, and plantings will be increased to make it 75 per cent. "It will save us $150 million," he said.

The National Assembly went back into plenary session, but by the time I arrived Wang Shih-chieh was reporting on the work of one of the examination committees, rather routine. Nathaniel Peffer, who had asked me to get him a visitor's pass, was there through the efforts of Lee Wei-kuo. At the session today there was being distributed a one-page "extra" of the *Social Welfare*

Evening News, a Catholic paper associated with Archbishop Paul
Yu Pin. The man who handed me one spoke little English, but
in French he explained that the leaflet quoted a critical editorial
on Stalin from the *Salvation Daily* which had caused that paper
to be suppressed for one week, and protested the suppression.
I met Fred Gruin, who had received a copy. He noted that
neither *Ta Kung Pao* nor *Wen Hui Pao* had bothered to protest
the suspension, and to have the Catholic paper do it was an interesting commentary on the double standard of "freedom of the
press" that exists here.

NANKING, December 19—Peng called me just before noon to
say that President Truman had issued a long statement on
China. Central News was sending over the brief story it had received pending arrival of text. It arrived while we were talking
and said that Truman reiterated his policy of December 15, 1945
—the one that launched Marshall on his mission to China.

Contrary to his usual reaction, Peng was all for having T.V.
or the Gimo issue a statement immediately, and we went to see
T.V. I backed Peng to the extent of saying that something probably could be said immediately but suggested that any snap
reaction issued before seeing the text would necessarily be innocuous and meaningless. I suggested that comment could be
ducked at Peng's press conference on the ground that the text
had not arrived. T.V. decided on that course. As it turned out
the correspondents did not ask about it because though they
knew about it they had not seen the text either.

T.V. asked if I thought Marshall knew about it. I said he probably had written it. T.V. thought, on the basis of the Central
News story, it forecast a "more realistic" U.S. policy.

I asked for a date with Marshall. Caughey said he was sick—
he had a cold—and was not seeing visitors, but if I would call
back later he would try to squeeze me in before dinner. I went
to the embassy but Stuart was out and Philip Fugh seemed to
know little about the statement. By this time the USIS was out
with the Truman text. I picked up half a dozen copies and had

the rare good sense to give five of them to Peng so he could get credit for distributing them to the Gimo, T.V., Wang Shih-chieh.

Reading of the statement led me to several conclusions:

It may not have been written by Marshall, since it came to no point, failed to outline any new U.S. policy.

It contained surprising emphasis on repatriation of Japanese in China, perhaps being directed in part at Russia and critics of U.S. China policy.

There was a touch in it of buck-passing, of apology, in its statement after a year of U.S. effort—one might say interference: it said that of course the Chinese had to solve their political difficulties by themselves.

It was significant that in two places it blamed the Communists for failure of negotiations, but with a studied casualness which avoided making a point of it.

It was solid in its reiteration of support for Chiang Kai-shek's government, held open the offer of aid from the U.S. if things are settled (without any face-destroying public demand for "reform"), though it repeated that the U.S. would not "interfere" in China's domestic affairs.

In sum I thought it indicated confusion in policy. The U.S. did not know what to do next.

I phoned C. P. Kiang, giving him a thumbnail sketch of the above to pass along to T.V., and said I had a 6 P.M. date with Marshall and would report to him in the morning.

Marshall had pretty well shaken his cold by staying in bed. I told him I wanted to interpret Truman's statement to the government and, before I did so, to check my reactions with his. I sparred around for a minute to see whether he wanted to proceed with an exposition or wanted to hear my reaction and check it. I decided on the latter, and proceeded to give it, skipping the bit about buck-passing. He checked me in general, but knocked down the idea that the statement was directed at Russia. The American public had not been told the story of Japanese repatriation, and the moving of three million men out of the country was a terrific job. He said that some time back he had notified the Russian ambassador, Petrov, that he would have ships free to transport Japanese from Russian-occupied ports and wanted from him some sort of schedule. There was no reply. He wrote another, saying that if he had to take it up at the Washington-Moscow level, just let him know, but quit stalling. No reply to this either. Not until he had heard from Bedell Smith in Moscow did he get word from Petrov.

But this was digression. Marshall seemed to enjoy demonstrating that the Russian ambassador had to take the simplest things to Moscow.

My mention of Truman's reference to non-interference got him launched into a discussion of that angle. Truman of course could not admit he was interfering in Chinese affairs—it would bring down not only Russia but China itself on the U.S. But as for interference, he had been considerably amused at the editorials back home which said he had been so wise to remain aloof politically in the PCC agreements. "Why, I drafted the bill of rights adopted by the PCC," he said. It was done in the utmost secrecy; only three persons knew. Not even Caughey was let in on it. The Gimo, he said, was very worried lest his connection with it should get out. "I interfered with a meat ax," he said, adding that the Gimo had told him personally he would have to go back on the PCC pledges. "That wasn't rumor, that was what he told me personally."

He said he still was working with Hu Lin and Mo Teh-hui, a prominent independent political figure, to bring the minor parties into a working group that would swing the balance of power, checking excesses by both the Communists and the KMT.

He noted that Teddy White had attacked him in a *New Republic* article (now under Henry Wallace's editorship) and he had Caughey look up the radio message he received today giving quotes. White, while saying that Marshall's "wisdom, integrity, and devotion" are beyond question, added: "But even Marshall cannot reconcile a policy of peaceful words and warlike deeds." He also said that "on those days when Marshall sends no cables from Nanking, Washington has no opinion on China. Never since the days of Roman proconsuls has a single man held in the name of a great republic such personal responsibility for security of its future and frontiers."

Marshall took this all more personally than I thought he should, but his point was that since Luce's publications were taking a favorable line on the Gimo, and since Scripps-Howard had been beating the drums for him, the U.S. enemies of this regime had concluded that Marshall was calling shots for Chiang and were attacking him personally and redoubling efforts to change policy. At this point Caughey came in to say Ambassador Stuart had arrived, and I left.

NANKING, December 20—I was still in my bathrobe when a phone call came from Dr. Soong's aide asking me to come over to the Executive Yuan right away. It took me twenty minutes to shave and dress and I got a second call. So when I got there I was ushered in to see T.V. immediately. He wanted, of course, to talk about the Truman message.

We talked it over for some time, after which he concluded: "This is not a bad statement. In fact, it is a good statement. They talk about withholding the $500 million loan. Actually I don't care about that. If this government goes ahead"—he was talking about the solidifying of political strength exclusive of the Communists, and the general progress it promised—"a loan is inevitable; if the whole thing collapses a loan would be of no use."

I told him I had pointed out to Marshall that in my recapitulation of what the National Assembly had accomplished there had been genuine progress on one side toward realization of the PCC agreements, the KMT side. Marshall had made no comment, but I suggested that if the occasion arose Ambassador Wellington Koo in Washington should bring this up with Truman, since Marshall knew only too well what progress had been made and where the parties had fallen down. T.V. scribbled a note on his copy of the text.

Then he said he was going to show me something and he wanted me to forget immediately that I had seen it. He got up and walked around the end of his desk to fish it out of his brief-case. It was a four-point statement of policy. The headings were: (1) military aid for China; (2) loans and material aid; (3) advisers; (4) reforms for the government to undertake. He said it was Stuart's idea of policy.

We discussed the points. With respect to military aid, I said I was not much impressed with the MAGIC setup, though I was not in a good position to judge. T.V. thought the trouble was that MAGIC had nothing much to do just now, and he thought basically it was a good idea. Chen Cheng, he went on, was comparatively junior, now boss as Chief of Staff of men who used to be his bosses, so that he had to move slowly.

He said China needed technical advisers but there were good ones and poor ones and they needed to have their work coordinated by a chief adviser. Stuart's outline had mentioned that some should be on the U.S., some on the Chinese payroll, and they should report to both governments and learn Chinese if the length of stay justified. T.V. said that if such a setup were created, Marshall would stay. (I presume as chief adviser; but I wonder if he would accept.)

As for the reforms, such as weeding out corruption, promoting and punishing officials, etc., T.V. commented: "Before the war, for one government to tell another it should do these things would mean war. But we are going to do them anyway." He said this seemed to him a good program under which China could go forward. He asked me which I thought was more advanced, Truman or Stuart? I said Stuart's; I could see no new policy in Truman's. Was there, he inquired, any preparation in Truman's for Stuart's? I thought only in that Truman reiterated support of the Central Government. He said Wang Ping-nan had told either Stuart or Marshall that with Russia and the U.S. getting along better these days (apparently judging from signs of better relations between Jimmy Byrnes and Molotov at the United Nations) maybe the Central Government and the Chinese Communists could work out something. T.V. thought the thing for China to do was to leave the door open for the Communists

but to go ahead in the meantime. He said he was much encouraged.

NANKING, December 21—At the Assembly this afternoon the
debate was rather riotous. Hu Shih presided at the morning session, which I did not attend, and railroaded the first reading
through by the "without objection" method. Supervising second
reading was the Minister of Education, who had tougher going.
The Gimo popped up to make one suggestion: omit mention in
the constitution that Nanking be the capital. The Assembly
agreed when it came to a vote. Later a delegate started a speech
by quoting what my translator said was a Chinese proverb to
this effect: "Please wash your ears and listen in silence to what
I have to say." Somehow it did not appeal to the delegates, who
broke out with shouts, hisses, and clapping. One shouted: "We
can't wash our ears; there's no water here." The speaker finally
gave up and stalked angrily back to his seat. The session ended
with only about one third of the articles approved.

Lee Wei-kuo looked me up and said he thought the Generalissimo should make a statement in reply to President Truman's,
and make it ahead of the Communists. Chiang will not be making
a closing speech to the Assembly, said Wei-kuo, since this is a
new situation in China and, while an opening speech was appropriate, a closing speech is not called for; thus he should reply
to Truman in some other way. He outlined what he thought
should be in such a statement: (1) appreciation of Truman's
reaffirmed recognition of China and her sovereignty; (2) of Marshall's services, as well as of the rank and file of U.S. armed
forces; (3) of the Chinese people's gratefulness for the material
and money aid they had received. I added a fourth point: determination to go ahead with the National Assembly and constitution, with reiteration that the door would still be held open
for the Communists. Wei-kuo had been talking about this to
Chen Pu-lei, who had asked him to consult me. In a drafty hall
upstairs I wrote one out in longhand embodying these ideas and
he went off to see Chen Pu-lei.

Betty and I had been invited to Peng's for a Mongolian dinner and a MOI-produced movie, *The Sacred City*. Soon after the movie started Peng called me out and we went upstairs to his second-floor office. Wei-kuo was there, and so was Hu Shih. Peng, it turned out, had seen Marshall, who thought it would be good for the Chinese government to put out a statement. Hu Shih did some editing of phrases, to good effect. He had some objections to parts of it and wanted to make it longer —as it stood it was one double-spaced page—and I was impressed with the way Wei-kuo diplomatically but firmly knocked down his objections and persuaded him against making it longer. Then Wei-kuo and I came home and typed out the final draft by candlelight, since the electric power was off. He left hoping to get the Gimo's consent to putting it out tomorrow, for use in the Monday morning U.S. papers.

The Mongolian dinner was something special. In the center of the table was a brass bowl in which a broth was simmering, heated by a charcoal fire within a cone which served as a brazier for it. There were platters of sliced meat at hand—beef, mutton, liver, kidney—and vegetables. Waiters placed dishes of various sauces at each place. The procedure was to select one's meat or vegetable with one's chopsticks, cook it briefly in the broth, dip it in the sauces, and eat it. Scrumptious.

NANKING, December 23—The Assembly is still droning through second reading of the constitution. I asked Lee Wei-kuo what had happened to our proposed statement. He said Wang Shih-chieh questioned the timing and felt the tone of thankfulness to the U.S. would have an adverse effect on young Chinese who might consider it too subservient. Wang had drafted a substitute and the Gimo will decide between them. I ran into Fred Gruin, who said Hu Shih had put out a statement of his own in which he praised Marshall's work for peace and added that the Chinese people have a hundred times the liberties they had a year ago. Hu had said, "I was away for eight years and I saw the difference when I got back." Hu has been a pillar for the government throughout the Assembly.

NANKING, December 24—Betty and I went to a Christmas Eve party at the Gimo's. It was quite an affair. There were twenty-four U.S. military and naval people and their wives; the Butterworths and ourselves were the only civilians. It gave my dinner jacket the first workout since I lugged it across the Pacific in a flight bag.

The invitation read 8 P.M. and we arrived in the family Pontiac a few minutes beforehand. Attendants took our coats in the hall and gave us checks. Then we went into the large living room of the east wing where Lieutenant Hsia announced us. Captain and Mrs. Kenny were present, with Madame Chiang, and several others. The Gimo entered in the midst of the arrivals. He wore a black mandarin costume. Madame Chiang was in a black silk gown with green and gold brocade. General Marshall, with Caughey and Underwood, was last to arrive.

There were old-fashioneds and martinis, and when the latter gave out Madame Chiang mixed some more herself. A fire was crackling in the big fireplace and in front of it a panda-skin rug. A lighted Christmas tree stood in a corner and a record player kept Christmas music going.

The Gimo encountered me during cocktails and through Hsia began to question me. Had I been to the Assembly? I had to confess I had not attended the afternoon session, but I understood they had completed second reading. That was right; the final session would be held tomorrow. What new trends did I find in American public opinion, and what should be done about them? This was getting beyond social-hour conversation and I wondered whether I had started him off and he was merely pursuing it to be polite. It seemed he was not. I said there seemed to be some misunderstanding about his speech in which he mentioned retirement, and possibly it might be necessary to say something to clarify it. He brushed that off by saying I knew what he meant; meanwhile, what did I think of the Assembly? I said it had made a very encouraging start on constitutionalism and I thought the U.S. got this impression too. What kind of publicity should be made of it? I said that at the close a summary should be issued of what it had done, and Minister Peng had arranged for this; beyond that, publicity on the program for the interim government.

This had been going on for some time, and at this point someone attracted the Gimo's attention and he left me. Walton Butterworth sidled up, if you can say that a man of that size sidles, and kiddingly said: "I see you were on the spot." I said I had scarcely expected to get into such a discussion. "Do you still feel about the Assembly as you did when you came to see Dr. Stuart?" he asked. I said yes; the fact of holding the Assembly, the participation of the Social Democrats and the Youth Party, their meeting together for more than a month all had combined to start a habit that was capable of growing and I felt it was something to be encouraged instead of complaining it is not good enough.

The dinner was an excellent Western meal, served amid Christmas decorations: tomato soup, gelatin salad, roast turkey with the usual trimmings, raisin pie, brandied fruitcake, and ice cream. We had a very sweet melon and coffee in the living room and were in the midst of it when Santa Claus, in the flesh—the too, too solid flesh, for he turned out to be J. L. Huang—came in from behind a screen. He put on a bit of an act and then distributed presents from his pack. General Marshall got a reading board of the kind you put on your lap in bed. Betty received a very fine porcelain Chinese desk set from Madame Chiang, I some tea. She took three candy canes off the Christmas tree for us to give the children. It was a most friendly affair. We had liqueurs and after Marshall left everyone else did.

NANKING, December 25—As Christmases go, today was a modest one for our family but the kids seemed to keep happy without much fuss. It was a cold, rainy day and the family stayed indoors while I attended the two final sessions of the National Assembly.

The morning session was for the third and formal reading of the constitution. It was presided over by bearded old Yu Yu-jen, president of the Control Yuan—most appropriately, as Fred Gruin remarked, since he looks like a Chinese Santa Claus. Ni Pi, an obstreperous delegate from Kiangsu, tried in violation of the rules to open it up for reconsideration of one clause. Old Yu stood pulling his beard, not knowing what to do. "Down with officialdom," Ni Pi kept yelling from his gallery seat. Finally the Gimo got up and said delegates should remember they were setting an example to the people they represent. He had to speak twice before Ni Pi subsided. There was genuine applause when old Yu took the final vote.

The afternoon session was devoted to pageantry. Wu Chih-hui, the KMT elder, formally handed the constitution to Chiang Kai-shek. It was contained in a gold-figured box with a ribbon of Chinese characters on the front, looking a bit like a five-pound box of chocolates. Chiang handed it to Wu Ting-chang, Secretary-General of the government, who went up to the platform with it. The applause was loud and one sensed a feeling of accomplishment in the air.

CHAPTER EIGHTEEN

Government seeks advice as to what further action U.S. favors. Marshall recommends organizing "liberal bloc" but economic deterioration makes political moves insignificant.

"Nothing ever happens in China, but something is always just about to happen," an Old China Hand advised me shortly after my arrival. It was one of those wry quips whose depth of meaning becomes apparent only with experience and helps put perspective in judgment. It was true and also not true, like so many features I discovered in the Chinese character.

Something *had* happened; the National Assembly had adopted a constitution deemed capable of providing the basis for democracy in China. It was, at least, a milestone that could be recognized and recorded. But had something *happened?* Was it for this the U.S. had been waiting? Not quite. The government itself had to be reorganized to take in minority representatives, whether the Communists came in or not. This was what was just going to happen.

There were, it was true, many Western-educated men of great ability who fully understood what Marshall advocated, and why. But there were many more whose way of life was scarcely a generation removed from Manchu despotism, as well as others who had grown up accustomed to the competitive individual struggle of the war-lord era. To imagine that the liberals could, in actual fact, step in and assume leadership was no more realistic than Stalin's hope about one of the U.S. presidential contests, when he was quoted as favoring the election of Henry Wallace. Thinking back to my own early contacts with the Generalissimo, was I justified in thinking of him as "ignorant" or "reactionary" because he did not appreciate the principle of a free press under which Communist papers might publish? Could he have been thinking of me in similar terms because I failed to see that a principle accepted in the United States did not necessarily apply in China? That a largely illiterate and politically unsophisticated country did not have the kind of strength to indulge Communist propaganda, especially at a time when they were in armed rebellion?

In one of his final press briefings Marshall commented that the Generalissimo had done about everything he had asked him to, "but always too late." Chiang, I felt, had to be the judge of how fast and how far he could move the Chinese government, how sure he could be of getting obedience from his military commanders. It was one of the ironies of the period that the U.S., in seeking to push China toward Jeffersonian democracy, subconsciously expected Chiang to use dictatorial power to apply it from above—an odd philosophical attitude entirely aside from the fact that his rule of China was tenuously based on personal prestige and ability to maneuver politically within the Chinese system. There was, of course, the additional difference in assessment of Communism: Chiang mistrusted it completely while the U.S. gave it credit for more national patriotism and "love of the people" than it possessed.

The task of promoting the next thing that had to happen fell to Ambassador Stuart. Negotiations had been going on for a year and the practice was carrying forward under the weight of its own momentum. I was surprised to learn that the decision of the small minority groups to join with the government in adopting the constitution did not immediately solve the problem of fitting them into the government.

NANKING, December 27—Spent the morning reading Teddy White's *Thunder Out of China*. He has some outlandish statements in it, such as: the tax collector always sees to it that the poorest farmer pays the largest tax. I cannot really accept his approach, though he does a magnificent job of writing and organizing the book, as far as I've gone.

Hu Shih came to lunch, and I also had Bill Powell of the *China Weekly Review*, and Fred Gruin. Dr. Hu is a man who is used to talking and having people listen, and he did a lot of talking with only minor leading by Fred and me. He thinks the constitution generally good, but bad in that it demands a fixed percentage of the budget for education (15 per cent of the national, 25 per cent of the provincial, and 35 per cent of the *hsien*). This, he said, will mean that the government will violate the constitution every day of the week, because under present conditions it is impossible to jump funds for education from the present 4 per cent to 15 per cent overnight. He also thought the section dealing with "basic national policies" was bad because it goes in for utopian ideas that cannot be implemented.

In answer to a feeler from me, based on reports that he may be Minister of Education, he denied any political ambition. He deplored the salary scale for public functionaries and teachers. His own salary as president of Peking University is 550,000 CNC, or about $75 U.S. a month, and he blamed T. V. Soong for being "a financier who is always trying to save money." He recalled how he had complained to the Gimo that Peking U. had only 4.3 million CNC to buy coal this winter—enough to buy thirty tons, when six thousand tons were needed. As a result he got 400 million. He seemed not to realize how such appeals to the Gimo's overriding priority messed up T.V.'s problem of keeping the government supplied with money.

At dinner, just as I was sitting down, I got a call to come over to see T.V. He seemed affable enough and with the exchange rate in mind I commented that his trip to Shanghai must have given him a hard week. With a hollow laugh he said, "When don't I have a tough week?" He motioned me to an easy chair and called for cigarettes. An aide brought in Egyptian Felluccas. "How is Marshall feeling?" he asked. I said I had not talked to him for a week or so.

The conversation lagged. He stared at the carpet without speaking. I talked idly just to keep it going, and occasionally he responded. I could sense he wanted me to stay and talk, but he seemed to be thinking about something he could not get himself to talk about. Finally, after about twenty minutes, he more or less shrugged a dismissal. On the way home I gave a lift to John Blandford, who said he also had been summoned without purpose, as far as he could see. We concluded he was stewing over China's chaotic finances and could see no solution.

NANKING, December 28—Marshall gave me an appointment at eleven-thirty. I told him how depressed T.V. had seemed last night, and I wondered if China had any prospect but to wait around, watching the economy go to hell from day to day, until the Communists chose to come into the government and fulfilled the reiterated Truman policy. It was, of course, an indirect way of asking what he wanted China to do now.

Marshall replied that it was China's fault that she was in this hole. They had told him in June it would take them only two months to clear the Communists out of northern Kiangsu and they weren't out yet. He repeated how he had told them their military miscalculations had created a financial vacuum into which they were expecting the U.S. to pour taxpayers' money, and he refused to recommend that. He had brought the two sides together in June, but the effort failed because of KMT refusal to let the Communists keep their local administrations. Soong had bucked him on that, and also had opposed reorganization of the Executive Yuan. When I got a chance I remarked that T.V. had, in August, expressed the idea that operating a cabinet would be impossible with Communists included because it was necessarily a vertical-authority organization, but that in September and thereafter he seemed resigned to it. "Always too late," Marshall interjected. T.V. had even told me a month ago, I went

on, that it was intended to give 50 per cent of the ministries to
non-KMT people.

Marshall said that if I wanted to know what was going on,
after the Assembly Chiang had asked him and Stuart for advice
on what to do next. Marshall had told him: You have now
passed a constitution which complies with the PCC. I didn't
think you would do it; I thought you might put in a clause that
would ruin the rest of it, but you didn't. This has not hurt you.
"I didn't say it had increased his prestige," said Marshall, "because that would have been too much encouragement." Now the
thing to do was to reorganize the Executive Yuan and the National Council, leaving places for the Communists, and then send
someone to Yenan. Further, he told the Gimo, the thing to do
was to organize a liberal bloc, pulling in people like Mo Teh-hui
and Hu Lin, and consult it for nominations. This would prove
that the interim government was a genuine liberal government
and not a cloak for continuation of KMT rule.

He said he had told the Gimo it was "almost impossible to
deal with the Communists now" and if they turned down this
final government gesture of offering to go to Yenan he thought
it was time to dismantle EHQ, since then it would only serve
as a means of transporting Communists around the country. He
had already pulled the EHQ organization out of Harbin because
it had become little more than a travel route for the Communists
on the weekly supply plane.

My net impression was that Marshall did not attach too much
importance to the nation's economic plight. He did mention that
the loans they had asked for were long-range, for spending in
the U.S. and not for bolstering the exchange market here. But
he is still thinking in terms of a political carpentry job without
a pressing economic deadline. Also, I felt he did not yet know
what to do if that failed, and probably had less conviction than
I that there will be any Communist cooperation.

Ed Bayne had been to see Marshall just before I had, and I
thought I would check with him before going back to see T.V.
He had the same question on his mind—What do you want

China to do now?—and got even less of an answer. Primarily, however, he was reporting to Marshall on a talk he had had with General Douglas MacArthur in Tokyo. Bayne said MacArthur had "climbed all over China" and said that if China's attacks on him continued he would "destroy the government of China." What attacks? I had seen only a couple of piddling editorial criticisms so inconsequential they failed to stick in my mind. "I tell you this guy MacArthur is crazy," Ed replied.

The Blandfords came to dinner. Blandford mentioned privately that there had been a terrific fight over the army budget. The army asked for 7000 billion CNC and he had urged a cut to 3500 billion. Last he heard, it had been fixed at 4800 billion. He said the army now takes about 59 per cent of national expenditures, not the 80 per cent which John Carter Vincent keeps harping on, and tentatively was budgeted for 40 per cent next year. But this, he added, failed to include expenses of other ministries which work for the army and he had no confidence the 40 per cent limit would hold.

NANKING, December 29—Around nine-thirty I called on T.V., suspecting he would be making use of a Sunday morning to avoid the distraction of visitors. He put aside his work immediately to hear about my conversation with Marshall. He listened without comment to the proposal for a liberal bloc. I said I had been disturbed by his distraction of Friday night—was he worried about the economy or his premiership?

Very seriously and with obvious emotional emphasis he replied: "I would to God, I would to God that Chang Chun could become Prime Minister. I have done it for two years and it has worn me out. Everything that happens wounds me." He looked at the map of China on the wall to his right and went on: "When coal fails to come out of Anshan it hurts me. There is no one who wants my job now. There is no one who is willing to do the things that are necessary, because they are unpopular. And if China collapses, it will be my responsibility."

I felt the weight of his responsibility as he mused a moment and went on: "We are in a blind alley. I'm almost afraid to talk to Marshall any more because he will think I want to borrow money. I don't want to borrow money. This isn't like America, where you can say, 'All right, let the Republicans run the country for a while.' The alternative here is Communism. If China collapses, the Communists will take over."

I left him to resume his work, but no sooner had I taken off my coat than I got a call to come back. I had noticed when I left that Han Li-wu, the Education Minister, was waiting to see him, and he was emerging when I returned.

Since we had talked, he said, he had received a visitor who had proposed formation of a "liberal bloc." Putting two and two together, did I think Marshall had put him up to it? Possibly, I suggested, through one of the men to whom he had been talking, Hu Lin or Mo Teh-hui.

A "bloc" was not too good, said T.V. It would immediately provoke a fight with the CC clique. Government efficiency would be slowed because it would constantly be under CC attack: "they control all the papers." Besides, consulting a bloc on appointments would bring up the question of patronage, and men would have to be named on other considerations than merit. "I am isolated," he said. "I have no political dependents. All these men around me are men who are useful to me. They could be earning more outside the government, and they stay only out of personal loyalty. I do not have to stay in this job because of any feeling that I must take care of dependents."

I agreed this technique made for greater inefficiency, but argued that it created broader acceptance of the government. Decisions had to be based on "equality of dissatisfaction"; ideas were compromised, but they had more people behind them. Critics who did not realize all the factors he had to weigh in deciding his course of action learned to know what those factors were, and came to support rather than criticize. It gave a basic strength to the decision.

He said he would be speaking to the Gimo this week about the new ministries. How about Shao Li-tze for vice-president of the

Executive Yuan? In effect, Vice-Premier. I asked if a Vice-Premier could "get in the way"—what did he do? Just presided in the Premier's absence, etc.; no administration. Shao was a good man for smoothing things over. I knew he was a liberal acceptable to Marshall, and said it seemed a good idea. "Well," said T.V., "let's think about it."

Nathaniel Peffer came over for an hour. He is leaving tomorrow for the States. I asked him if he could write anything about China now, since he had told me last time he couldn't. Possibly, he said. Two months ago he couldn't. The Assembly had given him some hope; not much, but some.

NANKING, December 30—The Generalissimo has invited me to a stag New Year's Eve dinner tomorrow night in honor of General Marshall's birthday. About fifty have been invited. Shen Chang-huan, in phoning, said Betty had mentioned we would be in Washington next summer. Was this because of a change in plans, he asked me, or a matter of contract? I said it was contract.

NANKING, December 31—Lee Wei-kuo came over to go with me to the Gimo's dinner. He says there is no question but that the Youth Party will take part in the government, but the Social Democrats have not made known their final decision. Reorganization will proceed slowly; probably first with the Legislative Yuan because of the laws that must be passed to conform with the new constitution and the third parties' interest in them.

The Gimo's dinner was fairly informal. Almost all the government and party ministers were there, including Chen Li-fu but not Chen Kuo-fu, and some third-party and independent figures, including Mo Teh-hui. Mo is a stoutish man of medium height with a bristly gray mustache. His habitat is Manchuria. The Yuan presidents also attended, including Yu Yu-jen, looking as always like a benign, tired Rabindranath Tagore. Americans, in addition to Marshall, were Dr. Stuart, Butterworth, Admiral Murray, General Lucas, and some of the MAGIC people, and Philip Fugh was with Stuart. While we waited Dr. Stuart said Luce had writ-

ten him of having received a letter from some crackbrain undertaking to prove that Chiang Kai-shek was really a Czech who
somehow got to China and while living in Shanghai adopted the
name "Shanghai Czech."

Madame Chiang was in the room to greet the guests, but left
after Marshall arrived. Dinner was at eight, in the big east-wing
living room where a U-shaped table had been set up. The older
Chinese wore Chinese-style dress (the Gimo was in black mandarin costume), the younger dark blue civilian uniform or Western clothes. There were a few dinner jackets and of course
military uniforms. The menu was tomato soup, fish, turkey (or
pheasant), sausages, sweet potatoes, peas, a cake dessert topped
by spun sugar, as well as fruit salad, and tea. A birthday cake had
been prepared for Marshall.

With T.V. translating, the Gimo proposed a toast to Marshall,
noting he had now been here a year and thanking him for all
his efforts for peace. Marshall replied with a toast to the Gimo,
put seriously with an air of holding emotion in check lest he
speak too encouragingly.

New Year's Day, 1947, was cold, crisp, and clear in Nanking.
Ambassador Stuart held a noon reception at which I heard
there had been a "riot" in Shanghai the previous day. It arose
out of a demonstration protesting reports that a Chinese girl
in Peking had been raped by two U.S. marines. The chap who
told me, a young member of the embassy staff, asked if I
thought the government had instigated it. I found myself
angered by the question, thinking of how hard the Chinese
were trying to please the U.S. What motive would the government have? I asked. Oh, he said, some liberals thought we
were just promoting civil war and wanted us out of China.
When the Shanghai papers arrived they were very depressing,
not because of any news of the "riot" but because of the
disturbing headlines: "Reds Claim Yenan Zone Under Attack," and "Students of Nine Colleges Strike" (protesting the
rape case), and "T. V. Soong Criticized at Meet."

NANKING, January 2, 1947—Someone told me that student demonstrators were scheduled to arrive at the U. S. Embassy at one-thirty. I drove over to take a look but found nothing. Harold Milks of AP called to say that yesterday's riot was not bad, though it could have been had the demonstrators been on schedule and met a crowd of G.I.s as they left the football game. During dinner I got a call saying a crowd of about a thousand had shown up at the embassy. Stuart was over seeing the Gimo, but thirty of the crowd presented a petition: punish the marines; compensate the girl; get out of China. Others plastered the nearby walls with slogans: G.I.s get out; mayor of Peking, have you a daughter? Then the demonstrators shifted over to the main street where they were literally swallowed up in the parades celebrating the completion of the constitution.

Peng called me around seven to talk about the rape case. He said he had issued circulars asking the KMT papers to play down the demonstrations and stress that it was an individual case that would be handled according to law and should not be allowed to harm Sino-American relations. He said the papers seemed loath to comply. He ascribed this to "competition"—a belief that readers were eager for this type of American-baiting news, and also feared their plants would be mobbed "by the opposition" if they did not print it. We decided we should go to see Stuart.

We arrived at nine, and Stuart had not returned from some missionary dinner he was attending. Philip Fugh told us, while we waited, that Stuart had gone to see the Gimo at five o'clock and the latter had insisted on going with him to see Marshall. The general was in bed, suffering from a heavy cold. [It was the only occasion I was aware of when the Gimo called on Marshall.]

When he returned to the embassy Stuart said he had mentioned to the Gimo that the Interior Ministry had banned Teddy White's book, and Chiang knew nothing about it. Peng said he hadn't heard of it either, and doubted it since normally Interior consulted his ministry in such cases, but he jotted down a note to look into it.

NANKING, January 4—The student demonstrators were back at the embassy last night. Philip Fugh said Stuart talked to five of them and seemed to have some effect. He said he sympathized with their indignation over the rape, if it turned out to be that, and with their patriotism, but was grieved to see Sino-American relations hurt in this fashion.

Looking back from this perspective, I marvel at the ease with which demonstrations which had previously been reflecting discredit on the "reactionary" Chinese government were suddenly directed at the United States. The Communist propaganda line had switched. With the U.S. seemingly capable of adopting a new policy of support now that the Chinese had met one of its requirements, it was to Communist advantage to get the U.S. to leave. It seems plain enough now that someone motivated by considerations other than sympathy for the girl seized on the Peking case for political ends. This was not something that could be blamed on "the CC clique," for U.S. marines were involved. At the time it put the Americans in Nanking on the defensive psychologically. It revived my periodic depression about being in the midst of a situation which had no clear shape and no solution and caused me to write one stream-of-consciousness entry in my journal reflecting this mood:

NANKING, January 6—So what the hell am I doing in China, anyway? I think to myself as I drive north on Chung Shan Road. It's raining, it's dusk, and I'm driving the old 1940 Pontiac (my chauffeur has been on New Year's leave) and getting pleasure out of the smooth purr she gives and remembering that Bill Turner, who brought a 1946 Ford out with him, thought I had a new car. It is driving the family car in China that usually gives me this feeling that I am in a strange place.

I round the circle into Shansi Road, skirting the ponds and avoiding the rickshaws and pedestrians ("as nonchalant as a Chinese pedestrian"), and I reflect that I came out here for new experiences, and I've had them; I came out to give the family a chance to see something of the world, and here they are.

So now I'm home in my office and it's raining harder outside and the wind whistles in around the metal casement windows and the 60-degree house temperature which seemed warm when I first came in has a chill to it. The single shaded-bulb street light outside the gate swings in the wind and seems to be dropping sparks, but it's only beads of water catching the light for an instant as they fall from the brim.

The amah who preys on my conscience by always bowing on sight and uttering "Master!" comes in with the evening edition of Central News, bows, says, "Master!" and hands it to me and I say, "Thank you," and she replies, "Don't mention it." What's left of our half ton of coal glistens wetly in the brick enclosure outside the window. I told Tang today I hoped the Fuel Control Commission would loosen up enough to let me have five tons to get through the winter; I would promise not to smuggle more than half of it to Shanghai.

CHAPTER NINETEEN

Marshall leaves for Washington to become Secretary of State. With U.S. knowledge, Soong evolves export subsidy program. Plan is promptly nullified, after its public announcement, by U.S. action. Soong resigns.

No one following the situation in China could have been surprised by General Marshall's departure. Yet his instinct for timing gave it dramatic impact in Nanking. I learned of it when Harold Milks of AP called me at home just after breakfast asking for reaction. It was January 7 in Nanking, still January 6 in North America. Word had come from Washington that he was being called back to report; Truman's press secretary refused to say whether he would return to China. It was a day when Truman's annual State of the Union message occupied most of the front-page space in America. The New York *Times* speculated that, since Dean Acheson was anxious to leave his post as Undersecretary of State, Marshall might be under consideration for a "high post" in the department but the story noted that Secretary James F. Byrnes had given no indication he was thinking of resigning in the near future.

In Nanking Marshall spent the day receiving farewell calls from Chinese officials and Americans. The question uppermost in Chinese minds—will he be coming back?—was left unanswered. My own impression was, "He certainly had the air of a man going home for good. He seemed in good spirits."

Next morning, just as he became airborne en route to

Honolulu to pick up Mrs. Marshall, the text of his farewell statement was released in Nanking and Washington. He blamed extremists on both sides for the failure of his mission: Communist extremists who did not hesitate to "wreck China to gain their own political ends" and Kuomintang extremists "dominated by a group of reactionaries." Simultaneously it was announced in Washington that he had been appointed Secretary of State. Byrnes had resigned on the advice of his doctors.

Picking up a copy of Marshall's statement, I went over to see Dr. Soong. "Marshall has resigned himself to a coalition without the Communists," he commented as we read it over. "Peng should issue a very enthusiastic statement about it."

The statement put out by Peng was noncommittal rather than enthusiastic, chiefly because Foreign Minister Wang Shih-chieh thought it was premature for the government to say anything and had himself gone on record with "no comment." I was a bit surprised that Wang, as one of those considered among the "liberal" group Marshall commended, was reacting so cautiously. Marshall's statement, interpreted in the United States as "a plague on both your houses," was privately assessed by Peng as "55 per cent for the government and 45 per cent for the Communists," a judgment in which I think most liberal elements in the government agreed. Chen Li-fu was unhappy. I noticed, however, that the smaller people around the MOI seemed to light up with genuine pleasure when I told them Marshall had been appointed Secretary of State.

Two days later I saw the Generalissimo for one of my regular conferences. He was suffering from a cold and had an electric heater placed high just behind his chair so that it would reflect heat on the back of his neck, and also wore a visored cap on his bald head; it appeared to me he had not shaved that morning. Among other things, he asked what I thought of another government offer to negotiate with the Communists. I assumed he had in mind Marshall's suggestion of an offer to send a mission to Yenan and replied that it seemed to me the government had nothing to lose by any offer it made to invite the Communists in.

Stuart told me later that at the Generalissimo's request he had made the proposal to Wang Ping-nan, who had been left in Nanking as the only Communist contact, and that Wang had said he would pass it along to Yenan. On the evening of January 18, in the midst of dinner, I got a call saying Stuart wanted to stop by the house on his way to some social affair. His news was that Wang had brought back the reply: unless the government invalidated the National Assembly and restored the military lines as they existed January 13, 1946, there was no use sending anyone. He had so informed the Generalissimo.

So ended General Marshall's mediation.

There were two moments during the year 1946 when coalition with the Communists could have come off. One was during the June truce when Marshall believed that the two sides were within inches of getting together, as set out in detail in the journal entries for that period. He blamed Chiang's stubborn holdout on the comparatively minor issue of permitting the Communists to retain local civil administration in northern Kiangsu Province for wrecking the whole structure. This judgment had to be based on a belief that if Chiang gave in on that point the Communists would accept as final all the other tentative agreements. Actually the belief was not that strong at the time—not in my mind, and I doubt in Marshall's. It was more a case of not yet having been convinced with finality that the Communists would not honor their tentative commitments, a double negative far short of a positive conviction. Subsequent Communist tactics, most notably their stony, unyielding opposition to the National Assembly, erased lingering doubts.

The other opportunity was one lost by the Communists themselves—if indeed they had desire at any time for coalition—when they boycotted the National Assembly. The well-known Communist genius for strictly disciplined political organization could have given Chou and his cohorts easy mastery of a convention made up of non-Communists unfamiliar with and confused by parliamentary procedure and split among themselves. The vertically authoritarian Communist organization, motivated by its clear, long-range goal of seizing power, able to judge every development in terms of that objective, could have easily exploited the divisions among the Kuomintang and the minor parties, which had no clear common objectives to guide them.

The point lost upon the Communists in rejecting that course was that the path to legal and peaceful assumption of power was open to them if they were willing to take the risk of entering the parliamentary battleground. They would have fought the battle under the protection of the United States, and had they won it, they would have had the blessing of the United States.

We have learned in the decades since then that Communists are inherently incapable of taking even the smallest of parliamentary or electoral risk; their only avenue to power is through the gun barrel. In China they spurned the peaceful and legal chance in favor of seizing power by force.

The Communists opted for a military solution at a time when their military fortunes were at a low ebb. As the State Department's White Paper recorded: "During the latter part of 1946 the Nationalists made impressive gains, clearing most of Shensi, Kansu, north Shansi, south Chahar, part of northern Hopeh and Jehol and nearly all of Kiangsu. The government seized Kalgan, Tatung, Chengteh, and gained control of the Ping-sui railway. In Shantung the Nationalists achieved a major advance, clearing much of the Tsin-pu (Tientsin and Pukow) railway. Communist gains during this period were limited to minor advances into Honan and Hupeh, and infiltration around government positions in Manchuria. By the close of 1946 the superiority of the government's forces was in most areas yet unchallenged."

It would seem that only in the military sphere were the Communists willing to take risks. But they did know that the U.S. had cut off arms to the Nationalists, and financial aid at a time when the currency was becoming more and more worthless; and that they themselves were well supplied with stocks of arms taken over from the Japanese. They may have known also that Russia was prepared to give them the moral and material support which the U.S. was denying the recognized government.

All during the year in China I was puzzled by the comparative restraint on Russia's part with respect to the Chinese Communists. Very important strategic aid was supplied—in making possible the seizure of Japanese munitions, in timing withdrawals to accommodate Communist seizure of vital centers—but it was not the type of all-out aid characteristic of the Russians once they decide where their interests lie.

I could only conclude that for a long time Russia was baffled by U.S. policy, probably on two counts. First by the naïveté, from the Communist standpoint, of policy designed to build the Communists into an official opposition to the existing government, and second by the failure to act once that policy had clearly failed. The Russian is suspicious by nature, as a Russian and doubly so as a Communist. To a suspicious government it must have seemed that the stated objectives of U.S. policy could not possibly be the real ones. Beneath it, they may have reasoned, there must be some deviously clever trap to be avoided. But after a year of watching they could only have reached the conclusion that the Americans were really as simple-minded as they appeared in their subordination of what to the Russians would have seemed their clear interest in terms of the world power struggle.

Indecision about U.S. policy continued after Marshall returned home. It left the Chinese in uncertainty. They had hoped for at least a statement of moral support, and, understandably, economic and perhaps arms support. Had the American government washed its hands of China forthwith they would at least have known where they stood. But they were left to fulfill another condition—reorganize the government—without any knowledge of what the U.S. intended to do.

This had several effects in China. For one, it stalled negotiations with the independents for places in the government. After three Chinese officials had complained to me in one week that everyone was acting "so Chinese" I sought enlightenment from Chen Li-fu, thinking he might be a stumbling block and perhaps could be persuaded that the process had to get finished before China collapsed economically. Chinese dislike direct talk, he said; ask how much they want for something and they reply by asking how much you will offer. Marshall had said independents should be in the coalition, and so had Senator Vandenberg, among other things, in a speech in Cleveland. This boosted their bargaining position.

The Youth Party was willing to come in but didn't want to do it alone, Chen said, lest they lay themselves open to Communist charges they had been "bought out" by the Kuomintang. Carson Chang's Social Democrats were willing too, but—Chen broke off to say it was like proposing to a girl; she wants to say yes but first she says no. Chen told me not to worry, it would all be fixed up before the Moscow Foreign Ministers' Conference, scheduled to start March 10. Actually it was April 18 before I was called on to write a release on the organization of the State Council: seventeen seats for the Kuomintang, four each for the Democratic Socialists, Youth Party, and independents. Eleven seats were offered the Communists in case they had a change of mind.

On the military side there was a development before the end of January which reminded me of T.V.'s remark that "if the Americans pull out it becomes a fight for the survival of the State," implying that in all-out war such democratic niceties as municipal reform and concessions to minorities would of necessity go by the board. I noted in the news that a general named Ho Peng-chu had defected from the Communists to the government, with 50,000 men under his command. The story said he did it out of disgust with Communist policy, and added that he had been appointed pacification commander for an area of southern Shantung.

It was obvious that individuals would be making their own assessments of which side was going to win and act to line up with the winners, but this was disgusting. I looked up Lee Wei-kuo and said this reeked to me of being the most blatant type of old war-lord deal.

"That's just what it was," said Wei-kuo. He described Ho Peng-chu as an arrant opportunist, once connected with Wang Ching-wei, war lord of the area and later the Japanese puppet. After the war Ho had joined the Communists' New Fourth Army. Now, with the fortunes of war apparently going against the Communists, he had come over to the Nationalists, with 20,000 men, not 50,000.

But surely, I protested, he didn't have to be appointed pacification commander. Wei-kuo said it probably was part of the deal. There were several angles to it, he went on. Communist General Chen Yi commands one of two columns advancing on Hsuchow, and suddenly he finds defecting General Ho a threat on his flank. The effect of this development, he said, helped the government retake Tsaochuang. Also, the area over which Ho's pacification command extends is now held by Chen Yi, so that Ho has to fight Chen to get it.

Loss of Hsuchow, junction of the Tientsin-Pukow and Lunghai railways, would be a heavy blow to the government. Conversely, defeat of the Communist attack would greatly damage the already deteriorating Communist morale. "General Ho will be dealt with later," Wei-kuo assured me. The government never did get a chance to deal with Ho, however, for a few days later he was captured by the Communists.

"It takes two to make peace, but only one to fight," T.V. remarked during one of our discussions after Marshall left. "I hope that now that he is back in the States he will see things in a different perspective."

The fallacy that peace can be promoted by withdrawing support from one side, lest you "feed a civil war," was clearly illustrated in China. The U.S. withdrew its support, but the war continued, until the Communists overran the mainland and set up their own government in Peking in October 1949. "You can't fight ideas with bullets," the United States kept telling China, blinded by propaganda to the fact that it was bullets the Communists were using: their ideology had already lost out to democracy in the competition for the minds of the independents. Yet the same fallacy infected U.S. thinking twenty years later with respect to Vietnam.

The greatest effect of continued U.S. indecision, however, was in the economic field. It was a curious logic with which the United States, after devoting so much of its national treasure to fighting a war, could counsel China not to spend so much on its armies, as if by reducing the military budget it could reduce the need for self-defense. Without the resources on which to draw, there was no alternative but printing money, though Dr. Soong wore himself out struggling to maintain financial control.

The exchange rate steadily deteriorated. The unofficial rate was uniformly described in the press as the "black market" rate, when actually private exchange transactions were legal until the spring of 1947.

The papers carried stories indicating a five-year economic program was in course of formulation, and I asked Dr. Soong about it. He laughed. "Don't pay any attention to it," he said. "Some people don't know what five years involves."

I asked him about the reports in the papers that exchange had touched an unofficial rate of 9200 to $1.00 in Shanghai and that note issuance had reached the total of 3 trillion since he became Prime Minister. His only answer was a gesture conveying the thought: well, what can you expect? I felt I had never seen him closer to admitting that he was at the end of his rope. But he was still fighting, seeking to devise an effective export program. "Forget about this," he said, "but I saw Stuart yesterday and I asked for a $150 million for cotton. I submitted a memorandum. I did not ask for long-term stuff." He paused and added: "I reminded him that last summer, when they said we could not go on, I said, 'No, we can hang on for several months.' But now . . ." It was plain he saw no alternative to throwing China on the mercy of the U.S.

The export subsidy program was an attempt to promote exports by means of a two-level exchange rate: 3350 to $1.00 for importers and 6700 to $1.00 for exporters. The objective was to conserve exchange by making it twice as costly to import as to export goods. But no sooner was it announced than the U.S. served notice that as far as exports to the U.S. were concerned the subsidy was nullified by a clause in the U.S. customs law. This was indeed strange, for the U.S. knew in advance about the program, through Sol Adler, treasury attaché in the embassy.

When I asked T.V. what had happened I found him unable to explain. He was angered on two counts: first, because Adler had been told about it beforehand and, second, because of the method by which the U.S. had made known the nullifying effect of its own statutes. Consul General Monnett B. Davis had circulated Shanghai businessmen with a notification, and word reached the Chinese government by this means. Furthermore, said Dr. Soong, France had some sort of export subsidy in operation and the U.S. raised no objection. He was hopeful that it would still have some effect, since tung oil and bristles were on the U.S. free list and constituted, between them, a large percentage of Chinese exports.

The whole episode, with its psychological overtones in the crude manner of U.S. action, created a temporary panic. In a couple of days the unofficial exchange rate zoomed to 17,000 to $1.00 and prices in nine major cities rose 80 per cent. It was felt all the way down, for even my cook, Chiao, was complaining about marketing prices that morning when he came in after breakfast for the daily consultation with my wife about meals and number of guests. But miraculously the panic subsided almost as quickly, for when I inquired at noon the rate had gone down to 12,000 and by 2 P.M. to 10,000. I went next day to the U. S. Embassy to see whether Adler had any explanation of the contretremps.

Adler said the export subsidy program had become academic—the rise in prices had nullified it. In any case, he said, the American tariff provisions were "peace legislation," and China was on a war psychology. He claimed to have no information on how the French system had overcome the U.S. restrictions, except that it got started during the war, and he likewise disclaimed information on the circumstances under which Consul General Davis had notified Shanghai businessmen. He was, I thought, rather sensitive about the whole episode.

Actually, he seemed less pessimistic about the economic situation than I expected. He said that from his experience in Chungking he had seen just how primitive China's agrarian economy was. Shanghai was not like New York; collapse in Shanghai would not mean collapse in China, as collapse in New York would mean collapse in the U.S. The two basic requirements in China were keeping the army in the field by providing it with food and retaining its loyalty; and giving the peasant, who produced for himself, a little salt and a little cotton cloth. Inertia, sheer governmental inertia, was one factor keeping the government in control, he said. The important thing for the government was to see that rice was for sale in Shanghai, to avoid food riots, which would give the Communists something to work with.

Adler was negative on every suggestion for doing something affirmative about the situation. Dr. Soong, however, was still seeking to evolve deflationary steps. He called me over to see a statement he was preparing for the Generalissimo to issue: devaluation of CNC to a rate of 12,000 to the U.S.

dollar, an end to the circulation of U.S. currency in China, with centralizing of exchange, and several other steps.

The worsening economic situation naturally had led to intensified criticism and the chief target was inevitably Dr. Soong. One day when I arrived at the Executive Yuan he was closeted with a group from the KMT's advisory council, answering questions about his policies. Afterward I asked him how the session had gone. "Very well," he said. "None of my enemies was there." He said the twenty who had come, including Shao Li-tze, had been sympathetic and understanding of his problems. I asked why none of his enemies had appeared. "I had invited them to tea," he said, "and they did not want to accept."

He had decided, he told me, it would be good for him to make a speech to the Legislative Yuan on March 1, as requested—something he had refused to do a year earlier. "It won't be bad," he said. "They won't be friendly, but I'm going to give them the statistics and publish the speech." We were riding up to his house on the hill. After a long pause he remarked: "It's a thankless job. I get the dirty jobs. When they wanted to appease Japan, I had to do it. When they wanted to deal with Moscow, I had to do it. But I don't mind. As I have told you, I won't lift a finger to keep my job."

The night before he made the speech he asked me to come up to his house and take a look at it. I thought it was frank and vigorous. I suggested he put greater emphasis on the need for everyone to take part in the enforcement of the economic emergency measures, with a quote from Chiang Kai-shek as a reminder that the nation's existence was at stake. Also, he had referred to himself as "Public Enemy No. 1" in the context of his attempt to protect the treasury against the demands for spending money. I could picture the Shanghai correspondents seizing on that phrase and prompting headlines pinning the label on him, and suggested he could substitute "Public Scapegoat." He asked me to work on the text while he had some conferences. Afterward he went over it again. He took out a sentence saying, "It has been suggested that I should resign," but left in the one following, which said, "What I have done has been in the line of duty." In a section where he said it had been his "evil fate" to suffer the humiliation at Moscow of giving up Outer Mongolia and leasing Port Arthur he wrote in a phrase referring to his having to bow to Yalta decisions to which China was not a party, and then struck out the whole section. Finally he gave it to his Chinese translator, who complained that "some of this will be very difficult to translate into Chinese." "Let's do it anyway," said T.V.

A few minutes later he got a phone call and came back to say, "The Generalissimo is not sure I should go before the Legislative Yuan." He seemed to be asking a question rather than making a statement, as if looking for support. "I think you should," I said. "It's been publicly announced and if you don't go now it will only increase the bad feeling. You can't explain that you didn't go because the Gimo wouldn't let you."

I started to leave but went back to the living room to get my pipe, and found several persons there, including Pei Tsu-i and General Yu Ta-wei. "Sit down a minute," said T.V. He seemed in need of reassurance that he should, after all, make the speech. I said he could not be more unpopular politically than he was, and that as I saw it he had nothing to lose, and might gain some understanding and sympathy. He nodded distractedly, and I left.

Wei-kuo had agreed to go with me to the Legislative Yuan next day for T.V.'s speech, since I had never seen the chamber in operation. He called that morning to let me know he was coming by. I had barely hung up the phone when it rang again. "Mr. Bee-er," said a voice I recognized as Dr. Soong's bodyguard, "please wait a minute." In a moment T.V. came on the wire. "Helloo, John?" he said. It was the first time he had used my first name; like Marshall, he normally used a plain Beal. "I have resigned," he said, "and the Generalissimo has accepted my resignation." I could muster nothing more than a startled "Oh," though I had known for weeks it was a possibility in view of the political pressure against him. He continued: "I am going to make my speech to the Legislative Yuan nevertheless. I shall put out a statement. Come up to my house afterward and look it over." I said I would.

I remember noting with surprise that my hand was shaking when I hung up the phone.

On the way down to the legislative building I told Wei-kuo the news in confidence. "But has the Generalissimo accepted his resignation?" he asked quickly. When I said yes, excitement showed on his face. He thought it over. "This is a momentous development in Chinese politics," he said. "The Generalissimo will have to rely on someone outside his family."

The Legislative Yuan chamber was relatively small as parliamentary chambers go, some fifty or sixty feet square. On one side was a stage, back of which was the inevitable portrait of Sun Yat-sen, festooned with the KMT banner and national emblem, and a four-character favorite saying of Sun's which Wei-kuo translated for me as meaning "The whole universe is for the public." The morning sun streamed through floor-to-ceiling windows to the east.

A big electric clock on the back wall said nine-fourteen when Sun Fo, the Yuan president, walked onto the stage from the wings, a fat sleek-haired butterball little man in black mandarin jacket and blue gown. Behind him was the tall figure of T.V., hatless but wearing his navy-blue overcoat and a light blue, red-figured muffler. Behind him came four of his cabinet. As heads were bowed while Sun Fo all but inaudibly mumbled the Sun Yat-sen will, Finance Minister O. K. Yui seemed like a man awaiting the executioner's stroke.

The preliminaries over, Sun Fo called on Soong, who rose, still wearing his overcoat and muffler, turned to address a word of salutation to Sun Fo, and began reading from his Chinese text. Almost immediately Wei-kuo tapped my arm and said: "He has announced his resignation and said the Gimo has accepted it." I looked around the floor to note what reaction it produced. I could see none whatever; from the intent but stolid faces it was as if he had said nothing more important than that it was a fine spring day outside. One of T.V.'s secretaries, sitting just behind me, nudged me and repeated what Wei-kuo had said. "It doesn't seem to create much of a sensation," I remarked. "Why aren't they excited?" He replied: "They didn't understand him." Wei-kuo added: "He is talking in Shanghai dialect. Many of them can't understand him at all; I can understand only about one third of it."

The speech took about twenty minutes. When he finished, T.V. sat down, and while five speakers got the floor one after another, he looked mostly at the ceiling with an air of detachment. At no time did he seem under strain. After the fifth speech he got up with an air of annoyance rather than anger—like a man who resents having his time wasted—and replied to some of the criticism. I heard him refer to *Ta Kung Pao*, which had printed a vicious attack on him, and across the room I saw Eric Chou at the press table duck his head and chuckle. After talking for several minutes T.V. gestured once by raising his hands, half clenched, turned and said something to Sun Fo, and then walked off the stage, leaving the others behind him.

At his house afterward the air was one of all passion spent. He was completely relaxed as he chatted with John Blandford and me for a few minutes before visitors started streaming in. He said he had refused to stay on as chairman of the Supreme Economic Council; he had promised Chiang Kai-shek to remain as long as necessary to pass the prime ministership along to his successor, Chang Chun, and then intended to live in Shanghai. How about that trip around the world with his family? I inquired. No, he said, it would give a bad impression to leave China at the moment—it would look as if he was running away.

Although my year's contract was almost over I overstayed

it several months at the Generalissimo's request. I did want to see the government reorganization completed, after which my wife and I had time for sightseeing trips to Peking and Hangchow. But with no sign of decision in U.S. policy and not wanting to abuse *Time*'s generosity in my leave of absence, I brought my family home in midsummer.

In Shanghai for three days prior to sailing aboard the President liner *General Gordon*, I consulted my banker on the problem of coming out even in Chinese currency, in view of the inflation which began to soar daily once T.V. had given his critics a chance to try for themselves to control it. The banker advised me to charge everything to my hotel bill and come down on the morning of departure to get enough to pay it.

The bill came to 3.6 million CNC. I went to the bank and borrowed 4 million—stacks of unopened 10,000 bills which filled a large briefcase. I paid the hotel bill and with the 400,000 left over I had enough to taxi with the family to the ship and tip the coolies. On the day I "borrowed four million" the CNC was worth about $300 U.S. Some weeks later, when I was back in Washington and paid off the loan, it was worth only $90.

CHAPTER TWENTY

The bitter tea of General Tu.

Several months after most of the events described in these chapters—in fact only a month or so before I left China—I received word one day that Colonel Amos Moscrip was in town and wanted to see me. I was naturally curious about this man, head of the SSU in China, whose subordinates often stopped for a visit on their trips through Nanking, and I had missed out on one invitation to call on him in Shanghai when I failed to make connections with the car he had sent.

In the several months since General Marshall's departure Nationalist Government troops had suffered serious reverses at the hands of the Communists. On that day, June 11, 1947, Nanking was uneasy about another threat. Outer Mongolian troops, consisting of some cavalry and motor lorries supported by four planes with Soviet markings, had penetrated two hundred miles into China. The Foreign Office had called a press conference to state that the government was "deeply concerned"; it felt the raid was more than a border incident and it considered Russia to have some responsibility. I picked up Moscrip after this press conference and took him to my home, where we talked for more than an hour. He said he was on the way back to Shanghai after making a tour of Nationalist lines where troops under General Tu Li-ming faced the Communists some distance north of Nanking. Many Nationalist units, said Moscrip, were literally down to one, two, and three rounds of ammunition per man, and without any prospect of further supply they were deserting or surrendering.

Moscrip's depressing information came to mind later whenever I read stories blaming the Nationalists for "lacking the will to fight," and again when the same accusation was leveled at the South Vietnamese. In the case of China, fatigue and despair were understandable in light of the fact that since 1928, when he led the expedition that saw the ending of the war-lord era and the beginning of national unity, Chiang Kai-shek had experienced only three peaceful years in China —until 1931, when Japan attacked in Manchuria. Coupled with this was the fact that the U.S. embargo on weapons invoked a year previously was in effect.

Why, Moscrip asked, did Secretary of State Marshall feel so bitter about General Tu? He conceded that Marshall felt Tu had upset his truce efforts on two occasions, once in an attack before my arrival, and again in the taking of Szepingkai. I had my own impression from Chou En-lai that Szepingkai was not as crucial to Marshall's success as he thought. The only answer I could offer Moscrip was that Marshall considered Tu to be one of the "reactionaries."

Moscrip talked for some time about General Tu, whom he described as "a very hep guy who has shown himself uncannily accurate about what he can do given certain support and logistics." Tu, he said, felt that Nanking had let him down. Moscrip's judgment was that Tu might "flop," not to the Communists, but against Nanking. (Tu, at least, did not lack the will to fight; he carried on until he was captured by the Communists.) The question in the back of Moscrip's mind became clear when he asked me: suppose Chiang Kai-shek were assassinated, who would emerge? What should the U.S. do, not in the sense of granting money, but in finding someone to back? The British, he observed, always have someone to back; sometimes it turned out they had picked the wrong man, but they always had someone. We had no one.

From this perspective it is possible to suggest that the U.S.

could have backed Chiang, had it decided on such a course promptly once the Communists had finally repudiated Marshall. Washington might indeed have thought about the alternatives even earlier. Conceivably—one can never be dogmatic about "what might have happened" in international affairs—it might have resulted in a friendly China as far north as the Yellow River instead of a mainland overrun by implacably hostile foes.

There were some in Congress who did advocate backing Chiang at the time of Marshall's departure. They were suspected of wanting to embroil the U.S. in a civil conflict that inevitably would lead to war with Russia. Their more responsible objective was the simple act of lifting the embargo against purchasing arms. Support of Chiang could have taken an even more limited form, with nothing more than a firm statement making clear which side we believed in. There come times when a people submerged in a flood of Communist propaganda depicting and wildly enlarging on their shortcomings sorely need public assurance that *someone* believes their fight to resist Communist enslavement is worth while. It was true in China at the end of 1946; it became true again in South Vietnam.

My contacts with Chiang convinced me that, whatever else he may or may not have been, he was a patriot sincerely dedicated to fulfilling Sun Yat-sen's objective of ending "political tutelage" and introducing democracy. It is difficult to make progress toward this goal while fighting a series of wars. If he failed to comprehend the concepts of democracy we pressed upon him, I found him extraordinarily willing to listen to outside advice when he felt it was well meaning, and to act on it if he thought it was practicable within the Chinese context. His repeated restraints on his generals in response to Marshall's pressure was an illustration of this.

In his two decades as exile on Taiwan Chiang has presided over a peaceful, prosperous country that raised its standard of living to second highest in the Far East, after Japan. The men who drove him off the mainland, who achieved a peace of their own except for such adventures as they sought for themselves, have with constant purging presided over a country still in the grip of ferment.

What would mainland China be today had the political progress of 1946 been nurtured and encouraged to take root? No one can say; but the question must nag at the minds of those now facing the task of coping with a seemingly irrational, nuclear-armed enemy. Some, surely, must have found it discouraging that a new generation of politicians included well-meaning individuals who forgot the costly results of the coalition-with-the-Communists formula when it was tried in China and wanted to apply it in Vietnam. Clemenceau's celebrated quip that war is too important to be left to the generals might be equally valid in reverse: peace is too important to be left to the politicians.

Chiang also suffered, I believe, from a popular psychology of battle fatigue of the kind Lyndon B. Johnson fell prey to. This was true in China when he was forced to yield his leadership for a time to Li Tsung-jen. It was true in the United States, where among the policy makers were those whose dislike of Chiang, the symbol of an insoluble problem, affected their capacity to make objective judgment on behalf of the national interest.

Except for one question, it avails nothing now to complain that the United States could have done better in China then, even though it remains true—as some fail to realize—that U.S. decision to "let the dust settle" was responsible for all of America's Far East problems ever since—all of them, without exception, including Vietnam. It was part of our postwar education to learn that the pressure of Communism is as constant and fluid as the pressure of water. Vietnam raised the question: was this education wasted? Did the swelling anti-war protest mean America had lost its will to resist Communist aggression, or did it mean we had been hypnotized by the ceaseless dinning of propaganda that it was our side that committed the aggression?

It still remains true, as it always has, that it takes only one to make a fight; the victim of aggression has the choice of submitting meekly or taking up arms to resist. Not many countries wishing no more than to be left alone are allowed to enjoy the privilege. And if a nation elects to fight, no way has yet been invented to escape the toll in killings or to avoid the personal sacrifices of individuals for the nation's benefit.

INDEX